华侨大学高层次人才科研启动项目资助项目名称:
"二十四史"的英语翻译案例建设
(项目编号:16SKBS106)

中国历史典籍英译：案例、教学与研究

吴国向 著

苏州大学出版社

图书在版编目(CIP)数据

中国历史典籍英译：案例、教学与研究/吴国向著. —苏州：苏州大学出版社，2021.8
ISBN 978-7-5672-3589-2

Ⅰ.①中… Ⅱ.①吴… Ⅲ.①古籍－英语－翻译－教学研究－中国 Ⅳ.①H315.9

中国版本图书馆 CIP 数据核字(2021)第 147957 号

中国历史典籍英译：案例、教学与研究
ZHONGGUO LISHI DIANJI YINGYI：ANLI JIAOXUE YU YANJIU
吴国向　著
责任编辑　金莉莉

苏州大学出版社出版发行
(地址：苏州市十梓街 1 号　邮编：215006)
镇江文苑制版印刷有限责任公司印装
(地址：镇江市黄山南路 18 号润州花园 6-1　邮编：212000)

开本 700 mm×1 000 mm　1/16　印张 19　字数 341 千
2021 年 8 月第 1 版　2021 年 8 月第 1 次印刷
ISBN 978-7-5672-3589-2　定价：75.00 元

图书若有印装错误，本社负责调换
苏州大学出版社营销部　电话:0512-67481020
苏州大学出版社网址　http://www.sudapress.com
苏州大学出版社邮箱　sdcbs@suda.edu.cn

前　言

中国历史典籍英译能为我国外语学科的发展和翻译专业的建设提供教学与研究的案例资源。尽管翻译实践与研究一直以来都是外语学科的主要内容之一，但翻译专业本身在我国的学科建设体系中起步较晚。自从 2006 年 3 月，教育部首次备案并批准部分高校设立本科翻译专业，该专业迅速成为我国外语学科发展的增长点。国务院学位委员会、教育部于 2007 年 8 月决定在我国设置翻译硕士专业学位，并且成立全国翻译硕士专业学位教育指导委员会，以"探索我国应用型、高层次翻译专门人才的培养模式，指导、协调全国翻译硕士专业学位教育活动，加强高等学校与实际部门的联系，推动我国翻译硕士专业学位教育的顺利发展和教育水平的不断提高"。此后，设置本科和硕士翻译专业的高等院校在数量上逐年增加，并且相继成立翻译系甚至翻译学院。翻译学科的发展有力地促进了翻译的教学与研究，同时也在翻译资源上形成新的需求。中国历史典籍英译所提供的语料资源能够在一定程度上满足这种需求，并反过来充实外语学科和翻译专业的内涵发展和建设，有利于强化我国翻译教育的中华文化主体特征。

本书正是在翻译教育的宏观背景下逐步形成的。笔者于 2008 年至 2010 年在中山大学翻译学院任教，了解了翻译专业和翻译学科的发展动向和学术困境，特别是深切体会到了在打造专业和学科特色上的艰难程度。在 2010 年至 2013 年期间，笔者在中山大学外国语学院黄国文教授的指导下撰写博士论文《〈论语〉翻译版本的语法复杂性研究》，对汉语文言的英语翻译及总体的汉英翻译乃至汉英两种语言的语际关系有些思考，形成一些适用于译文分析的概念和方法。在本书中用以分析和比较的译文词汇密度和译文语法难度等主要概念在博士论文中已经基本明确。自 2013 年开始，笔者大量翻译汉语学术著作，其中包括已于 2017 年由英国劳特利奇

（Routledge）出版社出版的北京大学中文系袁毓林教授的论文集《基于认知的汉语语法研究》的英文版（Cognition-based Studies on Chinese Grammar），进一步加深了对汉英翻译规律和翻译过程的认识。笔者于2015年进入华侨大学外国语学院任教，同年面向英语专业本科高年级的学生开设中国历史典籍英译课程。当年，学校批准开办翻译专业并设立翻译系，开始招收1个班的本科生。在此期间，华侨大学外国语学院正在筹备增设翻译专业硕士学位点。时任院长的黄小萍教授和主要筹备组成员既要考虑申报材料的师资力量和成果清单等实况，又要规划设立学位点以后的专业发展和教学研究等前景。笔者有幸成为一名优秀博士（后），学校给予了笔者一项"高层次人才科研启动项目资助"。经过权衡和思考，笔者最后决定把这项资助用在翻译教学与研究的案例资源建设上，并以"'二十四史'的英语翻译案例建设"为课题名称向学校申请立项，该课题被列入2016年度第一期高层次人才科研启动项目（项目编号为16SKBS106）。因此，本书也算是笔者近几年来对学校翻译专业和外语学科的建设所做的一种微小回报。笔者也为本书在多方不断的支持和鼓励下最后能够付梓出版而感到欣慰。

学校于2017年开始招收翻译专业硕士研究生，同年笔者开始面向英语笔译方向的学生开设中国历史典籍英译课程。载于本书附录的文本就是该课程所使用的展示译文以及由该年级的研究生张艳杰和薛嘉琪所完成的习作译文。这是继2015年和2016年连续两年分别面向2016届和2017届本科四年级学生开设同类课程之后在翻译教学上的一次重要调整。本科和硕士的课程设置直接影响毕业生的论文选题。至今，笔者指导的本科毕业生采用本书推荐的理论和方法已经完成多篇学士学位论文，其中包括《语法复杂性在汉文史籍翻译中的应用》（黄燕婷，2017届）和《〈三国演义〉译本对〈三国志〉外译的参考意义》（雷相奎，2017届）。后来的这些翻译实践、教学与研究不断地检验和修正笔者在博士论文中提出的概念体系，甚至对其加以扩充。例如，本书第9章"词字比与译文修订"在译文词汇密度的基础上提出"词字比"的概念，其中论涉的主体内容最早于2016年在福建省外国语文学会年会上宣读。实践证明，英汉词字比既可用于指导文言英译及其译文的修订，又可用于分析和比较不同的翻译文本，甚至能够用于反映翻译中的语言思维。已有多名华侨大学翻译硕士毕业生将"英汉词字比"作为分析方法完成了硕士学位论文，其中包括《"英汉词字比"对典籍译文信息与结构的影响》（王殿松，2019届）和《英汉字词比与典籍翻译中的语法自觉》（薛嘉琪，2019届）。多年的坚持与探索使笔者对此前的实践和研究有了更深的认识，而不断的总结与思考也逐步促成了一套适用于翻译实践、教学与研究的案例资源、操作模式和方法体系。可以说，本书的形成过程不仅从侧面见证了我国翻译专业和翻译学科建设的最新发展，而且直接反映了华侨大学外国语学院作为起步较晚的院校在本科和硕士翻译专业的建设中可能遇见的问题和需要处理的困难，其中包括种种体会与反思：作为一门新兴的专业，翻译教育如何形成特色？作为一门传统的学科，翻译研究如何守正创新？作为一种古典的文本，中国史籍如何译解传诵？

总体上，本书采用翻译案例、教学实践和分析研究相结合的模式，在案例中实践，在实践中研究，促成教研互长，为中国历史典籍英译实践、翻译专业教育及外语学科建设提供了一种翻译案例资源、一种教学实践模式和一种翻译研究思路。笔者希望本书能够对外语院校特别是设立本科和硕士翻译专业的学校有一定的借鉴意义和参考价值。

吴国向
2021 年 7 月 31 日
于华侨大学外国语学院

目 录 CONTENTS

绪论 ··· 001
  1. 协作翻译与标准样章 ·· 002
  2. 案例、教学与研究 ··· 003
  3. 本书结构 ··· 005

第1章　样章处理和翻译流程 ·· 007
  1. 原文的结构化处理 ··· 007
  2. 语法分析的基本框架 ·· 013
  3. 句读分析与类型标注 ·· 026
  4. 群组翻译 ··· 028
  5. 译文的整理与修订 ··· 030

第2章　天干地支记时及其英译 ······································· 032
  1. 天干地支记时及其结构 ··· 032
  2. 五代十国日历 ··· 038
  3. 天干地支记时的英译实例 ·· 045
  4. 小结 ··· 049

第3章　句读的语法解读及结构类型 ································· 050
  1. 句读的基本类型 ·· 050
  2. 普通体词性句读 ·· 051
  3. 简单谓词性句读 ·· 054
  4. 特殊谓词性句读 ·· 057
  5. 复杂句读 ··· 060
  6. 小结 ··· 063

第 4 章　普通体词性句读群组及其英语翻译 …………………… 066
   1. 完全体词性句读群组及其英译 …………………………… 066
   2. 名词性主语句读与名词性谓语句读 ……………………… 068
   3. 名词性状语句读群组及其英译 …………………………… 072
   4. 名词性列举句读群组及其英译 …………………………… 074
   5. 小结 ………………………………………………………… 075

第 5 章　简单谓词性句读群组及其英语翻译 …………………… 076
   1. 不及物动词谓语句读群组及其英译 ……………………… 076
   2. 单及物动词谓语句读群组及其英译 ……………………… 086
   3. 双及物动词谓语句读群组及其英译 ……………………… 099
   4. 小结 ………………………………………………………… 101

第 6 章　特殊谓词性句读群组及其英语翻译 …………………… 102
   1. 轻动词谓语句读群组及其英译 …………………………… 102
   2. 形容词谓语句读群组及其英译 …………………………… 105
   3. 形容词活用动词句读群组及其英译 ……………………… 108
   4. 名词活用动词句读群组及其英译 ………………………… 109
   5. 被动语态句读群组及其英译 ……………………………… 110
   6. 能愿动词句读群组及其英译 ……………………………… 112
   7. 小结 ………………………………………………………… 113

第 7 章　复杂句读群组及其英语翻译 …………………………… 114
   1. 双扇句读群组及其英译 …………………………………… 114
   2. 连动句读群组及其英译 …………………………………… 118
   3. 并列谓语句读群组及其英译 ……………………………… 121
   4. 主谓宾语句读群组及其英译 ……………………………… 129
   5. 主谓主语句读群组及其英译 ……………………………… 132
   6. 使役结构句读群组及其英译 ……………………………… 132
   7. 主副动词句读群组及其英译 ……………………………… 136
   8. 小结 ………………………………………………………… 143

第 8 章　翻译互文性与译文修订 ………………………………… 144
   1. 互文性与翻译互文性 ……………………………………… 144

   2. 中国史籍的翻译互文性 ··· 145
   3. 翻译互文性的应用 ··· 151
   4. 翻译互文性的语法实现形式 ··· 157
   5. 小结 ·· 159

第 9 章　词字比与译文修订 ··· 160
   1. 汉字和单词的比例关系 ·· 160
   2. 词字比与字词比 ·· 161
   3. 词字比在译文分析中的应用 ··· 165
   4. 词字比在译文修订中的作用 ··· 169
   5. 从词字比到译文词汇密度 ·· 175
   6. 小结 ·· 176

第 10 章　译文语法难度与译文修订 ···································· 178
   1. 引论 ·· 178
   2. 译文语法难度 ··· 179
   3. 译文语法难度在译文分析中的应用 ······························ 182
   4. 译文修订 ·· 186
   5. 译不厌修 ·· 191
   6. 小结 ·· 191

第 11 章　单语视角的语法复杂性 ·· 193
   1. 引论 ·· 193
   2. 单语语法复杂性 ·· 194
   3. 单语语法复杂性与译文修订 ··· 199
   4. 习作译文、修订译文与参照译文之间的互文关系 ········ 207
   5. 小结 ·· 208

第 12 章　译文的成长过程 ·· 209
   1. 案例一 ·· 209
   2. 案例二 ·· 217
   3. 案例三 ·· 224
   4. 案例四 ·· 233
   5. 译文语法复杂性的变化轨迹 ··· 241

6. 信息冗余分析 ·· 241

结论 ··· 246
　　1. 翻译流程和群组翻译的意义 ································ 246
　　2. 语法分析和翻译案例的意义 ································ 247
　　3. 翻译互文性和文本的再生 ·································· 247
　　4. 中国历史典籍英译在翻译教育中的作用 ···················· 248

参考文献 ·· 250

附录　部分"十国世家"的译文 ······························· 253
　　The Eighth Hereditary House of Min ························ 254
　　The Tenth Hereditary House of Eastern Han：Liu Min and Liu Chengjun
　　　··· 271
　　The Seventh Hereditary House of Wu and Yue：Qian Liu ······ 281

绪 论

中国典籍的英语翻译是中外语言文化交流的主要环节，一直以来存在一种明显的失衡现象。包括"四书五经"在内的先秦诸子经典的译本众多，而包括"二十四史"在内的后代典籍多数依然缺少翻译。究其原因，除了文本是否"经典"之外，文本的规模成为个体译者无法避开的最大挑战。相较于先秦典籍，后代典籍规模宏大。属于前一类别的《论语》全文共约1.5万字，其英语译本多达60多种；属于后一类别的"二十四史"每部少则几十万字，多则几百万字，其英语翻译不仅在范围上不够全面，而且在分布上极不平衡，因而显得非常"粗放"。例如，《史记》当前没有英语全译本，只有节选译本，其中包括 Bodde（1940）、Watson（1963）、Kierman（1962）和 Bolby & Scott（1974）的译本；《汉书》存在个别节选译本（Watson，1974）；《新五代史》的节选译本如 Davis（2004）的译本相对完整。其余史籍的英语翻译较少，甚至没有，更遑论"二十四史"之外的普通历史典籍。改变中国历史典籍英译的当前现状有赖于集体译者的共同努力。

以"二十四史"为主体内容的中国历史典籍全方位记录了中华文明的发展进程及中国朝代的改换更替，可大致分为前期七史、唐初八史和后期九史三部分。其中，"前期七史"包括《史记》《汉书》《三国志》《后汉书》《宋书》《齐书》《魏书》，"唐初八史"包括《梁书》《陈书》《北齐书》《周书》《隋书》《晋书》《南史》《北史》，"后期九史"包括《唐书》《五代史》《新五代史》《新唐书》《辽史》《金史》《宋史》《元史》《明史》。每段历史都承前启后，其叙事也宏伟浩荡，构建起一种相当完整的历史文化体系。对中国历史文化的认同既是捍卫我国完整统一的前提，也是促进中外文明互学互鉴的基础。从中西文明的交流历史来看，科学技术西方压倒东方，文化艺术则东方压倒西方，因而我们既要把西方的科学技术拿进来，又要把中国的文化艺术推出去（吴国向，2012：105）。中国历史典籍是世界文化艺术的瑰宝，包括其英语翻译在内的各种外语翻译是我国外语学界、翻译学界和世界史学界的共同愿望（周一平，2008）。

　　就我国当前的外语教育和翻译教育来说，中国历史典籍的英语翻译实践至少存在三个方面的现实意义。其一，传播并发扬中华优秀文化。其二，推动并促进中外语言文化交流。其三，巩固并强化我国外语教育的中华文化主体特征。中国历史典籍英译尽管以英语为终点，但其精神特质或灵魂依然是中国历史文化，因而文化主体特征保持不变。

1. 协作翻译与标准样章

　　中国历史典籍英译是中国典籍外译的重要组成部分。对于密集型的"四书五经"翻译，学界已经意识到需要专业的细化研究。至今举办多届的《论语》翻译研讨会的主旨就是为了"推广中国文化的对外传播和深化、细化典籍翻译的研究"（吴国向，2012：105）。实际上，"粗放型"的中国历史典籍英译也需要细化的研究。

　　中国历史典籍内容丰富，具有明确的结构体系，通常包含叙述帝王的本纪、讲述侯王的世家、记录名人的列传、列明事件的表、记载文化成果的书或志等，涉及人物、事件、地理、语言文学、天文历法等内容，文字规模宏大。例如，《史记》约有53万字，《汉书》约有74万字，《新五代史》约有29万字，《明史》约有280万字，《清史稿》约有451万字。对于如此规模的文本，个体译者根本无法独立应付，因而需要协作翻译。尽管如此，中国历史典籍文本的重复性特征同样显著，对其深入的研究能够为协作翻译提供有益的参考。协作翻译既能提高翻译效率，又能保证翻译质量。

　　协作翻译的基本单位称为样章，而样章规模的大小则取决于翻译实践的需要。本书按1个学期的翻译教学需要把包含200个句读的典籍文本称为1个标准样章，每个标准样章包含大约1 200个汉字。标准样章处理起来灵活方便，有利于阅读与翻译。例如，欧阳修的《新五代史》共约29万个汉字、5.2万个句读，即该书总体规模约为260个标准样章；其中的"闽世家第八"共有4 095个汉字、721个句读，即该卷总体规模约为3.5个标准样章。上述两种不同的标准样章表明，如果每名译员每个学期完成1个标准样章的翻译，那么译完整部《新五代史》需要260名译员，译完"闽世家第八"至少需要3名译员。在教学或实践中，可按具体的协作需要由不同的译员承担1个、1.5个、2个、3个或多个标准样章，自然而然地形成规模不等的协作翻译队伍。

2. 案例、教学与研究

翻译密切关联语言学，尤其是语言类型学。翻译关系其实是原文与译文之间在词与词、句与句、篇与篇等实例上的对等关系，能够直接反映源语言系统和目标语言系统之间的异同，而语际之间在系统上的异同又是语言类型学的主要内容。显然，翻译和类型学具有共同的核心，其研究对象均为语言。Halliday（2008：191）认为，二者之间的区别主要在于其所采取的视角各不相同：

> Whereas typology is the comparative linguistics of the system, translation is the comparative linguistics of the instance：here one text is being brought into relation with another—because that is how the translated text is constructed. ［类型学是语言系统的比较研究，而翻译则是语言实例的比较研究。实例的比较是译文所以形成的基本途径：译文和原文之间的对等关系在翻译中不断地被加强。］

尽管都是对语言的比较，研究视角的分化形成不同的研究范式：类型学是语际之间在系统上的比较研究，翻译是语际之间在实例上的比较研究。实际上，类型学的系统比较研究离不开翻译的实例比较研究，翻译的实例比较研究离不开类型学的系统比较研究。翻译与语言学相互交织，相互关联。正因为如此，在中国历史典籍英译实践中，采用翻译案例、教学实践和分析比较相结合的模式，在案例中实践，在实践中研究，能够促成教研互长，为语言学和翻译提供一种案例资源、一种实践模式和一种研究思路。

2.1 基于语法分析的汉语句读库与翻译案例库

汉语句读库和翻译案例库两种模块组合构成案例资源。其中，汉语句读库主要包括原文句读及其类型标注。每个原文句读都有明确的语法结构类型，即句读类型。句读类型既是语义理解的标记，也是句读群组的线索。一方面，句读类型是对句读作语法分析的结果。语义理解是翻译的前提基础。语义内容具有明显的综合性特征，语法结构具有明显的分析性特征。一般来说，只要能够明确给定句读的语法结构，也就基本确定了该句读的语义内容。因此，译者对句读的语法分析能够反映其对原文的语义理解。采用句读类型标记语义理解的完成情况，其实是把综合性的语义内容转换为分析性的语法结构。另一方面，句读类型又是形成句读群组的关键线索。通过添加句读类型的标注，原文文本以句读为单位转换为结构化的句读库。句读类型可用以检索并提取同类句读，形成句读群组，便于实施群组翻译。经过群组翻译，汉语单语的句读库转变为汉英双语的翻译案例库。

翻译案例库是一种以汉语句读为对齐单位的汉英平行语料库，其核心内容是原文句读及其英语译文。案例库中的每个汉英对齐单位构成一个翻译案例。在机器辅助翻译中，这种双语的资源库通常被称为记忆库。就处于同一群组但还未翻译的句读来说，翻译案例提供直接的翻译参考。群组翻译能够不断地添加翻译案例。直接利用现有的中国历史典籍英译文本也能扩充翻译案例库。其中的优秀译文往往能够提高翻译案例库的总体质量。翻译案例所提供的资源既方便教学与实践，又方便翻译知识的扩充积累与重复利用。

2.2 基于群组模式的翻译教学与实践

群组翻译是指以句读群组为单位的翻译教学与实践模式。处于同一群组的句读具有相同或相似的语法结构，而句读在语法上的重合有别于其在词汇上的重复。词汇重复在计算机辅助翻译中体现为重复率，表明句读之间在词汇项目上的相似度。语法重合不是句读在词汇项目上的相似度，而是其在语法结构上的相似度。同一群组内部的任何一对句读所包含的词汇项目既可能完全相同，又可能完全不同。

群组翻译涉及普通体词性句读、简单谓词性句读、特殊谓词性句读和复杂句读四种基本的句读类型。例如，《新五代史·闽世家第八》全文共有721个句读，其中包含94例普通体词性句读、271例简单谓词性句读、108例特殊谓词性句读、248例复杂句读。基本类型又可细分为不同的小类：普通体词性句读可细分为完全体名词性句读、名词性主语句读、名词性谓语句读、名词性状语句读、名词性列举句读等；简单谓词性句读可细分为不及物动词谓语句读、单及物动词谓语句读、双及物动词谓语句读等；特殊谓词性句读可细分为轻动词谓语句读、形容词谓语句读、形容词活用动词句读、名词活用动词句读、能愿动词句读、被动语态句读等；复杂句读可细分为双扇句读、连动句读、并列谓语句读、主谓宾语句读、主谓主语句读、使役结构句读、主副动词句读等。群组翻译属于一种流水作业模式，能够有效地利用同类句读在语法上的共性特征，达到提高翻译效率并确保译文质量的目的。在翻译教学中，群组翻译的结果就是习作译文的初稿。

2.3 基于参照的翻译修订与研究

习作译文需要经过多次修订才能得到终稿译文。在参照译文的基础上对习作译文的分析与研究可为译文的修订提供明确的指引。这种基于参照的译文修订程序主要包含四个步骤：第一，选定某种合适的中国典籍英译文本（辅以某种非汉译英文本）作为参照译文；第二，先后分析习作译文和参照译文的词汇语法特征；第三，比较习作译文与参照译文在词汇语法上的差距；第四，在多个维度上修订译文并缩小上述差距，以获得终稿。译文的词汇语法维度主要包括英汉词字比、译文词汇密度、译文语法难度等。多维的比较研究能够全面地反映习作译文的缺点和不足。

  作为参照的文本包括汉译英文本和非汉译英文本。汉译英文本主要包括中国典籍英译文本，特别是中国历史典籍英译文本。按照翻译教学与实践的需要，参照译文可从现有的历史典籍英语译本中选取，并以其具体的词汇语法指标作为参照数值。本书主要选取《史记》《汉书》等英语译本的部分片段作为参照译文。非历史典籍英译尽管有别于历史典籍英译，但是包括"四书五经"在内的经典文本的英语翻译全面、多样，因而必然存在一些合适的译文，可作为辅助的参照译文。非汉译英文本主要包括英文版的《塔西佗编年史》（*The Annals of Tacitus*）。该历史文本尽管不是汉译英文本，但也是一种译文，其原文为拉丁语。基于参照的翻译修订在本质上是一种翻译研究引领的译文修订方案，其目的是使习作译文在不同的维度上靠近参照译文。

3. 本书结构

  本书主要由12章、绪论和结论构成，可分为四个部分。第一部分包括绪论、第1章和第2章，主要概述本书论涉的案例、教学和研究三种主体及三者之间的关系。紧随本绪论之后，第1章介绍翻译样章的选定、原文的结构化处理、句读的结构分析与分类，以及翻译流程。第2章介绍天干地支记时方法和公元纪年的关系，以及天干地支的英译方法。

  第二部分包含5章，主要以《新五代史·闽世家第八》为例，分析句读的结构类型并实施群组翻译。第3章在句读库中逐句分析句读的语法结构，同时完成句读类型的标注，以完善句读库的内容。第4章、第5章、第6章和第7章分别讨论普通体词性句读群组及其英语翻译、简单谓词性句读群组及其英译、特殊谓词性句读群组及其英译，以及复杂句读群组及其英译。该部分在汉语句读库的基础上建立了翻译案例库。

  第三部分包含3章，主要在参照译文的基础上整合与修订习作译文。第8章主要探讨翻译互文性在中国历史典籍英译中的现实意义。第9章和第10章分别在英汉双语的词字比、译文词汇密度、译文语法难度上分析习作译文之于参照译文的差别，借以修订习作译文，使其在各种维度上不断地靠近参照译文。该部分提出一种能够确保译文质量的修订程式。

第四部分包含第 11 章、第 12 章和结论，进一步探讨译文形成的全过程及其在英语语境中的适应性特征。第 11 章在单语的词汇密度和语法难度两个维度上比较习作译文和参照译文，完成最后的译文修订，形成终稿。第 12 章总结并分析译文的成长过程。最后，本书总结案例、教学与研究。

另外，本书还有一个附录。附录载有《新五代史》部分世家的英语翻译，其中的 The Eighth Hereditary House of Min 及其原文"闽世家第八"是本书用以分析和研究的主要实例。

第1章

样章处理和翻译流程

规范的翻译流程是翻译质量的重要保障。译文尽管可以安排同行审校,但文责在译者,需要译者具有规范的翻译行为。规范的翻译流程是使翻译行为规范化的最稳妥、最保险的途径。这种流程要求译者严格约束自己的翻译行为,包括准确地理解原文、快速地生成初稿、不断地修订译文,直至高效地获得终稿。翻译行为的规范化能够明确译者的职责所在,确保准确的理解、高效的翻译和优美的行文。本章在教学与实践的基础上确立一种集理解、翻译和修订于一体的翻译流程。该流程主要包括四个步骤:第一步,在结构化原文的基础上建立原文句读库;第二步,在理解原文的基础上明确句读类型;第三步,在群组翻译的基础上建立翻译案例库;第四步,在比较分析的基础上修订译文。

1. 原文的结构化处理

建立翻译案例库的第一步是使原文结构化。只需使用当前通用的文字处理工具就可完成对原文的结构化处理,进而为译者提供一种关于原文的便捷视图。就《新五代史·闽世家第八》来说,该卷共有 4 095 个汉字,721 个句读,约等于 3.5 个标准样章(标准样章的长度为 200 个句读)。现从该卷中选取以下带有现代汉语标点符号的两段例文(以下简称"例文")来说明结构化原文的过程和步骤。

审知为人状儿雄伟,隆准方口,常乘白马,军中号"白马三郎"。乾宁四年,潮卒,审知代立。唐以福州为威武军,拜审知节度使,累迁同中书门下平章事,封琅琊王。唐亡,梁太祖加拜审知中书令,封闽王,升福州为大都督府。是时,杨行密据有江淮,审知岁遣使泛海,自登、莱朝贡于梁,使者入海,覆溺常十三四。

审知虽起盗贼,而为人俭约,好礼下士。王淡,唐相溥之子；杨沂，唐相涉从弟；徐寅，唐时知名进士，皆依审知仕宦。又建学四门，以教闽士之秀者。招来海中蛮夷商贾。海上黄崎，波涛为阻，一夕风雨雷电震击，开以为港，闽人以为审知德政所致，号为甘棠港。

最初的原文样章保存为独立的文件形式，添加文件名称，如"1号文件"。例文除了包含［，。；］等40个句读符号外，还包含3个非句读符号，即［、""］。为了方便统计文本的句读数量，可把非句读符号临时移除，仅保留句读符号。在"1号文件"的基础上移除全部非句读符号之后就可得到"2号文件"。移除非句读符号的具体方法如下（以微软公司的文字处理工具Word为例）：

第一步：打开文字处理工具的"替换"对话框，在其文本框"查找内容"中输入以下包括中括号在内的所有非句读符号的序列（倒数第二个符号为空格符），即［、《》（）""' '］；

第二步：文本框"替换为"保持空白，即不录入任何文字符号；

第三步：展开"更多"按键，在"搜索选项"中选择"使用通配符"；

第四步：单击"全部替换"按键。

经过上述替换处理，全部非句读符号均从原文中移除。例文变为：

审知为人状儿雄伟，隆准方口，常乘白马，军中号白马三郎。乾宁四年，潮卒，审知代立。唐以福州为威武军，拜审知节度使，累迁同中书门下平章事，封琅琊王。唐亡，梁太祖加拜审知中书令，封闽王，升福州为大都督府。是时，杨行密据有江淮，审知岁遣使泛海，自登莱朝贡于梁，使者入海，覆溺常十三四。

审知虽起盗贼，而为人俭约，好礼下士。王淡，唐相溥之子；杨沂，唐相涉从弟；徐寅，唐时知名进士，皆依审知仕宦。又建学四门，以教闽士之秀者。招来海中蛮夷商贾。海上黄崎，波涛为阻，一夕风雨雷电震击，开以为港，闽人以为审知德政所致，号为甘棠港。

移除非句读符号的文本另存为"2号文件"。上述例文当前只有［，。；］等40个句读符号，其余3个非句读符号均被移出文本，它们分别是1对引号和1个顿号。为了方便后续的文字处理，可临时使用文言句读符号［°］统一代替各类句读符号。具体的替代方法如下：

第一步：打开"替换"对话框，在其文本框"查找内容"中输入以下包括中括号在内的所有句读符号的序列，即［,。:!;?］；

第二步：在文本框"替换为"中输入文言句读符号，即°；

第三步：展开"更多"按键，在"搜索选项"中选择"使用通配符"；

第四步：单击"全部替换"按键；

第五步：当前的文件内容另存为新文件。

经过上述替换处理，现代句读符号均已改为文言句读符号。例文变为：

审知为人状儿雄伟°隆准方口°常乘白马°军中号白马三郎°乾宁四年°潮卒°审知代立°唐以福州为威武军°拜审知节度使°累迁同中书门下平章事°封琅琊王°唐亡°梁太祖加拜审知中书令°封闽王°升福州为大都督府°是时°杨行密据有江淮°审知岁遣使泛海°自登莱朝贡于梁°使者入海°覆溺常十三四°

审知虽起盗贼°而为人俭约°好礼下士°王淡°唐相溥之子°杨沂°唐相涉从弟°徐寅°唐时知名进士°皆依审知仕宦°又建学四门°以教闽士之秀者°招来海中蛮夷商贾°海上黄崎°波涛为阻°一夕风雨雷电震击°开以为港°闽人以为审知德政所致°号为甘棠港°

统一使用文言句读符号的文本另存为"3号文件"。为了方便统计文本的汉字数量，还可临时移除所有句读符号，得到"4号文件"。移除文言句读符号与移除非句读符号的方法类似。不同的是，文言句读符号只有一种，因而无须"使用通配符"的选项。具体的步骤如下：

第一步：打开带有文言句读符号的文件，另存为新文件；

第二步：打开"替换"对话框，在其文本框"查找内容"中输入文言句读符号，即°；

第三步：文本框"替换为"保持空白，即不录入任何文字符号；

第四步：展开"更多"按键，在"搜索选项"中取消"使用通配符"的选择；

第五步：单击"全部替换"按键。

第一步打开的文件即"3号文件"。经过上述移除处理，全部文言句读均被移除。例文变为：

> 审知为人状儿雄伟隆准方口常乘白马军中号白马三郎乾宁四年潮卒审知代立唐以福州为威武军拜审知节度使累迁同中书门下平章事封琅琊王唐亡梁太祖加拜审知中书令封闽王升福州为大都督府是时杨行密据有江淮审知岁遣使泛海自登莱朝贡于梁使者入海覆溺常十三四
>
> 审知虽起盗贼而为人俭约好礼下士王淡唐相溥之子杨沂唐相涉从弟徐寅唐时知名进士皆依审知仕宦又建学四门以教闽士之秀者招来海中蛮夷商贾海上黄崎波涛为阻一夕风雨雷电震击开以为港闽人以为审知德政所致号为甘棠港

上述新文件可命名为"4号文件"。该文件可方便地用以统计汉字数量。上述第三步的文本框"替换为"的内容如果不是空白，而是填入句读符号（°），那么替换的次数就是句读的总数。此外，在"3号文件"的基础上，还可借助文言句读符号使文本的所有句读分行排列。句读分行是结构化原文的中心环节，其操作步骤如下：

第一步：打开带有文言句读符号的文件，另存为新文件；

第二步：打开"替换"对话框，在其文本框"查找内容"中输入文言句读符号，即°；

第三步：在文本框"替换为"中输入分行符号，即^&^13；

第四步：展开"更多"按键，在"搜索选项"中取消"使用通配符"的选择；

第五步：单击"全部替换"按键；

第六步：按照此前的方法移除全部文言句读符号。

第一步打开的文件即"3号文件"。经过上述分行处理，文件以句读为单位分行排列。例文变为：

> 审知为人状儿雄伟
>
> 隆准方口
>
> 常乘白马
>
> 军中号白马三郎
>
> 乾宁四年
>
> 潮卒

审知代立
唐以福州为威武军
拜审知节度使
累迁同中书门下平章事
封琅琊王
唐亡
梁太祖加拜审知中书令
封闽王
升福州为大都督府
是时
杨行密据有江淮
审知岁遣使泛海
自登莱朝贡于梁
使者入海
覆溺常十三四
审知虽起盗贼
而为人俭约
好礼下士
王淡
唐相溥之子
杨沂
唐相涉从弟
徐寅
唐时知名进士
皆依审知仕宦
又建学四门
以教闽士之秀者
招来海中蛮夷商贾
海上黄崎
波涛为阻
一夕风雨雷电震击
开以为港
闽人以为审知德政所致
号为甘棠港

完成句读分行的新文件可命名为"5号文件"。该文件随即转为纯文本文件，并另存为"6号文件"。新建1个名为"7号文件"的表格文件，其中导入"6号文件"的内容（以微软公司的表格处理工具Excel为例）。在"7号文件"的基础上，添加表头和一些必要的字段就可得到如下"8号文件"（表1-1只列出例文第1段的内容）。

表1-1 汉语原文句读库及其结构

文本序号	句读类型	原文句读	译文语句	备注
		审知为人状儿雄伟		
		隆准方口		
		常乘白马		
		军中号白马三郎		
		乾宁四年		
		潮卒		
		审知代立		
		唐以福州为威武军		
		拜审知节度使		
		累迁同中书门下平章事		
		封琅琊王		
		唐亡		
		梁太祖加拜审知中书令		
		封闽王		
		升福州为大都督府		
		是时		
		杨行密据有江淮		
		审知岁遣使泛海		
		自登莱朝贡于梁		
		使者入海		
		覆溺常十三四		

表1-1共有5个基本字段。第3个字段"原文句读"就是"7号文件"的内容。其余4个字段暂时为空，将逐一补上。第1个字段"文本序号"填入当前句读在《新五代史》中所处的卷数。上述例文选自《新五代史》第68卷"闽世家第八"，因而句读的"文本序号"均为"68"。第2个字

段"句读类型"填入句读所属的结构类型。通过句读的语法分析就可明确句读类型。第 4 个字段"译文语句"填入群组翻译的结果，即原文语句的英语翻译。第 5 个字段"备注"用以记录翻译所涉及的疑问或遇到的困难。在教学与实践中，字段还可按需添加。上述"8 号文件"把原文结构化为一种更为有效的数据视图，方便译者阅读并理解原文。在明确并标注句读类型之后，原文就转化为便于实施群组翻译的原文句读库。在群组翻译并填入译文语句之后，句读库进而转化为翻译案例库。

2. 语法分析的基本框架

阅读并理解原文是翻译的前提。只有准确的理解，才会有准确的翻译。阅读理解既可获得句读的语义内容，又可获得语法结构。语义内容和语法结构两个方面关联密切。在一定程度上，明确句读的语法类型能够体现其语义理解。本书尝试把语义理解转化为语法分析。具体的操作程序是，先逐句阅读"8 号文件"，再明确每个句读的语法类型，然后在"句读类型"中标上具体的类型符号。语法分析主要以 Pulleyblank（1995）所明确的 20 余种句读类型为基本框架。这些类型又可归入四大类，分别是普通体词性句读（general nominal clause 或 general NC）、简单谓词性句读（simple predicative clause 或 simple PC）、特殊谓词性句读（special predicative clause 或 special PC）、复杂句读（complex clause）。

2.1 普通体词性句读

普通体词性句读是以名词性结构为主体成分的句读。其中，包含完整的主谓结构的类别称为完全体词性句读（complete nominal clause，CNC）。不完全体词性句读（incomplete nominal clause）本身不是一个完整的主谓结构，而是相关的上下文语句的主语、谓语、宾语或状语等成分，因而按其语法功能又可分为四类：名词性主语句读（nominal clause of subject，NCS）、名词性谓语句读（nominal clause of predicate，NCP）、名词性状语句读（nominal clause of adverbial，NCA）、名词性列举句读（nominal clause of enumeration，NCE）。如（PRN 表示代词，MOD 表示语气词）：

[1]　Tián　Dān　zhě　　Qí　　zhū　Tián　　shū　　shǔ　　yě
　　　田　　单　　者。　齐　　诸　　田　　　疏　　　属　　也
　　　Tian　Dan　PRN　Qi　 of　　Tian　distant　relative　MOD
　　　"Tian Dan was a distant relative of the royal Tian's clan in the state of Qi."《史记·田单列传》

第［1］例由"田单者"和"齐诸田疏属也"两个体词性句读构成：前者充当后者的主语，属于名词性主语句读；后者充当前者的谓语，属于名词性谓语句读。二者构成一个完整的主谓结构。在文言文中，主语省略或不在上文的现象比较普遍，形成大量的名词性谓语句读。如：

[2]　fēi　　wǒ　　yě　　bīng　　yě
　　　非　　我　　也。　兵　　　也
　　　not　　I　　MOD　weapon　MOD
　　　"It was not I; it was the weapon." (*Meng* 1A/3)

[3]　wèi　　tiān　　zhě　　yě
　　　畏　　 天　　　者　　 也
　　　fear　heaven　PRN　MOD
　　　"... is one who fears Heaven." (*Meng* 1B/3)

[4]　sōu　　zhī　　suǒ　　zhī　　yě
　　　叟　　 之　　 所　　 知　　也
　　　you　　PRN　　all　　know　MOD
　　　"It is what your reverence well knows." (*Meng* 1A/7)

第［2］例包含两个判断句读"非……也"和"……也"。Pulleyblank（1995：16）的译文是：It was not I; it was the weapon。其后的出处"*Meng* 1A/3"表明，该句引自《孟子》第1卷"梁惠王上"第3章。本章有标出处的译文均引自 Pulleyblank（1995）的译文。第［3］例整句译为 ... is one who fears Heaven，其中的"畏天者"（one who fears Heaven）是名物化的主谓结构。该句引自《孟子》第1卷"梁惠王上"第3章。第［4］例整句译为 It is what your reverence well knows，其中的"叟之所知"（what your reverence well knows）也是名物化的主谓结构。该句引自《孟子》第1卷"梁惠王上"第7章。第［5］例包含两个句读，其中之一为名词性状语句读。

[5]　qiū　　bā　　yuè　　Dì　　zhì　　zì　　fá　　Xiǎn
　　　秋　　 八　　月。　 帝　　至　　自　　伐　　 显
　　　Autumn　eight　moon　emperor　arrive　self　fight　Xian
　　　"In August at the Autumn, the emperor in person came to suppress Xian."《魏书·帝纪第二·太祖纪》

名词词组"秋八月"独立构成句读，充当第2个句读的状语。另有名词性列举句读，如《论语》中的"伯夷叔齐虞仲夷逸朱张柳下惠少连"，其中列举了7个人物的名称。

2.2 简单谓词性句读

以简单谓语动词为核心的句读就是简单谓词性句读，可分为不及物动词谓语句读（intransitive-verb clause, IVC）、单及物动词谓语句读（transitive-verb clause, TVC）、双及物动词谓语句读（ditransitive-verb clause, DVC）三类。如：

[1]　　yī　　lái
　　　　医　　来
　　　　physician　came
　　　　"The physician came."（*Meng* 2B/2）

第[1]例的"来"字为不及物动词，直接译为came。有些谓语动词虽然在形式上是及物的，但在英译中需要使用介词以连接动词和宾语，其实得到一种不及物的结构。如：

[2]　zé　　miáo　bórán　　xīng　zhī　yǐ
　　　则　　苗　　勃然　　兴　　之　　矣
　　　then　sprout　suddenly　spring up　PRN　MOD
　　　"… then the sprouts suddenly spring up in response to it [the rain]."（*Meng* 1A/6）

第[2]例的"兴之"为动宾结构，其译文 spring up in response to it 包含复杂介词词组 in response to，其中的 spring up 实为不及物动词词组。

[3]　qīshí　zhě　yī　bó　shí　ròu
　　　七十　　者　　衣　帛　食　肉
　　　seventy　PRN　wear　silk　eat　meat
　　　"When seventy year olds *wear* silk and *eat* meat …"（*Meng* 1A/3）

[4a]　láo　xīn　zhě　zhì　rén　láo　lì　zhě　zhì　yú　rén
　　　劳　　心　　者　　治　　人。劳　　力　　者　　治　　于　　人
　　　labour　mind　PRN　rule　man　labour　strength　PRN　rule　by　man
　　　"Those who labour with their minds [literally: labour their minds] rule others, those who labour with their strength are ruled by others."（Meng 3A/4）

[4b] zhì　yú　rén　zhě　sì　rén　zhì　rén　zhě　sì　yú　rén
　　　治　　于　　人　　者　　食　　人。治　　人　　者　　食　　于　　人
　　　rule　by　man　PRN　feed　man　rule　man　PRN　feed　by　man
　　　"Those who are ruled by others feed others, those who rule others are fed by others."（*Meng* 3A/4）

第［3］例包含"衣帛"和"食肉"两个并列的动宾结构，分别译为 wear silk 和 eat meat。第［4a］例和第［4b］例为前后相邻的两组语句，各自包含 2 个句读，共有 4 个句读。其中，第［4a］例的"治人"（rule others）和第［4b］例的"食人"（feed others）均为动宾结构，其被动形式分别是第［4a］例的"治于人"（are ruled by others）和第［4b］例的"食于人"（are fed by others）。

部分单及物动词后接地理名词或方位名词。如：

［5］　jiāng　　　zhī　　　Chǔ
　　　将　　　　之　　　　楚
　　　be going to　go to　　Chu
"… was going to go to Chu."（Meng 3A/1）

［6］　jiù　　zhī　　ér　　bù　　jiàn　　suǒ　　wèi　　yān
　　　就　　之　　而　　不　　见　　　所　　　畏　　　焉
　　　go up to　PRN　but　not　see　　thing　fear　MOD
"Going up to him, I did not see anything to fear (= awesome) in him."（Meng 1A/6）

［7］　jué　jǐng　jiǔ　rèn　ér　bù　jí　quán
　　　掘　　井　　九　　轫　　而　不　及　泉
　　　dig　well　nine　ren　and　not　reach　spring
"To dig a well to a depth of nine ren and not reach the spring …"（Meng 7A/29）

第［5］例的"之楚"和第［6］例的"就之"均译为不及物结构 go to Chu 和 going up to him。第［7］例的"及泉"译为动宾结构 reach the spring。

另有表示拥有或存在意义的句读。如：

［8］　xī　　Huáng　　Dì　　yǒu　　zǐ　　èrshíwǔ　　rén
　　　昔　　　黄　　　帝　　　有　　　子　　　二十五　　　人
　　　ancient　Yellow　Emperor　have　son　twenty-five　man
"The ancient Emperor Yellow had 25 sons."《魏书·帝纪第一·序纪》

［9］　yì　　yǒu　　rén　　yì　　ér　　yǐ　　yǐ
　　　亦　　有　　　仁　　义　　而　　已　　矣
　　　surely　have　benevolence　righteousness　and　only　MOD
"(I) surely have only benevolence and righteousness [to offer you]."（Meng 1A/1）

[10] rén   zhě   wú   dí
　　仁　　者　　无　　敌
　　benevolence PRN no match
"The man of benevolence has no match." (*Meng* 1A/5)

[11] wèi yǒu yì ér hòu qí jūn zhě
　　未　有　义　而　后　其　君　者
　　never there be righteous and last his ruler PRN
"There has never been one who was righteous and put his ruler last." (*Meng* 1A/1)

[12] wú   jūnzǐ   mò zhì yěrén   wú   yěrén   mò   yǎng   jūnzǐ
　　无　君子。莫 治 野人。无　野人。莫　养　　君子
　　no gentleman not rule rustics no rustics not support genetleman
"If there were no gentlemen, there would be no one to rule the rustics; if there were no rustics, there would be no one to support the gentlemen." (*Meng* 3A/3)

第[8]例的"有子[二十五人]"和第[9]例的"有仁义"均表示肯定的拥有关系，分别译为 had 25 sons 和 have only benevolence and righteousness。第[10]例的"无敌"表示否定的拥有关系，译为 has no match。第[11]例的"未有"和第[12]例的"无君子"与"无野人"均表示存在意义，分别译为 there has never been one、there were no gentlemen 和 there were no rustics。

例[13]—例[16]的"与、授、教、夺"后接两个宾语，均为双及物动词。

[13] néng yǔ   rén   guī   ju
　　能　　与　人　　规　　矩
　　can give man compass square
"… can give a man a compass and a square." (*Meng* 7B/5)

[14] shòu Mèngzǐ shì
　　授　　孟子　　室
　　give Mencius house
"… to give Mencius a house …" (*Meng* 3A/4)

[15] Hòujì jiāo rén jià sè
　　后稷　教　　人　稼　穑
　　Hou Ji teach people sow reaping
"Hou Ji taught the people sowing and reaping." (*Meng* 1A/3)

[16]　duó　　zhī　　shí
　　　　夺　　　之　　　食
　　　　rob　　PRN　　food

"… by robbing him of his food" (*Meng* 6B/1)

在第[13]例中,"与"字后接"人"和"规矩"两个宾语,其所构成的双宾结构"与人规矩"译为 give a man a compass and a square。在第[14]例中,"授"字后接"孟子"和"室"两个宾语,其所构成的双宾结构"授孟子室"译为 to give Mencius a house。在第[15]例中,"教"字后接"人"和"稼穑"两个宾语,其所构成的双宾结构"教人稼穑"译为 taught the people sowing and reaping。在第[16]例中,"夺"字后接"之"和"食"两个宾语,其所构成的双宾结构"夺之食"译为 by robbing him of his food。除了第[16]例的译文使用介词短语 of his food 之外,其余3例的译文均为双宾结构。

2.3　特殊谓词性句读

除了上述普通谓语动词之外,还有包括轻动词、形容词、形容词活用动词、名词活用动词、能愿动词、被动语态等在内的特殊谓语动词。以特殊谓语动词为核心的句读就是特殊谓词性句读。此类句读按其具体的动词类别可分为轻动词谓语句读(light-verb clause,LVC)、形容词谓语句读(adjective-predicate clause,APC)、形容词活用动词句读(deadjectival-verb clause,DAV)、名词活用动词句读(denominal-verb clause,DNV)、能愿动词句读(modal-verb clause,MVC)、被动语态句读(passive-voice clause,PVC)。如:

[1]　wù　　jiē　　rán　　xīn　　wéi　　shèn
　　　物　　皆　　然。心　　为　　甚
　　　thing　all　　like　　heart　is　　most

"Things are all like that and the heart is most so." (*Meng* 1A/7)

[2]　zé　　wú　　wàng　mín　　zhī　　duō　yú　　lín　　guó　　yě
　　　则　　无　　望　　民　　之　　多　　于　　邻　　国　　也
　　　then　not　hope　people　PRN　many　than　neighbour　country　MOD

"… then do not hope that your people will be more than [those of] the neighbouring countries." (*Meng* 1A/3)

第[1]例的轻动词"为"字后接形容词"甚"字,构成系补结构,表示程度最高(most so)。第[2]例的"多[于邻国]"字为形容词,直接充当谓词,译为 will be more than。

例[3]—例[6]的"大、远、安"均为形容词活用的及物动词,后接宾语。

[3] wáng qǐng dà zhī
王 请 大 之
king beg enlarge PRN
"I beg Your Majesty to make it great."(*Meng* 1B/3)

[4] sǒu bù yuǎn qiān lǐ ér lái
叟 不 远 千 里 而 来
you not far thousand *li* and come
"You have come, sir, not regarding 1,000 *li* as too far."(*Meng* 1A/1)

[5] bǎi xìng ān zhī
百 姓 安 之
common people peace PRN
"The common people were peaceful under him."(*Meng* 5A/5)

[6] zé bù néng ān Zǐsī
则 不 能 安 子思
then not can content Zisi
"… then he could not make Zisi content."(*Meng* 2B/11)

第[3]例的"大之"和第[6]例的"安子思"均译为使役结构 make it great 和 make Zisi content。第[4]例的"不远千里"译为 not regarding 1,000 *li* as too far。第[5]例的"安之"译为 were peaceful under him。第[4]例和第[5]例的使役特征明显减弱。

例[7]—例[10]的"臣、吴王、父、子、君"等均为名词活用的动词形式,可分为及物和不及物两种形式。

[7] gù Tāng zhīyú Yī Yǐn xué yān ér hòu chén zhī
故 汤 之于 伊 尹 学 焉 而 后 臣 之
thus Tang towards Yi Yin learn MOD and then subject PRN
"Thus Tang's [behaviour] towards Yi Yin was to learn from him and afterwards make him his subject."(*Meng* 2B/2)

[8] ěr   yù   Wú   Wáng   wǒ   hū
     尔   欲   吴   王   我   乎
     you   want Wu   King   me   MOD

"Do you want to King-of-Wu me (=treat me in the way the King of Wu was treated)?" (*Zuo Zhuan* 10/7)

[9] jūn   jūn   chén   chén   fù   fù   zǐ   zǐ
     君   君   臣   臣   父   父   子   子
     ruler ruler minister minister father father son   son

"Let the ruler act as a ruler should, the minister as a minister, the father as a father, the son as a son." (*Lun Yu* 12/11)

[10] wéi   chén   ér   jūn   ……   wáng   zhī   běn   yě
     为   臣   而   君   ……   亡   之   本   也
     for   minister but   ruler ... perdition's   root   MOD

"For one who is a minister to act as a ruler … is the root of perdition." (*Zuo Xiang* 7/7)

第[7]例的"臣"和第[8]例的"吴王"均为及物动词：前者及其宾语"之"字译为使役结构 make him as his subject；后者及其宾语"我"字译为 treat me in the way the King of Wu was treated，其中包含状语从句。第[9]例的"[君]君、[臣]臣、[父]父、[子]子"和第[10]例的"[为臣而]君"字均为不及物动词：前者译为 (let the ruler) act as a ruler should、(the minister) as a minister、(the father) as a father 和 (the son) as a son；后者译为 (for one who is a minister) to act as a ruler。

被动语态句读属于特殊谓词性句读，其谓语动词通常由"见、遇、所、受、被"等助动词复合特定的主动词，形成包括"见动（*jian*-passive）、遇动（*yu*-passive）、所动（*suo*-passive）、受动（*shou*-passive）、被动（*bei*-passive）"等在内的多种结构类型。其中的"被动"结构只是各类被动形式之一。在被动语态中，"见动"式最为普遍。如：

[1] yǐ   jǐn   hòu   jiàn   ài
     以   谨   厚   见   爱
     use   politeness honesty *jian*-passive appreciate

"He is appreciated for his politeness, innocence and honesty."
《新五代史·周本纪第十二》

[2] zì　　xiān　wáng　shí　cháng　jiàn　　yōu　jiǎ
　　 自　　先　　王　　时　　常　　见　　优　　假
　　 from　former　king　time　often　*jian*-passive　well　care

"These adopted sons had generally been treated with leniency from the time of the former king." 《新五代史·唐家人传第二》

[3] yóu　shì　Yánguǎng　yǐ　wǎn　qiáng　jiàn　chēng
　　 由　 是　　延广　　以　挽　　强　　见　　称
　　 for　this　Yanguang　time　draw the bow　*jian*-passive　adore

"Yanguang therefore was adored for his ability to draw the bow." 《新五代史·晋臣传第十七》

上述 3 例的"见"字分别后接"爱、[优]假、称",其所构成的"见爱、见[优]假、见称"分别译为 is appreciated、had [generally] been treated [with leniency] 和 was adored。有时"见"字后也接双字动词。如(CNJ 表示代词):

[4] pō　 jiàn　 xìn　yòng
　　 颇　 见　 信　 用
　　 well　*jian*-passive　trust　adopt

"[Shaohong] was well trusted and appointed."《新五代史·宦者传第二十六》

[5] ér　zhōng　chén　yǒng　shì　jiē　jiàn　shū　chì
　　 而　 忠　 臣　 勇　 士　 皆　 见　 疏　 斥
　　 CNJ　loyal　minister　brave　warrior　all　*jian*-passive　alienate　exclude

"… but all loyal ministers and brave warriors were alienated and excluded."《新五代史·杂传第三十二》

第[4]例的"信用"和第[5]例的"疏斥"均为双字动词,与"见"字构成复杂的被动结构"见信用"和"见疏斥",分别译为并列的被动结构 was trusted and appointed 和 were alienated and excluded。

[6] Zhuāngzōng　yù　shì
　　 庄宗　　　 遇　 弑
　　 Zhuangzong　*yu*-passive　murder

"Emperor Zhuangzong was murdered."《新五代史·晋本纪第八》

例[6]的"遇弑"通常涉及君臣或父子关系,可译为普通的被动形式 was murdered。

[7] ér   wàn   shì   suǒ   gòng   wù   zhě   yě
    而   万   世   所   共   恶   者   也
    CNJ myriad generation *suo*-passive commonly detest PRN MOD
    "… and you are the one who will be commonly detested by myriad generations."《新五代史·梁本纪第二》

[8] sì   fāng   suǒ   shàng   wù
    四   方   所   上   物
    four quarter *suo*-passive present object
    "Objects were presented from four quarters."《新五代史·唐本纪第六》

[9] Shěnchéng   Wēnyù   suǒ   jiàng   bù   guò   sān   qiān
    审澄   温裕   所   将   不   过   三   千
    Shencheng Wenyu *suo*-passive lead not surpass three thousand
    "The number of soldiers led by Shencheng and Wenyu was less than three thousand."《新五代史·梁臣传第十一》

[10] huànguān   língrén   yǒu   suǒ   qiú   qǐng
     宦官   伶人   有   所   求   请
     eunuch actor have *suo*-passive implore plea
     "The eunuchs and actors had something to implore or plea for."《新五代史·唐臣传第十二》

[11] Yìchéng   bīngzú   qǐ   gōng   suǒ   dé   zhǎn   yé
     义成   兵卒   岂   公   所   得   斩   邪
     Yicheng soldier how duke *suo*-passive can execute MOD
     "How can your reverence execute Yicheng's soldiers?"《新五代史·唐臣传第十三》

例[7]—例[11]的"所"字和"恶、上、将、求、斩"构成被动结构"所[共]恶[者]、所上[物]、所将、[有]所求、所[得]斩",分别译为 the one who will be (commonly) detested、(objects) were presented、the number of soldiers led by (Shencheng)、(had) something to implore or plea for 和 execute。除了最后两例的译文使用主动形式外,其余均用被动形式。

"受动"结构可分为三类:其一,"受"字后接名词和动词,形成"受字+名词+动词"结构;其二,"受字+名词+动词"结构因省略名词而转为"受字+动词"结构;其三,"受字+名词+动词"结构因省略动词而转为"受字+名词"结构。如:

[12] Cúnjié dōng xī shòu dí
存节 东 西 受 敌
Cunjie east west *shou*-passive enemy

"Cunjie was attacked by the enemy from both the east and the west."《新五代史·梁臣传第十》

[13] shòu guó ēn shēn
受 国 恩 深
shou-passive nation favour deep

"［I］have been deeply favoured by the nation." /
"［I］have accepted much favour from the nation."《新五代史·梁臣传第九》

[14] shǐ shòu sì fāng lù yí
始 受 四 方 赂 遗
begin *shou*-passive four quarter present donate

"［He］began to be presented and donated with goods or money by the four quarters/to accept donated goods or money from the people of different places."《新五代史·唐臣传第十二》

[15] wú bù néng chánchán zuò shòu líng ruò
吾 不 能 孱孱 坐 受 凌 弱
I not can passivly sit *shou*-passive insult weaken

"I cannot be passively insulted and thus simply weakened." /
"I cannot simply sit and passively accept the insult."《新五代史·杂传第二十八》

[16] Yíchāo guǒ bù shòu dài
彝超 果 不 受 代
Yichao sure not *shou*-passive substitute

"Yichao truly refused to be replaced by others." /
"Yichao did not accept the substitution as expected."《新五代史·杂传第二十八》

第［13］例的"受国恩［深］"和第［14］例的"受四方赂遗"均属第一类，分别译为 have been (deeply) favoured by the nation 和 be presented and donated with goods or money by the four quarters。第［15］例的"受凌弱"和第［16］例的"受代"均属第二类，分别译为 be insulted and thus simply weakened 和 be replaced by others。第［12］例的"受敌"属于第三类，译为 was attacked by the enemy，其中的（was）attacked 为添加的

内容。多数"受动"结构的"受"字还可译为主动的 accept。例如，第[13]例的"受[国]恩[深]"、第[14]例的"受[四方]赂遗"、第[15]例的"受凌弱"和第[16]例的"受代"可分别译为 have accepted（much）favour from the nation、to accept donated goods or money from the people of different places、accept the insult 和 accept the substitution。

"所动"结构之前都有"为"字结构，形成"为［名］所［动］"的复合结构。如：

[17] wèi   jiān   rén   suǒ   wù   ěr
　　　为　　奸　　人　　所　　误　　耳
　　　by treacherous man *suo*-passive mistake MOD
"［Jitao］was simply mistaken by the treacherous."《新五代史·义儿传第二十四》

[18] huàn zhě duō wèi zhū zhèn suǒ cángnì ér bù shā
　　　宦　者　多　为　诸　镇　所　藏匿　而　不　杀
　　　official PRN most by those town *suo*-passive hide CNJ not kill
"Most of the officials were hidden among those occupation forces and hence survived."《新五代史·宦者传第二十六》

[19] Wēn shù wèi Hézhōng Wáng Chóngróng suǒ bài
　　　温　数　为　河中　　王重荣　　　所　败
　　　Wen several by Hezhong Wang Chongrong *suo*-passive defeat
"Wen had been defeated by Wang Chongrong, the military commissioner of Hezhong, several times."《新五代史·梁本纪第一》

[20] gāo zǔ wèi Qìdān suǒ lì
　　　高　祖　为　契丹　所　立
　　　high ancestor by Khitan *suo*-passive enthrone
"The Founding Emperor was enthroned by Khitan."《新五代史·晋本纪第九》

[21] Róng sù wèi shūmìshǐ Wáng Jùn suǒ jì
　　　荣　素　为　枢密使　　王峻　　所　忌
　　　Rong always by privy chancellor Wang Jun *suo*-passive begrudge
"Rong had always been begrudged by Wang Jun, the privy chancellor."《新五代史·周本纪第十二》

上述第[17]例的"为［奸人］所［误］"、第[18]例的"为

[诸镇]所[藏匿]"、第[19]例的"为[河中王重荣]所[败]"、第[20]例的"为[契丹]所[立]"和第[21]例的"为[枢密使王峻]所[忌]"均属复合的"为[名]所[动]"结构，分别译为 was (mistaken) by (the treacherous)、were (hidden) among (those occupation forces)、had been (defeated) by (Wang Chongrong, the military commissioner of Hezhong)、was (enthroned) by (Khitan) 和 has been (begrudged) by (Wang Jun, the privy chancellor)。

[22] Chóngwēi   děng   bèi   wéi   liáng   jué
     重威   等   被   围   粮   绝
     Chongwei   and others bei-passive surround grain run out
     "Chongwei and others were surrounded and ran out of grain."《新五代史·四夷附录第一》

[23] èr   bǎi   kǒu   bèi   zhū
     二   百   口   被   诛
     two   hundred mouth bei-passive extinguish
     "Two hundred people were extinguished."《新五代史·杂传第三十二》

[24] jí   zhuī   fēng   qī   zǐ   zhī   bèi   shā   zhě
     及   追   封   妻   子   之   被   杀   者
     and   additionally confer wife child PRN bei-passive kill PRN
     "... and conferred additional titles to his wives and those children who had been killed."《新五代史·周家人传第八》

[25] Yǔ   děng   bèi   liú   jīng   suì
     羽   等   被   留   经   岁
     Yu   and others bei-passive detain pass year
     "Yu and others were detained for years."《新五代史·杂传第四十五》

例[22]—例[25]的"被"字后接"围、诛、杀、留"构成被动结构"被围、被诛、被杀、被留"，分别译为 were surrounded、were extinguished、had been killed 和 were detained。现代汉语广泛使用这种被动结构。

2.4 复杂句读

复杂句读包含两个或以上主谓结构，可细分为双扇句读（double-phased clause，DPC）、连动句读（serial-verb clause，SVC）、并列谓语句读

(coordinate-predicate clause，CPC)、主谓宾语句读（clause with a complex object，CCO)、主谓主语句读（clause with a complex subject，CCS)、使役结构句读（clause with a causative construction，CCC)、主副动词句读（clause with a verb and a coverb，CVC）等。如：

rén	jiē	wèi	wǒ	huǐ	míng	táng
人	皆	谓	我	毁	明	堂
man	all	tell	me	destroy	light	hall

"People all tell me to destroy the Hall of Light."（*Meng* 1B/5）

该例的"谓［我］毁［明堂］"构成使役结构，译为 tell (me) to destroy (the Hall of Light)。复杂句读通常是普通体词性句读、简单谓词性句读或特殊谓词性句读的复合形式，其内部涉及复合的逻辑关系。

3. 句读分析与类型标注

句读类型既是语义理解的标记，也是群组翻译的线索。一方面，句读类型用以标记语义理解的完成情况。句读库方便译者按顺序阅读并在语法框架中分析句读以理解其语法结构和语义内容，同时完成类型标注。句读类型的标注实际上把文本阅读从默会的语义理解变为明示的语法分析，充实了句读库的内容。换言之，句读类型虽然是语法分析的结果，但能反映语义理解的完成情况。阅读、理解、分析及标注上述例文的具体过程大致如下：

审知为人状儿雄伟［形容词作谓语核心，属于形容词谓语句读，标记为 APC］隆准方口［两个并列的名词词组，属于名词性谓语句读，标记为 NCP］常乘白马［动词后接单个宾语，标记为 TVC］军中号白马三郎［两个名词词组构成复合的主谓结构，属于名词性谓语句读，标记为 NCP］乾宁四年［时间名词充当状语，独立构成句读，属于名词性状语句读，标记为 NCA］潮卒［主语后接不及物动词构成句读，属于不及物动词谓语句读，标记为 IVC］审知代立［同上，标记为 IVC］唐以福州为威武军［两个动宾结构，前者包含副动词，后者包含主动词，属于主副动词句读，标记为 CVC］拜审知节度使［动词后接两个宾语，属于双及物动词谓语句读，标记为 DVC］累迁同中书门下平章事［动词后接单个宾语，属于单及物动词谓语句读，标记为 TVC］封琅琊王［轻动词后接补语名词，属于轻动词谓语句读，标记为 LVC］唐亡［主语后接不及物动词，构成不及物动词谓语句读，标记为 IVC］梁太祖加拜审知中书令［动词后接两个宾语，构成双及物动词谓语句读，标记为 DVC］封闽王［轻动词后接补语名词，构成轻动词谓语句读，标记为 LVC］升福州为大都督府［主动词和副动词构成主副动词句读，标记为 CVC］是时［时间名词充当状语，独立构成名词性状语句读，标记为 NCA］杨行密据有江淮［动词后接单个宾语，构成单及物动词谓语句读，标记为 TVC］审知岁遣使泛海［前后两个动词构成使役结构，属于使役结构句读，标记为 CCC］自登莱朝贡于梁［副动词和主动词构成主副动词句读，标记为 CVC］使者入海［动词后接单个宾语，构成单及物动词谓语句读，标记为 TVC］覆溺常十三四［不及物动词后接非宾语名词，属于单及物动词谓语句读，标记为 IVC］

审知虽起盗贼［同上，动词后接非宾语，实为不及物，标记为 IVC］而为人俭约［形容词充当谓语核心，属于形容词谓语句读，标记为 APC］好礼下士［动词后接单个宾语，构成单及物动词谓语句读，标记为 TVC］王淡［名词词组充当主语，独立构成名词性主语句读，标记为 NCS］唐相溥之子［名词词组充当谓语，独立构成名词性谓语句读，标记为 NCP］杨沂［名词词组充当主语，独立构成名词性主语句读，标记为 NCS］唐相涉从弟［名词词组充当谓语，独立构成名词性谓语句读，标记为 NCP］徐寅［名词词组充当主语，独立构成名词性主语句读，标记为 NCS］唐时知名进士［名词词组充当谓语，独立构成名词性谓语句读，标记为 NCP］皆依审知仕宦［包含名词活用的动词，属于名词活用动词句读，标记为 DNV］又建学四门［动词后接单个宾语，构成单及物动词谓语句读，标记为 TVC］以教闽士之秀者［属于连动句读的后半部分，标记为 SVC］招来海中蛮夷商贾［动词后接单个名词词组，构成单及物动词谓语句读，标记为 TVC］海上黄崎［名词词组充当主语，独立构成名词性主语句读，标记为 NCS］波涛为阻［属于被动语态句读，标记为 PVC］一夕风雨雷电震击［主语后接不及物动词，构成不及物动词谓语句读，标记为 IVC］开以为港［前后两个动词构成连动结构，属于连动句读，标记为 SVC］闽人以为审知德政所致［包含被动结构，属于被动语态句读，标记为 PVC］号为甘棠港［包含轻动词，属于轻动词谓语句读，标记为 LVC］

另一方面，句读类型是句读群组的线索，方便提取同类句读并组成句读群组。这是群组翻译得以实施的前提保障。有别于通常的顺序翻译，群组翻译不受限于句读在文本中的实际位置，属于一种"组装"的、"流水"的翻译活动：先按结构类型把句读归入不同的群组，再以群组为单位翻译句读，然后把翻译语句按原有的顺序重新装配并得到翻译文稿，最后从多重维度上修订译文而得到终稿。群组翻译的流水作业模式有利于提高翻译的速度与效率。

4. 群组翻译

在添加标注的句读库中，借助句读类型可直接把具有同类语法结构的句读检索并提取出来形成独立的群组。上述例文第 1 段包含 21 个句读：4 个普通体词性谓语句读，分别为 2 个名词性谓语句读（NCP）和 2 个名词性状语句读（NCA）；10 个简单谓词性句读，分别为 4 个单及物动词谓语句读（TVC）、4 个不及物动词谓语句读（IVC）和 2 个双及物动词谓语句读（DVC）；3 个特殊谓词性句读，分别为 1 个形容词谓语句读（APC）和 2 个轻动词谓语句读（LVC）；4 个复杂句读，分别为 3 个主副动词句读（CVC）和 1 个使役结构句读（CCC）。第 1 段一共涉及 9 种句读类型，可提取 9 个句读群组，每个群组包含 1~4 个句读。句读类聚成群组之后，便可实施群组翻译。例如，从句读库中可提取包含上述 2 个名词性状语句读的群组，并翻译如下：

［1］乾宁四年　in the fourth year of the Qianning period（A. D. 897）

［2］是时　at that time

又如，从句读库中还可提取包含上述 4 个单及物动词谓语句读的群组，并翻译如下：

［1］潮卒　Chao passed away

［2］审知代立　Shenzhi succeeded to his position

［3］唐亡　after the fall of the Tang dynasty

［4］覆溺常十三四　as many as three or four out of ten got drowned

群组翻译直接把汉语单语的句读库转变为汉英双语的翻译案例库。翻译案例库实质上是一种以句读为对齐单位的双语平行语料库。多数现有的双语平行语料库以句子为对齐单位。句子往往包含多个句读，不便于标注各个句读的类型结构。以句读为单位的句读库方便为句读逐一添加类型标注。除了复杂句读外，每个句读对应一种明确的语法结构，因而能够明确具体的类型归属。句读群组就是具有同类结构的句读的集合。在同一群组的翻译中，由于涉及的句读具有相同的语法结构，所以翻译无须在不同的句型之间变换。因此，译者只须把重心放在词汇项目的选择上，无须过多地关注语法结构。经过群组翻译，上述例文第 1 段对应如下翻译案例库（表 1-2）。

表 1-2 汉英翻译案例库及其结构（片段）

句读类型	原文句读	译文语句
APC	审知为人状儿雄伟	Shenzhi was a big, burly man
NCP	隆准方口	with his nose bridge highly upright and mouth widely square
TVC	常乘白马	he often rode a white horse
NCP	军中号白马三郎	so he earned himself the name of "White Knight the Third" in the army
NCA	乾宁四年	in the fourth year of the Qianning period (A.D. 897)
IVC	潮卒	Chao passed away
IVC	审知代立	Shenzhi succeeded to his position
CVC	唐以福州为威武军	the Tang dynastic court established a provincial-level institution entitled "Weiwu Military Government" in Fuzhou
DVC	拜审知节度使	appointed Shenzhi as military commissioner
TVC	累迁同中书门下平章事	since then, he had been promoted several times until he eventually became a joint manager of affairs with the secretariat chancellery
LVC	封琅琊王	was granted with the title of "King of Langya"
IVC	唐亡	after the fall of the Tang dynasty
DVC	梁太祖加拜审知中书令	the Founding Emperor Taizu of the Liang dynasty appointed Shenzhi as general secretary of the imperial secretariat
LVC	封闽王	granted him with "King of Min"
CVC	升福州为大都督府	promoted Fuzhou as Metropolitan Government

续表

句读类型	原文句读	译文语句
NCA	是时	at that time
TVC	杨行密据有江淮	Yang Xingmi occupied the Jianghuai area
CCC	审知岁遣使泛海	Shenzhi dispatched envoys to go by seaway every year
CVC	自登莱朝贡于梁	via the seaport commanderies of Dengzhou and Laizhou
TVC	使者入海	among the envoys sailing into the sea
IVC	覆溺常十三四	as many as three or four out of ten got drowned

在翻译实践中，原文规模较大，各个群组通常包含几十个或上百个同类句读。群组翻译使译者无须同时处理多种语法结构。在顺序的翻译中，相连的句读具有不同的语法类型，因而翻译往往涉及在各种语法结构之间的交替变换。例如，表1-2的前6种句读类型分别为APC、NCP、TVC、NCP、NCA、IVC。除了NCP出现2次之外，其余句读类型都不相同。翻译在不同的语法结构之间的交替变换必然会影响其速度和效率。相反，在群组翻译中，群组内部的所有句读都具有相同或相似的语法结构，可以明显减少因语法结构的交替变换而引起的翻译干扰。显然，群组翻译既可提高翻译效率，又可保证翻译质量。

5. 译文的整理与修订

在翻译案例库的基础上整理而成的翻译文稿就是译文初稿。与翻译案例库的建立类似，译文修订同样需要规范的流程。本书提出一种基于参照的译文修订方法，其流程主要包含以下三个步骤。

第一，从翻译案例库中提取"译文语句"字段的内容，添加必要的连接词语并适当调整语序，得到译文初稿。例如，表1-2的全部译文语句经过修订，可以得到如下译文初稿：

> Shenzhi was a big, burly man with his nose bridge highly upright and mouth widely square. He often rode a white horse, so he earned himself the name of "White Knight the Third" in the army. In the fourth year of the Qianning period (A.D. 897), Chao passed away and Shenzhi succeeded to his position. The Tang dynastic court established a provincial-level institution entitled "Weiwu Military Government" in

Fuzhou and appointed Shenzhi as military commissioner. Since then, he had been promoted several times until he eventually became a joint manager of affairs with the secretariat chancellery and was granted with the title of "King of Langya". After the fall of the Tang dynasty, the Founding Emperor Taizu of the Liang dynasty appointed Shenzhi as general secretary of the imperial secretariat and granted him with "King of Min". In addition, Fuzhou was promoted as Metropolitan Government. At that time, Yang Xingmi occupied the Jianghuai area. Shenzhi dispatched envoys to go by seaway every year via the seaport commanderies of Dengzhou and Laizhou. Among the envoys sailing into the sea, as many as three or four out of ten got drowned.

第二，选择合适的汉译英文本作为主要的参照译文，分别在英汉词字比、译文词汇密度、译文语法难度等多个维度上比较翻译文稿与参照译文之间在词汇语法上的差距，并且利用比较的结果来指导译文的修改，以获得不同的修订版本。例如，上述译文共有189个英语单词，其所对应的原文包含117个汉字。平均翻译每个汉字需要大约1.62个英语单词，即英汉词字比约为1.62。本书以Watson（1974）的《汉书》英语翻译为主要的参照译文。取样调研发现，参照译文的词字比普遍为1.90。显然，翻译文稿有待进一步的修订。本书的第9章和第10章将分别论述英汉词字比、译文词汇密度、译文语法难度在译文修订中的理论意义和实用价值。

第三，选择合适的非汉译英文本作为辅助的参照文本，分别在单语的词汇密度和单语的语法难度两个维度上比较修订译文与参照译文之间在词汇语法上的差距，并且利用比较的结果进一步指导译文的修订，以获得译文终稿。在教学场景中，此类翻译文稿就是习作译文。本书选取《塔西佗编年史》的英文版（*The Annals of Tacitus*）作为辅助的参照译文。该非汉译英文本既能充当习作译文在词汇语法上的定量参照，又能充当其在遣词造句上的定性参照，有利于不断地优化译文。

第 2 章

天干地支记时及其英译

中国历史典籍包含大量以天干地支为记时形式的名词性状语句读。在本纪中，名词性状语句读普遍超过 15%，甚至可达 30%。例如，《新五代史·梁本纪第一》包含 89 个名词性状语句读，在全篇 695 个句读中的占比约为 12.8%；《新五代史·梁本纪第二》包含 96 个名词性状语句读，在全篇 342 个句读中的占比约为 28.1%；《新五代史·梁本纪第三》包含 56 个名词性状语句读，在全篇 213 个句读中的占比约为 26.3%。在世家中，此类句读的占比尽管较低，但其数值可达 5%左右。例如，《新五代史·闽世家第八》包含 33 个名词性状语句读，在全篇 721 个句读中的占比约为 4.6%。其中，天干地支的记时形式是这些名词性状语句读的主体。尽管天干地支的记时法在形式上有别于公元纪年的记时法，但是二者所记录的时间内容能够准确地相互转换。翻译天干地支的核心任务就是转换两种记时体系。

1. 天干地支记时及其结构

历史典籍的天干地支记时通常由朝代年号、季度、月份、天干地支日子四部分构成。其中，年号后面有时添加天干地支岁次；月份区分平月和闰月；日子若逢月初，通常后加"朔"字，而若逢月中，则后加"望"字。以下第 1 段的时间句读选自《新五代史·梁本纪第一》，第 2 段的时间句读选自《新五代史·闽世家第八》。

开平元年春正月壬寅……夏四月壬戌……甲子……戊辰……五月丁丑朔……戊寅……乙酉……甲午……是月……六月甲寅……秋七月己亥……八月丁卯……九月……冬十月己未……十一月壬寅……二年春正月丁酉……

是时……光启二年……乾宁四年……同光三年……同光四

年……是岁……十月……十二月……长兴二年……长兴三年……龙启三年……是岁十月……晋天福二年……三年夏……是岁夏……六年三月……周世宗时……晋开运三年丙午……保大三年

第1段的"开平元年春正月壬寅"包含五种要素：年号为"开平"，年次为"元年"，季节为"春"，月份为"正月"，日子为"壬寅"；"五月丁丑朔"包含三种要素：月份为"五月"，日子为"丁丑朔"，其中的"朔"字表明月初。第2段的"晋天福二年"包含三种要素：朝代为"晋"，年号为"天福"，年次为"二年"；"周世宗时"包含两种要素：朝代为"周"，帝王的名号为"世宗"；"晋开运三年丙午"包含四种要素：朝代为"晋"，年号为"开运"，年次为"三年"，其中的"丙午"为天干地支岁次。总体上，天干地支主要用以记日，而用以记年的例子较少。

就上述两段引文来说，本纪在时间记录上较世家详细：前者通常具体到日子，后者通常具体到月份。正因如此，天干地支记时形式在本纪中的比重较大。天干地支记时主要涉及天干、地支与六十甲子。

1.1 天干及其英译

天干（heavenly stems）共有十项，包括甲[1]乙[2]丙[3]丁[4]戊[5]己[6]庚[7]辛[8]壬[9]癸[10]，通常关联阴阳及木、火、土、金、水五行。具体的关系是：甲乙属木，其中甲为阳木，乙为阴木；丙丁属火，其中丙为阳火，丁为阴火；戊己属土，其中戊为阳土，己为阴土；庚辛属金，其中庚为阳金，辛为阴金；壬癸属火，其中壬为阳水，癸为阴水。词汇区分阴阳，在印欧语系中也是普遍的现象，而五行又是日常的元素，因而五行和阴阳的直接翻译放在英语中不会遇到明显的理解障碍。其中，阴阳，可译为 Feminine 和 Masculine，分别缩写为 F. 和 M.；木、火、土、金、水，通常翻译如下：

木：Wood　火：Fire　土：Earth

金：Metal　水：Water

这样，阴阳五行的翻译与十个天干自然地形成如下对应情形：

甲——阳木：Masculine Wood 或 M. Wood

乙——阴木：Feminine Wood 或 F. Wood

丙——阳火：Masculine Fire 或 M. Fire

丁——阴火：Feminine Fire 或 F. Fire

戊——阳土：Masculine Earth 或 M. Earth

己——阴土：Feminine Earth 或 F. Earth

庚——阳金：Masculine Metal 或 M. Metal

辛——阴金：Feminine Metal 或 F. Metal
壬——阳水：Masculine Water 或 M. Water
癸——阴水：Feminine Water 或 F. Water

十个天干主要用以记数，其语义比较隐晦，代以常见的阴阳五行，可把隐晦的语义转变为明确的语义，同时保留记数的功能。

1.2 地支及其英译

十二地支（earthly branches）包括子^{1}丑^{2}寅^{3}卯^{4}辰^{5}巳^{6}午^{7}未^{8}申^{9}酉^{10}戌^{11}亥^{12}，通常关联民间的十二生肖（symbolic animals），即鼠、牛、虎、兔、龙、蛇、马、羊、猴、鸡、狗、猪，形成如下对应关系：子—鼠、丑—牛、寅—虎、卯—兔、辰—龙、巳—蛇、午—马、未—羊、申—猴、酉—鸡、戌—狗、亥—猪。这样，十二生肖的翻译与十二地支自然地形成如下对应情形：

子——鼠：Rat　　丑——牛：Ox　　寅——虎：Tiger
卯——兔：Rabbit　辰——龙：Dragon　巳——蛇：Snake
午——马：Horse　未——羊：Goat　申——猴：Monkey
酉——鸡：Rooster　戌——狗：Dog　亥——猪：Pig

跟天干类似，十二地支也主要用以记数，其语义比较隐晦，在翻译中代以日常的十二生肖，就可把隐晦的语义转化为明确的语义，同时保留记数的功能。

1.3 天干地支记时及其英译

天干地支按顺序两两组合用于记年记日，始于甲子^{01}乙丑^{02}，终于壬戌^{59}癸亥^{60}，共有60组，通常称为"六十甲子"。六十甲子的排列次序如下：

甲子^{01} 乙丑^{02} 丙寅^{03} 丁卯^{04} 戊辰^{05} 己巳^{06} 庚午^{07} 辛未^{08} 壬申^{09} 癸酉^{10}

甲戌^{11} 乙亥^{12} 丙子^{13} 丁丑^{14} 戊寅^{15} 己卯^{16} 庚辰^{17} 辛巳^{18} 壬午^{19} 癸未^{20}

甲申^{21} 乙酉^{22} 丙戌^{23} 丁亥^{24} 戊子^{25} 己丑^{26} 庚寅^{27} 辛卯^{28} 壬辰^{29} 癸巳^{30}

甲午^{31} 乙未^{32} 丙申^{33} 丁酉^{34} 戊戌^{35} 己亥^{36} 庚子^{37} 辛丑^{38} 壬寅^{39} 癸卯^{40}

甲辰^{41} 乙巳^{42} 丙午^{43} 丁未^{44} 戊申^{45} 己酉^{46} 庚戌^{47} 辛亥^{48} 壬子^{49} 癸丑^{50}

甲寅[51] 乙卯[52] 丙辰[53] 丁巳[54] 戊午[55] 己未[56] 庚申[57] 辛酉[58] 壬戌[59] 癸亥[60]

天干的翻译和地支的翻译相互组合，自然地与六十甲子形成以下对应关系：

01——甲子：Masculine Wood Rat 或 M. Wood Rat 或 Wood Rat

02——乙丑：Feminine Wood Ox 或 F. Wood Ox 或 Wood Ox

03——丙寅：Masculine Fire Tiger 或 M. Fire Tiger 或 Fire Tiger

04——丁卯：Feminine Fire Rabbit 或 F. Fire Rabbit 或 Fire Rabbit

05——戊辰：Masculine Earth Dragon 或 M. Earth Dragon 或 Earth Dragon

06——己巳：Feminine Earth Snake 或 F. Earth Snake 或 Earth Snake

07——庚午：Masculine Metal Horse 或 M. Metal Horse 或 Metal Horse

08——辛未：Feminine Metal Goat 或 F. Metal Goat 或 Metal Goat

09——壬申：Masculine Water Monkey 或 M. Water Monkey 或 Water Monkey

10——癸酉：Feminine Water Rooster 或 F. Water Rooster 或 Water Rooster

11——甲戌：Masculine Wood Dog 或 M. Wood Dog 或 Wood Dog

12——乙亥：Feminine Wood Pig 或 F. Wood Pig 或 Wood Pig

13——丙子：Masculine Fire Rat 或 M. Fire Rat 或 Fire Rat

14——丁丑：Feminine Fire Ox 或 F. Fire Ox 或 Fire Ox

15——戊寅：Masculine Earth Tiger 或 M. Earth Tiger 或 Earth Tiger

16——己卯：Feminine Earth Rabbit 或 F. Earth Rabbit 或 Earth Rabbit

17——庚辰：Masculine Metal Dragon 或 M. Metal Dragon 或 Metal Dragon

18——辛巳：Feminine Metal Snake 或 F. Metal Snake 或

Metal Snake

  19——壬午：Masculine Water Horse 或 M. Water Horse 或 Water Horse

  20——癸未：Feminine Water Goat 或 F. Water Goat 或 Water Goat

  21——甲申：Masculine Wood Monkey 或 M. Wood Monkey 或 Wood Monkey

  22——乙酉：Feminine Wood Rooster 或 F. Wood Rooster 或 Wood Rooster

  23——丙戌：Masculine Fire Dog 或 M. Fire Dog 或 Fire Dog

  24——丁亥：Feminine Fire Pig 或 F. Fire Pig 或 Fire Pig

  25——戊子：Masculine Earth Rat 或 M. Earth Rat 或 Earth Rat

  26——己丑：Feminine Earth Ox 或 F. Earth Ox 或 Earth Ox

  27——庚寅：Masculine Metal Tiger 或 M. Metal Tiger 或 Metal Tiger

  28——辛卯：Feminine Metal Rabbit 或 F. Metal Rabbit 或 Metal Rabbit

  29——壬辰：Masculine Water Dragon 或 M. Water Dragon 或 Water Dragon

  30——癸巳：Feminine Water Snake 或 F. Water Snake 或 Water Snake

  31——甲午：Masculine Wood Horse 或 M. Wood Horse 或 Wood Horse

  32——乙未：Feminine Wood Goat 或 F. Wood Goat 或 Wood Goat

  33——丙申：Masculine Fire Monkey 或 M. Fire Monkey 或 Fire Monkey

  34——丁酉：Feminine Fire Rooster 或 F. Fire Rooster 或 Fire Rooster

  35——戊戌：Masculine Earth Dog 或 M. Earth Dog 或 Earth Dog

  36——己亥：Feminine Earth Pig 或 F. Earth Pig 或 Earth Pig

  37——庚子：Masculine Metal Rat 或 M. Metal Rat 或 Metal Rat

  38——辛丑：Feminine Metal Ox 或 F. Metal Ox 或 Metal Ox

  39——壬寅：Masculine Water Tiger 或 M. Water Tiger 或

Water Tiger

40——癸卯：Feminine Water Rabbit 或 F. Water Rabbit 或 Water Rabbit

41——甲辰：Masculine Wood Dragon 或 M. Wood Dragon 或 Wood Dragon

42——乙巳：Feminine Wood Snake 或 F. Wood Snake 或 Wood Snake

43——丙午：Masculine Fire Horse 或 M. Fire Horse 或 Fire Horse

44——丁未：Feminine Fire Goat 或 F. Fire Goat 或 Fire Goat

45——戊申：Masculine Earth Monkey 或 M. Earth Monkey 或 Earth Monkey

46——己酉：Feminine Earth Rooster 或 F. Earth Rooster 或 Earth Rooster

47——庚戌：Masculine Metal Dog 或 M. Metal Dog 或 Metal Dog

48——辛亥：Feminine Metal Pig 或 F. Metal Pig 或 Metal Pig

49——壬子：Masculine Water Rat 或 M. Water Rat 或 Water Rat

50——癸丑：Feminine Water Ox 或 F. Water Ox 或 Water Ox

51——甲寅：Masculine Wood Tiger 或 M. Wood Tiger 或 Wood Tiger

52——乙卯：Feminine Wood Rabbit 或 F. Wood Rabbit 或 Wood Rabbit

53——丙辰：Masculine Fire Dragon 或 M. Fire Dragon 或 Fire Dragon

54——丁巳：Feminine Fire Snake 或 F. Fire Snake 或 Fire Snake

55——戊午：Masculine Earth Horse 或 M. Earth Horse 或 Earth Horse

56——己未：Feminine Earth Goat 或 F. Earth Goat 或 Earth Goat

57——庚申：Masculine Metal Monkey 或 M. Metal Monkey 或 Metal Monkey

58——辛酉：Feminine Metal Rooster 或 F. Metal Rooster 或

Metal Rooster

59——壬戌：Masculine Water Dog 或 M. Water Dog 或 Water Dog

60——癸亥：Feminine Water Pig 或 F. Water Pig 或 Water Pig

第一列为全称，第二列把阳性的英文 Masculine 或阴性的英文 Feminine 缩写为 M. 或 F.。由于子（鼠）¹、寅（虎）³、辰（龙）⁵、午（马）⁷、申（猴）⁹、戌（狗）¹¹ 只组合甲（阳木）¹、丙（阳火）³、戊（阳土）⁵、庚（阳金）⁷、壬（阳水）⁹ 五种阳性的天干，不组合乙（阴木）²、丁（阴火）⁴、己（阴土）⁶、辛（阴金）⁸、癸（阴水）¹⁰ 五种阴性的天干，所以上述两列的 Masculine（M.）均可省略，得到第三列的缩减形式。同理，丑（牛）²、卯（兔）⁴、巳（蛇）⁶、未（羊）⁸、酉（鸡）¹⁰、亥（猪）¹² 只组合阴性的天干，不组合阳性的天干，所以上述两列的 Feminine（F.）均可省略，得到第三列的缩减形式。

六十甲子主要用于记年记日，其具体的语义比较隐晦，在翻译中代以阴阳五行及十二生肖的组合，不仅能够起到记年记日的作用，而且能够把隐晦的语义转化为明确的语义，便于阅读，并在一定程度上传递汉语文化内涵。

2. 五代十国日历

五代包括后梁、后唐、后晋、后汉、后周五个朝代，自后梁开平元年春正月壬寅（公元 907 年 2 月 15 日）至后周显德六年十二月庚子（公元 960 年 1 月 30 日）历经整整 53 年。其中，后梁始于开平元年正月壬寅（公元 907 年 3 月 11 日），终于龙德三年三月甲辰（公元 923 年 4 月 18 日），历时 16 年；后唐始于同光元年四月乙巳（公元 923 年 4 月 19 日），终于清泰三年十月乙酉（公元 936 年 11 月 16 日），历时 13 年；后晋始于天福元年十一月丙戌（公元 936 年 11 月 17 日），终于开运四年正月丙辰（公元 947 年 2 月 23 日），历时 11 年；后汉始于天福十二年二月丁巳（公元 947 年 2 月 24 日），终于乾祐三年十二月壬戌（公元 951 年 2 月 8 日），历时 4 年；后周始于广顺元年正月癸亥（公元 951 年 2 月 9 日），终于显德六年十二月庚子（公元 960 年 1 月 30 日），历时 9 年。在此期间，先后出现十个较为显赫的世袭王国，包括吴、南唐、蜀、后蜀、南汉、楚、吴越、闽、南平。十国世家的英译是本书的主要对象。

后梁 16 年的国祚涉及唐天祐、唐天复、后梁开平、蜀武成、梁乾化、蜀永平、梁贞明、蜀通正、蜀天汉、南汉乾亨、蜀光天、吴武义、蜀乾德、梁龙德、吴顺义等年号。详细的年份[1]对照如下：

  公元 907 年 2 月 15 日—公元 908 年 2 月 4 日
  唐天祐四年丁卯、唐天复七年、梁开平元年
  公元 908 年 2 月 5 日—公元 909 年 1 月 24 日
  梁开平二年戊辰、唐天祐五年、蜀武成元年
  公元 909 年 1 月 25 日—公元 910 年 2 月 12 日
  梁开平三年戊辰、唐天祐六年、蜀武成二年
  公元 910 年 2 月 13 日—公元 911 年 2 月 1 日
  梁开平四年庚午、唐天祐七年、蜀武成三年
  公元 911 年 2 月 2 日—公元 912 年 1 月 21 日
  梁开平五年辛未、梁乾化元年、唐天祐八年、蜀永平元年
  公元 912 年 1 月 22 日—公元 913 年 2 月 8 日
  梁乾化二年壬申、唐天祐九年、蜀永平二年
  公元 913 年 2 月 9 日—公元 914 年 1 月 28 日
  梁乾化三年癸酉、唐天祐十年、蜀永平三年
  公元 914 年 1 月 29 日—公元 915 年 1 月 17 日
  梁乾化四年甲戌、唐天祐十一年、蜀永平四年
  公元 915 年 1 月 18 日—公元 916 年 2 月 5 日
  梁贞明元年乙亥、唐天祐十二年、蜀永平五年
  公元 916 年 2 月 6 日—公元 917 年 1 月 25 日
  梁贞明二年丙子、唐天祐十三年、蜀通正元年
  公元 917 年 1 月 26 日—公元 918 年 2 月 13 日
  梁贞明三年丁丑、唐天祐十四年、蜀天汉元年、南汉乾亨
元年

---

[1] 该年份的罗列以欧阳修《新五代史》为参考依据。一般认为，"五代十国"是从 907 年开始，至 960 年结束。其中的五个朝代的名称是：梁、唐、晋、汉、周。朝代名称本身没有"后"字，"后"字是后人为了方便区分而人为添加的，用来区分之前同名的朝代。例如，这个期间的"唐"代，就是"后唐"。欧阳修《新五代史》中的上述朝代的名字，都没有"后"字。但是，"后唐"只认"前唐"（907 年之前的大唐朝）为宗，不认"后梁"的年号。所以，在"（后）唐本纪"中，讲到唐末梁初的事件时，会用到唐朝的年号。

  例如：
  （天复）七年……梁灭唐，克用复称天祐四年。
  这一年就是 907 年。对于前唐朝来说，是"天复七年"（天复元年是 901 年），对于后梁来说，就是"开平元年"。李克用不认"开平元年"，所以他重新启用前唐朝 904 年开始使用的年号"天祐"。907 年即"天祐四年"。

公元918年2月14日—公元919年2月3日
梁贞明四年戊寅、唐天祐十五年、蜀光天元年、南汉乾亨二年

公元919年2月4日—公元920年1月23日
梁贞明五年己卯、唐天祐十六年、吴武义元年、蜀乾德元年、南汉乾亨三年

公元920年1月24日—公元921年2月10日
梁贞明六年庚辰、唐天祐十七年、吴武义二年、蜀乾德二年、南汉乾亨四年

公元921年2月11日—公元922年1月30日
梁龙德元年辛巳、唐天祐十八年、吴顺义元年、蜀乾德三年、南汉乾亨五年

公元922年1月31日—公元923年1月19日
梁龙德二年壬午、唐天祐十九年、吴顺义二年、蜀乾德四年、南汉乾亨六年

后唐13年国祚涉及唐同光、吴顺义、蜀乾德、南汉乾亨、蜀咸康、南汉白龙、唐天成、吴越宝正、吴乾贞、南汉大有、吴大和、唐长兴、闽龙启、唐应顺、唐清泰、后蜀明德、吴天祚、闽永和等年号。详细的年份对照如下：

公元923年1月20日—公元924年2月7日
唐同光元年癸未、吴顺义三年、蜀乾德五年、南汉乾亨七年

公元924年2月8日—公元925年1月26日
唐同光二年甲申、吴顺义四年、蜀乾德六年、南汉乾亨八年

公元925年1月27日—公元926年2月14日
唐同光三年乙酉、吴顺义五年、蜀咸康元年、南汉白龙元年

公元926年2月15日—公元927年2月4日
唐天成元年丙戌、吴顺义六年、南汉白龙二年、吴越宝正元年

公元927年2月5日—公元928年1月25日
唐天成二年丁亥、吴乾贞元年、南汉白龙三年、吴越宝正二年

公元928年1月26日—公元929年2月12日
唐天成三年戊子、吴乾贞二年、南汉大有元年、吴越宝正

三年

公元929年2月13日—公元930年2月1日

唐天成四年己丑、吴大和元年、南汉大有二年、吴越宝正四年

公元930年2月2日—公元931年1月21日

唐长兴元年庚寅、吴大和二年、南汉大有三年、吴越宝正五年

公元931年1月22日—公元932年2月8日

唐长兴二年辛卯、吴大和三年、南汉大有四年、吴越宝正六年

公元932年2月9日—公元933年1月28日

唐长兴三年壬辰、吴大和四年、南汉大有五年

公元933年1月29日—公元934年1月17日

唐长兴四年癸巳、吴大和五年、南汉大有六年、闽龙启元年

公元934年1月18日—公元935年2月5日

唐应顺元年、唐清泰元年甲午、吴大和六年、后蜀明德元年、南汉大有七年、闽龙启二年

公元935年2月6日—公元936年1月26日

唐清泰二年乙未、吴天祚元年、后蜀明德二年、南汉大有八年、闽永和元年

后晋11年国祚涉及晋天福、吴天祚、后蜀明德、南汉大有、闽通文、南唐昇元、后蜀广政、闽永隆、南汉光天、南唐保大、南汉应乾、南汉乾和、殷天德、晋开运等年号。详细的年份对照如下：

公元936年1月27日—公元937年2月12日

晋天福元年丙申、吴天祚二年、后蜀明德三年、南汉大有九年、闽通文元年

公元937年2月13日—公元938年2月1日

晋天福二年丁酉、南唐昇元元年、后蜀明德四年、南汉大有十年、闽通文二年

公元938年2月2日—公元939年1月22日

晋天福三年戊戌、南唐昇元二年、后蜀广政元年、南汉大有十一年、闽通文三年

公元939年1月23日—公元940年2月10日

晋天福四年己亥、南唐昇元三年、后蜀广政二年、南汉大有十二年、闽永隆元年

公元 940 年 2 月 11 日—公元 941 年 1 月 29 日

晋天福五年庚子、南唐昇元四年、后蜀广政三年、南汉大有十三年、闽永隆二年

公元 941 年 1 月 30 日—公元 942 年 1 月 19 日

晋天福六年辛丑、南唐昇元五年、后蜀广政四年、南汉大有十四年、闽永隆三年

公元 942 年 1 月 20 日—公元 943 年 2 月 7 日

晋天福七年壬寅、南唐昇元六年、后蜀广政五年、南汉光天元年、闽永隆四年

公元 943 年 2 月 8 日—公元 944 年 1 月 27 日

晋天福八年癸卯、南唐保大元年、后蜀广政六年、南汉应乾元年、乾和元年、殷天德元年

公元 944 年 1 月 28 日—公元 945 年 2 月 14 日

晋开运元年甲辰、南唐保大二年、后蜀广政七年、南汉乾和二年、殷天德二年

公元 945 年 2 月 15 日—公元 946 年 2 月 4 日

晋开运二年乙巳、南唐保大三年、后蜀广政八年、南汉乾和三年、殷天德三年

公元 946 年 2 月 5 日—公元 947 年 1 月 24 日

晋开运三年丙午、南唐保大四年、后蜀广政九年、南汉乾和四年、殷天德四年

后汉 4 年国祚涉及汉天福、南唐保大、后蜀广政、南汉乾和、汉乾祐等年号。详细的年份对照如下：

公元 947 年 1 月 25 日—公元 948 年 2 月 12 日

汉天福十二年丁未、南唐保大五年、后蜀广政十年、南汉乾和五年

公元 948 年 2 月 13 日—公元 949 年 1 月 31 日

汉乾祐元年戊申、南唐保大六年、后蜀广政十一年、南汉乾和六年

公元 949 年 2 月 1 日—公元 950 年 1 月 20 日

汉乾祐二年己酉、南唐保大七年、后蜀广政十二年、南汉乾

和七年

公元 950 年 1 月 21 日—公元 951 年 2 月 8 日

汉乾祐三年庚戌、南唐保大八年、后蜀广政十三年、南汉乾和八年

后周 9 年国祚涉及周广顺、东汉乾祐、南唐保大、后蜀广政、南汉乾和、周显德、东汉天会、南唐交泰、南汉大宝等年号。详细的年份对照如下：

公元 951 年 2 月 9 日—公元 952 年 1 月 29 日

周广顺元年辛亥、东汉乾祐四年、南唐保大九年、后蜀广政十四年、南汉乾和九年

公元 952 年 1 月 30 日—公元 953 年 1 月 17 日

周广顺二年壬子、东汉乾祐五年、南唐保大十年、后蜀广政十五年、南汉乾和十年

公元 953 年 1 月 18 日—公元 954 年 2 月 5 日

周广顺三年癸丑、东汉乾祐六年、南唐保大十一年、后蜀广政十六年、南汉乾和十一年

公元 954 年 2 月 6 日—公元 955 年 1 月 26 日

周显德元年甲寅、东汉乾祐七年、南唐保大十二年、后蜀广政十七年、南汉乾和十二年

公元 955 年 1 月 27 日—公元 956 年 2 月 14 日

周显德二年乙卯、东汉乾祐八年、南唐保大十三年、后蜀广政十八年、南汉乾和十三年

公元 956 年 2 月 15 日—公元 957 年 2 月 2 日

周显德三年丙辰、东汉乾祐九年、南唐保大十四年、后蜀广政十九年、南汉乾和十四年

公元 957 年 2 月 3 日—公元 958 年 1 月 22 日

周显德四年丁巳、东汉天会元年、南唐保大十五年、后蜀广政二十年、南汉乾和十五年

公元 958 年 1 月 23 日—公元 959 年 2 月 10 日

周显德五年戊午、东汉天会二年、南唐交泰元年、后蜀广政二十一年、南汉大宝元年

公元 959 年 2 月 11 日—公元 960 年 1 月 30 日

周显德六年己未、东汉天会三年、后蜀广政二十二年、南汉大宝二年

以上 53 年之内的具体天干地支日期都可在如下网址查到对应的公元纪年日期：http://flc.hqu.edu.cn/info/1166/10290.htm。在此范围之外的日期则需要通过其他途径获得，如由台北"中央研究院"在 http://sinocal.sinica.edu.tw/上所提供的电子日历。例如，后梁开平元年始于正月壬寅（公元 907 年 2 月 15 日），终于十二月壬申（公元 908 年 2 月 4 日）。这一整年的日历如图 2-1 所示。

唐天祐四年丁卯、唐天复七年、后梁开平元年：公元 907 年 2 月 15 日至 908 年 2 月 4 日

正月：公元 907 年 2 月 15 日至 3 月 16 日

戊寅 2/15	己卯 16	庚辰 17	辛巳 18	壬午 19	癸未 20	甲申 21	乙酉 22	丙戌 23	丁亥 24	戊子 25	己丑 26	庚寅 27	辛卯 28	壬辰 3/1
癸巳 2	甲午 3	乙未 4	丙申 5	丁酉 6	戊戌 7	己亥 8	庚子 9	辛丑 10	壬寅 11	癸卯 12	甲辰 13	乙巳 14	丙午 15	丁未 16

二月：公元 907 年 3 月 17 日至 4 月 16 日

戊申 3/17	己酉 18	庚戌 19	辛亥 20	壬子 21	癸丑 22	甲寅 23	乙卯 24	丙辰 25	丁巳 26	戊午 27	己未 28	庚申 29	辛酉 30	壬戌 31
癸亥 4/1	甲子 2	乙丑 3	丙寅 4	丁卯 5	戊辰 6	己巳 7	庚午 8	辛未 9	壬申 10	癸酉 11	甲戌 12	乙亥 13	丙子 14	丁丑 15

三月：公元 907 年 4 月 17 日至 5 月 14 日

戊寅 4/16	己卯 17	庚辰 18	辛巳 19	壬午 20	癸未 21	甲申 22	乙酉 23	丙戌 24	丁亥 25	戊子 26	己丑 27	庚寅 28	辛卯 29	壬辰 30
癸巳 5/1	甲午 2	乙未 3	丙申 4	丁酉 5	戊戌 6	己亥 7	庚子 8	辛丑 9	壬寅 10	癸卯 11	甲辰 12	乙巳 13	丙午 14	—

四月：公元 907 年 5 月 15 日至 6 月 13 日（后梁开平元年）

丁未 5/15	戊申 16	己酉 17	庚戌 18	辛亥 19	壬子 20	癸丑 21	甲寅 22	乙卯 23	丙辰 24	丁巳 25	戊午 26	己未 27	庚申 28	辛酉 29
壬戌 30	癸亥 31	甲子 6/1	乙丑 2	丙寅 3	丁卯 4	戊辰 5	己巳 6	庚午 7	辛未 8	壬申 9	癸酉 10	甲戌 11	乙亥 12	丙子 13

五月：公元 907 年 6 月 14 日至 7 月 12 日

丁丑 6/14	戊寅 15	己卯 16	庚辰 17	辛巳 18	壬午 19	癸未 20	甲申 21	乙酉 22	丙戌 23	丁亥 24	戊子 25	己丑 26	庚寅 27	辛卯 28
壬辰 29	癸巳 30	甲午 7/1	乙未 2	丙申 3	丁酉 4	戊戌 5	己亥 6	庚子 7	辛丑 8	壬寅 9	癸卯 10	甲辰 11	乙巳 12	—

六月：公元 907 年 7 月 13 日至 8 月 11 日

丙午 7/13	丁未 14	戊申 15	己酉 16	庚戌 17	辛亥 18	壬子 19	癸丑 20	甲寅 21	乙卯 22	丙辰 23	丁巳 24	戊午 25	己未 26	庚申 27
辛酉 28	壬戌 29	癸亥 30	甲子 31	乙丑 8/1	丙寅 2	丁卯 3	戊辰 4	己巳 5	庚午 6	辛未 7	壬申 8	癸酉 9	甲戌 10	乙亥 11

七月：公元 907 年 8 月 12 日至 9 月 10 日

丙子 8/12	丁丑 13	戊寅 14	己卯 15	庚辰 16	辛巳 17	壬午 18	癸未 19	甲申 20	乙酉 21	丙戌 22	丁亥 23	戊子 24	己丑 25	庚寅 26
辛卯 27	壬辰 28	癸巳 29	甲午 30	乙未 31	丙申 9/1	丁酉 2	戊戌 3	己亥 4	庚子 5	辛丑 6	壬寅 7	癸卯 8	甲辰 9	乙巳 10

八月：公元 907 年 9 月 11 日至 10 月 9 日

丙午 9/11	丁未 12	戊申 13	己酉 14	庚戌 15	辛亥 16	壬子 17	癸丑 18	甲寅 19	乙卯 20	丙辰 21	丁巳 22	戊午 23	己未 24	庚申 25
辛酉 26	壬戌 27	癸亥 28	甲子 29	乙丑 10/1	丙寅 2	丁卯 3	戊辰 4	己巳 5	庚午 6	辛未 7	壬申 8	癸酉 9	—	—

九月：公元 907 年 10 月 10 日至 11 月 8 日

乙亥 10/10	丙子 11	丁丑 12	戊寅 13	己卯 14	庚辰 15	辛巳 16	壬午 17	癸未 18	甲申 19	乙酉 20	丙戌 21	丁亥 22	戊子 23	己丑 24
庚寅 25	辛卯 26	壬辰 27	癸巳 28	甲午 29	乙未 30	丙申 31	丁酉 11/1	戊戌 2	己亥 3	庚子 4	辛丑 5	壬寅 6	癸卯 7	甲辰 8

十月：公元 907 年 11 月 9 日至 12 月 7 日

乙巳 11/9	丙午 10	丁未 11	戊申 12	己酉 13	庚戌 14	辛亥 15	壬子 16	癸丑 17	甲寅 18	乙卯 19	丙辰 20	丁巳 21	戊午 22	己未 23
庚申 24	辛酉 25	壬戌 26	癸亥 27	甲子 28	乙丑 29	丙寅 30	丁卯 12/1	戊辰 2	己巳 3	庚午 4	辛未 5	壬申 6	癸酉 7	—

十一月：公元 907 年 12 月 8 日至 908 年 1 月 6 日

甲戌 12/8	乙亥 9	丙子 10	丁丑 11	戊寅 12	己卯 13	庚辰 14	辛巳 15	壬午 16	癸未 17	甲申 18	乙酉 19	丙戌 20	丁亥 21	戊子 22
己丑 23	庚寅 24	辛卯 25	壬辰 26	癸巳 27	甲午 28	乙未 29	丙申 30	丁酉 31	戊戌 1/1	己亥 2	庚子 3	辛丑 4	壬寅 5	癸卯 6

十二月：公元 908 年 1 月 7 日至 2 月 4 日

甲辰 1/7	乙巳 8	丙午 9	丁未 10	戊申 11	己酉 12	庚戌 13	辛亥 14	壬子 15	癸丑 16	甲寅 17	乙卯 18	丙辰 19	丁巳 20	戊午 21
己未 22	庚申 23	辛酉 24	壬戌 25	癸亥 26	甲子 27	乙丑 28	丙寅 29	丁卯 30	戊辰 31	己巳 2/1	庚午 2	辛未 3	壬申 4	—

图 2-1　后梁开平元年全年日历

后梁开平元年岁次丁卯替换唐天祐四年，即唐天复七年，共 12 个月。

正月、二月、四月、六月、七月、九月和十一月为30天，其余5个月为29天，全年共355天。正月和二月共有60天：正月始于戊寅（公元907年2月15日），终于丁未（3月16日）；二月始于戊申（3月17日），终于丁丑（4月15日）。三月初一（4月16日）又从戊寅开始，以此类推。四月甲子（6月1日）改元开平。全年的最后一天为十二月壬申（公元908年2月4日）。癸酉（2月5日）为开平二年岁次戊辰正月初一。后梁开平二年正月的日历如图2-2所示：

后梁开平二年戊辰、唐天祐五年、蜀武成元年：公元908年2月5日至公元909年1月24日
正月：公元908年2月5日至3月4日

| 癸酉 2/5 | 甲戌 6 | 乙亥 7 | 丙子 8 | 丁丑 9 | 戊寅 10 | 己卯 11 | 庚辰 12 | 辛巳 13 | 壬午 14 | 癸未 15 | 甲申 16 | 乙酉 17 | 丙戌 18 | 丁亥 19 |
| 戊子 20 | 己丑 21 | 庚寅 22 | 辛卯 23 | 壬辰 24 | 癸巳 25 | 甲午 26 | 乙未 27 | 丙申 28 | 丁酉 29 | 戊戌 3/1 | 己亥 2 | 庚子 3 | 辛丑 4 | — |

图 2-2 后梁开平元年全年日历

后梁开平二年正月始于癸酉，终于辛丑（公元908年3月4日），共29天。

3. 天干地支记时的英译实例

本章第1节引用的第1段引文包含16个时间句读。除了第9个"是月"外，其余15个句读包含天干地支的记时形式，均可在上述日历词典中检索到公元纪年的具体日期。现把该段的时间句读翻译如下：

［1］开平元年春正月壬寅

on M. Water Tiger, January in the Spring of the first year of the Kaiping period (March 11, A. D. 907)

［2］夏四月壬戌 on M. Water Dog, April in the Summer (May 30)

［3］甲子 on M. Wood Rat (June 1)

［4］戊辰 on M. Earth Dragon (June 5)

［5］五月丁丑朔 on F. Fire Ox, May the First (June 14)

［6］戊寅 on M. Earth Tiger (June 15)

［7］乙酉 on F. Wood Rooster (June 22)

［8］甲午 on M. Wood Horse (July 1)

［9］是月 in this month

［10］六月甲寅 on M. Wood Tiger, June (July 21)

［11］秋七月己亥 on F. Earth Pig, July in the Autumn (September 4)

［12］八月丁卯 on F. Fire Rabbit, August（October 2）

［13］九月 in September（October or November）

［14］冬十月己未 on F. Earth Goat, October in the Winter（November 23）

［15］十一月壬寅 on M. Water Tiger, November（January 5, A.D. 908）

［16］二年春正月丁酉

on F. Fire Rooster, January in the Spring of the second year（February 29, A.D. 908）

第［1］句"开平元年春正月壬寅"为公元907年3月11日。该句包含年号"开平"、年次"元年"、季节"春"、月份"正月"及日子"壬寅"，分别译为 the Kaiping period, the first year, in the Spring, January, on M. Water Tiger，形成 on M. Water Tiger, January in the Spring of the first year of the Kaiping period，即 March 11, A.D. 907。第［16］句"二年春正月丁酉"（缺省年号）为公元908年2月29日。该句包含年次"二年"、季节"春"、月份"正月"及日子"丁酉"，分别译为 the second year, in the Spring, January, on F. Fire Rooster，形成 on F. Fire Rooster, January in the Spring of the second year，即 February 29, A.D. 908。第［2］句"夏四月壬戌"、第［11］句"秋七月己亥"、第［14］句"冬十月己未"都是季节、月份和天干地支日子的组合，分别译为 on M. Water Dog, April in the Summer（May 30）, on F. Earth Pig, July in the Autumn（September 4）, on F. Earth Goat, October in the Winter（November 23）。第［5］句"五月丁丑朔"为公元907年6月14日。该句包含月份"五月"、日子"丁丑"及新月标记"朔"，分别译为 May, on F. Fire Ox, the First，形成 on F. Fire Ox, May the First，即 June 14。除第［13］句"九月"跨越当年的10月或11月，译为 in September（October or November）外，其余的句读均为天干地支的日子。现把第1段的译文整理如下：

On M. Water Tiger, January in the Spring of the first year of the Kaiping period（March 11, A.D. 907）... On M. Water Dog, April in the Summer（May 30）... On M. Wood Rat（June 1）... On M. Earth Dragon（June 5）... On F. Fire Ox, May the First（June 14）... On M. Earth Tiger（June 15）... On F. Wood Rooster（June 22）... On M. Wood Horse（July 1）... In this month ... On M. Wood Tiger, June

(July 21)... On F. Earth Pig, July in the Autumn (September 4)... On F. Fire Rabbit, August (October 2)... In September (October or November)... On F. Earth Goat, October in the Winter (November 23)... On M. Water Tiger, November (January 5, A.D. 908)... On F. Fire Rooster, January in the Spring of the second year (February 29, A.D. 908)...

第 1 节引用的第 2 段引文包含 19 个时间句读。除了第 18 个"晋开运三年丙午"包含 1 个天干地支的记年表达之外，其余 18 个句读都不涉及天干地支的记时形式，其所记录的时间只精确到年份及月份。现将该段的时间句读翻译如下：

［1］是时 at this time

［2］光启二年 in the second year of the Guangqi period (A.D. 886)

［3］乾宁四年 in the fourth year of the Qianning period (A.D. 897)

［4］同光三年 in the third year of the Tongguang period (A.D. 925)

［5］同光四年 in the fourth year of the Tongguang period (A.D. 926)

［6］是岁 in this year

［7］十月 in October (November or December, A.D. 926)

［8］十二月 in December (January or February, A.D. 927)

［9］长兴二年 in the second year of the Changxing period (A.D. 931)

［10］长兴三年 in the third year of the Changxing period (A.D. 932)

［11］龙启三年 in the third year of the Longqi period (A.D. 935)

［12］是岁十月 in October of this year (October or November, A.D. 935)

［13］晋天福二年 in the second year of the Tianfu period of the Jin dynasty (A.D. 937)

［14］三年夏 in the Summer of the third year

〔15〕是岁夏 in the Summer of this year

〔16〕六年三月 in March of the sixth year（March or April，A. D. 941）

〔17〕周世宗时 during the reign of Emperor Shizong of the Zhou dynasty

〔18〕晋开运三年丙午 in M. Fire Horse, the third year of the Kaiyun period of the Jin dynasty（A. D. 946）

〔19〕保大三年 in the third year of the Baoda period（A. D. 945）

其中，第〔2〕句"光启二年"和第〔3〕句"乾宁四年"均不在五代十国的日历范围之内，需要通过其他手段获得。例如，检索台北"中央研究院"在 http://sinocal.sinica.edu.tw/ 上所提供的电子日历，就可得到两个年份分别为公元886年和公元897年。第〔4〕句"同光三年"、第〔5〕句"同光四年"、第〔9〕句"长兴二年"、第〔10〕句"长兴三年"、第〔11〕句"龙启三年"、第〔19〕句"保大三年"均为年号加年次的表达形式，可直接在五代十国日历中找到，分别译为 in the third year of the Tongguang period（A. D. 925）、in the fourth year of the Tongguang period（A. D. 926）、in the second year of the Changxing period（A. D. 931）、in the third year of the Changxing period（A. D. 932）、in the third year of the Longqi period（A. D. 935）、in the third year of the Baoda period（A. D. 945）。需要注意的是，尽管第〔5〕句"同光四年"和第〔11〕句"龙启三年"在五代十国日历中都无法找到与其对应的年份，但是二者的前一年"同光三年"和"龙启二年"都有直接对应的年份，分别为公元925年和公元934年，因而可推算得知，第〔5〕句"同光四年"为926年，第〔11〕句"龙启三年"为公元935年。第〔13〕句"晋天福二年"为公元937年。该句包含朝代"晋"、年号"天福"、年次"二年"，分别译为 of the Jin dynasty、of the Tianfu period、in the second year，形成 in the second year of the Tianfu period of the Jin dynasty，即 A. D. 937。第〔18〕句"晋开运三年丙午"为公元946年。除了朝代"晋"、年号"开运"及年次"三年"之外，该句还有天干地支的记年表达"丙午"，分别译为 of the Jin dynasty、of the Kaiyun period、in the third year、in M. Fire Horse，形成 in M. Fire Horse, the third year of the Kaiyun period of the Jin dynasty，即 A. D. 946。其余时间句读比较简单。现把第2段的译文整理如下：

At this time ... In the second year of the Guangqi period (A. D. 886) ... In the fourth year of the Qianning period (A. D. 897) ... In the third year of the Tongguang period (A. D. 925) ... In the fourth year of the Tongguang period (A. D. 926) ... In this year ... In October (November or December) ... In December (January or February, A. D. 927) ... In the second year of the Changxing period (A. D. 931) ... In the third year of the Changxing period (A. D. 932) ... In the third year of the Longqi period (A. D. 935) ... In October of this year (November or December, A. D. 935) ... In the second year of the Tianfu period of the Jin dynasty (A. D. 937) ... In the Summer of the third year ... In the Summer of this year ... In March of the sixth year (March or April, A. D. 941) ... During the reign of Emperor Shizong of the Zhou dynasty ... In M. Fire Horse, the third year of the Kaiyun period of the Jin dynasty (A. D. 946) ... In the third year of the Baoda period (A. D. 945) ...

4. 小结

天干地支既涉及历法科学，又涉及文化生活。在历史典籍英译中把天干地支的记时形式完整地译为英语，其实是科学知识和文化知识的同时转换。就阴阳概念来说，由于部分英语词汇区分阴阳［如男校友（alumnus）和女校友（alumna）］，所以英语读者能够很好地接受十个天干的阴阳区别。与此同时，五行和十二生肖都是源自生活的文化符号，并不会对实际的理解造成明显的困惑。总之，天干地支的英语翻译不但保留了历法的严肃性，而且引入了文化的趣味性。

第3章

句读的语法解读及结构类型

准确的中国史籍英译必须以准确的原文解读为基础。采用一种合适的语法框架来分析原文句读并识别其结构类型，能够确保解读及英译的准确性。在语法分析的基础上，原文语句转化为一种结构化、带标注的句读库。借助语法类型标记，我们可以简便地提取所有具有同类语法结构的句读，比较它们在词汇和语义上的异同，进而达到准确解读原文的目的，有利于后续的群组翻译。本章以《新五代史·闽世家第八》为例，建立一种基于语法分析的原文句读库。经过群组翻译，句读库将转化成一种可重复利用的汉英翻译案例库。

1. 句读的基本类型

译者往往以原文的字词、短语、语句或篇章为基本单位，按顺序一边解读一边翻译。解读与翻译两种语言处理行为不断地变换，形成一种类似正弦波动的交替现象。语法结构相同的句读往往产生相似的波动特征；相反，不同的语法结构具有不同的波动形式。翻译在语法结构上的不规则性直接影响其实际效率。显然，在翻译中只要提取语法结构相同的句读群组，就可集结波动特征相似的甚至重合的翻译行为，进而避免由不规则的变换所带来的影响。这种群组翻译相当于把解读环节明确地从翻译过程中离析出来：先从整体上解读原文，然后在此基础上翻译原文。由于中国史籍英译的规模较大，分类处理既有利于提高翻译效率，又能保证翻译质量。

本章主要在 Pulleyblank（1995）所提出的语法分析框架中分析《新五代史·闽世家第八》的原文句读，识别其语法结构，理解其语义内容，并在此基础上创建一种结构化的句读库。《新五代史·闽世家第八》全篇包含 4 095 个汉字，721 个句读，其汉字密度约为 5.68，即单位句读平均包含约 5.68 个汉字。因此，句读库共有 721 个记录，每个记录包含对应的句读及其语法类型标注等内容。在后续的翻译中，随着各个句读的英译语句被添加进来，该句读库逐渐转化为汉英双语的翻译案例库。

原文句读涉及四种基本类型，即普通体词性句读（general nominal clause 或 general NC）、简单谓词性句读（simple predicative clause 或 simple PC）、特殊谓词性句读（special predicative clause 或 special PC）、复杂句读（complex clause）。

2. 普通体词性句读

主体成分为名词性结构的句读称为普通体词性句读，可分为完全和不完全两种类型：完全体词性句读（complete nominal clause，CNC）包含完整的主谓结构；不完全体词性句读（incomplete nominal clause）则在上下文中充当相关语句的主语、谓语、宾语、状语等语法功能，因而其本身并不是一个完整的主谓结构。不完全体词性句读按其语法功能又可分为四类：名词性主语句读（nominal clause of subject，NCS）、名词性谓语句读（nominal clause of predicate，NCP）、名词性状语句读（nominal clause of adverbial，NCA）、名词性列举句读（nominal clause of enumeration，NCE）。此类句读与相关的上下文语句共同构成完整的主谓结构。在 721 个句读中，共有 94 例普通体词性句读：12 例 CNC、18 例 NCS、30 例 NCP、33 例 NCA、1 例 NCE。

2.1 完全体词性句读（CNC）

主要由名词性主语和名词性谓语构成的完整句读称为完全体词性句读（CNC），可分为简单和复杂两种类型。前者包含简单的主语和谓语。后者又可分为主谓主语句读和主谓谓语句读：主谓主语句读的主语部分本身又是一种主谓结构；同理，主谓谓语句读的谓语部分本身也是一种主谓结构。在 12 例 CNC 中，共有 4 例简单主谓句读、2 例主谓主语句读、6 例主谓谓语句读。四例简单主谓句读分别是：中国多故、匡范人中宝也、时开运元年也、此非常人也。它们均由简单的名词性主语（如：中国、匡范、时、此）和简单的名词性谓语（如：多故、人中宝、开运元年、非常人）构成。

2 例主谓主语句读分别是：生我者潮也、一岁中死者八十四人。它们的主语本身又是主谓结构，因而可称为"大主语"，其中的主语被称为"小主语"，谓语被称为"小谓语"。在前例的大主语"生我者"中，小主语是代词"者"，小谓语是动宾结构"生我"；在后例的大主语"［一岁中]死者"中,小主语是代词"者",小谓语是动状结构"[一岁中]死"。两个小谓语都不是名词性的,而是动词性的。

6例主谓谓语句读分别是:延翰字子逸、审知养子建州刺史延禀、国号闽、陛下左右多奸臣、审知婢金凤、此宗室将为乱之兆也。它们的谓语本身就是主谓结构,因而称为"大谓语",包含"小主语"和"小谓语"。在第1例的大谓语"字子逸"中,小主语是"字",小谓语是"子逸";在第2例的大谓语"建州刺史延禀"中,小主语是"建州刺史",小谓语是"延禀";在第3例的大谓语"号闽"中,小主语是"号",小谓语是"闽";在第4例的大谓语"左右多奸臣"中,小主语是"左右",小谓语是"多奸臣";在第5例的大谓语"婢金凤"中,小主语是"婢",小谓语是"金凤"。上述5个小谓语都是体词性的。第6例的大谓语"宗室将为乱之兆"虽然在整体上是名词性结构,但也包含动宾结构"为乱"。

2.2 名词性主语句读(NCS)

名词性主语句读(NCS)通常为专有名词或"者"字结构,充当下文语句的主语。在18例NCS中,共有13例专有名词和5例"者"字结构。专有名词主要包括人名、地名、职位名称。以人名为句读的例子有:王审知、王淡、杨沂、徐寅、鏻、继鹏、昶、延义、李仁遇、延政。它们通常后接解释语句。例如,"王审知"后接2个谓语句读"字信通°光州固始人也";"王淡"后接1个谓语句读"唐相溥之子"。以地名为句读的例子有:闽、海上黄崎。前者后接谓语句读"自古王国也";后者后接谓语句读"波涛为阻"。以职位名称为句读的例子有:凤阁舍人,后接1个名词化的句读"何偪(逼)下之甚也"。

5例"者"字结构分别是:部将有材能者、良家子之美者、敢有作威福者、不忠不孝者、而后人纪录者。此类结构本身具有主谓结构,通常以"者"字为其主语,以动宾结构或形容词为其谓语。例如,在"[部将]有材能者"中,代词"者"指代前面的"部将"并充当主语,其动宾结构为"有材能";在"[良家子之]美者"中,代词"者"为主语,其形容词性谓语为"美";在"[敢有]作威福者"中,动宾结构为"作威福";在"不忠不孝者"中,形容词性谓语为"不忠不孝";在"[而后人]纪录者"中,谓语由不及物动词"纪录"构成。此类句读通常后接复杂谓语结构。例如,"部将有材能者"后接"多因事杀之";"而后人纪录者"后接"乃用骑马来骑马去之谶以为据"。

2.3 名词性谓语句读(NCP)

名词性谓语句读(NCP)可分简单、复合和复杂三种类型。在30例

NCP 中，共有 2 例简单句读、3 例复合句读和 25 例复杂句读。2 例简单名词性谓语句读分别是：自古王国也、实五十五年也。3 例复合名词性谓语句读分别是：隆准方口、夷貊之君、皆王氏之诸子也。此类句读通常涉及两个处于并列关系的实体。例如，第 1 例是由"隆准"和"方口"两个并列词组构成的复合结构；第 2 例和第 3 例均属于偏正结构。

其余 25 例复杂名词性谓语句读本身又是一种主谓结构，通常用以叙述事实，大体上可分正向（obverse）和反向（reverse）两种叙述方式。属于正向叙述的句读共有 13 例：字信通、父恁、兄潮、军中号白马三郎、唐相溥之子、唐相涉从弟、唐时知名进士、年六十四、本姓周氏、庙号太祖、姓陈氏、号归郎、庙号太宗。此类句读前承名词性主语句读或谓词性句读。例如，第 1 例"字信通"前承名词性主语句读"王审知"，形成主谓谓语结构"［王审知°］字信通"；第 8 例"年六十四"前承谓词性句读"审知同光三年卒"，形成复合句子"［审知同光三年卒°］年六十四"；第 9 例"本姓周氏"前承主谓谓语句读"审知养子建州刺史延禀"，形成愈加复杂的主谓谓语结构"［审知养子建州刺史延禀°］本姓周氏"。正向叙述通常按由大到小、由老到少、由主到客的顺序来排列涉及的各种要素。

属于反向叙述的名词性谓语句读共有 10 例：光州固始人也、岂其本心哉、审知长子也、审知次子也、鏻长子也、审知少子也、曦甥也、审知子也、景保大四年也、南唐保大四年也。反向叙述通常按先小后大、先少后老、先分后总的顺序来排列涉及的各种要素。先小后大的叙述有：光州固始人也、景保大四年也、南唐保大四年也。在第 1 例"［王审知°］光州固始人也"中，先述个人"王审知"，后述地方"光州固始"；在第 2 例"［是岁°］景保大四年也"中，先述年份"是岁"，后述年号"景保大"。先少后老的叙述有：审知长子也、审知次子也、鏻长子也、审知少子也、曦甥也、审知子也。第 2 例"［鏻°］审知次子也"先述儿子后述父亲。先分后总的叙述有：［吾属弃坟墓妻子而为盗者°］岂其本心哉。反向叙述通常带有"也、哉、矣"等语气助词。被归为正向叙述的"［王淡°］唐相溥之子、［杨沂°］唐相涉从弟、［徐寅°］唐时知名进士"等 3 例缺少语气助词，但有先少后老的叙述顺序，因而具有中性叙述的特征。

另有 2 个名词化的主谓结构：延禀与鏻之谋杀延翰也、何偪（逼）下之甚也。前例是名词化的主谓结构，其主语是"延禀与鏻"，谓语是"谋杀延翰"；后例是名词化的动补结构，其动词是"偪（逼）下"，补语是"甚"。

2.4 名词性状语句读（NCA）

名词性状语句读（NCA）通常充当下文语句的状语，多数表示时间。在 33 例 NCA 中，共有 9 例年号及年份，7 例季度、月份、日子或时辰，13 例过去时间，4 例将来时间。

表示年号及年份的例子：光启二年、乾宁四年、同光四年、长兴二年、长兴三年、龙启三年、晋天福二年、晋开运三年丙午、保大三年。其中，第 7 例的"晋天福二年"还包括朝代名称"晋"；第 8 例的"晋开运三年丙午"除了朝代名称"晋"之外，还有天干地支纪年"丙午"。此类状语有时并不独立成句，而是融入其他句读并构成更加复杂的谓语，如"审知同光三年卒"。

在 7 例表示季度、月份、日子或时辰的句读中，共有 2 例季节：三年夏、是岁夏；4 例月份：十月、十二月、是岁十月、六年三月；1 例日子及时辰：明日晨朝。13 例表示过去时间的句读分别是：5 例"是时"、4 例"是岁"、3 例"初"、1 例"周世宗时"。4 例表示将来时间的句读分别是：2 个"明日"、1 个"明年"、1 个"六十年后"。

2.5 名词性列举句读（NCE）

名词性列举句读（NCE）包含多个并列的名词词组或专有名词。仅有的 1 例 NCE 是：控鹤都将连重遇拱宸都将朱文进［。皆以此怒激其军］，充当后句的主语。该句包含 14 个汉字。此类句读普遍较长。例如，《论语》全文最长的句读即为此类：伯达伯适仲突仲忽叔夜叔夏季随季骊，包含 16 个汉字。另有 1 例包含 15 个汉字：伯夷叔齐虞仲夷逸朱张柳下惠少连。

3. 简单谓词性句读

简单谓词性句读是以单个动词（词组）为核心的主谓结构，按动词是否后接宾语及其宾语的数量和特征可分为三类：不及物动词谓语句读（intransitive-verb clause，IVC）、单及物动词谓语句读（transitive-verb clause，TVC）、双及物动词谓语句读（ditransitive-verb clause，DVC）。此外，不同的句读按其所表示的过程特征又可分为物理和心理、言语和行为、存在和关系六种类型（Halliday，1994/2000）。在全文 721 个句读中，共有 271 例简单谓词性句读：108 例 IVC、143 例 TVC、20 例 DVC。

3.1 不及物动词谓语句读（IVC）

不及物动词谓语句读（IVC）的动词不接宾语，形成"主语+动词"句型（SV）。在 108 例 IVC 中，共有 49 例表示行为过程，11 例表示生理（行为）过程，21 例表示心理过程，18 例表示言语过程，9 例表示物理过程。

在 49 例表示行为过程的例子中，表示普通行为的句读有 8 例：唐末群盗起、延禀之兵先至、明日鏻兵始至、伏兵发、军士踊跃、鏻使者至、陈氏与归郎奸、损还。此类句读的否定形式有 6 例：潮不许、唐不报、已不及、仁达不从、不叶、遂不纳。表示登基继位的句读有 9 例：子延翰立、延翰立、而延钧立、既立、延义立、既立、曦既立、自曦立、曦立。与反身代词"自"连用的句读有 4 例：绪后自杀、吾当自往、欲自立、乃自立。后接表示方位短语的句读有 9 例：伏篁竹间、鏻饯于郊、奔于钱塘、奔于钱塘、宿于野次、挂于木、遂降于吴越、迁于金陵、其始年则牵于谶书。如果涉及的动词能带宾语（实际不带），那么它们通常具有被动意义。例如，"挂于木"的"挂"字、"其始年则牵于谶书"的"牵"字和"迁于金陵"的"迁"字都有一定的被动特征。另外，不及物行为动词有时后接时间、数量、身份等补语成分。此类句读有 4 例：吾属不自保朝夕、士卒伤死甚众、覆溺常十三四、审知虽起盗贼。它们的动词具有较大的语义分量，因而有别于"主语+连系动词+补语"结构（SVC）。行为动词可两两组合构成双音节的不及物动词（词组）。此类句读有 7 例：召置军中、审知代立、英自诬伏、走匿九龙帐中、遣归、曦出游、醉归。另有 2 例是行为动词的列举句读：起居动静、其赐予给赏。

表示生老病死苦等生理（行为）的句读有 11 例：将吏之材能者必死、景福元年岩卒、潮卒、审知同光三年卒、崔氏后病、今皆已毙、头痛、鏻妻早卒、鏻已病、而俶已死、久而乃绝。

在 21 例表示心理过程的例子中，表示喜、怒、哀、乐等普通心理的句读有 15 例：前锋将大悟、崔氏性妒、延钧怒、闽人皆怨、皆怨、鏻惭、其次子继韬怒、继鹏惧、重遇惧、曦怒、曦喜、曦怒、重遇等惧、曦怒、文缜惧。与反身代词"自"搭配的句读有 2 例：潮颇自惧、而心常自疑。心理动词经常两两组合构成双音节的不及物动词词组。此类句读有 4 例：绪性猜忌、今绪雄猜、乙羞愧、而昶愈惑乱。

在 18 例表示言语过程的例子中，表示普通言语的句读有 15 例：前锋将曰、曰、英曰、巫言、曰、文杰曰、英曰、曰、仁达曰、俶曰、曦曰、谏议大夫郑元弼切谏、元弼曰、曦曰、《江南录》云。此类动词实为及物动词，只因其后接的言语内容独立成句而被归为不及物动词谓语句读。言语动词也可两两组合构成双音节的不及物动词词组。此类例子有 3 个：潮报曰、自占云、国人歌曰。

在 9 例表示物理过程的例子中，表示普通物理过程的句读有 6 例：唐亡、既成、虹见其宫中、后兴事败、皇后土贡何在、王氏灭。否定形式的句读有 2 例：久不克、昼夜声不辍。另有 1 例天气现象：一夕风雨雷电震击。

3.2 单及物动词谓语句读（TVC）

单及物动词谓语句读（TVC）的动词后接一个宾语，形成"主+动+宾"句型（SVO）。143 例 TVC 包含 99 例行为过程、16 例心理过程、2 例言语过程、10 例物理过程、16 例存在或关系过程。

在 99 例表示行为过程的例子中，8 例表示普通行为过程的句读：常乘白马、登舟、鏻欣然逊位、既而复位、他日损遇乙于途、群臣侍酒、诸子继柔弃酒、昔太祖武皇帝亲冒矢石。3 例表示视觉察看等行为过程的句读：闻败、文杰多察民间阴事、鏻闻鼓噪声。13 例表示攻城略地的句读：陷漳浦、攻其西门、延禀子继升守建州、吴人攻建州、程赟守漳州、许文缜守汀州、富沙王兵收福州矣、延政已得三州、而南唐兵方急攻延政、唐兵攻建州、景已破延政、据泉漳二州、李景兵破建州。14 例表示烧杀抢夺的句读：磔文杰于市、枭其首于市、烧启圣门、夺仿首、并杀其赞者一人、连重遇杀昶、连重遇已杀曦、州人共杀绍颇、亦杀赟、重遇亦杀文进、福州裨将林仁翰又杀重遇、已而又杀俨明、而留从效亦逐景守兵、虏王氏之族。22 例表示施礼管教奖罚的句读：乃选壮士数十人、且益兵、而犹禀唐正朔、善继先志、仁达伏甲舟中、受册于宝皇、置百官、又荐妖巫徐彦、将罢公、英尝主闽兵、而典亲兵、惟贮一归郎、鏻飨军于大酺殿、既立昶、陛下方示大信、高祖乃赦元弼、昶弟继严判六军诸卫事、曦尝嫁女、百姓与能、称晋年号、送款于李景、迁延政族于金陵。12 例表示时空迁移的句读，其动词通常后接地名、职位或时代。其中，后接地名的例子：军次南安、使者入海、延禀还建州、入北庙、损至闽、间道至京师。后接职位的例子：累迁同中书门下平章事、累加检校太师中书令、六十年后将安归、鏻乃即皇帝位。后接时代的例子：及其子孙、至保大四年。17 例句读的单及物行为动词后接代词"之"：因之军中、逾年克之、辄幽之别室、遂杀之、送者闻之、赦之、族灭之而已、鏻怏怏与之、昶闻之、及之、斩之、朝士有不贺者笞之、弃之水中、有诉及私弃酒者辄杀之、延政逐之、王氏子弟在福州者无少长皆杀之、漳州闻。另有 10 例双音节行为动词句读：寿州人王绪攻陷固始、审知请班师、杨行密据有江淮、好礼下士、招来海中蛮夷商贾、刺杀之、谋杀继鹏、射杀数人、昶相王倓每抑折之、而景兵攻破建州。

在 16 例表示心理过程的例子中，7 例表示普通心理过程：鏻好鬼神道家之说、宫人不忍其苦、不知礼义、昶亦好巫、曦亦惮倓、李氏妒尚妃之宠、今天厌王氏。另有 9 例句读的单及物心理动词后接代词"之"：鏻衔之、继雄信之、镛心忌之、陛下皆知之、镛劈之、其子继鹏蒸之、与皇城使李仿图之、昶患之、曦心疑之。

2例表示言语过程的例子是：谁谓九龙帐、其婿范晖自称留后。后例与反身代词"自"字搭配。

在10例表示物理过程的例子中，6例表示普通物理过程：彻其几筵、镛遂绝朝贡、日焚龙脑薰陆诸香数斤、掷弓于地、而新罗复献剑、廷英进买宴钱千万。另有4例表示建制过程：又建学四门、立五庙、乃更其制、铸大铁钱。

在16例表示存在或关系的例子中，3例表示事物存在：有众数万、果有之邪、遂启有闽。13例表示拥有关系：何待之有、文杰与内枢密使吴英有隙、无他苦也、得其军士心、镛有嬖吏归守明者、镛后得风疾、又有百工院使李可殷、镛婢春燕有色、镛无恙、仿有弑君之罪、当求有德、其能有此土也、然其奄有闽国。

3.3 双及物动词谓语句读（DVC）

双及物动词谓语句读的动词后接两个名词词组，形成"主+动+宾$_1$+宾$_2$"句型（SVO$_1$O$_2$）或"主+动+宾+补"句型（SVOC）。后者又称为复杂宾语结构。构成第一种句型的动词一般都是物理过程或言语过程。其中，3例表示物理过程：枭其首西门、致书晋大臣、廷英又献皇后钱千万。1例表示言语过程：不质诸鬼神，其中的代词"诸"为直接宾语。

构成第二种句型的动词一般都是行为过程或言语过程。其中，9例表示行为过程：福建观察使陈岩表潮泉州刺史、拜审知节度使、梁太祖加拜审知中书令、唐拜延翰节度使、唐即拜镛节度使、请授臣尚书令、拜其子继恭临海郡王、贬峻漳州司户参军、景犹封从效晋江王。7例表示言语过程：更名镛、改元永和、更名昶、改元通文、更名曦、改元永隆、改元天德。

4. 特殊谓词性句读

除了普通的不及物动词和及物动词之外，构成谓语核心的词语还包括轻动词、形容词、形容词活用的动词、名词活用的动词、能愿动词及被动结构，分别形成轻动词谓语句读（light-verb clause, LVC）、形容词谓语句读（adjective-predicate clause, APC）、形容词活用动词句读（deadjectival-verb clause, DAV）、名词活用动词句读（denominal-verb clause, DNV）、能愿动词句读（modal-verb clause, MVC）、被动语态句读（passive-voice clause, PVC）。在全文721个句读中，共有108例特殊谓词性句读：34例

LVC、23 例 APC、4 例 DAV、9 例 DNV、17 例 MVC、21 例 PVC。

4.1　轻动词谓语句读（LVC）

包括"为、作、加、封、如、似、以"等在内的轻动词（light verb；Huddleston & Pullum, 2002：290-296）虽然后接名词词组，但并不传递主要的语义内容。轻动词谓语句读（LVC）主要用以表达身份、称号、类比、数量、行为等意义。在 34 例 LVC 中，8 例表示身份：世为农、为县史、延禀自以养子、楚王马殷吴越王钱镠皆为尚书令、后当为六十年天子、当为大罗仙人、曦弟延政为建州节度使、吾属世为王氏臣。4 例表示称号：号为甘棠港、谥曰忠懿、谥曰惠皇帝、谥曰景宗。6 例表示封官授爵：封琅琊王、封闽王、封闽王、封富沙王、封鄱阳王、拜观察使。5 例表示普通行为过程：将为乱、作乐于台下、将加笞、曦常为牛饮、为淫虐。

表示比喻关系的句读有 3 例：倓面如生、卿何如魏郑公、陛下似唐太宗。表示数量关系的句读有 4 例：朝廷官不满百、已而岁入不登其数、故为六十一年、惟《江南录》又差其末年也。表示类属关系的句读有 1 例：其后事具国史。另有 3 例表示疑问：奈何、此将何为、奈何。

4.2　形容词谓语句读（APC）

形容词谓语句读（APC）是以形容词为谓语核心的句读。在 23 例 APC 中，8 例用以描写为人处事的状态：泉州刺史廖彦若为政贪暴、而军行整肃、审知为人状儿雄伟、而为人俭约、延翰为人长大、美皙如玉、乙衣冠伟然、骖僮甚盛。5 例表示行为品性：其妻崔氏陋而淫、秦二世愚、今陛下聪明、仁达智略、曦性既淫虐。4 例表示事物范围：兵与将俱尽、而闽地狭、廥食立尽、独厚于他军。3 例表示否定意义：国用不足、事无大小、上心不平于二公。2 例表示评价意义：谬也、谬矣（二者属于形容词性句读）。另有 1 例带有动词性的补语：曦自昶世倔强难制（其中的动词"制"补足形容词"难"）。

4.3　形容词活用动词句读（DAV）

形容词活用动词句读（DAV）的谓语动词通常是由形容词后接宾语转变而来的，因而属于及物动词。4 例 DAV 分别是：泉人苦之、文杰善数术、曦由此恶其宗室、以安此土。第 1 例的宾语为代词"之"，其余 3 例的宾语均为名词词组。

4.4　名词活用动词句读（DNV）

名词活用动词句读（DNV）的谓语动词是由名词转变而来的，既可为及物动词，又可为不及物动词。在 9 例 DNV 中，3 例及物动词：率百官北面而臣之、率诸将吏北面而臣之、谋迎延政都福州。6 例不及物动词：皆依审知仕宦、吾今不王、审知丧未期、布衣芒屦而已、而宫中火、从效仍臣于南唐。

4.5 能愿动词句读（MVC）

能愿动词句读（MVC）以能愿动词后接普通动词所构成的复合动词词组为谓语核心，用以表达情态意义，其中的能愿动词主要包括"能、愿、敢、可、欲"。在 17 例 MVC 中，5 例"能"字后接普通动词：延翰不能制、予不能继先志、延禀不能对、非高能愚二世也、富沙王不能自保。3 例"敢"字后接普通动词：汝何敢谋反、乃敢强谏、群臣皆莫敢议。4 例"可"字后接普通动词：未可信也、在吾世可用、不可遗后世患、过三日可无患（其中的"无"为存在动词）。另有 5 例其他能愿动词后接普通动词：况欲图成事哉、愿伏斧锧、兵士在道不肯进、乃得不刭、求置邸内属（其中的能愿动词分别为"欲、愿、肯、得、求"）。

4.6 被动语态句读（PVC）

单音节的"见、遇、被、为、所"等动词也能后接及物动词构成双音节的动词词组，表示被动意义，分别得到"见"动句（*jiàn*-passive clause，JPC）、"遇"动句（*yù*-passive clause，YPC）、"被"动句（*bèi*-passive clause，BPC）、"为"动句（*wéi*-passive clause，WPC）、"所"动句（*suǒ*-passive clause，SPC）等。此类句读统称为被动语态句读（PVC）。在 21 例 PVC 中，共有 7 例 JPC、1 例 YPC、2 例 BPC、2 例 WPC、9 例 SPC。

"见"动句就是"见"字后接及物动词所构成的被动结构。此类例子有：绪已见废、晖见杀、延禀见执、道士陈守元以左道见信、见杀、以色见倖、而妖人林兴以巫见幸。"遇"动句就是"遇"字后接及物动词所构成的被动结构。此类例子有：遇弑。该词仅用于皇帝遇害，如：庄宗遇弑。在狭义上，由"被"字后接动词所构成的被动语句称为"被动句"。此类例子有：亦被杀、首被其毒。第 2 例在"被"字后面添加代词"其"。"为"动句就是"为"字后接动词所构成的被动结构。此类例子有：波涛为阻、为绝之。"所"动句就是"所"字后接动词所构成的被动结构，通常需要搭配"为"字结构，构成"为……所……"句式。此类例子有：为绪所胁尔、闽人以为审知德政所致、见英为崇顺王所讯、继韬及陈后归郎皆为仿所杀、内学士陈郯素以便佞为昶所亲信、惧为国人所讨、为延政所败。"所"动结构可搭配包括"有、无"在内的存在动词，因而在功能上转化为名词性结构，如：昶无所答、不敢有所发。

除了以上被动结构外，部分不带宾语的及物动词后接"于"字也能表达被动意义（本章 3.1 节）。

5. 复杂句读

复杂句读包含双重谓语动词或双重主谓结构，可细分为双扇句读（double-phased clause, DPC）、连动句读（serial-verb clause, SVC）、并列谓语句读（coordinate-predicate clause, CPC）、主谓宾语句读（clause with a complex object, CCO）、主谓主语句读（clause with a complex subject, CCS）、使役结构句读（clause with a causative construction, CCC）、主副动词句读（clause with a verb and a coverb, CVC）等。在全文 721 个句读中，共有 248 例复杂句读：25 例 DPC、25 例 SVC、65 例 CPC、25 例 CCO、1 例 CCS、41 例 CCC、66 例 CVC。

5.1 双扇句读（DPC）

双扇句读（DPC）包含一组因"而"字相连的双重谓语或主谓结构（马建忠，2007：386），通常表达连动、并列、转折、因果、时间等逻辑关系。在 25 例 DPC 中，15 例具有连动关系：吾属弃坟墓妻子而为盗者、见以为崇而卒、已执延翰而杀之、推镰而立之、疾驰二日而至、退而谓人曰、仿惧而出、与继鹏率皇城卫士而入、兴辄以宝皇语命之而后行、昶疑而罢之、昶挟爱姬子弟黄门卫士斩关而出、继业执而杀之、欲图曦而立其子亚澄、重遇等遣壮士拉于马上而杀之、安能交臂而事贼乎。4 例具有并列关系：与潮相持而泣、以手掩面而走、兵部员外郎李知损上书请籍没其物而禁锢使者、而妻李氏悍而酗酒。2 例具有转折关系：继室金氏贤而不见答、曦命卫士鞭之百而不死。2 例具有因果关系：贤妃尚氏有色而宠、醉而不胜。1 例表达时间关系：岁复在丙午而灭。另有 1 例以"乃"字为连词：得文杰乃进（该句表达条件关系）。

5.2 连动句读（SVC）

连动句读（SVC）包含个组因"以"字相连的双重谓语结构，通常表达目的、结果等逻辑关系。在 25 例 SVC 中，11 例属于完全的普通连动句读：蔡州秦宗权方募士以益兵、刻木为人手以击颊、建宝皇宫以居之、而籍没其货以佐用、其子继鹏请与之以纾难、而募勇士为宸卫都以自卫、昶举以示俅曰、国计使陈匡范增算商之法以献、乃借于民以足之、与朱文进连姻以自固、传首建州以自归。4 例属于不完全的普通连动句读：以教闽士之秀者、以愚二世、以来远人、以赎昶罪。"以"字后接轻动词"为"的句读共有 6 例：开以为港、遂立以为后、多养死士以为备、后立以为皇后、用以为相、乃用骑马来骑马去之谶以为据（其中的"为"字的功能详见本章第 4.1 节）。除了第 1 例表示结果关系外，其余 5 例均表示目的关系。另有4例缺省前一谓语动词：英以为然、鏻以语文杰、鏻以为然、郯反以告重遇。

5.3 并列谓语句读（CPC）

并列谓语句读（CPC）的谓语部分是由不带连词的双重谓语所构成的，通常表达时间、互补、对象、方式、连动、因果、转折等逻辑关系。在65例CPC中，4例表示同时关系：所至剽掠、延翰建国称王、坐中昏然、曦居旁色变。10例表示互补关系：绪迟留不行、鏻惜之不与、下诏暴其罪、归其贡物不纳、臣将命无状、及其妻子皆死无遗类、血流被体、乃释赟不答、淫虐不道、更其名曰弘义。13例表示言语对象：潮说其前锋将曰、延禀临诀谓鏻曰、鏻诮之曰、守元谓鏻曰、文杰谓英曰、文杰因教英曰、尝问仁达曰、谥昶曰康宗、曦谓元弼曰、谏议大夫黄峻昇橇诣朝堂极谏、集闽群臣告曰、泉州军将留从效诈其州人曰、福州将李仁达谓其徒曰。8例表示目的：绪率众南奔、跃出擒之、其耆老相率遮道留之、于是军府将吏上书劝进、伪立白帜请降、赐与金帛慰安之、昶徙南宫避灾、校书郎陈光逸上书疏曦过恶五十余事。8例表示方式：审知乃亲督士卒攻破之、延翰乃取司马迁史记闽越王无诸传示其将吏曰、鏻上书言、守元传宝皇语曰、昶称疾不见、元弼俯伏曰、重遇等流涕自辨、延政数贻书谏之。17例表示连动关系：潮即引兵围彦若、执延翰杀之、延禀率兵击鏻、卒诬以罪杀之、鏻立十年见杀、伏甲擒仿杀之、仿部曲千人叛、而其子继恭遣其佐郑元弼随损至京师贡方物、狱具引见、夜率卫士纵火焚南宫、重遇迎延义立之、泉州刺史余廷英尝矫曦命掠取良家子、数举兵相攻、剖棺断尸、曦乃举兵攻延政、乃擒继昌杀之、执王继勋送于金陵。3例表示因果关系：其兵见之皆溃去、英病在告、御史中丞刘赟坐不纠举。1例表示转折关系：卫士刺之不殂。另有1例表示条件关系：动辄触之。

5.4 主谓宾语句读（CCO）

言语和心理两类动词时常以主谓结构为其后接的宾语，构成主谓宾语句（CCO）。在25例CCO中，15例包含言语类动词：绪闻潮兄弟材勇、闻潮略地至其境、当言头痛而已、宜问其疾如何、军士闻英死、以谓古制疏阔、言见延禀来、问仿杀可殷何罪、述昶意求以敌国礼相往来、云如此可求大还丹、林兴传神言、术者言昶宫中当有灾、南唐李景闻闽乱、留从效闻延政降唐、今诸家记其国灭丙午是也。8例包含心理类动词：仿以为鏻病已甚、怒损侵辱之、高祖怒其不逊、昶疑重遇军士纵火、昶知不免、曦思俊前言、其后知其借于民也、惧众不附。2例包含行为类动词：伺绪至、据王潮实以唐景福元年入福州。

5.5 主谓主语句读（CCS）

以主谓结构为主语的句读称为主谓主语句读（CCS）。唯一的例子是：臣为魏郑公可矣。该句的主语部分"臣为魏郑公"本身就是一个轻动词谓语句读，其谓语部分是形容词谓语结构"可矣"。此类结构通常被划分为两个或多个句读。例如，在"今诸家记其国灭丙午是也。其始年则牵于谶书。谬矣"中，"谬矣"独立成句。

5.6 使役结构句读（CCC）

以使役结构为谓语核心的句读称为使役结构句读（CCC），其中的使役结构通常由"遣、使、命、令"等引导，分别构成"遣"字句、"使"字句、"命"字句、"令"字句等。在41例CCC中，共有17例"遣"字句：潮遣审知攻晖、审知岁遣使泛海、鏻遣王仁达拒之、遣守元问宝皇、即上遣人问公疾、鏻遣人问之、鏻遣其将王延宗救之、昶遣使朝贡京师、高祖遣散骑常侍卢损册昶闽王、又遣中书舍人刘乙劳损于馆、又遣医人陈究以空名堂牒卖官、遣使者朝贡于晋、新罗遣使聘闽以宝剑、遣杜建崇监其军、延政遣其从子继昌守福州、遣人召李仁达入朝、从效遣牙将蔡仲兴为商人。5例"使"字句：使其子继雄转海攻其南门、鏻使彦视鬼于宫中、讽鏻使巫视英疾、损使人诮之曰、乃使人谓重遇等曰。6例"命"字句：宝皇命王少避其位、命其子继鹏权主府事、命文杰劾之、鏻命锦工作九龙帐、乃命兴率壮士杀审知子延武延望及其子五人、命发冢戮其尸。4例"令"字句：令上下通、乃令壮士先杀李可殷于家、令继恭主之、延义令其子继业率兵袭昶。另有9例使役结构由其他动词引导：召其兵会击黄巢、宗权发兵攻绪、又请潮自临军、毋烦老兄复来、果烦老兄复来、守元教昶起三清台三层、召下御史劾之、乃掖朱文进升殿、发兵攻之。

5.7 主副动词句读（CVC）

有别于主动词，包括"以、为、自、因"等在内的字词虽然能够后接宾语，但其谓语功能很弱，通常无法直接构成独立的主谓结构，只能起到辅助功能，因而被称为副动词（coverb; Pulleyblank, 1995：47-57）。包含主、副两类动词的句读称为主副动词句读（CVC），可分"以"字句、"为"字句、"自"字句、"因"字句等。在66例CVC中，共有42例"以"字句、15例"为"字句、4例"自"字句、5例"因"字句。

在42例"以"字句中，12例"以"字后接人物并以"为"字为主动词：以潮为军校、乃以绪为光州刺史、唐即以潮为福建观察使、潮以审知为副使、唐以福州为威武军、以其弟延钧为泉州刺史、以福州为长乐府、以中军使薛文杰为国计使、景以仁达为威武军节度使、李景以泉州为清源军、以从效为节度使、遂以王潮光启二年岁在丙午拜泉州刺史为始年。8 例"以"字后接人物并以其他动词为主动词：延禀延钧皆以兵入、上以公居近密、即以英下狱、以李仿判六军诸卫事、于是以元弼下狱、文进以重遇判六军诸卫事、以黄绍颇守泉州、以雪峰寺僧卓俨明示众曰。19 例"以"字后接事物，通常表示工具、方式或原因：又以铁锥刺之、以黄龙见真封宅、致富人以罪、而屡以疾告、以金槌击其首、乃以槛车送文杰军中、闽人争以瓦石投之、中以铁芒内向、以黄金数千斤铸宝皇及元始天尊太上老君像、皆以此怒激其军、昶以火事语之、以一当十、多以事诛之、以绳系颈、匡范以忧死、以色嬖之、常以语消重遇等、延政乃以建州建国称殷、以汀州降于延政。另有 3 例因主动词不接宾语而使"以"字后置：系以大械、代以季弟继镛、被以衮冕。

在 15 例"为"字句中，共有 13 例"为"字实属轻动词，其所构成的动宾结构充当另一动宾结构的补足成分：乃推潮为主、升福州为大都督府、又多选良家子为妾、改元为龙启、追谥审知为昭武孝皇帝、赵高指鹿为马、故高指鹿为马、拜道士谭紫霄为正一先生、又拜陈守元为天师、立父婢春燕为淑妃、迎王继勋为刺史、迎王继成为刺史、世宗与李景画江为界。另有 2 例"为"字后接事物用以表示目的：文杰为鏻造槛车、王仁达为鏻杀延禀有功。

"自"字句表示动作开始的地方或时间。此类例子有：自南康入临汀、自登莱朝贡于梁、自审知时与延翰不叶、则当自景福元年为始。

"因"字句表示动作的原因或方式。此类例子有：多因事杀之、二人因谋作乱、因归郎以通陈氏、继鹏因陈氏以求春燕、因大享军。其中，第 5 例"因大享军"单独成句。

6. 小结

在全文 721 个句读中，共有 94 例普通体词性句读，其占比约为 13.04%：12 例 CNC（完全体词性句读）、18 例 NCS（名词性主语句读）、30 例 NCP（名词性谓语句读）、33 例 NCA（名词性状语句读）、1 例 NCE（名词性列举句读）。271 例简单谓词性句读，其占比约为 37.59%：108 例 IVC（不及物动词谓语句读）、143 例 TVC（单及物动词谓语句读）、20 例 DVC（双及物动词谓语句读）。108 例特殊谓词性句读，其占比约为 14.98%：34 例 LVC（轻动词谓语句读）、23 例 APC（形容词谓语句读）、4 例 DAV（形容词活用动词句读）、9 例 DNV（名词活用动词句读）、17 例 MVC（能愿动词句读）、21 例 PVC（被动语态句读）。248 例复杂句读，其占比约为 34.40%：25 例 DPC（双扇句读）、25 例 SVC（连动句读）、65 例 CPC（并列谓语句读）、25 例 CCO（主谓宾语句读）、1 例 CCS（主谓主语句读）、41 例 CCC（使役结构句读）、66 例 CVC（主副动词句读）。具体情况见表 3-1。

表 3-1　《新五代史·闽世家第八》各类句读的类型比重一览表

大类	句读类型	数量/例	占比/%
普通体词性句读	CNC	12	1.66
	NCS	18	2.50
	NCP	30	4.16
	NCA	33	4.58
	NCE	1	0.14
	小计	94	13.04
简单谓词性句读	IVC	108	14.98
	TVC	143	19.83
	DVC	20	2.77
	小计	271	37.59
特殊谓词性句读	LVC	34	4.72
	APC	23	3.19
	DAV	4	0.55
	DNV	9	1.25
	MVC	17	2.36
	PVC	21	2.91
	小计	108	14.98
复杂句读	DPC	25	3.47
	SVC	25	3.47
	CPC	65	9.02
	CCO	25	3.47
	CCS	1	0.14
	CCC	41	5.69
	CVC	66	9.15
	小计	248	34.40
合计		721	100

在简单谓词性句读中，不及物动词谓语句读和单及物动词谓语句读的数量分别为108例和143例，均超过100例。本章已按物理和心理、言语和行为、存在和关系等6类动词对及物和不及物两类动词谓语句读做了进一步的分类。例如，108例不及物动词句读被细分为49例行为过程、11例生理（行为）过程、21例心理过程、18例言语过程、9例物理过程。复杂句读的数量位列第二，其占比略低于简单谓词性句读，通常涉及两个或两个以上主谓结构，其及物性特征具有双重性。其中的并列谓语句读和主副动词句读的数量分别为65例和66例，均超过60例。本章按主谓结构之间的逻辑关系或连接词语对两类句读做了进一步的分类。例如，在65例并列谓语句读中，4例表示同时关系，10例表示互补关系，13例表示言语对象，8例表示目的，8例表示方式，17例表示连动，3例表示因果关系，1例表示转折关系，1例表示条件关系。

第4章

普通体词性句读群组及其英语翻译

本章及接下来的3章将在语法分类的基础上以句读群组为单位讨论中国史籍的英语翻译。群组翻译不是以零散的句读为单位，而是以类聚的句读为单位，因而有利于呈现同类句读在翻译上的个性差异和共性特征。具体的句读以语法结构为依据归入对应的群组。语法结构的重合有别于词汇形式的重复。后者在计算机辅助翻译软件中体现为重复率，表明语句之间在词汇形式上的相似程度。语法结构的重合只涉及语法结构的相似程度，不涉及词汇形式的相似程度，处于同一群组的任何一对句读所包含的词汇项目既可能完全相同，又可能完全不同。群组翻译从句读所共享的语法结构入手。

本章主要讨论体词性句读群组及其英语翻译。该组包括完全体词性句读（CNC）、名词性主语句读（NCS）、名词性谓语句读（NCP）、名词性状语句读（NCA）和名词性列举句读（NCE）。它们的共同特点是完全由名词性成分所构成。在群组英译中，通常需要构建新的主谓结构。

1. 完全体词性句读群组及其英译

完全体词性句读普遍缺少谓语动词，其主语和谓语都是名词词组。因此，翻译通常需要引入谓语动词以重新构建语句的主谓结构。如：

[1] 中国多故 the nation witnessed radical changes

[2] 匡范人中宝也 Kuang Fan is rare and precious among men

[3] 时开运元年也 it was the first year of the Kaiyun period of the Jin dynasty (A.D. 944)

[4] 此非常人也 this is not a common person

其中，第[1]句"中国多故"的译文以witnessed为谓语动词。第[2]句、第[3]句和第[4]句都带有语气助词"也"，其译文均以连系动词 be 为谓语动词；第［2］句的"人中宝"被译为形容词词组 rare and precious among men；第［3］句的译文补足"后晋"及具体的年份，即 the Jin dynasty（A. D. 944）；第［4］句的译文相对直观。

对于以主谓结构为主语的完全体词性句读，其中的主语是否必须译为小句，取决于具体的情况。如：

［1］生我者潮也 it is Chao who has given us a second life

［2］一岁中死者八十四人 within one single year eighty-four of them were killed

第［1］句的主语"生我者"属于 SVO 句型，其中包含作为主语的代词"者"、谓语动词"生"和作为宾语的代词"我"；该主谓结构译为小句（who）has given us a second life，并置于 it is ... who 结构中构成分裂句。第［2］句的主语"死者"属于 SV 句型，其中包含作为主语的代词"者"和不及物的谓语动词"死"；该主谓结构译为被动结构（of them）were killed，直接充当主句谓语的核心。原文的名词性谓语"八十四人"则被译为 eighty-four（of them），在译文中充当主语。

以主谓结构为谓语的完全体词性句读涉及多个主体，因而不同主体之间的关系是翻译的重点问题。如：

［1］延翰字子逸 Yanhan, with Ziyi as his courtesy name

［2］审知养子建州刺史延禀 Yanbing, adopted as a son by Shenzhi, was appointed as magistrate of Jianzhou

［3］国号闽 and named the state "Min"

［4］陛下左右多奸臣 there are too many crafty ministers by your left and right sides

［5］审知婢金凤 Jinfeng, who had been Shenzhi's maidservant

［6］此宗室将为乱之兆也 this is an omen which shows that a revolt be staged within the loyal clan

第［1］句"延翰字子逸"不仅涉及"延翰"和"子逸"两个专有名词，而且涉及二者互为名字的关系。译文通过复杂的介词短语 with Ziyi as his courtesy name 来处理二者及其关系。第［2］句"审知养子建州刺史延禀"涉及"审知、养子、建州刺史、延禀"四个主体及两层关系。译文用非限定小句 adopted as a son by Shenzhi 来处理"审知"与"延禀"之间的父子关系，用限定小句 was appointed as magistrate of Jianzhou 来处理"建州刺史"与"延禀"之间的身份关系。第［3］句"国号闽"的译文用双及物动词 named 来处理其中涉及的"国"与"闽"之间的称谓关系。第[4]句主要涉及"陛下左右、多奸臣"两个主体，其译文以存在结构为框架，以介词 by 把二者的英语翻译 too many crafty ministers（多奸臣）和 your left and right sides（陛下左右）联结起来。第[5]句声明"审知"与"金凤"为主婢关系，其译文用限定的关系分句 who had been Shenzhi's maidservant 来描述两个主体之间的身份关系。第[6]句的谓语部分"宗室将为乱之兆"是主谓结构"宗室将为乱"的名词化形式，其译文用关系分句（an omen）which shows that 来处理主语 this（此）、补语 an omen（兆）和主谓结构 a revolt be staged within the loyal clan（宗室将为乱）的关系。

显然，汉语的体词性句读主要依靠语序来处理各类主体之间的关系，而在其英译中通常需要建立新的主谓结构以把涉及的各类关系描述清楚。

2. 名词性主语句读与名词性谓语句读

名词性主语句读和名词性谓语句读都是不完全的主谓结构。前者只有名词性主语部分，后者只有名词性谓语部分。尽管如此，二者均独立成句。两种句读群组均可参考完全体词性句读群组的翻译方法。

2.1 名词性主语句读群组及其英译

名词性主语句读区分为简单、复合、复杂三类。简单的名词性主语句读一般为人名和地名两类专有名词，通常后接详细的说明语句。汉语的单名现象比较普遍，而在中国史籍的行文中往往又省略姓氏，因此单音节的专有名词很常见。对于单字名称的翻译，多数译者（如 Watson，1974）倾向于添加姓氏。如：

[1] 王审知 Wang Shenzhi
[2] 王淡 Wang Dan
[3] 杨沂 Yang Yi
[4] 徐寅 Xu Yin
[5] 闽 "The state of Min," he said
[6] 鏻 Wang Ling
[7] 继鹏 Wang Jipeng
[8] 昶 "Wang Chang," he said
[9] 延义 Wang Yanyi
[10] 李仁遇 Li Renyu
[11] 延政 Wang Yanzheng

其中，第［1］句、第［2］句、第［3］句、第［4］句和第［10］句直接给出音译词项，全都包含姓氏及名称。第［6］句、第［7］句、第［8］句、第［9］句和第［11］句统一补上姓氏Wang。第［5］句把"闽"字解释为the state of Min，这种处理方法类似添加姓氏。

复合的名词性主语句读通常包含修饰成分。如：

［1］海上黄崎 the merchant ships, however, could only berth across the sea at the Huangqi Island

［2］凤阁舍人 "Secretary of the Phoenix Cabinet," the man said

翻译需要处理的主要问题是中心词和修饰成分之间的关系。第［1］句按上下文的语义在译出across the sea at the Huangqi Island（海上黄崎）的基础上添加解释性语句the merchant ships, however, could only berth。第［2］句"凤阁舍人"是官职名称，其中的"凤阁"译为the Phoenix Cabinet，而"舍人"则译为secretary。

复杂的名词性主语句读本身包含的主谓结构是翻译的要点。如：

［1］部将有材能者 those commanders who were capable and talented

［2］良家子之美者 those well-bred girls who were beautiful

［3］敢有作威福者 if any one dares to abuse his power or stage any rebel

［4］不忠不孝者 those who lack loyalty or filial piety

［5］而后人纪录者 with regard to the final year, recorders of the later generations

第［1］句、第［2］句均以those ... who ... 结构为框架。第［1］句"部将有材能者"的代词"者"先译为those ... who ... 结构，而后代入主谓结构"部将有材能"的译文 ... commanders ... were capable and talented。第［2］句"良家子之美者"先使用those ... who ... 结构，然后代入"良家子之美"的译文well-bred girls were beautiful。第［4］句"不忠不孝者"由于缺少一个主体，所以译文直接把lack loyalty or filial piety（不忠不孝）置于those who ... 结构之后，其中的those变为不定代词。第［3］句"敢有作威福者"使用条件状语从句any one ... ；该句也可使用关系分句（those）who ... 。第［5］句则用介词of来处理the later generations（后人）和recorders（纪录者）之间的关系。

2.2 名词性谓语句读群组及其英译

在英语中，限定谓语必须是动词性的。因此，如果名词性谓语句读译为限定形式，就必须引入相应的谓语动词。如：

［1］自古王国也 has been a kingdom since ancient times

［2］实五十五年也 it is actually fifty-five years

两例均为简单的名词性谓语句读。其中，第［1］句"自古王国也"引入连系动词 been；第［2］句"实五十五年也"引入 it is 结构。

复合的名词性谓语句读涉及修饰成分或并列结构。如：

［1］隆准方口 with his nose bridge highly upright and mouth widely square

［2］夷貊之君 is simply a barbarian king of the ethnic minorities

［3］皆王氏之诸子也 they were all princes of the Wang's house

第［1］句包含"隆准、方口"两个并列的名词词组，译文采用介词 with 引入二者，并将其分别译为无动词分句 his nose bridge highly upright 和 mouth widely square。第［2］句是涉及两个主体的偏正结构，译文引入连系动词 is；两个主体通过介词 of 连接起来，并被译为 a barbarian king of the ethnic minorities。第［3］句也是涉及两个主体的偏正结构，译文引入 were；其中涉及的 princes（诸子）和 the Wang's house（王氏）两个主体通过介词 of 连接。

在复杂的名词性谓语句读群组中，正面叙述涉及的句式比较多样，因而译文的结构相对复杂。如：

［1］字信通 whose courtesy name was Xintong

［2］父恁 his father was Wang Nen

［3］兄潮 and his brother was Wang Chao

［4］军中号白马三郎 so he earned himself the name of "White Knight the Third" in the army

［5］唐相溥之子 whose father is Wang Pu, the Prime Minister of the former Tang dynasty

［6］唐相涉从弟 whose elder brother is Yang She, the Prime Minister of the former Tang dynasty

［7］唐时知名进士 a famous scholar during the former Tang dynasty

[8] 年六十四 when he was 64 years old and

[9] 本姓周氏 originally born in a Zhou family

[10] 庙号太祖 consecrated in the ancestral temple in name of "Taizu", that is, the "Founding Emperor"

[11] 姓陈氏 had come from a Chen family

[12] 号归郎 he was known as Brother Gui

[13] 庙号太宗 and was consecrated in the ancestral temple in name of "Taizong", that is, the "Grand Emperor"

第［1］句、第［4］句、第［9］句、第［11］句和第［12］句涉及名称或姓氏：第［1］句的"字"字译为 whose courtesy name；第［4］句的"号"字译为 he earned himself the name of；第［9］句的"姓"字译为动词词组（was）born in；第［12］句的"号"字译为 was known as。第［2］句"父恁"和第［3］句"兄潮"各自引入其他人物，分别译为 his father was Wang Nen 和 his brother was Wang Chao。第［5］句和第［6］句的"唐相"的译文 the Prime Minister of the former Tang dynasty 较长且后置，因而分别使用 whose father 和 whose elder brother 来处理"之子"和"从弟"两个名词词组。第［7］句"唐时知名进士"相对简单，译为 a famous scholar during the former Tang dynasty。第［8］句涉及年龄，译为状语从句 when he was 64 years old。第［10］句和第［13］句都有"庙号"，译为(was) consecrated in the temple in name of。

反面叙述通常涉及判断，其译文的结构相对单一。如：

[1] 光州固始人也 was a native of Gushi County of Guangzhou Commandery

[2] 岂其本心哉 It isn't our own wish, is it?

[3] 审知长子也 was the eldest son of Wang Shenzhi

[4] 审知次子也 was the second son of Wang Shenzhi

[5] 鏻长子也 was the eldest son of Wang Lin

[6] 审知少子也 was the youngest son of Wang Shenzhi

[7] 曦甥也 was one of Wang Xi's nephews and

[8] 审知子也 was one of Wang Shenzhi's sons

[9] 景保大四年也 was the fourth year of the Baoda period during the reign of Li Jing (A.D. 946)

[10] 南唐保大四年也 was the fourth year of the Baoda period of

the state of Southern Tang (A. D. 946)

其中，第［1］句、第［3］句、第［4］句、第［5］句、第［6］句、第［7］句和第［8］句涉及人物介绍，其译文普遍使用属格结构或介词短语。第［2］句"岂其本心哉"用反问句式来总结上文所述的内容，其译文使用反意疑问句。第［9］句和第［10］句涉及时间，其译文均使用介词短语。

当名词性谓语句读包含名词化的主谓结构时，通常需要把该结构还原为普通的主谓结构。如：

［1］延禀与鏻之谋杀延翰也 when Yanbing and also Lin were to murder Yanhan

［2］何偪（逼）下之甚也 how can Your Reverence embarrass me in such an extent

两个例句读的翻译方法基本一致。第［1］句的主语"延禀与鏻"和谓语"谋杀延翰"被"之"字封装为名词性结构，其在翻译中被拆解为从句（when）Yanbing and also Lin were to murder Yanhan。第［2］句的动宾结构"偪（逼）下"和状语"甚"同样被"之"字封装为名词性结构，其在翻译中被拆解为主句（how can）Your Reverence embarrass me in such an extent。

3. 名词性状语句读群组及其英译

名词性状语句读多数由时间名词词组构成，通常译为复合的介词短语。其中，涉及具体年份的译文均在括号里添加公元纪年。如：

［1］光启二年 in the second year of the Guangqi period (A. D. 886)

［2］乾宁四年 in the fourth year of the Qianning period (A. D. 897)

［3］同光四年 in the fourth year of the Tongguang period (A. D. 926)

［4］长兴二年 in the second year of the Changxing period (A. D. 931)

［5］长兴三年 in the third year of the Changxing period (A. D. 932)

[6] 龙启三年 in the third year of the Longqi period (A. D. 935)

[7] 晋天福二年 in the second year of the Tianfu period of the Jin dynasty (A. D. 937)

[8] 晋开运三年丙午 in M. Fire Horse, the third year of the Kaiyun period of the Jin dynasty (A. D. 946)

[9] 保大三年 in the third year of the Baoda period (A. D. 945)

第[1]句、第[2]句、第[3]句、第[4]句、第[5]句、第[6]句和第[9]句都涉及年号和年份两个主体，译文均以介词of为连接词语。第[7]句和第[8]句的译文均在年号和年份上外加朝代名称(of) the Jin dynasty（晋）。第2章已经详细讨论天干地支记时形式的英语翻译。同时，可以在 https://flc.hqu.edu.cn/info/1166/10290.htm 直接查到五代十国每个天干地支日子或年份所对应的公元纪年日子或年份。

季节月份时辰的译法类似年份，通常添加具体的公元纪年。如：

[1] 十月 in October (November or December, A. D. 926)

[2] 十二月 in December (January or February, A. D. 927)

[3] 是岁十月 in October of this year (October or November, A. D. 935)

[4] 明日晨朝 on the next morning

[5] 三年夏 in the summer of the third year (A. D. 938)

[6] 是岁夏 in the summer of this year

[7] 六年三月 in March of the sixth year (March or April, A. D. 941)

第[1]句和第[2]句的月份分别译为 in October 和 in December，其后添加公元纪年的具体年月（November or December, A. D. 926）和（January or February, A. D. 927）。第[3]句和第[7]的年份及月份分别译为 in October of this year 和 in March of the sixth year，其后添加公元纪年的具体年月（October or November, A. D. 935）和（March or April, A. D. 941）。第[4]句"明日晨朝"译为 on the next morning，不再添加年月。第[5]句和第[6]句的年份及季节分别译为 in the summer of the third year 和 in the summer of this year，仅在前者的译文之后添加年份（A. D. 938）。

表示过去某个时间节点的名词多数比较简单。如：

[1] 是时₁ at that time

[2] 是时₂ at that time

[3] 是时₃ at that time

[4] 是岁₁ in the same year

[5] 初₁ earlier

[6] 是岁₂ later in that year

[7] 初₂ earlier

[8] 初₃ earlier

[9] 是时₄ at that time

[10] 周世宗时 during the reign of Emperor Shizong of the Zhou dynasty

[11] 是时₅ at that time

[12] 是岁₃ in this year

其中，5个"是时"都译为 at that time；3个"是岁"的翻译有些区别；3个"初"字都译为 earlier。第［10］句"周世宗时"包含具体的朝代及其帝王，译为 during the reign of Emperor Shizong of the Zhou dynasty。

表示将来某个时间节点的名词也相对简单。如：

[1] 六十年后 after sixty years

[2] 明日₁ on the next day

[3] 明日₂ on the next day

[4] 明年 in the next year

其中，第［1］句"六十年后"译为 after sixty years 或 in sixty years；2个"明日"都译为 on the next day；第［4］句"明年"译为 in the next year。

4. 名词性列举句读群组及其英译

名词性列举句读包含两个或多个并列的主体，通常充当上下文语句的主语或宾语。如：

[1] 控鹤都将连重遇拱宸都将朱文进 at that time, the general-in-chief of "Konghe Du" was Lian Chongyu and the general-in-chief of "Gongchen Du" was Zhu Wenjin

该句充当下句"皆以此怒激其军"的主语。译文采用解释的方法分别介绍 Lian Chongyu（连重遇）和 Zhu Wenjin（朱文进）二人，而 Konghe Du（控鹤都）和 Gongchen Du（拱宸都）二部则在上句"独厚于他军"的译文中加以解释：including the other two divisions of loyal guards called "Konghe Du" and "Gongchen Du"。

5. 小结

普通体词性句读的数量在《新五代史·闽世家第八》中占 13.04%。其中，名词性状语句读（NCA）超过三分之一。名词性状语句读的多数例子因涉及天干地支的记时形式而需要检索五代日历。虽然检索难度不大，但耗时费力，而把此类句读作为一种独立的群组来翻译，有利于群组翻译的流水作业模式。

第5章

简单谓词性句读群组及其英语翻译

翻译是用译入语的词汇语法形式（即译文）来识解（construe）原文所表达的功能语义内容，因而多重译文的词汇语法形式能够体现多重识解。对于等同的语义内容，英汉两种语言都有多种互补的识解方式。例如，"他用斧头把树砍倒"在英语中至少可以译为以下四种形式（Halliday, 2014: 18）：

[1] he took an axe and felled the tree

[2] using an axe he felled the tree

[3] he felled the tree with an axe

[4] he felled the tree axewise

此类多重识解是普遍的语言现象，只是语际之间在具体形式的选择上存在不同的倾向。总体上，英语倾向于使用[3]，其中的介词短语 with an axe 置于动宾结构 felled the tree 之后；汉语倾向于使用[2]，其中的次要动宾结构 using an axe 置于主要动宾结构 felled the tree 之前。尽管如此，在英语中上述四种表达都是正确的语法形式，因而相互之间处于互补关系。交错使用不同的语法形式，能够使行文更加生动。

本章主要讨论简单谓词性句读群组及其英语翻译。该群组包括不及物动词谓语句读（IVC）、单及物动词谓语句读（TVC）和双及物动词谓语句读（DVC）三类。由于简单谓词性句读在全部句读中的占比较大，所以需要对其再做细分。群组翻译有利于实施多样化的措辞策略，避免过度集中的词汇语法选择，使译项分布趋于合理。

1. 不及物动词谓语句读群组及其英译

单音节的不及物动词数量众多，大体上可再细分为行为、心理、言语、物理等类别。虽然双音节的不及物动词数量相对较少，但其结构较单音节的不及物动词复杂，因而在翻译中也不容忽视。

1.1 行为类不及物动词

汉语文言的不及物动词通常都能在英语中找到对应的不及物项。因此，该群组的翻译主要采取 SV 句型。如：

[1] 唐末群盗起 in the late Tang dynasty, as an increasing number of bandits were rising up

[2] 延禀之兵先至₁ the troops of Yanbing had come first

[3] 明日磷兵始至₂ whereas the troops of Lin did not arrive until the next day

[4] 磷使者至₃ messengers who had been sent by Lin arrived

其中的"起、至₁、至₂、至₃"分别译为 were rising up、had come、did not arrive、arrived，涉及过去进行时、过去完成时、一般过去时多种时态形式，以及肯定、否定两种极性形式。三个"至"字的翻译在词汇和语法上均存在分化现象。只有充分认识和理解上下文语句的逻辑关系，才能明确此类语法范畴。例如，第[2]句"延禀之兵先至"的下文句读是"明日磷兵始至"，上下两句在时间上存在先后关系。只要以下文句读的一般过去时形式作为参照，就可确定当前句读的译文需要使用过去完成时时态。显然，群组翻译并未把当前语句从上下文中完全分离出来。

如果不及物动词涉及两个或以上主体，可把不同的主体分开。如：

[1] 陈氏与归郎奸 Mrs Chen fornicated with Brother Gui

其中的"与"字译为介词 with。该句的翻译也可使用连词 and 以构成并列主语：Mrs Chen and Brother Gui fornicated with each other。

主动的不及物动词有时译为被动结构。如：

[1] 伏兵发 only to be ambushed by the soldiers

[2] 军士踊跃 the soldiers got excited

两句译文都用被动结构，不仅能够有效地传递原文的语义，而且能够使译文的语义更加明确、丰满。例如，第[1]句的译文 be ambushed by the soldiers 既能体现原句的"伏兵"，又能包含"发"字的意义，即 came out 或 rushed out。

部分带有否定副词的及物动词经常形成不及物的结构模式，其英译既需要注意否定形式的变换，又需要注意语态形式的交替。该群组的句读有时译为被动或中动结构。如：

［1］潮不许 but it was disapproved of by Chao

［2］唐不报 the Tang dynastic court made no reply to the application

［3］已不及 but it was too late

［4］不叶 they had not been in a good term with each other

［5］仁达不从 Renda was unwilling to submit to the state of Southern Tang

［6］遂不纳 tribute was no longer paid to the Zhou dynasty

除了"叶"字外，尽管"许、报、及、从、纳"等在肯定的条件下通常后接宾语，但在以上否定的句读中都构成不及物的结构模式。第［1］句的"不许"和第［5］句的"不从"分别译为被动形式 was disapproved of 和主动形式 was unwilling to submit to，两句译文均使用否定的前缀：前者使用 dis-，后者使用 un-。第［2］句的"不报"译为动宾结构 made no reply to，其中包含否定限定词 no。第［3］句的"不及"和第［4］句的"不叶"均以 SVC 句型为结构框架：前句译为肯定形式 it was too late，其中包含程度副词 too；后句译为否定形式 had not been in a good term with，其中包含否定副词 not。第［6］句的"不纳"译为被动的否定形式 tribute was no longer paid to，其中包含否定副词词组 no longer。

包含"立"字的句读通常表示登基，其语义相对简单，一般译为 succeeded/came to the throne。如：

［1］子延翰立 his son Yanhan succeeded to the throne

［2］延翰立 Yanhan later succeeded to the throne

［3］而延钧立 Yanjun succeeded to the throne soon afterwards

［4］既立 after he was enthroned

［5］延义立 Yanyi came to the throne

［6］既立 after he came to the throne

［7］曦既立 after Xi came to the throne

［8］自曦立 since Wang Xi came to the throne

［9］曦立 Xi succeeded to the throne

除了第［4］句外，其余 8 句的译法基本相同，要么译为 succeeded to the throne，要么译为 came to the throne。第［4］句"既立"关联下文的"既立昶"，明显存在"拥立"的语义，因而可译为被动结构 was enthroned。

第5章 简单谓词词性句读群组及其英语翻译

对于"生、老、病、苦、死"等生理动词，需要特别注意措辞的礼节。如：

［1］将吏之材能者必死₁ that all capable commanders and talented officials are sure to be killed

［2］景福元年岩卒₁ Yan passed away in the first year of the Jingfu period（A. D. 892）

［3］潮卒₂ Chao passed away and

［4］审知同光三年卒₃ Shenzhi passed away in the third year of the Tongguang period（A. D. 925）

［5］崔氏后病₁ Mrs Cui later got sick

［6］今皆已薨 now that they all have passed away（demised）

［7］头痛 it is a headache

［8］鏻妻早卒₄ after his wife died（passed away）earlier

［9］鏻已病₂ after Lin began to suffer from sickness

［10］而倓已死₂ Tan had died

［11］久而乃绝 only to die（to stop breathing/to run out of breath）after a long time

关于"死"类动词，中国史籍的选词普遍符合《礼记·曲礼下》所记载的如下礼节：天子死曰崩，诸侯死曰薨，大夫死曰卒，士曰不禄，庶人曰死。Yuan & Wu（2017：102）对该节的翻译如下：

> The Son of Heaven dies, which is called "collapse"; a king dies, called "demise"; a minister dies, called "pass away"; a scholar [dies], called "not salaried"; the common [die], called "die".

第［1］句的"死₁"字和第［10］句的"死₂"字分别译为被动形式 be killed 和主动形式 died。第［2］句的"卒₁"字、第［3］句的"卒₂"字和第［4］句的"卒₃"字均译为 passed away，但第［8］句的"卒₄"字译为 died。由于第［8］句在语境上跟第［2］句、第［3］句和第［4］句不存在明显的区别，所以"卒₄"字的翻译 died 可改为 passed away。第［6］句的"薨"字译为 passed away，可改为 demised。第［5］句的"病₁"字和第［9］句的"病₂"字分别译为形容词（got）sick 和名词（to suffer from）sickness。第［7］句的"头痛"译为名词词组（it is）a headache。最后，第［11］句的"绝"字译为 to die，略显简单，因而可改为复杂的动词结构 to stop breathing 或 to run out of breath。

搭配行为动词的反身代词"自"时常不译。如：

［1］绪后自杀 later he committed suicide

［2］吾当自往 I shall surely go fighting myself (in person)

［3］欲自立₁ he wanted to claim the kingship

［4］乃自立₂ then he claimed the kingship

在4个"自"字的翻译中，只有第［2］句"吾当自往"的"自"字译为反身代词 myself，也可译为介词短语 in person。第［1］句的"自杀"译为 committed suicide；第［3］句和第［4］句的"自立₁、自立₂"译为 claim/claimed the kingship。

对于后接方位的不及物动词，在翻译中需要注意介词短语的使用。特别是当部分不带宾语的及物动词后接"于"字时，可能涉及主动与被动之间的语态转换问题，而解决语态问题则有赖于上下文的语义关系。如：

［1］伏篁竹间 to ambush Xu in the midst of the bamboo forest

［2］犒饯于郊 Lin treated him with food and wine in the suburbs

［3］奔₁于钱塘₁ he escaped to the region of Qiantang in haste

［4］奔₂于钱塘₂ then sought refuge into the Qiantang area

［5］宿于野次 and made camp in the wild

［6］挂于木 was hung to a tree

［7］遂降于吴越 so he surrendered to the state of Wu and Yue

［8］迁于金陵 moved them to the capital city of Jinling

［9］其始年则牵于谶书 but the initial year was misled by books of prediction

第［1］句"伏篁竹间"的不及物动词"伏"直接译为及物动词 ambush Xu，其后的方位结构"篁竹间"则译为介词短语 in the midst of the bamboo forest。其余8句都有"于"字，后接方位名词。其中，第［2］句"犒饯于郊"的"饯"字和第［8］句"迁于金陵"的"迁"字分别译为及物的动宾结构 treated him with food and wine 和 moved them；第［3］句"奔于钱塘₁"的"奔₁"字译为不及物动词 escaped (to)，而第［4］句"奔于钱塘₂"的"奔₂"字则译为动宾结构 sought refuge (into)；第［5］句"宿于野次"的"宿"字译为动宾结构 made camp；第［6］句"挂于木"的"挂于"和第［9］句"其始年则牵于谶书"的"牵于"均有明显的被动意义，因而分别译为 was hung to 和 was misled by；第［7］句"遂降于吴越"的"降"字与"奔₁"字类似，译为不及物动词 surrendered （to）。

不及物动词有时后接其他非宾语成分。涉及的句读会因此而变得更加复杂，其翻译的难度也会相应地提高。如：

［1］吾属不自保朝夕 none of us can guarantee our own safety even for a single day

［2］士卒伤死甚众 resulted in a large number of injuries and casualties

［3］覆溺常十三四 as many as three or four out of ten often got drowned

［4］审知虽起盗贼 Shenzhi, though having risen up among the bandits

其中，第［1］句的"自保"后接时间名词"朝夕"："朝夕"译为介词短语 even for a single day；"自保"则译为动宾结构 can guarantee our own safety。第［2］句"士卒伤死甚众"的"众"字和第［3］句"覆溺常十三四"的"十三四"均表示数量关系，分别译为复杂限定词 a large number of 和复杂名词词组 as many as three or four out of ten，而其中的"伤死、覆溺"两个动词则分别译为名词词组（resulted in）injuries and casualties 和动词词组 got drowned；第［4］句"审知虽起盗贼"的"盗贼"表示身份，译为介词短语 among the bandits。

列举的动词序列在翻译中通常需要采用概述策略。如：

［1］起居动静 of whose daily life and behaviours

［2］其赐予给赏 what this troop of loyal guards were awarded

第［1］句用名词词组 daily life and behaviours 来概述"起居动静"。

第［2］句用主语从句 what were awarded 来概述"赐予给赏"。

1.2 心理类不及物动词

不及物的心理动词多数表达喜、怒、哀、乐等心理状态，通常译为动词的体分词（如-ed 分词）、形容词或动宾结构。如：

［1］前锋将大悟 the forward commander was thoroughly disillusioned by what Chao had said

［2］崔氏性妒 Mrs Cui was so jealous-tempered that

［3］延钧怒 for which Yanjun flew into a rage

［4］闽人皆怨 for this reason, much resentment arose among

people in the Min state

　　[5] 皆怒₂ all of them burst into a rage

　　[6] 镣惭 Lin felt so ashamed

　　[7] 其次子继韬怒₃ Lin's second son Jitao, however, was enraged by this

　　[8] 继鹏惧₁ having overheard Jitao's plan, Jipeng was frightened into

　　[9] 重遇惧₂ Chongyu was frightened into

　　[10] 曦怒₄ for this reason, Xi flew into a rage

　　[11] 曦喜 Xi was so pleased

　　[12] 曦怒₅ Xi flew into a rage

　　[13] 重遇等惧₃ Chongyu and his colleagues were frightened

　　[14] 曦怒₆ Xi flew into a rage

　　[15] 文缜惧₄ Wenzhen was frightened

第［1］句"前锋将大悟"的"[大]悟"译为被动结构 was [thoroughly] disillusioned by。第［2］句"崔氏性妒"的"性妒"二字合译为 was so jealous-tempered。在 6 个"怒"字中，第［3］句、第［5］句、第［10］句、第［12］句和第［14］句的"怒₁、怒₂、怒₄、怒₅、怒₆"五字译为主动结构 flew into a rage 或 burst into a rage，而第［7］句的"怒₃"字则译为被动结构 was enraged by this。显然，"怒"字的选项集中在主动结构 flew into a rage 上，因而后续的调整可适量增加被动结构或包括 flew into a fury 和 burst into anger 在内的其他主动结构。第［4］句"闽人皆怨"的"怨"字译为名词 resentment，使原句的心理过程转变为物理过程：much resentment arose among people in the Min state。第［6］句"镣惭"的"惭"字译为动补结构 felt so ashamed。第［8］句、第［9］句、第［13］句、第［15］句的"惧₁、惧₂、惧₃、惧₄"四字均译为体分词（was）frightened 或（were）frightened，其遣词造句比较集中。最后，第［11］句"曦喜"的"喜"字也使用体分词结构 was so pleased。

心理动词也时常搭配反身代词"自"。如：

　　[1] 潮颇自惧 Chao himself was quite frightened that he might also be killed one day

　　[2] 而心常自疑 he himself had been suspicious ever since he supported Chang to the throne

第[1]句的"[颇]自惧"译为 himself was [quite] frightened，其中的"惧"字跟此前所述的4个"惧"字一样译为 was frightened。第[2]句的"自疑"译为 himself had been suspicious，而"心"字的翻译则直接用代词 he。前后2个"自"字都译为反身代词 himself。

1.3 言语类不及物动词

普通的言语类动词都可后接言语内容。然而，如果表达言语内容的语法形式不是直接依附于此类动词，而是构成独立的句读，那么此类动词就体现出不及物的特征。在英语中，言语类动词时常因上下文的需要而使用倒装结构。如：

[1] 前锋将曰$_1$ said the forward commander

[2] 曰$_2$ "Your Majesty," he said

[3] 英曰$_3$ Ying asked

[4] 巫言 The wizard said

[5] 曰$_4$ asked the king

[6] 文杰曰$_5$ Wenjie said

[7] 英曰$_6$ Ying answered

[8] 曰$_7$ "We won't march on," they said

[9] 仁达曰$_8$ Renda replied

[10] 倓曰$_9$ said Tan

[11] 曦曰$_{10}$ said Xi

[12] 谏$_1$议大夫郑元弼切谏$_2$ Minister of Remonstrance Zheng Yuanbi tried his best to dissuade the punishment

[13] 元弼曰$_{11}$ Yuanbi answered

[14] 曦曰$_{12}$ Xi said

[15]《江南录》云 according to *Records of Jiangnan*

该组共有12个句读包含"曰"字。其中，"曰$_1$、曰$_2$、曰$_5$、曰$_7$、曰$_9$、曰$_{10}$、曰$_{12}$"7个译为 said；"曰$_3$、曰$_4$"2个译为 asked；"曰$_6$、曰$_{11}$"2个译为 answered；另有"曰$_8$"译为 replied。尽管 said 具有最高的使用频次7，但从上下文来看该词并不是其余5个"曰"字的最优译项。按照英语的习惯，当置于引言的后方时，言语小句通常需要使用倒装结构，如第[1]句的 said the forward commander、第[10]句的 said Tan 和第[11]句的 said Xi。另外，第[4]句的"[巫]言"字也译为 said。在第[12]句"谏$_1$议大夫郑元弼切谏$_2$"中，"谏$_1$"字已经译为其本义名词

remonstrance；"谏₂"字的翻译不再使用 remonstrate，而是使用 dissuade the punishment，将其所谏的内容直接展开。最后，第[15]句的"云"字直接译为介词短语 according to，消解掉1个言语过程。

1.4 物理类不及物动词

不及物的物理类动词往往涉及朝代或事物的存亡、更替或成败，以及天气现象或事件状态的转变等内容。如：

[1] 唐亡 after the fall of the Tang dynasty

[2] 皇后土贡何在 "What have you presented to the queen?" asked Xi.

[3] 王氏灭 the reign of the Wang's house came to an end

第[1]句"唐亡"和第[3]句"王氏灭"均指政权的终结：前句译为复杂的介词短语 after the fall of the Tang dynasty；后句译为小句 the reign of the Wang's house came to an end。第[2]句"皇后土贡何在"的"土贡"译为动词形式（what have you）presented，直接改变句子的结构特征。

涉及事件成败的物理类动词存在主动与被动之间的语态分化现象。如：

[1] 既成 this done

[2] 后兴事败 but Xing failed when he carried out Chang's order

第[1]句"既成"译为被动的非限定小句 this done，也可将其详细地解释为 after the newly-designed prison van was completed。第[2]句"后兴事败"的"败"字译为主动结构 but Xing failed，其主语因而改为 Xing，而"事"字则扩展为 when he carried out Chang's order。

以下2句涉及天气现象：

[1] 虹见其宫中 a rainbow was seen in the palace

[2] 一夕风雨雷电震击 one evening, after a fearful tempest had arisen with thunder and lightning

与原句一样，两句译文都以名词词组为其主语。第[1]句的"虹"字直接译为 a rainbow，而其动词"见"字既可译为被动结构 was seen，又可译为主动结构 appeared。第[2]句的"风雨雷电"在翻译时不好逐一列举 wind, rain, thunder, lightning，只好把"风雨、雷电"分开处理：以名词词组 a fearful tempest（风雨）为主语，以添加的 had arisen 为谓语，以介宾结构 with thunder and lightning（雷电）为状语，构建包含上述四种天气现象的小句 a fearful tempest had arisen with thunder and lightning。

部分及物的物理类动词在否定的条件下也会形成不及物的结构模式。例如，"克、辍"二字在肯定的条件下通常后接宾语，但以下否定的"不克、不辍"均不后接宾语，因而形成不及物的结构模式。

　　[1] 久不克 but the war turned out to be a long stalemate
　　[2] 昼夜声不辍 with instrumental music continued all day and all night

第[1]句的译文 the war turned out to be a long stalemate 从侧面解释"久不克"，即"战争进入相持阶段"。第[2]句的译文则把否定结构明确为肯定的被动结构 continued all day and all night。显然，该组的英译既要注意肯定和否定的极性变换，又要注意主动和被动的语态交替。

1.5　双音节的不及物动词

在中国史籍中，多数双音节动词具有较强的分析性特征，既有词法功能，又有句法功能，通常需要按音节将其译为两个英语单词，才能充分表达其语义。如：

　　[1] 召置军中 so he summoned them into the army
　　[2] 审知代立 Shenzhi succeeded to his position
　　[3] 英自诬伏 Ying submitted, though acknowledging the false accusation
　　[4] 走匿九龙帐中 Lin retreated and he himself hid in the midst of the nine-dragon curtain
　　[5] 遣归$_1$ repatriated him soon afterwards
　　[6] 醉归$_2$ he drank and returned

第[1]句"召置军中"的"召"字译为动词 summoned (them)，而"置"字则译为介词 into (the army)；第[2]句"审知代立"的"代立"整体译为动词词组 succeeded to (his position)，其中包含不及物动词 succeed 和介词 to；第[3]句"英自诬伏"的"[自]诬伏"二字被拆解，分别译为从句 though acknowledging the false accusation 和主句（Ying）submitted；第[4]句"走匿九龙帐中"的"走匿"二字也被拆解，译成2个并列分句（Lin）retreated 和（he himself）hid in the midst of (the nine-dragon curtain)。第[5]句和第[6]句均有"归"字：前句的"遣归$_1$"在整体上译为具有较强使役意义的单个动词 repatriated (him)；后句的"醉

归$_2$"则可拆译为 2 个并列的谓语动词 drank 和 returned。

双音节的不及物动词有时被译为动宾结构。如：

[1] 曦出游 after Xi took an excursion

该句的"出游"二字译为动宾结构 took an excursion，其中包含轻动词 took 及其宾语 an excursion。

双音节的心理类动词多数译为形容词或体分词，其所涉及的译文语句通常以 SVC 句型为其结构框架。如：

[1] 绪性猜忌 Xu was so suspicious and jealous in nature
[2] 今绪雄猜 now Xu is so stubborn and skeptical
[3] 乙羞愧 Yi felt so embarrassed and ashamed
[4] 而昶愈惑乱 now that Chang became even more confused and reckless

第［1］句的"猜忌"和第［2］句的"雄猜"分别译为复合的形容词词组 suspicious and jealous 和 stubborn and skeptical。第［3］句的"羞愧"译为复合的体分词结构 embarrassed and ashamed。第［4］句的"惑乱"被译为体分词 confused 和形容词 reckless 的复合结构。

双及物的言语类动词通常也需拆译。如：

[1] 潮报曰 Chao replied with a simple report … he said
[2] 自占云 so he made a prediction for himself and said
[3] 国人歌曰 this rumor was then composed into a song and the song was chanted among the nationals as follows

第［1］句的"报"字被扩展为 replied with a simple report，"曰"字译为 said。第［2］句的"占"字译为动宾结构 made a prediction，"云"字译为 said。第［3］句其中的"歌"字译为一分句 this rumor was then composed into a song，"曰"字译为另一分句 the song was chanted as follows，因而（among）the nationals（国人）不再充当主语。

2. 单及物动词谓语句读群组及其英译

以单及物动词为核心的 SVO 句型基本匹配英语的 SVO 句型，因而单及物动词谓语句读的翻译具有相对固定的结构模式。该组动词数量众多，可将其细分为行为、心理、言语、物理等类别。

2.1 行为类单及物动词

单及物的行为类动词通常以人物作为宾语。尽管多数动词可以找到英语的单及物词项，但在翻译中也需注意少数动词在及物性上的分化现象。如：

［1］常乘白马 he often rode a white horse

［2］登舟 he embarked onto the boat

［3］镤欣然逊位 Lin was so pleased to abdicate the throne

［4］既而复位 shortly afterwards Lin restored the dominion

［5］他日损遇乙于途 on another day, Sun incidentally met Yi on the way

［6］群臣侍酒 the ministers served by his side and catered for the drinking

［7］诸子继柔弃酒 after discarding some wine on one occasion, Jirou, one of the princes

［8］昔太祖武皇帝亲冒矢石 in the past, the Founding Emperor went through the battlefield in spite of arrows and stones

其中，第［1］句的"乘白马"、第［3］句的"逊位"、第［4］句的"复位"、第［5］句的"遇乙"、第［7］句的"弃酒"分别译为 rode a white horse、abdicate the throne、restored the dominion、met Yi、discarding some wine，均为单及物的动宾结构。第［2］句的"登［舟］"字和第［8］句的"冒［矢石］"字译为 embarked (onto the boat) 和 went (through the battlefield)，均为不及物动词后接介宾结构。第［6］句的"侍酒"可译为两个并列的谓语结构 served by his side 和 catered for the drinking，具有明显的解释性痕迹。

单及物的生理类动词在译法上与行为类动词相似。如：

［1］闻$_1$败 but, on hearing the failure

［2］文杰多察民间阴事 Wenjie had many studies on his observation over various secret affairs among the folk

［3］镤闻$_2$鼓噪声 on hearing the sounds of drums

其中，"闻$_1$、闻$_2$"均译为及物动词（on）hearing；第［2］句的"多察"二字则译为复杂的动宾结构 had many studies on his observation (over)。

表示攻城略地的单及物动词主要包括"陷、攻、守、收、得、破、据"，可译为 capture、attack、defend、recapture、control、conquer、occupy。如：

[1] 陷漳浦 soon afterwards they captured the county of Zhangpu

[2] 攻₁其西门 he himself launched an attack at the west gate

[3] 延禀子继升守₁建州 Jisheng, another son of Yanbing, had stayed back to defend Jianzhou

[4] 吴人攻₂建州 the state of Wu sent troops to attack Jianzhou

[5] 程赟守₂漳州 Chen Yun was sent to defend Zhangzhou

[6] 许文缜守₃汀州 Xu Wenzhen was sent to defend Tingzhou

[7] 富沙王兵收福州矣 Fusha King has sent troops to capture Fuzhou

[8] 延政已得三州 Yanzheng now took control of three military commanderies

[9] 而南唐兵方急攻₃延政 the troops of Southern Tang were launching a quick attack on Yanzheng

[10] 唐兵攻₄建州 the troops of Southern Tang were now attacking Jianzhou

[11] 景已破₁延政 Jing had crushed the defence of Yanzheng

[12] 据泉漳二州 occupied the commanderies of Quanzhou and Zhangzhou

[13] 李景兵破₂建州 Li Jing's troops conquered the commandery of Jianzhou

其中，capture、occupy、attack、defend、conquer 等及物动词后接 Zhangpu、Jianzhou、Zhangzhou、Tingzhou、Fuzhou 等城市名称。如果后接其他类型的名词，那么此类动词可译为相应的名词形式。例如，第 [4] 句的"攻₂"和第 [10] 句的"攻₄"后接城市，均译为及物动词 attack，而第 [2] 句的"攻₁"后接具体的城门，第 [9] 句的"攻₃"后接具体的人物，二者均译为动宾结构 launched/were launching an attack：前句的"其西门"译为介宾短语 at the west gate，后句的"延政"译为 on Yanzheng。第 [3] 句、第 [5] 句和第 [6] 句的"守₁、守₂、守₃"后接城市名称，均译为 defend。第 [7] 句的"[兵] 收"可译为 [has sent troops] to capture，也可使用词组动词 to take over。第 [8] 句的"得"字译为词组动词 took control of。第 [13] 句的"破₂"后接城市名称"建州"，直接译为 conquered the commandery of Jianzhou，而第 [11] 句的"破₁"后接人物名称"延政"，可译为 crushed the defence of Yanzheng。

第 5 章　简单谓词性句读群组及其英语翻译

表示烧杀抢夺的单及物动词主要包括"磔、枭、烧、夺、杀、逐、虏",可译为 dismember、behead、burn、seize、kill、expel、capture。如:

［1］磔文杰于市 dismembered Wenjie in the downtown area

［2］枭其首于市 Fang was beheaded and his cut-off head was hung over the downtown area

［3］烧启圣门 burn down the Qisheng gate

［4］夺仿首 take away the head of Fang

［5］并杀$_1$其赞者一人 was killed together with one of his emcees

［6］连重遇杀$_2$昶 since Lian Chongyu killed Chang

［7］连重遇已杀$_3$曦 after Lian Chongyu killed Xi

［8］州人共杀$_4$绍颇 men in the military commandery rose up together to kill Shaopo

［9］亦杀$_5$赟 men in Zhangzhou also killed Yun

［10］重遇亦杀$_6$文进 Chongyu also killed Wenjin

［11］福州裨将林仁翰又杀$_7$重遇 but Lin Renhan, assistant general of Fuzhou, in turn killed Chongyu

［12］已而又杀$_8$俨明 and then also killed Yanming

［13］而留从效亦逐景守兵 and Liu Congxiao also expelled the garrison dispatched by Li Jing

［14］虏王氏之族 Li Jing captured the Wang's clan

该组译文在语态上存在明显的分化。第［1］句的"磔"字译为主动结构 dismembered (Wenjie),而第［2］句的"枭"字则译为被动结构 was beheaded,且在其后使用(his) cut-off (head)加以补充说明。在 8 个"杀"字中,只有第［5］句的"杀$_1$"字译为被动语态 was killed,其余 7 个译为主动形式 killed。第［3］句的"烧"字和第［4］句的"夺"字分别译为词组动词 burn down 和 take away。第［13］句的"逐景守兵"译为复杂的动宾结构 expelled the garrison dispatched by Li Jing。第［14］句"虏王氏之族"译为类似的动宾结构 captured the Wang's clan。

施礼管教奖罚的单及物动词数量较多,主要包括"选、益、礼、教、禀、继、伏、受、置、荐、罢、主、典、贮、飨、嫁、贬"。如:

［1］乃选壮士数十人 Chao and the forward commander selected dozens of vigorous soldiers

［2］且益兵 that more soldiers be summoned and sent

［3］好礼下士 treated his subordinates with courtesy

　　［4］以教闽士之秀者 educate talented men in the region of Min

　　［5］而犹禀唐正朔 though still observing the calendar of the Tang dynasty

　　［6］善继先志 uphold the good will of our forefather

　　［7］仁达伏甲舟中 in which he first concealed soldiers in his boat

　　［8］受册于宝皇 accepting edicts that were conferred by Baohuang

　　［9］置百官 one hundred ranking officials were nominated

　　［10］又荐妖巫徐彦 he also recommended the seductive wizard Xu Yan to Lin

　　［11］将罢公 His Majesty is going to dismiss Your Reverence from the office

　　［12］英尝主闽兵 Ying had taken command of the Min army

　　［13］而典亲兵 he had been in charge of the loyal bodyguards

　　［14］惟贮一归郎 it accommodates more than one brother

　　［15］镣绘军于大酺殿 when a banquet was held to entertain the army in the Dapu Palace

　　［16］既立昶 since he had supported Chang to the throne

　　［17］陛下方示大信 Your Majesty shows generous trustworthiness

　　［18］高祖乃赦元弼 on hearing this, the Founding Emperor remitted Yuanbi from punishment

　　［19］昶弟继严判六军诸卫事 Chang's younger brother Jiyan had taken command of the six legions and general security affairs

　　［20］曦尝嫁女 Xi once married his daughter

　　［21］百姓与能 the common people recommended men of talent

　　［22］称晋年号 adopted the designation of the Jin dynasty

　　［23］送款于李景 sent his sincerity to Li Jing

　　［24］迁延政族于金陵 migrated the clan of Yanzheng to the capital of Jinling

　　该组译文多数使用及物的动宾结构：第［1］句的"选壮士"译为 selected [dozens of] vigorous soldiers；第［4］句的"教［闽士之］秀者"译为 educate talented men [in the region of Min]；第［5］句的"禀唐正朔"

译为 observing the calendar of the Tang dynasty；第［6］句的"继先志"译为 uphold the (good) will of our forefather；第［7］句的"伏甲"译为 concealed soldiers；第［10］句的"荐［妖巫］徐彦"译为 recommended [the seductive wizard] Xu Yan；第［17］句的"示大信"译为 shows generous trustworthiness；第［20］句的"嫁女"译为 married his daughter；第［21］句的"与能"译为 recommended men of talent；第［22］句"称晋年号"译为 adopted the designation of the Jin dynasty；第［23］句的"送款"译为 sent his sincerity；第［24］句的"迁延政族"译为 migrated the clan of Yanzheng。

其余句读的译文有所不同。其中，第［3］句的"好礼"使用介词短语（treated）with courtesy；第［18］句的"赦元弼"添加具体的动作对象（remitted Yuanbi from）punishment；第［16］句"既立昶"添加动词 had supported（Chang to the throne）；第［12］句的"主"字、第［13］句的"典"字和第［19］句的"判"字分别译为动词词组 had taken command of，had been in charge of 和 had taken command of。第［2］句和第［15］句的英译使用被动结构：前者的"益兵"译为 more soldiers be summoned and sent，后者的"飨军"译为 a banquet was held to entertain the army。

后接地理位置的迁移动词主要有"次、入、还、至"等，通常直接译为 arrive、step、return、went 等。如：

［1］军次南安 when the troops arrived in the county of Nan'an
［2］使者入₁海 among the envoys sailing into the sea
［3］延禀还建州 Yanbing was now returning to Jianzhou
［4］入₂北庙 I had stepped into the Northern Temple
［5］损至₁闽 when Sun arrived in the Min state, however
［6］间道至₂京师 went through some bypaths to the capital

其中，第［1］句的"次［南安］"译为 arrived in [the county of Nan'an]；第［3］句的"还［建州］"译为 returning to [Jianzhou]。两个"入"字的翻译因其后接不同类型的地理名称而有所不同：第［2］句的"入₁［海］"译为 sailing into [the sea]；第［4］句的"入₂［北庙］"译为 stepped into [the Northern Temple]。同理，两个"至"字的翻译也各不相同：第［5］句的"至₁［闽］"译为 arrived in [the Min state]；第［6］句的"至₂［京师］"译为 went (through some bypaths) to [the capital]。

后接职位的动词主要包括"迁、加、即"等，翻译的重点在于职位名称。如：

[1] 累₁迁同中书门下平章事 he had been promoted several times until he eventually became a joint manager of affairs with the secretariat chancellery

[2] 累₂加检校太师中书令 promoted him several times until he became the grand police inspector and the general secretary of the imperial secretariat

[3] 六十年后将安归 "What destination," he said, "will I turn to after sixty years?"

[4] 镠乃即皇帝位 Lin came to the imperial throne

第[1]句的"（累₁）迁"和第[2]句的"（累₂）加"分别译为被动结构 had been promoted（several times until he eventually became）和主动结构 promoted him（several times until he became），其中的副词"累₁、累₂"均译为 several times。第[3]句的"将安归"译为 what destination will I turn to，其中的"安"字译为疑问词组 what destination。第[4]句的"即皇帝位"直接译为 came to the imperial throne。

由迁移动词后接时代而构成的句读在上下文中表达逻辑关系。如：

[1] 及其子孙 his sons and grandsons, however

[2] 至保大四年 to the fourth year of the Baoda period (A.D. 946)

第[1]句"及其子孙"表达转折的逻辑关系，其译文在添加转折副词 however 的前提下把"其子孙"译为 his sons and grandsons，直接充当后句译文的主语。第2句"至保大四年"表达时间关系，直接译为介宾结构 to the fourth year of the Baoda period (A.D. 946)。

2.2 心理类单及物动词

单及物的心理类动词主要包括"好、忍、知、惮、妒、厌"，在英语中大体上对应 adhere、bear、know、fear、envy、hate。如：

[1] 镠好₁鬼神道家之说 Lin believed in theories of ghosts and gods and adhered to practices of Taoism

[2] 宫人不忍其苦 his men in the palace could not bear the bitterness from which he suffered

[3] 不知礼义 he does not know what are rite and righteousness

［4］昶亦好₂巫 Chang was also intrigued by sorcerers

［5］曦亦惮倓 Xi also feared Tan

［6］李氏妒尚妃之宠 Mrs Li envied Princess Shang for being favoured

［7］今天厌王氏 but now the heaven hates the Wang's house

其中，两个"好"字的译法不同：由于第［1］句的"好₁"字因后接复杂宾语"鬼神道家之说"而译为两个并列的动宾结构：believed in theories of ghosts and gods 和 adhered to practices of Taoism；第［4］句的"好₂"字因后接简单宾语"巫"而译为单个被动结构 Chang was also intrigued by sorcerers。第［2］句的"不忍"译为 could not bear，而其后的宾语"其苦"译为包含关系分句的名词词组 the bitterness from which he suffered。第［3］句的"不知"二字译为 does not know，而其后的宾语"礼义"则译为名词性分句 what are rite and righteousness。第［5］句的"惮倓"和第［7］句的"厌王氏"分别译为简单的动宾结构 feared Tan 和 hates the Wang's house。第［6］句的"妒"字译为 envied，而其后的宾语"尚妃之宠"则译为 Princess Shang for being favoured，包含 1 个嵌入于介词短语的非限定小句 being favoured。

2.3 言语类单及物动词

包括"谓、告、称"等在内的部分言语类动词后接简单宾语时就形成动宾结构。如：

［1］谁谓九龙帐 for whom is the nine-dragon curtain woven

［2］其婿范晖自称留后 his son-in-law Fan Hui pronounced himself as the successor

两句均未直接译为对应的单及物动宾结构。第［1］句原文为主动的问句，译为被动的问句 for whom is the nine-dragon curtain woven，其中的"谓"字并未直接翻译出来。第［2］句的"自称留后"译为包含介词短语的复杂动宾结构 pronounced himself as the successor。

2.4 物理类单及物动词

以物体为宾语的动词一般归入物理类动词。该组动词数量较少。如：

［1］彻其几筵 Yanhan removed the sacrificial offerings

［2］鏻遂绝朝贡 so Lin paid no further loyal tribute to the Tang dynasty

［3］日焚龙脑薰陆诸香数斤 borneol, frankincense and other

incenses were burnt daily in a large amount

［4］掷弓于地 he threw his bow onto the ground

［5］而新罗复献剑 the state of Silla presented another sword

［6］廷英进买宴钱千万 Tingying handed in ten thousand grands of money for banquet expenditure to Xi

第［1］句的"彻其几筵"、第［2］句的"绝朝贡"、第［4］句的"掷弓"、第［5］句的"复献剑"和第［6］句的"进买宴钱"都具有明确的主语，因而分别译为动宾结构：removed the sacrificial offerings, Lin paid no further loyal tribute, threw his bow, presented another sword 和 handed in (ten thousand grands of) money for banquet expenditure。第［3］句的"日"字处于主位，但不是主语，因而"日焚"译为被动结构 were burnt daily，其中的"日"字译为副词 daily；此外，该句的"数斤"译为介词短语 in a large amount。

包括"建、立、更、铸"在内的建制类动词可直接译为 establish、revise、cast 等，而且经常使用被动语态。如：

［1］又建学四门 in addition, a national academy was established

［2］立五庙 five temples were established to consecrate the past five generations of forefathers

［3］乃更其制 so he revised the traditional structure

［4］铸大铁钱 he also ordered to cast big metal coins

其中，第［1］句的"建"字译为被动结构 was established，而"［建学］四门"译为 a national academy 作主语。第［2］句"立五庙"除了译为被动语句 five temples were established 之外，还添加不定式结构 to consecrate the past five generations of forefathers，用以解释五庙所供的五代先祖。第［3］句"更［其制］"和第［4］句"铸［大铁钱］"均译为主动形式 revised [the traditional structure] 和 cast [big metal coins]。

2.5 存在类单及物动词

事物的存在时常使用及物的"有"字。该群组的译文并非全部使用 there be 句型。如：

［1］有$_1$众数万 now there were tens of thousands of soldiers in the army

［2］果有$_2$之邪 is it truly the case

［3］遂启有$_3$闽 since then the state of Min has been founded

三个"有"字的译法各不相同：第［1］句的"有₁"字译为存在结构 there were，第［2］句的"有₂"字译为 IT 句式 is it，第［3］句的"有₃"字译为 has been founded。

表示所属关系的"有、得"等动词的具体翻译通常取决于其后所接的名词词组。如：

［1］何待之有₁ what then should I be waiting for

［2］文杰与内枢密使吴英有₂隙 Wenjie and Wu Ying, the inner military affairs commissioner, had been dissatisfied with and resented each other to some extent

［3］无他苦也 I have suffered from nothing (but a headache)

［4］得₁其军士心 was strongly supported by soldiers

［5］鐻有₃嬖吏归守明者 a government clerk named Gui Shouming was favoured by Lin

［6］鐻后得₂风疾 Lin later got a paralytic stroke

［7］又有₄百工院使李可殷 the directorate of general production Li Keyin (also)

［8］鐻婢春燕有₅色 Lin's maidservant Chunyan was born with adorable appearance

［9］仿有₆弑君之罪 Fang, however, was well aware that he had committed regicide

［10］当求有₇德 we should accept those who are virtuous

［11］其能有₈此土也 how can he possess this land

［12］然其奄有₉闽国 the time, however, when the Wang's house had a sudden control over the state of Min

该组共有 9 个句读包含"有"字。第［1］句"何待之有₁"译为 what then should I be waiting for，其中的"有₁"字没有直接译出。第［2］句的"有₂隙"在整体上译为 had been dissatisfied with and resented each other，其中的"有₂"字也没有译出。第［5］句"鐻有₃嬖吏归守明者"译为 a government clerk named Gui Shouming was favoured by Lin；该句译文可在句首添加存在结构 there is。第［7］句"又有₄百工院使李可殷"的译文 the directorate of general production Li Keyin (also) 在使用定冠词后不再使用 there be 句式。第［8］句的"有₅色"在整体上译为 was born with adorable appearance，其中的"有₅"字译为介词 with。第［9］句的"有₆弑君之

罪"译为 was well aware that he had committed regicide，其中的 was well aware that 为解释成分。第 [10] 句的"有₇德"译为 those who are virtuous，即"道德高尚的人"。第 [11] 句的"有₈"字直接译为 possess。第 [12] 句的"奄有₉"译为动词词组 had a sudden control (over)。显然，"有"字的翻译存在明显的选择分化。

另外，第 [3] 句的"无"字译为代词 (have suffered from) nothing。两个"得"字的翻译完全不同：第 [4] 句"得₁其军士心"在整体上译为被动结构 was strongly supported by soldiers，而第 [6] 句的"得₂"字则直接译为及物动词 got，后接疾病 a paralytic stroke (风疾)。

2.6　以"之"字为宾语的单及物动词

当单及物动词以"之"字为宾语时，在翻译中特别需要注意主动与被动之间的语态交替。总体上，被动结构特别适合用以翻译行为类或物理类动词后接"之"字的情况。如：

[1] 囚之军中 Xu was then imprisoned in the army

[2] 逾年克之 occupied Quanzhou the next year

[3] 辄幽之别室 tended to be confined in a special room

[4] 遂杀₁之 so he was killed soon afterwards

[5] 送者闻₁之 this, however, was overheard by those who escorted him

[6] 赦之 remit Wenjie from punishment

[7] 族灭之而已 it is simple to extinguish his entire clan

[8] 镔怏怏与之 though Lin was dissatisfied with the request, he allowed Jipeng to have Chunyan

[9] 昶闻₂之 these words were soon passed on to Chang

[10] 及之 and they caught up with Chang soon afterwards

[11] 斩之 will be chopped with this

[12] 朝士有不贺者笞之 those officials in the central court who failed to congratulate were whipped

[13] 弃之水中 discarded it into the water

[14] 有诉及私弃酒者辄杀₂之 those who complained or discarded any wine in private were often killed

[15] 延政逐之 but he was expelled by Yanzheng

[16] 王氏子弟在福州者无少长皆杀₃之 those sons and nephews of the Wang's house who resided in Fuzhou were mostly killed regardless

of their ages

[17] 漳州闻₃之 on hearing this, men in Zhangzhou

其中，译为主动结构的句读包括：第[2]句的"克之"译为 occupied Quanzhou，第[6]句的"赦之"译为 remit Wenjie from punishment，第[7]句的"族灭之"译为 extinguish his entire clan，第[8]句的"与之"译为 he allowed Jipeng to have Chunyan，第[10]句的"及之"译为 and they caught up with Chang，第[13]句的"弃之"译为 discarded it into the water，第[17]句的"闻₃之"译为 on hearing this。

其余 10 句均译为被动结构：第[1]句的"囚之"译为 was imprisoned，第[3]句的"幽之"译为 be confined，第[4]句的"杀₁之"、第[14]句的"杀₂之"和第[16]句的"杀₃之"分别译为 was killed 和 were killed，第[5]句的"闻₁之"和第[9]句的"闻₂之"分别译为 this was overheard（by those who escorted him）和 these words were soon passed on（to Chang），第[11]句的"斩之"译为 will be chopped（with this），第[12]句的"笞之"译为 were whipped，第[15]句的"逐之"译为 was expelled（by Yanzheng）。

与行为类或物理类动词不同，多数以"之"字为宾语的心理类动词都译为主动结构。如：

[1] 鏻衔之 Lin had borne this grudge in mind ever since

[2] 继雄信之 Jixiong was so gullible that he was tricked into the trap

[3] 鏻心忌之 Lin scrupled about this

[4] 陛下皆知之 Your Majesty is kept well informed

[5] 鏻嬖之 was favoured by Lin

[6] 其子继鹏蒸之 and she intrigued Lin's son Jipeng to a considerable degree

[7] 与皇城使李仿图之 that he turned to the director of the imperial city Li Fang and worked out a solution

[8] 昶患之 this, in turn, alerted and troubled Chang to such an extent

[9] 曦心疑之 Xi was suspicious with Chongyu and those who were concerned

其中，第[1]句的"衔[之]"译为动词词组 had borne [this

grudge] in mind，第［2］句的"信［之］"译为形容词（was so）gullible，第［3］句的"忌［之］"译为动词词组 scrupled about [this]，第［6］句的"蒸［之］"译为复杂的动补结构 [she] intrigued (Lin's son Jipeng) to a considerable degree，第［7］句的"图［之］"译为复杂的动宾结构 worked out a solution，第［8］句的"患［之］"译为并列谓语 [this] alerted and troubled (Chang)，第［9］句的"疑［之］"译为形容词（was）suspicious。其余 2 句译为被动结构：第［4］句的"知［之］"译为 is kept well informed，第［5］句的"嬖［之］"译为 was favoured (by Lin)。

2.7　双音节的单及物动词

类似单音节的不及物动词，多数双音节的单及物动词也是可分析的，因而在翻译中通常被拆解为双重的谓语动词或动宾结构。如：

　　［1］寿州人王绪攻陷固始 Wang Xu, a native from the commandery of Shouzhou, led a group of soldiers to attack and occupy the county of Gushi

　　［2］审知请班师 Shenzhi first requested to withdraw the troops

　　［3］杨行密据有江淮 Yang Xingmi occupied the area of Jianghuai, blocking the land route in the region between Yangtze River and Huai River

　　［4］招来海中蛮夷商贾 and managed to invite overseas and foreign merchants to boost the domestic economy

　　［5］刺杀之 but was stabbed by Renda's soldiers to death

　　［6］谋杀继鹏 so he drafted a plot to kill Jipeng

　　［7］射杀数人 Chang shot a number of them to death

　　［8］昶相王倓每抑折之 when Chang's prime minister Wang Tan suppressed him

　　［9］而景兵攻破建州 and Li Jing's troops attacked and conquered Jianzhou

其中，第［1］句的"攻陷"译为并列谓语动词 attack and occupy；第［2］句的"请班［师］"译为复杂谓语动词 requested to withdraw [the troops]；第［3］句的"据有"译为主从结构 occupied ..., blocking ...；第［4］句的"招来"译为复杂谓语结构 managed to invite ... to boost ...；第［5］句的"刺杀"译为被动的动补结构 was stabbed to death；第［6］句的

"谋杀"译为复杂谓语结构 drafted a plot to kill；第［7］句的"射杀"译为动补结构 shot (a number of them) to death；第［9］句的"攻破"译为并列谓语动词 attacked and conquered。

少数双音节的单及物动词也译为单个英语动词。例如，第［8］句的"抑折"译为 suppressed，第［6］句的"谋杀"也可译为 was to murder。总体上，多数此类动词需要译为两个英语动词，才能完整解释其语义。

3. 双及物动词谓语句读群组及其英译

双及物的物理类和行为类动词在翻译中通常转化为单及物结构。如：

［1］枭其首西门 his head was transferred and hung over the west gate

［2］致书晋大臣 in addition, Jigong also wrote to the ministers of the Jin dynasty

［3］廷英又献皇后钱千万 Tingying presented another ten million grands of money to the queen

上述3例均为物理过程。第［1］句"枭其首西门"的"枭"字译为并列的被动结构 was transferred and hung over：前一结构 was transferred 组合表示动作对象的直接宾语 his head（其首），而后一结构（was）hung over 组合表示方位的间接宾语 the west gate（西门）；第［2］句"致书晋大臣"的"致书"直接译为不及物动词 wrote，而"晋大臣"则译为复杂介宾结构 to the ministers of the Jin dynasty；第［3］句"廷英又献皇后钱千万"的"皇后"译为介宾结构 to the queen，也可保留双及物结构 presented the queen another ten million grands of money。行为类动词的双及物特征在翻译中通常被消解。如：

［1］福建观察使陈岩表潮泉州刺史 Chen Yan, surveillance commissioner of Fujian, nominated Chao as magistrate of Quanzhou

［2］拜审知节度使 appointed Shenzhi as military commissioner

［3］梁太祖加拜审知中书令 the Founding Emperor Taizu of the Liang dynasty appointed Shenzhi as general secretary of the imperial secretariat

［4］唐拜延翰节度使 the Tang dynastic court appointed Yanhan as military commissioner

［5］唐即拜鏻节度使 The Tang dynastic court soon afterwards

appointed him as military commissioner

［6］请授臣尚书令 please grant me with the title of general secretary

［7］拜其子继恭临海郡王 also to granted his son Jigong with the title of "Prince of Linhai County"

［8］贬峻漳州司户参军 demonted Jun to an adjutant fiscal officer

［9］景犹封从效晋江王 Jing still granted Congxiao with the title of "King of Jin River"

以上 9 例的双及物结构分别被 as，with（the title of）和 to 等介词所消解。

类似双及物的物理类和行为类动词，言语类动词的双及物性在翻译中通常被介宾结构所化解。如：

不质诸鬼神 if we don't reproach and rectify them against ghosts and spirits

该句的"鬼神"译为介宾结构 against ghosts and spirits。

包括"更、改"等在内的双及物动词经常用以更换名称，其双及物特征可被介词 into 所消解。如：

［1］更名$_1$镵 with his given name changed into "Lin"

［2］改元$_1$永和 the designation of the reign was changed into "Yonghe", that is, Everlasting Harmony

［3］更名$_2$昶 he revised his name into "Chang"

［4］改元$_2$通文 the designation of the reign was changed into "Tongwen", that is, Fairly Cultured

［5］更名$_3$曦 he changed his name into "Xi"

［6］改元$_3$永隆 changed the designation of the reign into "Yonglong", that is, Everlasting Prosperity

［7］改元$_4$天德 the designation of the reign was changed into "Tiande", that is, Heavenly Virtue

其中，第［1］句"更名$_1$［镵］"、第［3］句"更名$_2$［昶］"和第［5］句"更名$_3$［曦］"分别译为 with his given name changed into、revised his name into 和 changed his name into。第［2］句"改元$_1$［永和］"、第

[4] 句"改元$_2$ [通文]"、第 [6] 句"改元$_3$ [永隆]"和第 [7] 句"改元$_4$ [天德]"分别译为 the designation of the reign was changed into、the designation of the reign was changed into、changed the designation of the reign into、the designation of the reign was changed into。该组所有的双宾结构在翻译后均转化为单及物结构和介宾结构的复合形式。

4. 小结

简单谓词性句读的数量在《新五代史·闽世家第八》中占 37.6%。该群组一半以上为不及物动词谓语句读,其余接近一半为单及物和双及物动词句读。群组翻译使同组语句之间的译文形成直接的对照,不仅有利于确保译文的准确性和多样性,而且有利于保证合理的词汇选择和结构分布,使译文更为生动活泼。

第6章

特殊谓词性句读群组及其英语翻译

除了普通的不及物、单及物和双及物谓语动词之外，还有轻动词、形容词、形容词活用的动词、名词活用的动词等特殊谓词。此外，由两个动词所构成的被动结构和能愿动词结构也属特殊谓词结构。本章主要讨论特殊谓词性句读群组的英语翻译规律。该群组主要包括轻动词谓语句读（LVC）、形容词谓语句读（APC）、形容词活用动词句读（DAV）、名词活用动词句读（DNV）、被动语态句读（PVC）和能愿动词句读（MVC）。

1. 轻动词谓语句读群组及其英译

包括"为、以"等在内的轻动词后接职业或职位名词时通常表示"从事、担任、成为、身为"等语义，其译项的选择需要参考具体的名词。如：

［1］世为农 who had been engaged in farming throughout his whole life

［2］为县史 who had served as a petty official in the county administration

［3］延禀自以养子 nevertheless, regarding himself as the adopted son

［4］楚王马殷吴越王钱镠皆为尚书令 both Ma Yin, the king of Chu, and Qian Liu, the king of Wu and Yue, were appointed as general secretary of the imperial secretariat

［5］后当为六十年天子 and then Your Majesty will become the son of heaven in the future 60 years

［6］当为大罗仙人 Your Majesty will become the saint of Daluo

[7] 曦弟延政为建州节度使 Xi's younger brother of Yanzheng had been appointed as military commissioner of Jianzhou

[8] 吾属世为王氏臣 we have been ministers at the service of the Wang's house for all our life

涉及"从事"的句读有3例：第［1］句的"为［农］"译为 had been engaged in [farming]，第［2］句的"为［县史］"译为 had served as [a petty official in the county administration]，第［8］句的"为［王氏臣］"译为 have been [ministers at the service of the Wang's house]。涉及"担任"的句读有2例：第［4］句的"为［尚书令］"译为 were appointed as [general secretary of the imperial secretariat]，第［7］句的"为建州节度使"译为 had been appointed as [military commissioner of Jianzhou]。涉及"成为、身为"的句读有3例：第［3］句的"［自］以［养子］"译为 regarding [himself as the adopted son]，第［5］句的"为六十年天子"译为 will become the son of heaven in the future 60 years，第［6］句的"为大罗仙人"译为 will become the saint of Daluo。

包括"为、曰"等在内的轻动词后接名字或称号时通常表示"称为、名为"等语义，其在翻译中需要注意主动和被动之间的语态转换。如：

[1] 号为甘棠港 so they called it "Gantang Port", that is, the Sweet-Pear Port

[2] 谥曰₁忠懿 was honoured with the posthumous title of "Zhongyi", that is, the "Loyal Virtuous"

[3] 谥曰₂惠皇帝 he was honoured with the posthumous title of "Hui Emperor", that is, the "Clement Emperor"

[4] 谥曰₃景宗 Xi was honoured with the posthumous title of "Jingzong", that is, the "Lofty Emperor"

除了第［1］句"号为甘棠港"译为主动结构 they called it "Gantang Port"之外，其余3句的"谥曰"均译为被动结构 was honoured with the posthumous title of。

包括"封、拜"等在内的动词紧接官职名称时也可看作轻动词，表达"任命、册封"等语义，其在翻译中需要注意主动和被动的语态转换。如：

[1] 封₁琅琊王 was granted with the title of "King of Langya"

[2] 封₂闽王 granted him with the title of "King of Min"

[3] 封₃闽王 and finally granted him with the title of "King of

Min"

[4] 封₄富沙王 was granted with the title of "King of Fusha"

[5] 封₅鄱阳王 was granted with the title of "King of Boyang"

[6] 拜观察使 and was appointed as surveillance commissioner

在5个"封"字中，第［1］句、第［4］句和第［5］句的"封₁、封₄、封₅"均译为被动结构 was granted with，而第［2］句和第［3］句的"封₂、封₃"则译为主动结构 granted him with。此外，第［6］句的"拜"字也译为被动结构 was appointed as。

涉及比喻关系的句读可从词项和语法结构两个角度切入翻译。如：

[1] 俊面如生 Tan's face looked as if he were still alive

[2] 卿何如魏郑公 how can you compare yourself to Duke Zheng of the Wei state

[3] 陛下似唐太宗 if Your Majesty compare yourself to the founding emperor Taizong of the Tang dynasty

第［1］句的"如生"从语法结构入手，译为1个分句（looked）as if he were still alive。第［2］句和第［3］句存在互文关系，二者的译文可相互参照，前者的"如"字和后者的"似"字均从词汇入手译为复杂的动宾结构 compare yourself to。

包括"满、登、为、差"等在内的轻动词后接数量名词时表示数量关系，其译项选择需要参考具体的数量特征。如：

[1] 朝廷官不满百 and the number of officials in the dynastic court is no more than one hundred

[2] 已而岁入不登其数 the annual revenue, however, failed to reach to the expected amount

[3] 故为六十一年 it is therefore 61 years

[4] 惟《江南录》又差其末年也 though the initial year was correct in Records of Jiangnan, the final year was incorrect

第［1］句的"不满［百］"译为动补结构 is no more than ［one hundred］，并在"朝廷官"的译文 officials in the dynastic court 之前添加 the number of，明确数量关系。第［2］句的"不登［其数］"译为复杂动词结构 failed to reach to ［the expected amount］。第［3］句的"［故］为［六十一年］"译为 IT 句式 it is ［therefore 61 years］。第［4］句的"差"译

为 (was) incorrect，其中的"其末年"转为主语 the final year；而"惟《江南录》"则译为 though the initial year was correct in *Records of Jiangnan*。

表示类属关系的轻动词有 1 例，涉及"具"字：

其后事具国史 what came after was documented in the *Hereditary House of Southern Tang*

该句的"具"字表明"后事"和"国史"之间具有从属关系，译为被动结构 was documented in。

指称行为的名词前加"为、作、加"等轻动词时形成的动宾结构可表达完整的行为过程。如：

［1］将为$_1$乱 they will commit rebellion
［2］作乐于台下 he enjoyed himself at the foot of the terrace
［3］将加答 was to be whipped for his unwillingness to impeach other ministers
［4］曦常为$_2$牛饮 Xi often boozed
［5］为$_3$淫虐 was dissolute and tyrannical

其中，3 个"为"字的译法各不相同：第［1］句的"为$_1$乱"译为动宾结构 commit rebellion；第［4］句的"为$_2$牛饮"译为不及物谓语动词 boozed；第［5］句的"为$_3$淫虐"译为系补结构 was dissolute and tyrannical。第［2］句的"作乐"译为 enjoyed himself。第［3］句的"加答"译为被动结构 be whipped。

包括"奈、为"等在内的轻动词搭配疑问代词"何"时构成疑问句，其译项的选择直接受到具体语境的影响。如：

［1］奈$_1$何 how should I cope with this
［2］此将何为 what will this be used for
［3］奈$_2$何 how could this situation be coped with

第［1］句"奈$_1$何"译为主动形式 how should I cope with this；第［3］句"奈$_2$何"译为被动形式 how could this situation be coped with。2 个"奈"字均选用动词词组 cope with。第［2］句的"何为"则译为 what will ... be used for。

2. 形容词谓语句读群组及其英译

表达品性的形容词谓语句读多数在翻译中可使用 SVC 句型直接新建主

谓结构。如：

[1] 其妻崔氏陋而淫 whereas his wife Mrs Cui was ugly in appearance but dissolute in nature

[2] 秦二世愚 but that the Second Generation of Qin was a fool

[3] 今陛下聪明 now that Your Majesty is intelligent

[4] 仁达智略 Renda is wise

[5] 曦性既淫虐 Xi was dissolute and tyrannical in nature

其中，第［3］句和第［4］句的译文以形容词为补语：前者的"聪明"译为（is）intelligent，后者的"智略"译为（is）wise。第［2］句的译文以名词为补语，其中的"愚"字译为（was）a fool。其余两句的译文均添加具体的方面：第［1］句的"陋而淫"译为 was ugly in appearance but dissolute in nature，添加 appearance（相貌）和 nature（品性）两个具体的方面；第［5］句的"淫虐"译为 was dissolute and tyrannical in nature，同样添加具体的方面 nature（品性）。该组译文的补语成分交替使用形容词词组和名词词组。

包括"尽、狭、厚"等在内的形容词表示事物的范围，其在翻译中需要注意动词与形容词的选择分化。如：

[1] 兵与将俱尽$_1$ if both soldiers and commanders have died out

[2] 而闽地狭 the state of Min, however, was narrow in terms of its terrain

[3] 脔食立尽$_2$ and then carved up his flesh and bones

[4] 独厚于他军 was considerably favourable over other armed forces

两个"尽"字的译文存在及物动词与不及物动词的分化：第［1］句的"尽$_1$"字译为不及物的动词词组 died out，而其"兵与将"的译文 both soldiers and commanders 充当主语；第［3］句"尽$_2$"字译为不及物的词组动词 carved up，而其"脔食"的译文 his flesh and bones 充当宾语。第［2］句的"狭"字和第［4］句"厚"字分别译为形容词补语（was）narrow 和（was considerably）favourable。其中，第［2］句的"地"字译为 in terms of its terrain，表示具体的方面。

同理，否定的形容词谓语句读也有时译为动词词组。如：

[1] 国用不足 the revenue fell short of the expenditure

[2] 事无大小 no matter how big or small an event might be
　　[3] 上心不平于二公 His Majesty does not treat both of you in a fair manner

第［1］句和第［3］句的形容词在翻译中均转化为动词：前者的"国用不足"译为 the revenue fell short of the expenditure，其中添加 the revenue（收入）；后者在整体上译为及物的复杂动词结构 does not treat … in a fair manner。第［2］句的"事无大小"译为状语从句 no matter how big or small an event might be，其中的形容词"大小"译为形容词词组 big or small。

部分形容词谓语句读的主语本身又是主谓结构，其翻译的重点是妥善处理形容词谓语与大主语的小主语或小谓语之间的关系。如：

　　[1] 泉州刺史廖彦若为政贪暴 Liao Yanruo, magistrate of Quanzhou, led a corruptive, atrocious government
　　[2] 而军行整肃 that the army paraded in a disciplined order
　　[3] 审知为人₁状儿雄伟 Shenzhi was a big, burly man
　　[4] 而为人₂俭约 led a frugal, thrifty life
　　[5] 延翰为人₃长大 Yanhan had a tall, large figure
　　[6] 乙衣冠伟然 Yi looked brilliant with his hat and dress
　　[7] 驺僮甚盛 even his servants who drove the carriage were gorgeous

此类形容词多数为双音节词语。第［1］句的小谓语"为政"是由轻动词"为"后接名词"政"所构成的，译为动宾结构 led a government，而形容词谓语"贪暴"则译为名词 government 的修饰成分 corruptive, atrocious。第［2］句的"军行"实为主谓结构，译为主谓结构 the army paraded，其后的"整肃"则译为介宾短语 in a disciplined order，充当状语。三个"为人"都是轻动词与名词的组合结构，其译法有所不同：第［3］句的"为人₁"译为系补结构 was a man，而形容词谓语"状儿雄伟"译为名词修饰成分 big, burly；第［4］句的"为人₂"译为动宾结构 led a life，而形容词谓语"俭约"译为名词 life 的修饰成分 frugal, thrifty；第［5］句的"为人₃"译为动宾结构 had a figure，而形容词谓语"长大"译为名词 figure 的修饰成分 tall, large；第［6］句的小谓语"衣冠"属于名词活用动词，译为介宾结构 with his hat and dress，而小主语和形容词谓语"乙……伟然"则在整体上译为 Yi looked brilliant；第［7］句结构相对简单，而"驺僮"则译为复杂的名词词组 his servants who drove the carriage,

其中包含 1 个关系分句。

与名词性谓语句读类似，当形容词词组独立成句时就会组成形容词性谓语句读。如：

[1] 谬₁也 it is erroneous

[2] 谬₂矣 this is an error

两个"谬"字分别与"也、矣"组成形容词性句读，充当上文语句的谓语，均译为 SVC 句式：第 [1] 句的"谬"字译为形容词性补语（is）erroneous，第 [2] 句的"谬"字译为名词性补语（is）an error。

形容词谓语有时后接动词性补语成分。对此，英语的同类结构往往不便应用，如 difficult to do something。如：

[1] 美皙如玉 he looked as beautiful and fair as a piece of jade

[2] 曦自昶世倔强难制 although Xi had been obstinate and unyielding since Chang's time

第 [1] 句缺少主语部分，属于不完全的谓语句读，可分中心形容词"美皙"及其补语"如玉"两部分：前者译为动补结构 looked as beautiful and fair；后者译为比较结构 as a piece of jade，充当前者的补足成分。第 [2] 句的中心形容词"倔强"后接补足成分"难制"：前者译为形容词 obstinate，后者译为体分词 unyielding；显然，原文的从属结构已被译为并列结构。上述两种情况均已构成复杂句读。第 7 章将详细讨论复杂句读群组及其英语翻译的相关问题。

3. 形容词活用动词句读群组及其英译

形容词活用动词的例子数量不多，但其译法较为多样。如：

[1] 泉人苦之 from which the people of Quanzhou suffered very much

[2] 文杰善数术 Wenjie was good at numerology

[3] 曦由此恶其宗室 therefore, Xi hated his clan and house

[4] 以安此土 so as to make this land peaceful

第 [1] 句的"苦"字和第 [3] 句的"恶"字分别译为不及物动词 suffered (from) 和及物动词 hated。第 [2] 句的"善"字译为形容词词组（was）good（at）。第 [4] 句的"安"字译为使役结构 make ... peaceful。

4. 名词活用动词句读群组及其英译

不及物的名词活用动词在形式上与体词性谓语类似。二者在翻译中的主要区别在于：前者的译文一般需要建构 SVO 句型，后者的译文通常构建 SVC 句型。如：

［1］皆依审知仕宦 those who took office in Shenzhi's government included

［2］吾今不王 if I do not claim the kingship now

［3］布衣芒屩而已 only to find that Yi simply wore cotton clothes and grass shoes

上述 3 例名词活用动词均译为动宾结构：第［1］句的"仕宦"译为 took office；第［2］句的"王"字译为 claim the kingship；第［3］句的"布衣芒屩"译为 wore cotton clothes and grass shoes。

该组例子有时需要译为补语成分。如：

［1］从效仍臣于南唐 Congxiao was still subject to the state of Southern Tang

［2］而宫中火 only to find his palace on fire

［3］审知丧未期 before the mourning period for Shenzhi was over

上述 3 例均译为补语成分：第［1］句的"臣"字译为主语 Congxiao 的补语（was）subject（to），第［2］句的"火"字译为宾语 his palace 的补语 on fire，第［3］句的"未期"被重新组织成 SVC 句式并译为（before）the period was over。

至于及物的名词活用动词，通常需要构建复杂的动宾结构。如：

［1］率百官北面而臣$_1$之 led a hundred officials to face north and submit to him

［2］率诸将吏北面而臣$_2$之 led generals and officials to face north and submit to him as ministers

［3］谋迎延政都福州 received Yanzheng to move the capital to Fuzhou

第［1］句和第［2］句的"臣$_1$［之］、臣$_2$［之］"均译为 submit to ［him］；第［3］句的"都［福州］"译为 move the capital to［Fuzhou］，其"都"字被还原为名词形式 the capital，因而引入动词 move 以构建新的

动宾结构。

5. 被动语态句读群组及其英译

包括"见动、遇动、被动"等在内的多数被动句读都能够直接译为被动句。如：

[1] 绪已见废 now that Xu had been deposed
[2] 晖见杀$_1$（Hui's troops were eventually defeated and）Hui was also killed
[3] 延禀见执 Yanbing was then captured
[4] 道士陈守元以左道见信 the Taoist Chen Shouyuan was trusted with a heterodox belief
[5] 见杀$_2$ and soon afterwards he was killed
[6] 以色见倖 was favoured because of his beauty
[7] 而妖人林兴以巫见幸 in addition, another wizard Lin Xing was favoured for his witchcraft
[8] 庄宗遇弑 Emperor Zhuangzong was murdered
[9] 亦被杀$_3$ so he was also killed

第[1]句的"见废"译为 had been deposed。第[2]句、第[5]句和第[9]句的"见杀$_1$、见杀$_2$、见杀$_3$"均译为 was killed。第[3]句的"见执"译为 was captured。第[4]句的"见信"译为 was trusted。第[6]句的"见倖"和第[7]句的"见幸"同义，均译为 was favoured。第[8]句的"遇弑"仅限于其主语为尊者，译为 was murdered。

如果被动结构的"被"字后接名词，那么翻译需要处理更加复杂的语义关系。如：

[1] 首被其毒 Wenjie was the first victim of this new prison van

该句的"其"字指代 this new prison van，因而"[首]被[其]毒"译为名词性补语（was）the [first] victim [of this new prison van]，并未使用被动结构。

尽管"为动"结构具有被动意义，但通常译为主动形式，因而需要重构句型。如：

[1] 波涛为阻 between which and the mainland the mighty waves remained the last obstacle

［2］为绝之 so they helped in ending his life

第［1］句的"为阻"译为 remained the last obstacle，其中的"为"字译为 remained。第［2］句的"为绝"译为 helped in ending his life，其中的"为"字译为 helped。两句译文都消解了原文的被动结构。

多数"所动"结构搭配"为名"结构，形成复杂的"为名所动"句式，表达更加完整的被动情景。由于句式变换的原因，部分"所动"结构的被动特征在翻译中被弱化。如：

［1］为绪所胁尔 it is because of the threat under Xu

［2］闽人以为审知德政所致 the Min people believed that this was what the virtue of Shenzhi and his government had brought about

［3］见英为崇顺王所讯 only to see Ying being questioned by the King of Chongshun

［4］继韬及陈后归郎皆为仿所杀 Jitao, Empress Chen and Brother Gui were all killed by Fang

［5］内学士陈郯素以便佞为昶所亲信 the grand secretariant academician Chen Tan had been favoured and trusted by Chang because he was good at flattery

［6］惧为国人所讨 he had feared that he would be sanctioned by the nationals

［7］为延政所败 only to be defeated by Yanzheng

除了第［1］句和第［2］句外，其余5句的"所动"结构均译为被动结构，后接以 by 为核心的介宾结构：第［3］句的"为崇顺王/所讯"译为 being questioned | by the King of Chongshun；第［4］句的"为仿/所杀"译为 were killed | by Fang；第［5］句"为昶/所亲信"译为 had been favoured and trusted | by Chang；第［6］句的"为国人/所讨"译为 be sanctioned | by the nationals；第［7］句的"为延政/所败"译为 to be defeated | by Yanzheng。第［1］句和第［2］句的译文均使用因果关系以消解被动结构：前句采用介词词组 because of，后句采用动词词组 had brought about。

搭配"有、无"的"所动"结构通常已经转化为名词性成分，因而在翻译中需要按具体的动词引入对应的名词。如：

［1］昶无所答 Chang gave nothing in return

［2］不敢有所发 restrained himself from making further troubles

上述2例均使用主动结构：第［1］句的"无所答"译为 gave nothing in return，引入否定代词 nothing；第［2］句的"有所发"译为 making further troubles，引入名词 troubles。

6. 能愿动词句读群组及其英译

能愿动词主要包括"能、敢、可、愿"等，与其后接的动词形成"能动、敢动、可动、愿动"等动词结构。它们都有直接对应的英语结构。其中，"能动"结构通常译为 can do 或 be able to do。如：

［1］延翰不能$_1$制 from which situation Yanhan was not able to restrain himself

［2］予不能$_2$继先志 My elder brother! I cannot uphold the will of our forefather

［3］延禀不能$_3$对 Yanbing could not make any reply

［4］非高能愚二世也 it is not that Gao could make a fool of the Second Emperor of the Qin dynasty

［5］富沙王不能$_4$自保 the King of Fusha is not able to even protect himself

除了第［4］句译为肯定的 could 外，其余4句都是否定形式，分别译为 cannot/could not 或 is/was not able to。其中，多数否定形式可用肯定的动词形式 failed/fail to：第［1］句的"不能$_1$［制］"可译为 failed to［restrain］；第［2］句的"不能$_2$［继］"可译为 fail to［uphold］；第［3］句的"不能$_3$［对］"可译为 failed to［make any reply］。

在"敢动"结构的译文中，dare 经常充当助动词。如：

［1］汝何敢$_1$谋反 how dare you have plotted a rebel

［2］乃敢$_2$强谏 and how dear you have dissuaded so far

［3］群臣皆莫敢$_3$议 no ministers dared to raise any further suggestions

第［1］句和第［2］句的"敢$_1$、敢$_2$"均为助动词，而第［3］句的"敢$_3$"字译为主动词。

部分"可动"结构在翻译中转化为形容词词组。如：

［1］未可信也 they are not yet believable for the moment

［2］过三日可无患 there will be no worry for any ill luck in

three days

　　［3］在吾世可用 though fairly usable in my generation

　　［4］不可遗后世患 is too wise to be left over as a danger in the coming generation

其中，第［1］句的"可信"译为 believable；第［3］句的"可用"译为 usable。第［2］句因时态要求而把"可"字译为 will。第［4］句则采用 too … to … 结构直接改变原来的句式，消解了"可动"结构本身。

其他类型的能愿动词在翻译中体现一定程度的多样化特征。如：

　　［1］况欲图成事哉 let alone achieve any success

　　［2］兵士在道不肯进 but the soldiers stationed on the road and were unwilling to march forward

　　［3］愿伏斧锧 I wish I lay prone on the stake and were axed across the waist

　　［4］乃得不劾 as a result, he was not impeached

　　［5］求置邸内属 requested to establish a representative office and to submit to the Zhou dynasty as a dependent state

第［1］句的"欲"字没有直接译出，而是用 let alone；第［2］句的"肯"字译为 were unwilling；第［3］句的"愿"字译为 wish，后接虚拟的宾语从句；第［4］句的"得"字没有直接的译文；第［5］句的"求"字译为 requested。

7. 小结

特殊谓词性句读在《新五代史·闽世家第八》中的占比为 15.0%。该群组大约三分之一包含轻动词，后接名词形成动宾结构；大约三分之一为形容词或词类活用的形式；另有三分之一为被动结构和能愿结构两类复合的动词词组。特殊谓词性句读虽然占比较小，但其结构较简单谓词性句读和普通名词性句读复杂，具有独特的翻译规律。

第7章

复杂句读群组及其英语翻译

复杂句读所包含的双重或多重主谓结构是引起译文语法难度大于1的主要因素。除了使役结构句读之外，双扇句读、连动句读、并列谓语句读、主谓宾语句读、主谓主语句读、主副动词句读6种句读类型的实例多数都可以明确地译为双重或多重谓语结构，而不少双重或多重谓语结构又可进一步识别为两个或多个小句。这在实际上增加了译文的小句数量。使役结构句读则通常译为复杂谓语结构。复杂句读群组之间在连接方式、逻辑语义、主次关系上存在明显的区别，并对实际的翻译产生明确的影响。甚至，同类句读的不同例子在翻译中也存在不同的分化。该句读群组在其英语翻译上的类聚与分化在一定程度上反映了汉英两种语言在词汇和语法的实现方式上既存在可通约的方面，又存在不可通约的方面。

1. 双扇句读群组及其英译

表示两个动作前后相连的双扇句在英译中可分化为并列结构、复杂动词词组、主从复合语句等。如：

[1] 吾属弃坟墓妻子而为盗者 We have abandoned our ancestral tombs and left our wives and children. We are now nothing but thefts and robbers

[2] 见以为祟而卒 died of being reported to have seen their ghosts

[3] 已执延翰而杀之 who captured and killed Yanhan

[4] 推鏻而立之 Yanbing recommended Lin to succeed to the throne

[5] 疾驰二日而至 so they speeded up and arrived at the destination within two days

[6] 退而谓人曰 after Lin retreated, however, he warned his trusted followers against Renda

[7] 仿惧而出 Fang was frightened and rushed out of the court

[8] 与继鹏率皇城卫士而入 together with Jipeng, he led the security guards of the imperial city and invaded the palace

[9] 兴辄以宝皇语命之而后行 Chang would act according to the words expressed by him on behalf of Baohuang

[10] 昶疑而罢之 Chang was so suspicious that he removed Jiyan from the position

[11] 昶挟爱姬子弟黄门卫士斩关而出 taking his concubines and sons together, Chang led his security guards to fight a way out of the Yellow Gate

[12] 继业执而杀之 Jiye captured and killed Chang

[13] 欲图曦而立其子亚澄 she conspired against Xi and intended to enthrone her son Yacheng

[14] 重遇等遣壮士拉于马上而杀之 Chongyu and his colleagues dispatched soldiers to drag him down from the horse and killed him

[15] 安能交臂而事贼乎 how can we surrender to and serve for these traitors

在上述 15 例句读中，共有 8 例译为并列动词、并列动宾或并列谓语结构。第 [3] 句的"执延翰而杀之"包含"执延翰"和"[而] 杀之"两个并列的动宾结构，其中的名词性宾语"延翰"和代词性宾语"之"的所指相同。该双扇结构被译为并列动词后接同一宾语：captured and killed Yanhan。第 [12] 句的译文类似第 [3] 句，其中的"执而杀之"包含两个并列的动词后接相同的代词"之"，译为 captured and killed Chang。第 [5] 句包含"疾驰 [二日]"和"[而] 至"两个并列的不及物动词，分别译为 speeded up 和 arrived at (the destination)，构成并列谓语结构。第 [15] 句的译文类似第 [5] 句，其中的"交臂而事贼"包含两个并列的动宾结构"交臂"和"[而] 事贼"，分别译为 surrender to 和 serve for (these traitors)，形成并列谓语结构。第 [7] 句的"惧而出"涉及因果关系，其中的心理过程"惧"是原因，而行为过程"出"则是结果，译为并列谓语 was frightened and rushed out。第 [8] 句的"率皇城卫士而入"涉及"率皇城卫士"和"[而] 入"两个表示先后关系的动作，分别译为 led the security guards of the imperial city 和 invaded the palace，构成并列动宾结构。第［13］句涉及目的关系，包含"欲图曦"和"［而］立其子亚澄"两个并列的动宾结构，译为并列动宾结构 conspired against Xi and intended to enthrone her son Yacheng。第［14］句包含使役结构"遣壮士拉于马上"和动宾结构"［而］杀之"，分别译为 dispatched soldiers to drag him down from the horse 和 killed him，构成并列谓语结构。

译为复杂谓语结构的句读共有4例。在第［2］句的"见以为祟而卒"中，"［而］卒"字译为谓语动词 died，而"见以为祟"则译为复杂的介宾结构 of being reported to have seen their ghosts，其中包含1个-ing分词分句。第［9］句的"以宝皇语命之而后行"在结构上与第［2］句类似，其中的"［而后］行"字译为谓语动词（would）act，而"以宝皇语命之"则译为复杂的介宾结构 according to the words expressed by him on behalf of Baohuang，其中包含1个-ed分词分句。第［4］句"推磷而立之"虽在结构上与第［3］句"执延翰而杀之"类似，但未被译为并列谓语结构，而是译为复杂的动词词组 recommended Lin to succeed to the throne。第［11］句的前半部分"挟爱姬子弟黄门卫士斩关"包含"挟爱姬子弟黄门卫士"和"斩关"两个动宾结构，前者译为非限定分句 taking his concubines and sons together，后者译为主句 Chang led his security guards，与后半部分为"［而］出"的译文 to fight a way out of the Yellow Gate 构成复杂谓语结构。

译为主从复合句的句读共有2例。在第［6］句"退而谓人曰"中，"退"字译为时间状语从句 after Lin retreated，而"［而］谓人曰"则译为主句 he warned his trusted followers against Renda。第［10］句包含的"疑"和"［而］罢"两个动词后接同一代词"之"，其在结构上与第［12］句的"执而杀之"类似，但其译法不同："疑"字译为主句（Chang）was（so）suspicious；"罢之"译为从句（that）he removed Jiyan from the position。

此外，第［1］句被分解为两个句子：前半部分"吾属弃坟墓妻子"译为 we have abandoned our ancestral tombs and left our wives and children，后半部分"［而］为盗者"译为 we are now nothing but thefts and robbers。

表示平行关系的双扇句通常译为并列结构或复杂谓语。如：

［1］与潮相持而泣 they supported each other with their arms, with tears trickling down from their eyes

［2］以手掩面而走 he went away quickly with his hands covering his face

［3］兵部员外郎李知损上书请籍没其物而禁锢使者 vice minister of war Li Zhisun submitted a written statement to the emperor, requesting that his goods should be confiscated and his envoy should be arrested

[4] 而妻李氏悍而酗酒 his wife Mrs Li was ferocious and indulged in drinking

第［1］句包含"相持"和"［而］泣"两个不及物动词，分别译为动宾结构（they）supported each other with their arms 和介宾结构 with tears trickling down from their eyes，构成以前者为核心的复杂谓语，而后者则嵌入 1 个-ing 分词分句 tears trickling down from their eyes。第［2］句"以手掩面而走"在结构上与第［1］句类似，包含动宾结构"以手掩面"和不及物动词"［而］走"，分别译为介宾结构 with his hands covering his face 和动状结构（he）went away quickly，构成以后者为核心的复杂谓语，而前者则包含 1 个-ing 分词分句 his hands covering his face。第［3］句包含的两个动宾结构"籍没其物"和"禁锢使者"分别译为两个并列分句 his goods should be confiscated 和 his envoy should be arrested，充当 requested（that）的复合宾语从句。第［4］句包含的形容词性补语"悍"和动宾结构"［而］酗酒"译为并列谓语结构 was ferocious and indulged in drinking。

表示转折关系的双扇句或者译为并列结构，或者译为从属结构。如：

[1] 继室金氏贤而不见答 Lin accepted Mrs Jin as his second wife, who was taciturn though amiable

[2] 曦命卫士鞭之百而不死 Xi ordered his guards to whip Guangyi a hundred times but he was still alive

第［1］句包含的"贤"和"［而］不见答"两个并列谓语分别译为主要成分（who）was taciturn 和次要成分 though amiable，构成从属结构。第［2］句的"鞭之百"和"［而］不死"实为两个主谓结构，分别译为 whip Guangyi a hundred times 和（but）he was still alive，二者以 but 为连词构成并列复合句。

双扇句所表示的因果关系在翻译中或隐或现。如：

[1] 贤妃尚氏有色而宠 his concubine Mrs Shang was favoured for her good appearance

[2] 醉而不胜 they often failed to sustain the excessive drinking and got heavily drunk

第［1］句包含的原因"有色"和结果"［而］宠"分别译为表示原因的介宾结构 for her good appearance 和表示结果的被动结构 was favoured，其中的因果关系在词汇上主要通过介词 for 得以体现。第［2］句包含的原因"醉"和结果"［而］不胜"在整体上译为并列结构 failed to sustain the excessive drinking and got heavily drunk，其中的连词 and 并未明确涉及因果关系。

双扇句所表示的时间关系通常被译为时间状语。如：

岁复在丙午而灭 the state of Min ended in the second successive year of M. Fire Horse

该句包含的"岁复在丙午"和"［而］灭"两个主谓结构分别译为充当状语的介词短语 in the second successive year of M. Fire Horse 和主句 the state of Min ended。由于其中涉及的时间关系比较突出，所以该句又可译为 it is in the second successive year of M. Fire Horse that the state of Min ended。

由其他词语连接的双扇句在翻译中需要注意连词的选用。如：

得文杰乃进 we won't march on, until we have got Wenjie

该句通过"乃"字连接"得文杰"和"进"前后两个谓语，其中的"乃"字译为从属连词 until，而两个谓语分别译为从句 until we have got Wenjie 和主句 we won't march on。

2. 连动句读群组及其英译

普通的连动句读多数表达方式与目的之间的关系。该关系通常转换为不定式结构，有时也被介宾结构所化解。如：

［1］蔡州秦宗权方募士以益兵 Qin Zongquan, who took control of the Caizhou commandery, was managing to recruit soldiers to expand his own troops

［2］刻木为人手以击颊 hit in the face with a bat which was made of wood and carved into a hand-like shape

［3］建宝皇宫以居之 so Lin built a holy palace to accommodate him, in which the god of Baohuang was consecrated

［4］而籍没其赀以佐用 deprive them of their goods in order to aid national expenditure

［5］其子继鹏请与之以纾难 but his son Jipeng made a plea to

trade him for a possible relief of the emergent situation

[6] 而募勇士为宸卫都以自卫 in addition, Chang recruited soldiers and organised them into a division entitled "Chenwei Du" to ensure his own safety

[7] 昶举以示俨曰 Chang lifted the sword and showed it to Tan ... he said ...

[8] 国计使陈匡范增算商之法以献 the minister of finance Chen Kuangfan presented a method of increasing taxes on merchants

[9] 乃借于民以足之 so he made use of private borrowing to make it up

[10] 与朱文进连姻以自固 so he made use of a marriage with Zhu Wenjin's family to strengthen his position and ensure his safety

[11] 传首建州以自归 and submitted to Yanzheng by transferring Wenjin's head to Jianzhou

其中，第［4］句、第［6］句和第［9］句以"而"字或"乃"字开头，属于双扇句的后半部分，只是独立构成句读。第［4］句包含的方式"籍没其赀"和目的"［以］佐用"分别译为动宾结构 deprive them of their goods 和不定式结构（in order）to aid national expenditure。第［6］句包含的"募勇士为宸卫都"和"［以］自卫"分别译为复杂动宾结构（Chang）recruited soldiers and organised them into a division entitled "Chenwei Du" 和不定式结构 to ensure his own safety。第［9］句包含的"借于民"和"［以］足之"分别译为动宾结构 made use of private borrowing 和不定式结构 to make it up。以上3句的"以"字在翻译中均体现为表示目的关系的不定式标记（in order）to。同类例子还包括第［1］句、第［3］句和第［10］句。第［1］句包含的"募士"和"［以］益兵"两个动宾结构分别译为 was managing to recruit soldiers 和 expand his own troops。第［3］句包含的"建宝皇宫"和"［以］居之"两个动宾结构分别译为 built a holy palace 和 accommodate him；其中，"宝皇宫"译为（a holy palace ... ,）in which the god of Baohuang was consecrated。第［10］句包含的方式"与朱文进连姻"和目的"［以］自固"分别译为复杂谓语（he）made use of a marriage with Zhu Wenjin's family 和不定式结构 to strengthen his position and ensure his safety。

第［2］句和第［11］句的连动结构在翻译中转化为介宾结构。在第［2］句"刻木为人手以击颊"中，用以表示方式的前一个动宾结构"刻木为人手"被译为复杂的介宾结构 with a bat which was made of wood and carved into a hand-like shape，其中包含 1 个关系分句。在第［11］句"传首建州以自归"中，用以表示方式的前一个动宾结构"传首建州"被译为介宾结构 by transferring Wenjin's head to Jianzhou，其中包含 1 个-ing 分词结构。相反，在第［5］句"其子继鹏请与之以纾难"中，用以表示目的的后一个动宾结构"［以］纾难"被译为介宾结构 for a possible relief of the emergent situation，而用以表示方式的"请与之"则译为语句的主干（but his son Jipeng）made a plea to trade him。

第［7］句的"举"和"［以］示倓"两个动词结构分别译为 lifted the sword 和 showed it to Tan，二者通过连词 and 构成并列语句。另外，第［8］句在翻译中被简化为动宾结构，其中的"增算商之法"和"［以］献"分别译为宾语 a method of increasing taxes on merchants（包含 1 个-ing 分词）和谓语动词 presented。

不完全的连动句缺少表示方式意义的前半部分，仅保留表示目的意义的后半部分，因而在翻译中往往会使用不定式（in order）to 或目的状语从句 so that ...。如：

［1］以教闽士之秀者 to educate talented people in the region of Min

［2］以愚二世 in order to fool the Second Emperor

［3］以来远人 to invite people to the nation from a far distance

［4］以赎昶罪 so that the crime of Chang might be atoned

第［1］句的"以［教］"和第［3］句的"以［来］"分别译为 to (educate) 和 to (invite ... to the nation from a far distance)。第［2］句的"以［愚］"译为 in order to (fool)。第［4］句的"以［赎］"译为 so that (... might be atoned)，充当前文的状语（从句）。

"以"字与轻动词"为"所构成的连动结构在英译中通常被介宾结构所转换。如：

［1］开以为港 the sea was then split into two by a road leading to the island and the island became a seaport

［2］遂立以为后 was nominated as queen

［3］多养死士以为备 so a large number of loyal soldiers were raised to prepare for any unexpected incident

［4］后立以为皇后 later nominated her as empress

[5] 用以为相 employed him as prime minister

[6] 乃用骑马来骑马去之谶以为据 made use of the superstitious prediction as evidence that the Wang's clan come with one (year of) horse and go with another (year of) horse

第[2]句的"以为后"、第[4]句的"以为皇后"、第[5]句的"以为相"和第[6]句的"以为据"分别译为 as queen、as empress、as prime minister 和 as evidence，其中的"以为"均译为介词 as。第[3]句包含的方式"多养死士"和目的"[以]为备"分别译为被动结构 a large number of loyal soldiers were raised 和不定式结构 to prepare for any unexpected incident。第[1]句的"以为港"则译为独立分句 and the island became a seaport。

缺少前一谓语动词的连动结构在翻译中通常需要考虑上下文的语义关系，添加一些必要的补足成分。如：

[1] 英以为然 Ying took it seriously

[2] 镈以语文杰 Lin consulted with Wenjie on the wizard's words

[3] 镈以为然 Lin took it seriously

[4] 郑反以告重遇 but Tan in turn told Chongyu about Chang's suspicion

第[1]句和第[3]句的"以为然"均译为 took it seriously，添加了代词 it。第[2]句的"以语[文杰]"译为 consulted [with Wenjie] on the wizard's words，添加了（on）the wizard's words。第[4]句的"以告[重遇]"译为 told Chongyu about Chang's suspicion，添加了前文提到的、关于火事的疑虑 Chang's suspicion。

3. 并列谓语句读群组及其英译

存在同时关系的并列谓语结构通常被译为从属或并列的结构。如：

[1] 所至剽掠 they plundered everywhere they arrived

[2] 延翰建国称王 Yanhan founded the kingdom and pronounced himself as king

[3] 坐中昏然 Lin was sleepily seated

[4] 曦居旁色变 Xi was sitting aside and was shocked by what Tan had said

其中，第［1］句的"所至"和"剽掠"分别译为 they plundered 和（everywhere）they arrived 两个分句，二者通过连词 everywhere 构成主从复合句。第［2］句和第［4］句的译文都通过连词 and 构成并列谓语：前者的"建国"和"称王"分别译为 founded the kingdom 和 pronounced himself as king 两个动宾结构，后者的"居旁"和"色变"分别译为 was sitting aside 和 was shocked (by what Tan had said)。第［3］句的"坐中"和"昏然"分别译为被动结构 was seated 和副词 sleepily，因而涉及的并列关系被简化为动状关系。

存在互补关系的并列谓语结构有时译为并列结构，有时也被其他语法结构所转换。如：

［1］绪迟留不行 Xu, however, hesitated to submit his soldiers under the command of Zongquan

［2］鳞惜之不与 Lin took pity on Wenjie and hesitated to give him up

［3］下诏暴其罪 so he issued an imperial decree to expose his crimes

［4］归其贡物不纳 returned all his presents and rejected any tribute he had paid

［5］臣将命无状 I have obeyed the order humbly yet it has turned out to be offensive

［6］及其妻子皆死无遗类 none of his wife and sons were spared

［7］血流被体 and his body was covered all over with blood

［8］乃释赞不答 that Zan was released and exempted from the punishment of whipping

［9］淫虐不道 was dissolute and tyrannical, and ran far away from the right way

［10］更其名曰弘义 changed his name into Hongyi

在上述 10 例中，共有 5 例译为并列结构：第［2］句的"惜之"和"不与"两个动词结构分别译为 took pity on Wenjie 和 hesitated to give him up，第［4］句的"归其贡物"和"不纳"分别译为 returned all his presents 和 rejected any tribute he had paid，第［8］句的"释赞"和"不答"分别译为 Zan was released 和 exempted from the punishment of whipping，第［9］句的"淫虐"和"不道"分别译为 was dissolute and tyrannical 和

ran far away from the right way。上述 4 例均使用连词 and 把译文连成并列谓语。第［5］句的"将命"和"无状"分别译为 have obeyed the order humbly 和 it has turned out to be offensive，二者则通过连词 yet 构成表示转折关系的并列复合句。

第［1］句和第［10］句均译为由动宾结构和介宾结构所构成的复合谓语结构：前者的"迟留"和"不行"分别译为 hesitated to submit his soldiers 和 under the command of Zongquan，后者的"更其名"和"曰弘义"分别译为 changed his name 和 into Hongyi。

第［6］句和第［7］句的并列结构均被转化为简单的被动结构：前者的"及其妻子皆死"和"无遗类"在整体上被译为 none of his wife and sons was spared，后者的"血流"和"被体"被一起译为 his body was covered all over with blood。

此外，第［3］句的"下诏"和"暴其罪"分别译为动宾结构 issued an imperial decree 和不定式结构 to expose his crimes，体现明显的连动意义。

涉及言语对象、关联言语内容的并列谓语结构通常被译为两个相关的小句。如：

［1］潮说其前锋将曰 Chao persuaded his forward commander to start up a revolt against Xu … he said …

［2］延禀临诀谓镣曰 as they bade farewell to each other, Yanbing instructed Lin in the tone of an elder brother … he said …

［3］镣诮之曰 Lin mocked Yanbing in the tone of a younger brother … he said …

［4］守元谓镣曰 later Shouyuan made a prediction about Lin's fortune … he said …

［5］文杰谓英曰 Wenjie informed Ying of a piece of false news … he said …

［6］文杰因教英曰 Wenjie instructed Ying … he said …

［7］尝问仁达曰 on one occasion he made an inquiry to Renda … he said …

［8］谥昶曰康宗 honoured Chang with the posthumous title of "Kangzong", that is, the "Peaceful Emperor"

［9］曦谓元弼曰 so Xi turned to Yuanbi … he said …

［10］谏议大夫黄峻舁榇诣朝堂极谏 the grand master of remonstrance Huang Jun carried a coffin to the court and tried his best to remonstrate

［11］集闽群臣告曰 he summoned all the ministers in the state of Min and persuaded them to establish a new government … he said …

［12］泉州军将留从效诈其州人曰 the general commander of Quanzhou Liu Congxiao deceived the men of Quanzhou … he said …

［13］福州将李仁达谓其徒曰 the general of Fuzhou Li Renda persuaded his followers … he said …

除了第［8］句和第［10］句外，其余11句均译为含有两个小句的句子，其中的"曰"字译为 he said 且置于下文引语的中间。例如，第［1］句的"［潮］说其前锋将"涉及言语对象"其前锋将"，译为小句（Chao）persuaded his forward commander（to start up a revolt against Xu），而"曰"字关联下文的言语内容，译为另一小句 he said，并且插入下文译文的语句中间。又如，第［2］句的"谓鏻"译为小句 Yanbing instructed Lin（in the tone of an elder brother），而"曰"字译为 he said。另外，第［3］句的"诮之"译为小句 Lin mocked Yanbing（in the tone of a younger brother），第［4］句的"谓鏻"译为 made a prediction about Lin's fortune，第［5］句的"谓英"译为 informed Ying of a piece of false news，第［6］句的"教英"译为 Wenjie instructed Ying，第［7］句的"问仁达"译为 made an inquiry to Renda，第［9］句的"谓元弼"译为 Xi turned to Yuanbi，第［11］句的"告"字译为 persuaded them to establish a new government，第［12］句的"诈其州人"译为 deceived the men of Quanzhou，第［13］句的"谓其徒"译为 persuaded his followers。这些涉及言语对象的谓语结构均和关联言语内容的"曰"字分开翻译。

第［8］句和第［10］句的并列结构均转化为介宾结构：前者的"谥昶"译为 honoured Chang，而其"曰"字译为 with the posthumous title of "Kangzong",（that is, the "Peaceful Emperor"）；相反，后者的"诣朝堂"译为 to the court，而其"极谏"译为 tried his best to remonstrate。

表示目的关系的并列结构在翻译中的分化较为明显。如：

［1］绪率众南奔 Xu led his men and fled southwards

［2］跃出擒之 then jumped out from the forest to capture him

［3］其耆老相率遮道留之 the elder people leading their youngsters blocked the way with the hope that Chao and his troops would stay so as to replace the government by Yanruo

［4］于是军府将吏上书劝进 so generals and officials in the military government submitted written statements and advised him to proceed to establish a kingdom

［5］伪立白帜请降 then held up a white flag, making a false plea for surrender

［6］赐与金帛慰安之 that he granted money and silks to Renda as a comfort

［7］昶徙南宫避灾 so Chang moved to the South Palace to keep away from the fire

［8］校书郎陈光逸上书疏曦过恶五十余事 the editor Chen Guangyi presented a written document in which more than fifty faults that Xi had or misdeeds that he committed were sorted out

在上述 8 例中，第［1］句和第［4］句的译文均通过连词 and 构成并列谓语结构：前者的"率众"和"南奔"分别译为 led his men 和 fled southwards，后者的"上书"和"劝进"分别译为 submitted written statements 和 advised him to proceed (to establish a kingdom)。另外，第［5］句和第［8］句的译文通过分句结构形成主从复合语句。其中，第［5］句的"伪立白帜"和"请降"分别译为主句 then held up a white flag 和-ing 分词分句 making a false plea for surrender；第［8］句"上书"译为主句的动宾结构 presented a written document，而"疏"字译为关系分句的谓语成分 were sorted out。

其余 4 例的并列结构均转化为不定式或介宾结构。其中，第［2］句、第［7］句的并列结构均转化为不定式，体现明显的连动特征：第［2］句的"跃出"和"擒之"两个动宾结构分别译为 jumped out from the forest 和 to capture him，第［7］句的"徙南宫"和"避灾"分别译为 moved to the South Palace 和 to keep away from the fire。第［3］句和第［6］句的并列结构转化为介词短语，形成复杂的谓语结构：第［3］句的"相率遮道"和"留之"分别译为 leading their youngsters blocked the way 和 with the hope that Chao and his troops would stay so as to replace the government by Yanruo，第［6］句的"赐与金帛"和"慰安之"分别译为 he granted money and silks to Renda 和 as a comfort。

表示方式的并列结构在翻译中同样分化明显，形成跨句结构、并列结构、从属结构、不定式结构、介宾结构等。如：

［1］审知乃亲督士卒攻破之 Shenzhi had no choice but to launch another campaign, leading commanders and soldiers in person

［2］延翰乃取司马迁《史记》闽越王无诸传示其将吏曰 Yanhan took out *Historical Records* by the grand historian Sima Qian of the Han dynasty and showed the "Biography of Wuzhu the King of Min and Yue" to his generals and officials … he said …

［3］鏻上书言 Lin submitted a written application to the imperial court of the Tang dynasty … he said …

［4］守元传宝皇语曰 Shouyuan returned the words of Baohuang and said

［5］昶称疾不见 Chang did not receive him in person with the excuse of being in bad health

［6］元弼俯伏曰 he lay prone and submitted … he said …

［7］重遇等流涕自辨 they could do nothing but to defend themselves with a running nose

［8］延政数贻书谏之 Yanzheng submitted several written statements to remonstrate him

除了第［1］句外，其余 7 句都涉及言语过程。在这些言语过程中，"曰、言"等字通常单独译为小句 he said，并且置于引语中间，形成跨句结构，如第［2］句和第［6］句的"曰"字，以及第［3］句的"言"字。第［4］句的译文通过连词 and 构成并列谓语，其中的"传宝皇语"和"曰"分别译为 returned the words of Baohuang 和 said。第［8］句的并列关系转化为不定式结构，其中的"贻书"和"谏之"分别译为 submitted several written statements 和 to remonstrate him。第［5］句和第［7］句的并列结构均被介宾结构所化解：前者的"称疾"和"不见"分别译为介宾结构 with the excuse of being in bad health 和动宾结构 did not receive him in person，后者的"流涕"和"自辨"分别译为 with a running nose 和 could do nothing but to defend themselves。此外，第［1］句的译文通过非限定分句译为主从复合结构，其中的"亲督士卒"和"攻破之"分别译为主句 had no choice but to launch another campaign 和 -ing 分词从句 leading commanders and soldiers in person。

表示连动关系的并列谓语句读数量较多，其在逻辑语义上类似连动句读，因而在翻译中也存在明显的结构分化现象。如：

第 7 章　复杂句读群组及其英语翻译

　　［1］潮即引兵围彦若 Chao then led his troops to outflank Yanruo

　　［2］执延翰杀之 Yanhan was captured and killed

　　［3］延禀率兵击鏻 Yanbing commanded his troops to assault Lin

　　［4］卒诬以罪杀之 soon afterwards Renda was killed on a false accusation of crime

　　［5］鏻立十年见杀 Lin got killed ten years after he had came to the throne

　　［6］伏甲擒仿杀之 he ordered ambushing soldiers to capture and kill Fang

　　［7］仿部曲千人叛 his division became disobedient and more than one thousand of his men revolted

　　［8］而其子继恭遣其佐郑元弼随损至京师贡方物 his son Jigong sent his adjuvant Zheng Yuanbi to keep company with Sun to the imperial capital, paying loyal tribute and presenting local products

　　［9］狱具引见 Yuanbi was then bound up with shackles and introduced before the emperor

　　［10］夜率卫士纵火焚南宫 that he led his soldiers to set fire on the South Palace one night

　　［11］重遇迎延义立之 Chongyu received Yanyi and enthroned him

　　［12］泉州刺史余廷英尝矫曦命掠取良家子 the magistrate of Quanzhou Yu Tingying once took a false command from Xi and seized girls of good breeding

　　［13］数举兵相攻 they dispatched their troops to attack each other several times

　　［14］剖棺断尸 so he split up Kuang Fan's coffin and dismembered his body

　　［15］曦乃举兵攻延政 then Xi raised troops to attack Yanzheng

　　［16］乃擒继昌杀之 so he arrested Jichang and killed him

　　［17］执王继勋送于金陵 so he captured and escorted Wang Jixun to Jinling

　　其中，第［8］句和第［10］句均包含 3 个动词：第［8］句的"遣其佐郑元弼""随损至京师""贡方物"分别译为限定的动宾结构（his son

Jigong) sent his adjuvant Zheng Yuanbi、不定式结构 to keep company with Sun to the imperial capital 和现在分词分句 paying loyal tribute and presenting local products，构成主从复合结构；第［10］句的"夜率卫士""纵火""焚南宫"分别译为限定的动宾结构 led his soldiers (one night)、不定式结构 to set fire 和介宾结构 on the South Palace，构成复杂的谓语结构。

其余15句均包含2个动词，其译文在语法结构上分化明显。其中，有2句的连动关系译为复合句：第［5］句的"［璘］立十年"和"见杀"分别译为 ten years after he had came to the throne 和 (Lin) got killed，二者通过连词 (ten years) after 构成主从复合句；第［7］句的"［仿部］曲"和"［千人］叛"分别译为 (his division) became disobedient 和 (more than one thousand of his men) revolted，二者通过连词 and 构成并列复合句。

有6句的连动关系译为并列谓语结构，均通过 and 连接：第［2］句的"执延翰"和"杀之"分别译为 Yanhan was captured 和 killed 两个被动结构；第［9］句的"狱具"和"引见"分别译为 (was) bound up with shackles 和 introduced before the emperor 两个被动结构；第［11］句的"迎延义"和"立之"分别译为 received Yanyi 和 enthroned him 两个主动结构；第［12］句的"矫曦命"和"掠取良家子"分别译为 took a false command from Xi 和 seized girls of good breeding；第［14］句的"剖棺"和"断尸"分别译为 split up Kuang Fan's coffin 和 dismembered his body；第［16］句的"擒继昌"和"杀之"分别译为 arrested Jichang 和 killed him。

共有3句的连动关系通过不定式转化为复杂谓语结构：第［1］句的"引兵"和"围彦若"分别译为动宾结构 led his troops 和不定式结构 to outflank Yanruo；第［3］句的"率兵"和"击璘"分别译为 commanded his troops 和 to assault Lin；第［13］句的"举兵"和"相攻"分别译为 dispatched their troops 和 to attack each other。此外，第［4］句的并列关系被介宾结构所化解，其中的"诬以罪"和"杀之"分别译为介宾结构 on a false accusation of crime 和 Renda was killed，构成复杂谓语结构。

另有2句简化为以 and 为连词的并列动词结构：第［6］句的"［伏甲］擒仿"和"杀之"分别译为 (ordered ambushing soldiers) to capture 和 kill Fang；第［17］句的"执王继勋"和"送于金陵"分别译为 captured 和 escorted Wang Jixun to Jinling。

表示因果关系的并列谓语句读数量较少，其英译通常需要使用 for 等介词或 because 等连词。如：

［1］其兵见之皆溃去 on seeing this, the soldiers of Yanbing all

fled away

　　［2］英病在告 on one occasion Ying was off duty because he was in bad health

　　［3］御史中丞刘赞坐不纠举 vice censor-in-chief Liu Zan was to be punished for his unwillingness to impeach other ministers

第［2］句和第［3］句的译文均包含表示因果关系的词汇：前句的原因"［英］病"和结果"在告"分别译为（because）he was in bad health 和［Ying］was off duty，两个小句通过连词 because 构成表示因果关系的主从复合句；后句的原因"不纠举"和结果"坐"分别译为（for）his unwillingness to impeach other ministers 和 was to be punished，二者通过介词 for 构成复杂的谓语结构。至于第［1］句，其因果关系在词汇上则没有明确的体现：其原因"见之"和结果"溃去"分别译为 on seeing this 和（the soldiers of Yanbing）all fled away，体现为两个动作的同时关系。

类似表示因果关系的并列谓语句读，表示转折或条件关系的并列谓语句读在翻译中通常需要使用连词或介词。如：

　　［1］卫士刺之不殂 the security guards stabbed him but he did not die

　　［2］动辄触之 so that the prisoner would be pricked whenever the carriage moved

第［1］句的"刺之"和"不殂"两个谓语结构存在转折关系，分别译为 stabbed him 和（but）he did not die，二者通过连词 but 构成并列结构。第［2］句的"动辄"和"触之"两个谓语结构存在条件关系，分别译为（whenever）the carriage moved 和 the prisoner would be pricked，二者通过连词 whenever 构成主从复合句。

4. 主谓宾语句读群组及其英译

多数主谓宾语句读涉及言语和心理两类动词，其宾语通常译为言语或心理的投射小句。如：

　　［1］绪闻潮兄弟材勇 Xu heard that Chao and his brothers were intrepid and talented

　　［2］闻潮略地至其境 when it was heard that Chao had invaded across territories to the border

[3] 当言头痛而已 please do say that you have suffered from nothing but a headache

[4] 宜问其疾如何 it would be better if we could inquire into Ying's health condition in person

[5] 军士闻英死 when the news came that Ying died

[6] 以谓古制疏阔 he regarded the existing carriage as loose and wide

[7] 言见延禀来 murmured that he saw Yanbing coming

[8] 问仿杀可殷何罪 asked Fang about the crime that Li Keyin had committed

[9] 述昶意求以敌国礼相往来 narrating that Chang was intending to seek for a mutual relation with the Jin dynasty so that the state of Min could be acknowledged as independent

[10] 云如此可求大还丹 it was said that the elixir of life could be extracted in this way

[11] 林兴传神言 so Lin Xing conveyed the words of the god … he said …

[12] 术者言昶宫中当有灾 the prophets said that a disaster was to take place in Chang's palace

[13] 南唐李景闻闽乱 the news came to the state of Northern Tang and Li Jing heard that the state of Min was in disorder

[14] 留从效闻延政降唐 Liu Congxiao heard that Yanzheng surrendered to the state of Southern Tang

[15] 今诸家记其国灭丙午是也 now it is correctly recorded by a number of historians that the final year is the year of M. Fire Horse

共有12句的译文包含言语小句，充当言语动词的宾语。第［1］句、第［2］句、第［5］句、第［13］句和第［14］句均包含言语动词"闻"。其中，第［1］句、第［2］句和第［14］句的"闻"字译为主动的 heard（that …）或被动词的 it was heard（that …）。第［5］句的"闻"字译为 when the news came（that …）。第［13］句则综合了以上两种形式，得到1个并列结构：the news came to（…）and Li Jing heard（that …）。第［3］句、第［7］句和第［12］句均包含言语动词"言"：第［3］句和第［12］句的"言"译为 say/said（that …）；第［7］句的"言"字译为 murmured（that …）。第［9］句的"述"字译为 narrating（that …）；第

[10]句的"云"字译为 it was said (that ...);第[11]句的"传"字译为 conveyed (that ...);第[15]句的"记"字译为 it is recorded (that ...)。

其余 3 句的译文没有使用言语小句:第[4]句和第[8]句均包含"问"字,分别译为 inquire into 和 asked ... about;第[6]句的"谓"字译为 regarded ... as。

主谓宾语句读的心理动词类似言语动词,多数例子的译文使用宾语从句。如:

[1]仿以为鏻病已甚 Fang believed that Lin had been seriously sick

[2]怒损侵辱之 he felt offended at the thought that Sun had insulted him

[3]高祖怒其不逊 the Founding Emperor burst into rage at Chang's impertinence

[4]昶疑重遇军士纵火 he suspected that Chongyu's soldiers had set the fire

[5]昶知不免 knowing that he could not escape

[6]曦思倓前言 which reminded Xi of Tan as well as what he had said before

[7]其后知其借于民也 later, Xi discovered that Kuang Fan had used private lending

[8]惧众不附 but he was afraid that no one supported him

除了第[3]句外,其余 7 句的译文均使用宾语从句:第[1]句的"以为"译为 believed (that ...);第[2]句的"怒"字译为 felt offended at the thought (that ...);第[4]句的"疑"字译为 suspected (that ...);第[5]句和第[7]句的"知"字分别译为 knowing (that ...) 和 discovered (that ...);第[6]句的"思"字译为 reminded ... of ... what (...);第[8]句的"惧"字译为 was afraid (that ...)。第[3]句的宾语"其不逊"译为名词词组 Chang's impertinence。

后接主谓结构的行为动词较少,其译法有别于涉及言语或心理动词的句读。如:

[1]伺绪至 these soldiers awaited Xu passing by

[2]据王潮实以唐景福元年入福州 it was in the first year of

the Jinfu period of the Tang dynasty (A. D. 892) that Wang Chao entered Fuzhou

第［1］句"伺绪至"译为 awaited Xu passing by, 第［2］句的"据"字译为 it is ... that ... 。

5. 主谓主语句读群组及其英译

充当主语的主谓结构往往自成句读，因而主谓主语句读的数量很少。在《新五代史·闽世家第八》的721个句读中，只有如下1例：

臣为魏郑公可矣 I can humbly compare myself to Duke Zheng of the Wei state

该句的谓语"可矣"可译为情态动词 can（compare）。该谓语也可译为主句 it is acceptable（that ... ）。

6. 使役结构句读群组及其英译

用以引导使役结构的"遣、使、命、请"等动词通常译为 dispatch、send、order、request。其中，"遣"字结构的翻译通常使用 dispatch/send somebody to do something。如：

［1］潮遣审知攻晖 Chao sent Shenzhi to attack Hui

［2］审知岁遣使泛海 Shenzhi dispatched envoys to go by seaway

［3］鏻遣王仁达拒之 Lin dispatched Wang Renda to resist the attack launched by Jixiong

［4］遣守元问宝皇 dispatched Shouyuan to enquire Baohuang again

［5］即上遣人问公疾 if His Majesty sends someone to inquire your health

［6］鏻遣人问之 Lin then sent someone to inquire Ying

［7］鏻遣其将王延宗救之 Lin dispatched his general Wang Yanzong to run a rescue campaign

［8］昶遣使朝贡京师 Chang sent envoys to pay loyal tribute to the imperial court of the Jin dynasty

［9］高祖遣散骑常侍卢损册昶闽王 the Founding Emperor in return sent the cavalier attendant-in-ordinary Lu Sun to confer Chang with the title of "King of Min"

[10] 又遣中书舍人刘乙劳损于馆 the council secretary Liu Yi was additionally sent to treat Sun in the guest-house

[11] 又遣医人陈究以空名牒卖官 furthermore, he also sent the physician Chen Jiu to sell official titles with blank letters of appointment

[12] 遣使者朝贡于晋 dispatched envoys to pay loyal tribute to the Jin dynasty

[13] 新罗遣使聘闽以宝剑 the state of Silla dispatched envoys and presented a precious sword

[14] 遣杜建崇监其军 so he sent Du Jiancong to supervise his army

[15] 延政遣其从子继昌守福州 Yanzheng sent his nephew Jichang to defend Fuzhou

[16] 遣人召李仁达入朝 men was sent to summon Li Renda to the court

[17] 从效遣牙将蔡仲兴为商人 Congxiao dispatched his company commander Cai Zhongxing in the guise of a merchant

在上述 17 句中，只有第 [13] 句的使役结构被转化为并列结构 dispatched envoys and presented a precious sword。第 [1] 句、第 [5] 句、第 [6] 句、第 [8] 句、第 [9] 句、第 [10] 句、第 [11] 句、第 [14] 句、第 [15] 句、第 [16] 句的"遣"字结构均译为 send someone to do something 或 someone was sent to do something；第 [2] 句、第 [3] 句、第 [4] 句、第 [7] 句、第 [12] 句、第 [17] 句的"遣"字结构均译为 dispatch someone to do something。

与"遣"字结构类似，"使"字结构也通常译为 send someone to do something。如：

[1] 使其子继雄转海攻其南门 sent his son Jixiong to make another attack on the South Gate by seaway

[2] 镈使彦视鬼于宫中 Lin then sent Yan to watch the ghosts in the palace

[3] 讽镈使巫视英疾 Wenjie hinted Lin into sending a wizard to watch the health condition of Ying

[4] 损使人诮之曰 Sun sent someone to mock him in the tone of an inferior ... he said ...

[5] 乃使人谓重遇等曰 so she sent someone to take words to Chongyu and his colleagues ... he said ...

其中，第［1］句的"使……攻……"译为 sent ... to make another attack ... ；第［2］句和第［3］句的"使……视……"均译为 sent ... to watch ... ；第［4］句的"使……诮……"译为 sent ... to mock ... ；第［5］句的"使……谓……"译为 sent ... to take words to ... 。

"命"字句的翻译通常使用 order/appoint someone to do something 或用 order 的名词形式。如：

[1] 宝皇命王少避其位 Baohuang orders Your Majesty to refrain yourself from the throne for a short while

[2] 命其子继鹏权主府事 that he appointed his son Jipeng to take charge of the government affairs

[3] 命文杰劾之 ordered Wenjie to impeach him

[4] 璘命锦工作九龙帐 Lin ordered the brocade craftsmen to weave a curtain with the pattern of nine dragons

[5] 乃命兴率壮士杀审知子延武延望及其子五人 Xing then received an order to lead a group of soldiers to kill five of Shenzhi's sons or grandsons, including Yanwu, Yanwang, and their sons

[6] 命发冢戮其尸 so Xi gave an order to excavate his tomb and expose his corpse

第［3］句和第［4］句均使用动词不定式结构：前者的"命……劾……"译为 ordered ... to impeach ... ，后者的"命……作……"译为 ordered ... to weave ... 。第［1］句的"命"字译为 orders，而其后接的成分"王少避其位"也可译为宾语从句 that Your Majesty refrain yourself from the throne for a short while。第［2］句的"命……权……"结构则译为 appointed ... to take charge of ... 。第［5］句和第［6］句均使用 order 的名词形式：前者的"命……率……"译为 ... received an order to lead ... ；后者的"命"字缺少宾语，因而"命发"译为 ... gave an order to excavate ... 。

"令"字句的译文在语法结构上分化明显。如：

[1] 令上下通 the upper part and the lower part were combined into one single cell

第 7 章 复杂句读群组及其英语翻译

[2] 乃令壮士先杀李可殷于家 so he immediately ordered soldiers to break into Li Keyin's house and kill him

[3] 令继恭主之 Jigong was instructed to host him

[4] 延义令其子继业率兵袭昶 Yanyi commanded his son Jiye to make a final raid on Chang with a troop of soldiers

其中，第[1]句"令上下通"的使役表达直接译为被动结构 the upper part and the lower part were combined into one single cell，其中的"令"字并未直接译出。第[2]句的"令……杀……"译为主动结构 ordered ... to kill ...。第[3]句的"令……主……"译为被动结构 ... was instructed to host ...。第[4]句的"令……率……袭……"译为 commanded ... to make a final raid ... with ...，其译文中的介词 with 化解了原文的动宾结构"率……"。

用以引导使役结构的"召、发、请、烦、教、掖"等动词通常译为 assemble、dispatch、request、bother、instruct、support 等。如：

[1] 召其兵会击黄巢 then tried to assemble Xu's soldiers to suppress the anti-imperial rebellion led by Huang Chao

[2] 宗权发兵攻绪 who therefore dispatched his own troops to trounce Xu

[3] 又请潮自临军 so he further requested that Chao should lead the troop in person

[4] 毋烦老兄复来 never bother me to come over again

[5] 果烦老兄复来 ever bother you to come over again

[6] 守元教昶起三清台三层 Shouyuan instructed Chang to build a three-storey terrace called "Sanqing Tai"

[7] 召下御史劾之 ordered censors to impeach him

[8] 乃掖朱文进升殿 so he supported Zhu Wenjin to ascend the palace

[9] 发兵攻之 dispatched his soldiers to attack the state of Min

除了第[3]句外，其余 8 句的译文均使用不定式结构。第[1]句的"召……会击……"和第[7]句的"召……劾……"分别译为 assemble ... to suppress ... 和 ordered ... to impeach ...；第[2]句和第[9]句的"发……攻……"译为 dispatched ... to trounce ... / to attack ...；第[4]句和第[5]句的"烦……来"均译为 bother ... to come over；第[6]句的

"教……起……"译为 instructed ... to build ... ；第 [8] 句的"掖……升……"译为 supported ... to ascend ...。第 [3] 句的译文则使用宾语从句，其"请……临……"译为 requested that ... lead ...。

7. 主副动词句读群组及其英译

对于"以……为……"结构，"以"是副动词，"为"是主动词（轻动词）。该结构按其主副动词后接的宾语可区分两种情况：其一，当"以"字后接人物、"为"字后接官职时，该结构通常译为 appoint ... as ...；其二，当"以"字后接城市名称、"为"字后接行政区域时，其译文的语法结构有所分化。如：

[1] 以潮为军校 appointed Chao as military commander

[2] 乃以绪为光州刺史 for this purpose, Zongquan appointed Xu as magistrate of the Guangzhou commandery

[3] 唐即以潮为福建观察使 the Tang dynasty soon afterwards appointed Chao as surveillance commissioner of Fujian

[4] 潮以审知为副使 Chao in turn appointed Shenzhi as assistant

[5] 唐以福州为威武军 the Tang dynasty established a provincial-level institution entitled "Weiwu Military Government" in Fuzhou

[6] 以其弟延钧为泉州刺史 appointed his younger brother Yanjun as magistrate of Quanzhou

[7] 以福州为长乐府 Fuzhou was taken as the capital in the name of "Changle Fu", that is, Government of Long-lasting Joy

[8] 以中军使薛文杰为国计使 the military secretary Xue Wenjie was appointed as minister of finance

[9] 景以仁达为威武军节度使 Li Jing appointed Li Renda as military commissioner of Weiwu Military Government

[10] 李景以泉州为清源军 Li Jing established a provincial-level institution entitled "Qingyuan Military Government" in Quanzhou

[11] 以从效为节度使 appointed Congxiao as military commissioner

[12] 遂以王潮光启二年岁在丙午拜泉州刺史为始年 so the

second year of the Guangqi period (A. D. 886) was taken as the initial year when Wang Chao was appointed as magistrate of Quanzhou

除了第［5］句、第［7］句和第［10］句外，其余9句都为第一种情况，其中，第［8］句"以中军使薛文杰为国计使"译为被动结构 the military secretary Xue Wenjie was appointed as minister of finance；第［12］句也译为被动结构，其余几句分别译为 appointed Chao (Xu, Chao, Shenzhi, his younger brother, Li Renda, Congxiao) as military commander (magistrate, surveillance commissioner, assistant, magistrate, minister of finance, military commissioner)；第［5］句、第［7］句和第［10］都有明显的解释痕迹，属于第二种情况。例如，第［5］句译为 the Tang dynasty established a provincial-level institution entitled "Weiwu Military Government" in Fuzhou，其中引入的 a provincial-level institution 消解了原文的主副动词结构。

当副动词"以"后接人物、主动词不是轻动词时，主副动词结构的译文分化明显，形成主从复合句、不定式结构、介宾结构或简单动宾结构。如：

［1］延禀延钧皆以兵入 leading their soldiers respectively, Yanbing and Yanjun launched an invasion

［2］上以公居近密 His Majesty entrusts your honour with an important position in the imperial court

［3］即以英下狱 so he imprisoned Ying

［4］以李仿判六军诸卫事 Li Fang was then appointed to take charge of the six legions of armed forces and all security affairs

［5］于是以元弼下狱 thus Yuanbi was imprisoned

［6］文进以重遇判六军诸卫事 Wenjin appointed Chongyu to take charge of the six legions of armed forces and all security affairs

［7］以黄绍颇守泉州 Huang Shaopo was sent to defend Quanzhou

［8］以雪峰寺僧卓俨明示众曰 he showed Monk Zhuo Yanming from the Snow-Peak Temple to the public … he said …

第［1］句被译为主从两个小句，其中的"延禀延钧［皆］……入"译为主句 Yanbing and Yanjun launched an invasion，而"以兵"译为非限定的从句 leading their soldiers respectively。第［4］句"以李仿判六军诸卫事"、第［6］句"文进以重遇判六军诸卫事"、第［7］句"以黄绍颇守泉州"的副动词"以"字均被译为具体的动词 appointed 或 sent，而主动词"判、守"则被译为动词不定式 to take charge of 和 to defend。第 [2] 句的主动词"居 [近密]"被译为介词 with (an important position)，而副动词"以 [公]"则译为具体的 entrusts。同理，第 [8] 句的主动词"示 [众]"被译为介词 to (the public)，而副动词"以 [雪峰寺僧卓俨明]"则译为具体的动词 showed (Monk Zhuo Yanming from the Snow-Peak Temple)。另外，第 [8] 句还包含 1 个并列的主动词"曰"，译为 he said。第 [3] 句的"以英下狱"和第 [5] 句的"以元弼下狱"直接简化为动宾结构 imprisoned Ying 和被动结构 Yuanbi was imprisoned。

当副动词"以"后接事物时，其译文往往因事物的类别不同而有所分化。如：

[1] 又以铁锥刺之 then stabbed them with an iron spike

[2] 以黄龙见真封宅 the yellow dragon was used as a symbol to mark his mansion

[3] 致富人以罪 tended to convict those who were rich of various crimes

[4] 而屡以疾告 but you have been off duty successively with the excuse of illness

[5] 以金槌击其首 then hit Ying in the head with a metal hammer

[6] 乃以槛车送文杰军中 as a result, Wenjie was escorted in a prison van on a trip to the army

[7] 闽人争以瓦石投之 in addition, onlookers rushed to throw tiles and stones at him

[8] 中以铁芒内向 within which sharp iron thorns were equipped, pointing to the center

[9] 以黄金数千斤铸宝皇及元始天尊太上老君像 several thousand *jin* of gold was used to cast the statues of the god Baohuang and the Founding Sovereign of Heaven, that is, the Lofty Laozi

[10] 皆以此怨激其军 both of them used this unfair treatment to irritate their own soldiers

[11] 昶以火事语之 Chang consulted him about the fire

[12] 以一当十 each of which was set to be worth ten old coins

[13] 多以事诛之 killed them for one or another reason

第 7 章　复杂句读群组及其英语翻译

[14] 以绳系颈 he was hung in the neck with a rope

[15] 匡范以忧死 Kuang Fan died of worries for this

[16] 以色嬖之 was favoured by Xi for his good appearance

[17] 常以语诮重遇等 he often blamed Chongyu and his colleagues for the guilt

[18] 延政乃以建州建国称殷 Yanzheng founded a new state called Yin on the basis of the Jianzhou commandery

[19] 以汀州降于延政 so he surrendered the Tingzhou commandery to Yanzheng

当"以"字后接工具类名词时，通常译为介词 with。例如，第 [1] 句的副动词"以 [铁锥]"和主动词"刺 [之]"分别译为介词 with (an iron spike) 和单及物动词 stabbed (them)，第 [5] 句的副动词"以 [金槌]"和主动词"击 [其首]"分别译为介词 with (a metal hammer) 和单及物动词 hit (Ying in the head)，第 [14] 句的副动词"以 [绳]"和主动词"系 [颈]"分别译为介词 with (a rope) 和被动结构 (he) was hung (in the neck)。

当"以"字后接材料类或方式类名词时，通常译为 use 或 set 等动词，或者译为不同的介词。例如，第 [2] 句的副动宾结构"以黄龙见真"在翻译中转为被动结构 the yellow dragon was used as a symbol，而主动宾结构"封宅"则译为不定式结构 to mark his mansion；第 [9] 句的副动宾结构"以黄金数千斤"和主动宾结构"铸……像"分别译为被动结构 several thousand *jin* of gold was used 和不定式结构 to cast the statues of …；第 [10] 句的副动宾结构"以此"在翻译中转为动宾结构 used this unfair treatment，而主动宾结构"怒激其军"则译为不定式结构 to irritate their own soldiers。第 [12] 句译文使用动词 set，其副动宾结构"以一"译为 each of which was set，而主动宾结构"当十"则译为不定式结构 to be worth ten old coins。共有 3 例此类句读的译文使用了不同的介词：第 [6] 句的副动词"以 [槛车]"和主动词"送 [文杰军中]"分别译为介词 in (a prison van) 和被动结构 (Wenjie) was escorted (on a trip to the army)；第 [11] 句的副动词"以 [火事]"和主动词"语 [之]"分别译为介词 about (the fire) 和动词 consulted (him)；第 [18] 句的主动宾结构"建国称殷"和副动宾结构"以建州"分别译为 founded a new state called Yin 和 on the basis of the Jianzhou commandery。

当"以"字后接原因类名词时，通常译为 of 或 for 等介词。共有 3 句使用 for：第［13］句的主动词"诛［之］"和副动词"以［事］"分别译为动词 killed（them）和介词 for（one or another reason）；第［16］句的主动词"嬖［之］"和"以［色］"分别译为被动结构 was favoured（by Xi）和介词 for（his good appearance）；第［17］句的主动词"诮［重遇等］"和副动词"以［语］"分别译为动词（he often）blamed（them）和介词 for（the guilt）。共有2句使用 of：第［3］句的主动词"致［富人］"和副动词"以［罪］"分别译为及物动词 convict（those who were rich）和介词 of（various crimes）；第［15］句的主动词"死"和副动词"以［忧］"分别译为（Kuang Fan）died 和 of（worries for this）。另外，第［4］句的译文使用 with，其主动词"告"和副动词"以［疾］"分别译为（you）have been off duty（successively）和介词 with（the excuse of illness）。

第［7］句和第［17］句的及物关系发生转化：第［7］句的主动词"投［之］"和副动词"以［瓦石］"分别译为 at（him）和（were rushing to）throw（tiles and stones），其中的及物动词 throw 消解了原文的"以……投"结构，后接 tiles and stones（瓦石），而介词 at 则用来引入 him（之）；第［19］句的副动词"以［汀州］"和主动词"降［于延政］"在整体上被译为（he）surrendered the Tingzhou commandery（to Yanzheng），其中的 surrendered 消解了原文的"以……降"结构，后接 the Tingzhou commandery（汀州），而介词 to 则用来引入 Yanzheng。另外，第［8］句则使用复合语句消解了"以……向"结构，其主动词"［内］向"和"以［铁芒］"分别译为非限定分句 pointing（to the center）和限定分句（sharp iron thorns）were equipped。

当主动词缺少宾语时，译文通常需要补上对应的宾语或使用被动结构。如：

［1］系以大械 they were fastened to a punishment device

［2］代以季弟继镛 appointed his third younger brother Jiyong to take over the position

［3］被以衮冕 he wore him with the dragon crown

上述3句的译文均补上必要的对象：第［1］句的译文使用被动结构 they were fastened，补上 they；第［2］句的译文补上宾语 the position；第［3］句补上宾语 him。

在上述"以……为……"结构中，"为"字充当主动词。相反，"为"字句的"为"字则充当副动词，而其主动词则另由其他动词充当。此类

第 7 章 复杂句读群组及其英语翻译

"为"字句的译文通常使用不定式结构或介宾结构。如：

[1] 乃推潮为主 so Chao was recommended to be the lord

[2] 升福州为大都督府 promoted Fuzhou as Metropolitan Government

[3] 又多选良家子为妾 eagerly rushed into the act of selecting girls of good breeding to be his concubines

[4] 改元为龙启 he changed the designation of the reign into "Longqi", that is, dragons' rising up

[5] 追谥审知为昭武孝皇帝 added to Shenzhi the posthumous title of "Bright Martial Filial Emperor", or "Emperor Wu"

[6] 赵高指鹿为马 Zhao Gao referred to a deer as a horse

[7] 故高指鹿为马 so Gao referred to a deer as a horse

[8] 拜道士谭紫霄为正一先生 He granted Tan Zixiao, a Taoist, with the title of "Sir Right-One"

[9] 又拜陈守元为天师 also granted Chen Shouyuan with the title of "Master of Heaven"

[10] 立父婢春燕为淑妃 he nominated his father's maidservant Chunyan as his concubine

[11] 迎王继勋为刺史 received Wang Jixun as magistrate

[12] 迎王继成为刺史 received Wang Jicheng as magistrate

[13] 世宗与李景画江为界 Emperor Shizong and Li Jing took the Yangtze River as the border

当"为"字后接身份类、职能类或头衔类名词时，通常译为不定式 to be 或介词 as 或 with（the title of）。共有 2 个"为"字译为不定式 to be：第[1] 句的主动词"推［潮］"和副动词"为［主］"分别译为 (Chao) was recommended 和 to be (the lord)；第 [3] 句的主动词"选［良家子］"和副动词"为［妾］"分别译为 selecting (girls of good breeding) 和 to be (his concubines)。共有 7 个"为"字译为介词 as：第 [2] 句的主动词"升［福州］"和副动词"为［大都督府］"分别译为 promoted (Fuzhou) 和 as (Metropolitan Government)；第 [6] 句和第 [7] 句的主动词"指［鹿］"和副动词"为［马］"均分别译为 referred to (a deer) 和 as (a horse)；第 [10] 句的主动词"立［父婢春燕］"和副动词"为［淑妃］"分别译为 nominated (his father's maidservant Chunyan) 和 as (his concubine);第［11］句和第［12］句的主动词"迎［王继勋/王继成］"和副动词"为［刺史］"分别译为 received (Wang Jixun/Wang Jicheng) 和 as (magistrate);第［13］句的主动词"画［江］"和副动词"为［界］"分别译为 took (the Yangtze River) 和 as (the border)。共有2个"为"字译为 with (the title of):第［8］句的主动词"拜［道士谭紫霄］"和副动词"为［正一先生］"分别译为 granted (Tan Zixiao, a Taoist) 和 with (the title of "Sir Right-One");第［9］句的主动词"拜［陈守元］"和副动词"为［天师］"分别译为 granted (Chen Shouyuan) 和 with (the title of "Master of Heaven")。另有1个"为"字译为 into:第［4］句的译文使用介词 into,其主动词"改［元］"和副动词"为［龙启］"分别译为 changed (the designation of the reign) 和 into ("Longqi")。

另外,第［5］句的"谥……为……"直接译为 added to ... the posthumuous title of ... ,其中使用及物动词 added 消解了"为"字结构。

如果副动词"为"前置,则其目的性比较明显。如:

［1］文杰为鐻造槛车 when Wenjie built the prison van at the service of Lin

［2］王仁达为鐻杀延禀有功 since Wang Renda took credit for killing Yanbing at the service of Lin

两句的"为"字都译为 at the service of。

以"自"字为副动词的句读通常关联起始地点或时间,其译文往往会使用 via、since 等介词。如:

［1］自南康入临汀 until they entered the county of Linting via Nankang

［2］自登莱朝贡于梁 paid loyal tribute to the Liang dynasty via Dengzhou and Laizhou

［3］自审知时与延翰不叶 but had been in a bad term with Yanhan ever since Shenzhi's reign

［4］则当自景福元年为始 the time should begin with the first year of the Jinfu period (A. D. 892)

第［1］句的"南康"和第［2］句的"登莱"均为地点名词;两例"自"字均译为 via。第［3］句的"审知时"和第［4］句的"景福元年"均为时间名词:前句的"自"字译为 since (Shenzhi's reign),后句的"自"字译为 (begin) with (the first year of the Jinfu period)。其中,第

［4］句包含"为"字，后接"始"字，二者合译为 begin with。

以"因"字为副动词的句读通常涉及凭借的方式，其译文往往会使用 for 或 by way of 等介词（词组）。如：

［1］多因事杀之 were mostly killed for one or another reason

［2］二人因谋作乱 Yanbing and Yanjun worked out a conspiracy to rebel against Yanhan

［3］因归郎以通陈氏 also colluded with Mrs Chen by way of Brother Gui

［4］继鹏因陈氏以求春燕 Jipeng made a proposal to Chunyan by way of Mrs Chen

［5］因大享军 in a grand banquet which was held to entertain the army

除了第［2］句和第［5］句外，第［1］句的副动词"因［事］"和主动词"杀［之］"分别译为介词 for（one or another reason）和被动结构 were mostly killed；第［3］句的副动词"因［归郎］"和主动词"［以］通［陈氏］"分别译为 by way of（Brother Gui）和 colluded with（Mrs Chen）；第［4］句的副动词"因［陈氏］"和主动词"［以］求［春燕］"分别译为 by way of（Mrs Chen）和 made a proposal to（Chunyan）。其中，第［3］句和第［4］句均有"以"字用以连接两个动宾结构，因而又属连动句读。

另外，第［2］句的主副动词结构"因谋作乱"被转化为不定式结构，其中的"因谋"译为 worked out a conspiracy，而"作乱"译为 to rebel against Yanhan。第［5］句"因大享军"缺少主动词，直接译为介宾结构 in a grand banquet which was held to entertain the army，其中包含 1 个关系分句。

8. 小结

复杂句读在《新五代史·闽世家第八》中的占比达到 34.40%，仅次于简单谓词性句读的比例（37.59%）。在本章中，复杂句读的类型划分不是按照某个动词的及物性特征，而是按其所包含的并列或多重谓语之间的连接逻辑或主次关系。至于复杂句读的及物性分析，可参考普通体词性句读、简单谓词性句读和特殊谓词性句读的方法。

第8章

翻译互文性与译文修订

互文性（intertextuality）是指文本之间在语义上相互关联的特征，其在翻译语境中体现为翻译互文性，可按源语言和译入语两种语言基础区分两种翻译互文性，即基于源语言的翻译互文性和基于译入语的翻译互文性。前者的主体是不同的原文，它们围绕相关的译文形成互文性；后者的主体是不同的译文，它们围绕相关的原文形成互文性。

汉英两种语言的交往历史为汉英翻译提供深厚的互文性基础。当前，包括"四书五经"在内的汉语经典文本普遍存在多重译文，而新的译本依然不断出现。这表明汉英翻译的互文性在程度上依然被不断地加深。新的译本并未取代旧的译本，而是两类译本在功能上相互补充，围绕特定的原文形成一种翻译共生状态。这种翻译生态已经普遍地涉及汉英两种语言及其具体的文本。因此，尽管大量的汉语文本依然缺少英语译本，其在英语中的翻译互文性已经普遍存在。

1. 互文性与翻译互文性

语言中普遍存在以"辞意相连而功能不同"为基本特征的互文性现象，可在宏观、中观、微观三种语境视角下，识别语义、文本、语句三种主体。在宏观的文化语境中，任何一种语义内容都有不同的社会功能，总会因普遍的语境而形成直接或间接的互动。此时，互文性的主体是语义内容本身（王洪涛，2010：6）。在中观的情景语境中，互文性是个体文本相互参照的基本形式，其主体是文本自身。在微观的上下文语境中，互文性是给定文本的内部语句相互照应的体现形式，其主体是文本的内部要素（蒋骁华，1998：21）。例如，《三国演义》主要是在《三国志》的基础上演绎而成的一部长篇历史章回小说，二者因密切关联的叙事线索而维持很强的互文性特征。

汉英两种语言文化的相互交往逐渐促使汉语文本的语内互文性衍化为汉英之间的语际互文性。汉英翻译互文性是语际互文性的主要形式之一。就处于翻译互文关系的任何一组文本来说，只要其中一种文本存在译文，其译文就可为另一种文本的翻译提供参考。总体上，相关文本的翻译程度越深，其翻译互文性就越强，因而它们之间在翻译中的参考作用就越明显。

深谙翻译互文性是译者能力与素养的重要体现。早在 20 世纪 90 年代，国内学者已经开始重视互文性与翻译之间的关系，并认为"处理好翻译中遇到的互文性问题，说到底是译者的文化修养问题"（杨衍松，1994：13）。此类能力和素养的提高自然离不开大量的译文阅读，掌握大量的翻译互文线索。充分吸收并有效利用相关文本的翻译互文线索，不仅能够提高翻译的效率，而且能够确保译文的质量。例如，只要见到以下英语句对：to acquire knowledge and, as you go on acquiring, to put into practice what you have acquired 和 to learn with constant perseverance and application，就可判断它们是围绕汉语原文"学而时习之"而形成的互文性语句。积累类似的翻译知识有利于塑造良好的译者素养。在深谙翻译互文性的译者看来，由于"原型"译文早已存在，所以翻译其实就是在原型译文的基础上重新创作。

翻译互文性在文字上的体现形式就是文本重复，可分完全重复和部分重复两类。完全重复是指文字完全相同，即重复率为 100%。部分重复是指文字部分相同，即重复率处于 0 到 100% 之间。在机器辅助翻译中，重复率就是翻译互文性在技术上的应用形式。该技术以重复的原文为基础来检索原型译文的基本要素。换言之，原型译文是在翻译互文性中提取出来的。本章先分析中国史籍英译的翻译互文性特点，然后以《新五代史》节选片段的英语翻译为例，讨论在翻译创作中如何处理上下文的翻译互文性问题。

2. 中国史籍的翻译互文性

当前，包括"四书五经"在内的汉语典籍已有比较充分的英语翻译，其翻译互文性的程度较高。例如，现有的 60 多种《论语》英语译本为翻译互文性提供了一种坚实的文本基础。相反，中国史籍的英语翻译却还不充分、不完整，而其翻译互文性的程度依然很低。尽管如此，由于汉语文本之间普遍存在的互文关系，包括汉语古典小说英译在内的汉英翻译在更大的语境中强化了中国史籍的翻译互文性。本节分别以《三国志》《三国演义》与《汉书》《史记》两组文本为例，阐述汉英翻译互文性的类型特征。

2.1 《三国志》《三国演义》的翻译互文性

对于具有互文关系的任何两种汉语文本，一方的译文总能为另一方在翻译互文性上提供参考。由于历史典籍《三国志》和历史小说《三国演义》存在推演关系，所以从前者到后者在互文性上的方向明确。然而，二者在翻译互文性上却存在相反的方向。当前，还未见《三国志》的英语全译本，而《三国演义》已有包括 Robert（1994）的译本在内的多种译本，形成一种从后者到前者为方向的翻译互文性。这种文本关系自然引出一个翻译实践问题：文学著作的英语翻译是否能够促进历史典籍的英语翻译？带着这个问题，雷相奎（2017）从语句重复的角度来分析 Robert 的《三国演义》英译本对《三国志》的英语翻译具有的参考价值。其中，语句重复分为基本重复和部分重复两类。基本重复是指在两种文本中文辞基本一致的语句。如：

[1a] 程昱说公曰："观刘备有雄才而甚得众心，终不为人下，不如早图之。"公曰："方今收英雄时也，杀一人而失天下之心，不可。"（陈寿，2005：11）

[2a] 程昱谏曰："刘备终不为人下，不如早图之。"操曰："方今正用英雄之时，不可杀一人而失天下之心。"（罗贯中，2009：91）

前段选自历史典籍《三国志》，以"公"敬称曹操，共有8个句读：第2句"观刘备有雄才而甚得众心"的"有雄才"和"而甚得众心"分别与第6句"方今收英雄时也"的"英雄"和第7句"杀一人而失天下之心"的"天下之心"形成互文关系。后段选自历史小说《三国演义》，直呼曹操的名字，共有6个句读。其中，"有雄才而甚得众心"因有互文语句而被省略。另外，前段的最后两个句读在后段中合二为一，成为复杂句读"不可杀一人而失天下之心"。尽管后段的篇幅短于前段，但是其与省略的语句构成互文关系的其他语句得到保留，所以后段所表达的语义在整体上并未因文辞的省略而受到明显的影响。以下是 Robert（1994：203）对上述《三国演义》语句的译文：

[2b] Cheng Yu advised, "With great talent and the ability to win people's loyalties, Liu Bei will not remain long under anybody. You'd better deal with him before it is too late." "At a time," Cao Cao replied, "when we are calling for outstanding men to serve us, we cannot afford to lose the world to fail to inspire others' loyalties by killing one person."

在后段原文中对部分重复文字的删减只是弱化了后段原文内部的互文

性特征，而对前后两段原文之间的互文关系则影响不大。对于那些在后段原文中删除的字词，在后段译文中依然可以为这些字词找到可供参照的词句。例如，前段"有雄才而甚得众心"的"有雄才"对应后段"英雄"的译文 outstanding men，前段的"得众心"则对应后段"失天下之心"的译文 to lose the world to fail to inspire others' loyalties。因此，尽管前后两段原文存在不对应的文字，后段的译文也能为前段的翻译提供互文性的参考，构成很强的翻译互文性特征。对于此类基本重合的原文语句，现有译文具有很强的参考价值，只要"稍加修改"（雷相奎，2017：21），便可形成特定版本的译文。

当然，毕竟《三国演义》《三国志》分属不同的著作，部分重合才是普遍的互文性形式。尽管如此，前者的译文依然能够为后者的翻译提供遣词造句、逻辑语义、篇章结构等方面的现实参考。我们对《论语》多重译本的研究表明（吴国向，2013），由于翻译目的的不同和文化语境的变迁，即使以前人的译本为参考，后来的译者往往也会避免抄袭。新的译本和旧的译本最终不是构成前后重复的关系，而是在词汇选择、语法使用、语义诠释、话语结构上构成互补关系。

2.2 《汉书》《史记》的翻译互文性

同为"二十四史"的《汉书》《史记》记录了部分相同的历史人物，具有较强的互文性特征。同时，二者均有英语选译本，因而二者之间又存在翻译互文性。本小节以 Watson 的《汉书》译文和 Yang & Yang 的《史记》译文为例，来解释历史典籍之间围绕现有译文而形成的翻译互文性。此类汉英双语的翻译互文性又以汉语单语的互文性为前提。例如，《史记·李将军列传》和《汉书·李广苏建传》分别有如下涉及李广由于迷路而耽误行军的叙述。

[3a] 至莫府，广谓其麾下曰："广结发与匈奴大小七十余战，今幸从大将军出接单于兵，而大将军又徙广部行回远，而又迷失道，岂非天哉！且广年六十余矣，终不能复对刀笔之吏。"（司马迁，1999：2202—2203）

[4a] 至莫府，谓其麾下曰："广结发与匈奴大小七十余战，今幸从大将军出接单于兵，而大将军徙广部行回远，又迷失道，岂非天哉！且广年六十余，终不能复对刀笔之吏矣！"（班固，1999：1866）

上述两段原文基本一致，均包含9个句读，其中的第1、第3、第4和第

7句完全相同。前段的第2句较后段的第2句多1个"广"字，第5句较后段的第5句多1个"又"字，第6句较后段的第6句多1个"而"字，第8句较后段的第8句多1个"矣"字，第9句较后段的第9句少1个"矣"字。前段的汉字总数为68个，后段的汉字总数为65个，前后两段相差3个汉字。除了"广"字外，其余4处涉及的汉字均为虚字，在翻译中其对语义重构的总体影响不大。由于"广"字是句读的主语，即使在原文中省去该主语，在译文中通常也会重新补上，所以同样不会对总体语义造成明显的影响。Yang & Yang（2007）对前段和 Watson（1974）对后段的翻译如下：

[3b] When he reached headquarters he turned to his officers. "Since I was old enough to wear my hair bound up, I have fought more than seventy battles, great and small, against the Huns," he said. "This time I was fortunate enough to set out under Grand Marshal Wei Qing to fight the khan; but the grand marshal transferred me to another post and sent me by a longer route. And then I lost my way. This must be fate. I am over sixty now, too old to face up to the questions of these clerks."（Yang & Yang, 2007: 158-159）

[4b] Then he went in person to headquarters and, when he got there, said to his officers, "Since I was old enough to wear my hair bound up, I have fought over seventy engagements, large and small, with the Hsiung-nu. This time I was fortunate enough to join the general in chief in a campaign against the soldiers of the Shan-yü himself, but he shifted me to another division and sent me riding around by the long way. On top of that, I lost my way. Heaven must have planned it like this! Now I am over sixty—much too old to stand up to a bunch of petty clerks and their list of charges!"（Watson, 1974: 22）

上述译文[3b]对应原文[3a]，译文[4b]对应原文[4a]。现将存在字词差别的原文语句及其译文逐一分析如下：

[3a-1] 至莫府，广谓其麾下曰：……

[3b-1] When he reached headquarters he turned to his officers ... he said.

[4a-1] 至莫府，谓其麾下曰：……

[4b-1] Then he went in person to headquarters and, when he got there, said to his officers, ...

第 8 章　翻译互文性与译文修订

后段原文的第 1 句虽然省略主语 "广"字，但其译文并未受此影响。前后两句的译文均选用相同的代词 he 作为小句的主语。后句的译文补齐了在其原文中省略的主语。

　　［3a-5］而大将军又徙广部行回远
　　［3b-5］but the grand marshal transferred me to another post and sent me by a longer route
　　［4a-5］而大将军徙广部行回远
　　［4b-5］but he shifted me to another division and sent me riding around by the long way

对于前段原文的第 5 句较后段原文的第 5 句多出的 "又"字，在译文［3b-5］中并未出现与之对应的副词。然而，两句译文都有限定词（to）another（post/division）。该词在一定程度上补足了 "又"字的语义。这种译法表明，Watson 与 Yang & Yang 在翻译中都采用了相近的理解。

　　［3a-6］而又迷失道
　　［3b-6］And then I lost my way
　　［4a-6］又迷失道
　　［4b-6］On top of that, I lost my way

前后两句原文在 "而"字上的区别对译文的具体选词产生了影响。前句的 "而"字在译文［3b-6］中直接译为连词 and；后句缺少 "而"字，在其译文［4b-6］中也相应地缺少对应的词项。尽管如此，后句译文的介词短语 on top of that 包含代词 that，能够指向上文的 the long way，这在逻辑上起到承前启后的衔接作用。

　　［3a-8+9］且广年六十余矣，终不能复对刀笔之吏。
　　［3b-8+9］I am over sixty now, too old to face up to the questions of these clerks.
　　［4a-8+9］且广年六十余，终不能复对刀笔之吏矣！
　　［4b-8+9］Now I am over sixty—much too old to stand up to a bunch of petty clerks and their list of charges!

前后两段原文的第 8 句和第 9 句汉字总数相同，只是语气助词 "矣"字从前段的第 8 句末尾移至后段的第 9 句末尾。此处调整对概念意义的影响不大，但对人际意义的影响明显，其中影响集中体现在前后两段原文的第 9 句上。前段第 9 句的译文使用普通的陈述式，而后段第 9 句的译文则使用感叹句。

上述分析显示，前后两段译文的区别并不是由前后两段原文的差别所引起的。虽然前段原文［3a］较后段原文［4a］多出 3 个汉字，但后段译文［4b］较前段译文［3b］多出 19 个单词。前段译文［3b］的单词总数为 95 个，后段译文［4b］的单词总数为 114 个。这说明，Watson 的译文较 Yang & Yang 的译文在词汇的使用上富余不少。在缺少多重译文可供选择的条件下，此类处于互文关系的译文选段可用以比较不同译者的翻译风格。

我们在翻译教学和研究中发现，充分理解和有效利用翻译互文性，不仅能够提高翻译的效率，而且能够获得具有某种词汇语法特征的译文。例如，在比较 Watson 的《汉书》译文选段和 Yang & Yang 的《史记》译文选段的基础上，黄燕婷（2017）以前者为参照译文，以《新五代史·汉家人传第六》为习作原文，在翻译中使习作译文在词汇和语法特征上尽量向参照译文靠近。

2.3　翻译互文性的模式类型

翻译互文性的主体语境可分为源语言和译入语两类。在源语言中，不同的原文围绕特定的译文形成翻译互文关系。例如，由于《三国演义》和《三国志》存在较强的互文关系，所以前者与后者围绕前者的译文形成翻译互文关系。在译入语中，不同的译文围绕特定的原文形成互文关系。例如，《论语》现有包括 Pound（1950/1969）的译本、Legge（1893/1971）的译本、Waley（1938）的译本和 Ku（1898）的译本等 60 多种译本。多重译本之间围绕《论语》原文形成翻译互文关系。基于源语言的翻译互文性和基于译入语的翻译互文性可能同时存在。例如，由于《汉书》与《史记》之间存在很强的互文关系，二者的译文之间自然存在基于译入语的翻译互文性；同理，《汉书》与《史记》又因二者的译文而形成基于源语言的翻译互文性。翻译互文性的模式类型如图 8-1 所示。

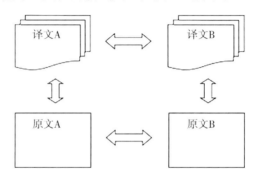

图 8-1　翻译互文性的模式类型示意图

从源语言的角度来看，处于互文关系的原文 A 和原文 B 不仅会因二者的译文（译文 A 和译文 B）而形成翻译互文性，而且会因任何一方的译文（译文 A 或译文 B）而形成翻译互文性。从译入语的角度来看，译文 A 和译文 B 会因二者的原文（原文 A 和原文 B）之间存在的互文性而形成翻译互文性。在原文 A 和原文 B 为同一文本的条件下，译文 A 和译文 B 形成双重译文。双重译文和多重译文之间围绕相同的原文形成翻译互文性。经典文本普遍存在多重翻译，因而翻译互文性程度较深。相对来说，中国史籍的翻译互文性尚浅，因而需要在汉英翻译的宏观语境中寻找各类线索，以加强其翻译互文性特征。

上文提到的翻译互文性都是文本之间的关系。对于翻译互文性很低的文本，只能在其翻译中不断地创造出各种翻译互文性的关联。此时往往需要从文本内部的语句片段入手。例如，同一文本的前后语段之间时常存在互文关系，前段的译文为后段的翻译提供翻译互文性的参考。这样，在文本的翻译过程中翻译互文性的网络被逐渐地搭建起来，而不同的语段会围绕相同的译文形成文本内部的翻译互文性。

3. 翻译互文性的应用

本节分别从概念功能、人际功能、语篇功能（Halliday，1994/2000）三种互补的语句分析视角出发，以《新五代史·闽世家第八》的篇内互文语段为例，阐明中国史籍英译的互文性及其在实践中的应用。

3.1 翻译互文性与概念功能

文本内部的语段之间在概念功能上存在的互文关系称为翻译的概念互文性，通常涉及事件相同而叙述不同的情形。对于相同的事件，不同的叙述形成不同的语段，而不同的语段又围绕相同的事件形成互文关系。如：

[5a] 二人因谋作乱，十二月，延禀延钧皆以兵入，执延翰杀之，而延钧立，更名鏻。

[6a] 初，延禀与鏻之谋杀延翰也，延禀之兵先至，已执延翰而杀之，明日鏻兵始至，延禀自以养子，推鏻而立之。

前后两段虽然讲述相同的事件，但采取了不同的叙事角度。前段的叙事角度突出延钧（即鏻，下同）与延翰之间的关系：从事件的结果来看，在延禀和延钧同谋作乱并杀死延翰后，延钧取代延禀。后段的叙事角度突出延禀与鏻（即延钧，下同）之间的关系：从事件的经过来看，延禀杀死延翰之后，鏻才带兵前来。显然，两种叙事在概念功能上的重点有所不同。前段原文的翻译如下：

[5b] Therefore, they conspired with one another to revolt against their elder brother Yanhan. In December (January, A. D. 927), Yanbing and Yanjun invaded with their own forces. Yanhan was captured and then killed. Soon afterwards, Yanjun came to the throne and renamed himself as Lin.

在此段译文的基础上，后段原文与前段原文之间形成翻译互文性。现逐句分析与比较两段原文，同时以前段译文为参照来翻译后段原文。前段原文的第1句、第2句和第3句大体上对应后段原文的第1句和第2句。

[5a-1+2+3] 二人因谋作乱，十二月，延禀延钧皆以兵入

[5b-1+2+3] Therefore, they conspired with one another to revolt against their elder brother Yanhan. In December (January, A. D. 927), Yanbing and Yanjun invaded with their own forces

[6a-1+2] 初，延禀与镠之谋杀延翰也

[6b-1+2] Four years before, when Yanbing conspired with this younger brother Lin to murder their elder brother Yanhan

前段译文的要素确立了后段原文的翻译基调。除了前段译文 [5b-1+2+3] 的 Yanhan 和 Yanjun 等专有名词之外，包括 conspire 在内的动词及相关的其他词语均可直接用于后段原文的翻译，形成的后段译文为 [6b-1+2]。另外，由于前段讲述的事件发生在公元926年年底至公元927年年初，而后段是在大约4年后（即公元931年）重提前段所讲述的事件，所以把后段原文的"初"字直接译为 four years before，进一步明确了具体的时间关系。

[5a-4] 执延翰杀之

[5b-4] Yanhan was captured and then killed

[6a-3+4+5] 延禀之兵先至，已执延翰而杀之，明日镠兵始至

[6b-3+4+5] Yanbing led his soldiers arrived first, and not until the next day after they had captured and then killed Yanhan did Lin arrive with his soldiers

前段原文的第4句大体上对应后段原文的第3句、第4句和第5句。后段详细地解释前段所述的事件，明确谁的兵先到，谁的兵后到，是谁执

杀延翰。前段译文的 capture 和 kill 等词语均可直接用于后段原文的翻译，形成的后段译文为 [6b-3+4+5]。

　　[5a-5+6] 而延钧立，更名鏻。

　　[5b-5+6] Soon afterwards, Yanjun came to the throne and renamed himself as Lin.

　　[6a-6+7] 延禀自以养子，推鏻而立之。

　　[6b-6+7] Yanbing regarded himself as an adopted son, so he recommended Lin to come to the throne.

前段原文的第 5 句和第 6 句大体上对应后段原文的第 6 句和第 7 句。后段原文解释鏻的年纪虽小但继位的原因是：延禀虽为长兄，但实为养子。后段译文的 to come to the throne 呼应前段译文的 came to the throne。现将完整的后段译文整理如下：

　　[6b] Four years before, when Yanbing conspired with this younger brother Lin to murder their elder brother Yanhan, Yanbing led his soldiers to arrive first, and not until the next day after they had captured and then killed Yanhan did Lin arrive with his soldiers. Yanbing regarded himself as an adopted son, so he recommended Lin to come to the throne.

上述两段原文的互文性体现为叙述视角的互补关系，即两种不同的叙述视角获得两种互补的故事版本。语段之间的互文性还体现为总分关系。如：

　　[7a] 长兴二年，延禀率兵击鏻，攻其西门，使其子继雄转海攻其南门，鏻遣王仁达拒之。仁达伏甲舟中，伪立白帜请降，继雄信之，登舟，伏兵发，刺杀之，枭其首西门，其兵见之皆溃去，延禀见执……遂杀之。

　　[8a] 龙启三年，改元永和。王仁达为鏻杀延禀有功，而典亲兵……

前段原文详细地描述战争的过程及王仁达对打胜仗起到的决定性作用。后段原文的第 3 句则是对前段原文的总述。前段原文的翻译如下：

　　[7b] In the second year of the Changxing period (A.D. 931), Yanbing commanded his troops to assault Lin. He himself launched an attack at the west gate and sent his son Jixiong simultaneously to make

another attack by seaway. Lin dispatched Wang Renda to resist the attack launched by Jixiong. Renda designed a trap in which he first concealed soldiers in his boat and then held up a white flag, making a false plea for surrender. Jixiong was so gullible that he was tricked into the trap. He embarked onto the boat only to be ambushed and killed by Renda's soldiers. His head was transferred and hung over the west gate. On seeing this, the soldiers of Yanbing all fled away and Yanbing was then captured ... and he was killed soon afterwards.

前段译文为后段原文的翻译提供详尽的铺垫。只要精简包括 Wang Renda、Lin 和 Yanbing 在内的人物关系及相关的事件，就可获得以下译文：

[8b] In the third year of the Longqi period (A. D. 935), the designation of the reign was changed into Yonghe. Wang Renda took credit at the service of Lin for having killed Yanbing four years before, so he had been in charge of the loyal bodyguards.

在前后两段译文的形成过程中，其在概念功能上的翻译互文性逐渐加强。一方面，前段译文可直接用以确立后段原文的翻译基调；另一方面，在后段译文的形成过程中，前段译文能够得到重新检视，并且按检视的结果得到进一步的修订与完善。

翻译互文性是在双语语境中文本之间存在的一种双向关系。充分利用已有的译文所建立起来的翻译互文基础，既有利于理解处于互文关系的原文，又有利于提高翻译的效率，从而确保译文的质量。

3.2 翻译互文性与人际功能

译文内部的语段之间在人际功能上存在的互文关系称为翻译的人际互文性，涉及对话各方的视角和关系。不同的人际视角往往传达不同的语义。如：

[9a] 延禀还建州，鏻饯于郊，延禀临诀谓鏻曰："善继先志，毋烦老兄复来！"鏻衔之。

[10a] 长兴二年，延禀率兵击鏻……延禀见执。鏻诮之曰："予不能继先志，果烦老兄复来！"延禀不能对，遂杀之。

前段的"善继先志，毋烦老兄复来"是由兄长延禀亲口对其兄弟鏻所讲的话，以"老兄"指代自己；后段的"予不能继先志，果烦老兄复来"是由鏻对延禀所讲的话，以"老兄"指代对方。在后段中，鏻引用延禀的话讥讽后者，让后者无言以对。这使前后两段产生了很强的互文性效果。对于前后两段都有的"志"字，可以在 Legge 的《论语》译文中找到翻译互文性的线索。

[11a] 子曰："父在观其志，父没观其行，三年无改于父之道，可谓孝矣。"

[11b] The Master said, "While a man's father is alive, look at the bent of his will; when his father is dead, look at his conduct. If for three years he does not alter from the way of his father, he may be called filial." (Legge, 1983/1971)

该节原文讲叙的是，只要一个人"志于父之道、行于父之道"就可称其为"孝"。虽然原文的"志"字不是其父的遗志，但 Legge 还是选用了跟"遗志"直接相关的单词 will。这跟如下另一节的"志"字有所不同。

[12a] 颜渊、季路侍。子曰："盍各言尔志？"

[12b] Yen Yüan and Chî Lû being by his side, the Master said to them, "Come, let each of you tell his wishes." (Legge, 1983/1971)

这里的"志"字指个人的志向，跟遗志无关，因而 Legge 选用了跟"愿望"相关的 wishes。显然，"善继先志"的"志"字指先父的遗志，可直接选用单词 will。现把[9a]翻译如下：

[9b] Yanbing was now returning to Jianzhou and Lin saw him off in the suburbs. At their departure, Yanbing instructed Lin in a superior tone, referring himself as the elder brother, and said, "Uphold the will of our forefather and never bother me to come over again!" Lin had borne this in mind ever since.

其中，对应"老兄"的地方使用代词 me："老兄"的翻译 the elder brother 没有在引语中出现，而是在引语外转化为一个由介词短语和非限定小句所构成的组合，即 in a superior tone, referring himself as the elder brother。显然，在原文中人际语义的直接表达在译文中转化为概念语义的间接描写，人际功能变成概念功能。尽管如此，前段译文[9b]对后段原文[10a]的翻译提供坚实的基础。后段原文的翻译如下：

[10b] In the second year of the Changxing period (A.D. 931), Yanbing commanded his troops to assault Lin … Lin mocked Yanbing

in a subordinate tone, referring himself as the younger brother, and said, "I fail to uphold the will of our forefather and ever do bother my elder brother to come over again!" Yanbing could reply nothing and he was killed soon afterwards.

其中,"老兄"的翻译 my elder brother 很自然地嵌入引语里,形成强烈的讥讽效果。前段原文的铺垫最终也是为了在后段原文中形成讥讽效果。尽管前段译文无法提供直接的人际铺垫,由人际表达转化而来的概念描写却实际上充当后段译文的铺垫,进而在后段译文的引语中产生与其原文等同的讥讽效果。此外,在译文的引语外同样使用 in a subordinate tone, referring himself as the younger brother 来回应前段译文中的 in a superior tone, referring himself as the elder brother。

显然,由于人际功能在汉英两种语言中存在不同的表达形式,所以中国史籍英译既要注意人际功能的直接翻译,又要注意其转化为包括概念功能在内的其他功能形式。

3.3 翻译互文性与语篇功能

译文内部的语段之间在语篇功能上存在的互文关系称为翻译的语篇互文性,主要涉及主位和述位之间的逻辑结构。不同的逻辑结构往往传递不同的语篇意义。如:

[13a] 王仁达……而典亲兵,鏻心忌之,尝问仁达曰:"赵高指鹿为马,以愚二世,果有之邪?"

[14a] "秦二世愚,故高指鹿为马,非高能愚二世也。今陛下聪明,朝廷官不满百,起居动静,陛下皆知之,敢有作威福者,族灭之而已。"鏻惭,赐与金帛慰安之。退而谓人曰:"仁达智略,在吾世可用,不可遗后世患。"卒诬以罪杀之。

前段的语句"赵高指鹿为马,以愚二世,果有之邪"和后段的语句"秦二世愚,故高指鹿为马,非高能愚二世也"具有不同的逻辑结构。前后两段的因果关系相反,得到正反两种不同的结论。值得注意的是,此处的语篇互文性是以概念互文性为基础的:前后两段均有"指鹿为马"的事件描述。

此外,"秦二世、二世、吾世、后世"等名词及"愚、能愚、聪明、智略"等形容词构成的语篇线索,使前后两段在翻译互文性上的关系更加紧密。前段原文的翻译如下:

[13b] ... Wang Renda ... so he had been in charge of the loyal

bodyguards. Lin had scruple over this, so he turned to Renda on one occasion, making an inquiry about the second emperor of the Qin dynasty and Zhao Gao, the prime minister of the dynasty. "Is it truly the case," he asked, "that Zhao Gao referred to a deer as a horse in order to fool the Second Generation of Qin?"

就一般的语法规则来看，由于汉语习惯先摆事实而后加评论，英语习惯先置评论而后摆事实，所以原文和译文在事实和评论的顺序上正好相反：评论句读"果有之邪"在原文中处于句末，与该句对应的译文 is it truely the case 在译文中则置于句首。另外，类似在本章第3.2小节中对称呼的解释，前段译文在引语外分别对"赵高"和"秦二世"做了相应的解释。现将后段原文翻译如下：

[14b] "The Second Generation of Qin was a fool," Renda replied, "so Gao referred to a deer as a horse. It is not the case that Gao could make a fool of the Second Generation. Now, Your Majesty is wise, and the number of court officials is no more than one hundred, of whose daily life and behaviours Your Majesty is kept well informed. If any one dares to abuse his power, it is simple to extinguish his entire clan." Lin felt so ashamed that he granted money and silks as a comfort to Renda. After he retreated to his trusted followers, however, he warned them to guard against Renda. "Renda is so intelligent," he said, "that he can be used in my generation, but cannot be left over as a danger for the coming generation." Soon afterwards, Renda was killed on a false accusation of crime.

前后两句的因果关系对调，论据和论点重新组织，最终获得完全不同的结论。另外，the Second Generation of Qin、the Second Generation、in my generation、the coming generation 等名词词组及 was a fool、can make a fool of、wise、intelligent 等结构或词语为前后两段译文的互文性提供词汇基础。

综上所述，在中国史籍英译中处理好概念、人际和语篇互文性，有利于提高翻译效率，确保译文质量。

4. 翻译互文性的语法实现形式

结构分化是翻译互文性在语法上的主要实现形式。翻译互文性既不是完全相同的语义内容，也不是完全重复的文本形式，而是相关的语义内容在不同的语境中形成相同的、相近的、不同的或相反的功能形态，因而在语法上也存在相同的、相近的、不同的或相反的实现形式。例如，《论语》中的短语"喟然叹曰"存在以下多重译文：

  Lau："heaving a sigh, said"（限定动词+分词动词-名词词组）

  Ku："speaking in admiration［…］, remarked"（限定动词+分词动词+介词短语）

  Ware："heaved a long sigh and said"（限定动词+限定动词-名词词组-形容词词组）

  Waley："sighed heavily and said"（限定动词+限定动词-副词词组）

  Legge："in admiration［…］, sighed and said"（限定动词+限定动词+介词短语）

  Pound/Xu："said with a deep sigh"（限定动词+介词短语-形容词词组）

  Collie："in admiration［…］exclaimed"（限定动词+介词短语）

  上述多重译文在语法结构上存在明显的分化现象：译文L（Lau）和K（Ku）均使用1个限定动词（said及remarked）和1个非限定动词（heaving a sigh及speaking in admiration）的组合，得到heaving a sigh, said和speaking in admiration［…］, remarked；译文Wr（Ware）、Wl（Waley）和Lg（Legge）均使用2个限定动词，得到heaved a long sigh and said，sighed heavily and said，in admiration［…］, sighed and said；译文Pd（Pound）／X（Xu）和Cl（Collie）使用1个限定动词，得到said with a deep sigh和in admiration［…］exclaimed。此外，各种译文在细节上的区别包括是否附加名词（如sigh）、介词短语（如in admiration）、形容词（如long）或副词（如heavily）等短语。

  显然，基于译入语的翻译互文性最终通过不同的语法结构体现出来，在限定小句（如heaved a long sigh）与非限定小句（如heaving a sigh）、非限定小句（如speaking in admiration）与介词短语（如with a deep sigh）、复合动词词组（如sighed and said）与简单动词（如exclaimed）等结构关系之间形成互文性。结构分化直接影响译文的词字比和译文的语法难度：前者是指翻译单位原文汉字所需的平均译文单词数量，将在第9章讨论；后者是指翻译单位原文语句所需的平均译文小句数量，将在第10章讨论。

  结构分化使翻译互文性显得更加错综复杂。例如，实现概念功能可用不同的及物性结构，实现人际功能可用不同的语气结构，实现语篇功能可用不同的主位结构。深入认识翻译互文性的结构分化形式，有助于塑造双语语法的知识结构体系。

5. 小结

翻译互文性可分基于源语言的和基于译入语的两种类型。基于源语言的翻译互文性主要体现为原文重复。在翻译实践中，充分利用文本的重复率能够直接提高翻译效率并保证翻译质量。基于译入语的翻译互文性主要体现为多重译文，其在语法上形成相同的、相近的、不同的或相反的各种互补结构。在英语教学和汉英翻译教学中，此类多重表达的翻译知识有利于提炼翻译实务技巧和提升语言表达能力，以及提高英语写作水平。

功能的视角有助于理顺翻译互文性的线索，充分发挥其在翻译实践与教学中的作用。翻译互文性以"辞意相连而功能不同"为其基本特征，因而翻译的任务既包括辞意的转换，又包括功能的转换。就概念、人际和语篇三种功能维度来说，语际之间在概念功能上的对等往往较人际功能对等或语篇功能对等容易实现。这种现状既表明概念功能对等的基础性，又反衬人际功能对等和语篇功能对等的重要性，使后两种对等在翻译实践中优先取得更高的权值。当然，尽管概念功能对等在权值上低于人际功能对等或语篇功能对等，但是翻译必须以概念功能对等为前提。在中国史籍英译中，通常需要使用具有基础对等权值的概念功能来转换具有较高对等权值的人际功能或语篇功能。概念功能的转换往往在译文中产生大量的解释性语句，用以补偿在人际功能对等或语篇功能对等上的不足。

第 9 章

词字比与译文修订

在汉英互译中，译文的字词数量与原文的字词数量之间的比值称为"字词比"，可分为汉译英的词字比（RWC）和英译汉的字词比（RCW）两种不同的情形：前者是指翻译单位汉字平均使用的英语单词数量；后者是指翻译单位英语单词平均使用的汉字数量。对于相同的或同类的原文，不同的译文往往具有不同的字词比。字词比能够直观地反映原文和译文之间在字词数量上的关系，因而适用于多重译文的分析和比较。

习作译文和参照译文在词字比上的差值可用来指导译文修订。给定合适的参照译文，词字比既可直接反映习作译文的当前状态，又可迅速呈现习作译文与参照译文之间的差距。该值明确了进一步修订习作译文的方向，有利于提高译文质量。本章以词字比的差值为指标，以 Watson 的《汉书》译文为参照，以欧阳修的《新五代史》为习作原文，为中国史籍英译提供一种行之有效的译文修订程式。

1. 汉字和单词的比例关系

字词比值是指译文的字词数量与原文的字词数量之间存在的字词比例的具体数值。对于给定的原文，不同的译文通常具有长短不一的篇幅，其所包含的字词数量也就各不相同。译文篇幅越长，字词数量越多，其字词比值就越大；相反，译文篇幅越短，字词数量越少，其字词比值就较小。汉英互译的字词比按实际的翻译方向可分为汉译英的词字比和英译汉的字词比。词字比（the ratio of words to characters，RWC）是指翻译单位汉字平均使用的英语单词数量，即单词对汉字的比例。字词比（the ratio of characters to words，RCW）是指翻译单位英语单词平均使用的汉字数量，即汉字对单词的比例。在不做方向性的区分时二者可统称为字词比。

20 世纪 60 年代以前，语言学视角的翻译研究普遍使用"对等"

(equivalence; Catford, 1965) 这一定性概念, 借以分析译文与原文之间在单词、词组或短语、小句等语法级阶上的多维对等关系 (Halliday, 1966/2007)。现有的英汉翻译研究与实践较少以字词比为指标来呈现译文特点或评价译文质量。这是因为现有的证据不足以说明汉英两种语言之间在翻译上存在某种固定的字词比。例如, 在汉语文言的英语翻译中, 词字比可能高于 1.6, 即翻译单位汉字平均可能需要 1.6 个多英语单词; 相反, 在现代汉语的英语翻译中, 词字比可能只有 0.8, 即翻译单位汉字平均可能只需 0.8 个英语单词。对于同类原文, 各类译文在字词比上都存在较大的差别。更甚的是, 同一译文的不同片段都有不同的词字比。显然, 字词比是一种动态的概念, 其实际数值具有较大的波动, 因而在翻译实践与教学中存在操作困难。词字比的应用首先需要解决此类实际问题。

我们的翻译实践、教学与研究表明, 在汉语文言的英语翻译中, 词字比既可评价译文的词汇特征, 又可为翻译的遣词造句提供策略性的方案, 特别是在习作译文的修订中具有很强的实效性。

2. 词字比与字词比

汉英互译的字词比值因存在汉译英和英译汉两种语言转换方向而区分为词字比和字词比两种形式。词字比是在汉译英中英语单词数量和汉字数量的比值。字词比是在英译汉中汉字数量和英语单词数量的比值。在汉译英中, 汉字数量是常量, 英语单词数量是变量, 因而需要考察词字比。相反, 在英译汉中, 英语单词数量是常量, 汉字数量是变量, 因而需要考察字词比。

2.1 汉语文言英译的词字比

在汉译英中, 词字比反映英语单词与汉字之间在数量上的对等关系。汉语典籍的多重英译表明, 词字比具有明显的波动性特征。例如,《论语·学而第一》全篇包含 493 个汉字, 而 Ku (1898)、Waley (1938)、Legge (1893/1971) 和 Pound (1950/1969) 分别翻译的四种英语译文所使用的英语单词数量分别为 1 009 个、924 个、881 个和 635 个 (表 9-1)。

表 9-1 四种《论语·学而第一》英语译文的词字比对照表

序号	译者	汉字数量/个	英语单词数量/个	词字比
1	Ku	493	1 009	2.05
2	Waley	493	924	1.87

续表

序号	译者	汉字数量/个	英语单词数量/个	词字比
3	Legge	493	881	1.79
4	Pound	493	635	1.29

四种词字比的区别显著：Ku 的译文的词字比是 2.05，表明翻译单位汉字平均使用 2.05 个英语单词；Waley 的译文的词字比是 1.87，表明翻译单位汉字平均使用 1.87 个单词；Legge 的译文的词字比是 1.79，表明翻译单位汉字平均使用 1.79 个单词；Pound 的译文的词字比是 1.29，表明翻译单位汉字平均使用 1.29 个单词。显然，Ku 的译文最耗词，Pound 的译文最省字，二者分处词字比渐变体的两端。包括 Waley 的译文和 Legge 的译文在内的其余译文则处于 Ku 的译文和 Pound 的译文之间。现以该篇 Waley 的译文第 1 节为例比较四种译文在字词使用上的区别性特征。

[1a] 子曰：学而时习之，不亦说乎？有朋自远方来，不亦乐乎？人不知而不愠，不亦君子乎？

[1b] It is indeed a pleasure to acquire knowledge and, as you go on acquiring, to put into practice what you have acquired. A greater pleasure still it is when friends of congenial minds come from afar to seek you because of your attainments. But he is truly a wise and good man who feels no discomposure even when he is not noticed of men. (Ku, 1898)

该节共有 32 个汉字。上述译文 K 使用 64 个单词，其词字比计算如下：$RWC_{1b} = 64/32 = 2.00$。该值略低于全篇的词字比 2.05。以下是 Pound 的译文：

[1c] Study with the seasons winging past, is not this pleasant? To have friends coming in from far quarters, not a delight? Unruffled by men's ignoring him, also indicative of high breed. (Pound, 1893/1971)

此译文使用 31 个单词，其词字比计算如下：$RWC_{1c} = 31/32 \approx 0.97$。该值明显低于全篇的词字比 1.29。以下是 Waley 和 Legge 的译文：

[1d] The Master said, "To learn and at due times to repeat what one has learnt, is that not after all a pleasure? That friends should come to one from afar, is this not after all delightful? To remain

unsoured even though one's merits are unrecognised by others, is that not after all what is expected of a gentleman?"(Waley, 1938)

[1e] The Master said, "Is it not pleasant to learn with a constant perseverance and application? Is it not delightful to have friends coming from distant quarters? Is he not a man of complete virtue, who feels no discomposure though men may take no note of him?"(Legge, 1893/1971)

Waley 的译文使用 58 个单词，其词字比计算如下：$RWC_{1d} = 58/32 \approx 1.81$；Legge 的译文使用 46 个单词，其词字比计算如下：$RWC_{1e} = 46/32 \approx 1.44$。两节译文的词字比均小于全篇的词字比。显然，在相同的译文中不同的片段之间在词字比上存在明显的波动性特征。在汉语文言英译中，词字比总体上大于 1。

2.2 现代英语汉译与字词比

在英译汉中，字词比反映汉字与英语单词在数量上的对等关系。现代英语的多重汉译表明，字词比具有明显的波动性特征。例如，F. 培根的《新工具》有以下语句：

[2a] For men converse by means of language, but words are formed at the will of the generality, and there arises from a bad and unapt formation of words a wonderful obstruction to the mind.

该句语法古典，用词经济，共有 3 个分句、34 个单词。现有多种《新工具》的汉语译文，其中两种对上述语句的翻译如下：

[2b] 人们的交流是通过谈话来实现的，用的则是约定俗成的文字，而用词不当往往会妨碍理解。（培根，2008：17）

[2c] 人们是靠言语沟通联系的而所利用的文字则是依照一般俗人的了解。因此，选用文字之失当害意就惊人地阻碍着理解力。（培根，2008：136）

译文 [2b] 包含 37 个汉字，其字词比计算如下：$RCW_{2b} = 37/34 \approx 1.09$。译文 [2c] 包含 50 个汉字，其字词比计算如下：$RCW_{2c} = 50/34 \approx 1.47$。前者翻译单位英语单词平均使用约 1.09 个汉字，后者翻译单位英语单词平均使用约 1.47 个汉字。二者的词字比差为 0.38。在现代英语汉译中，字词比总体上大于 1。

2.3 现代汉语英译与词字比

现代汉语英译和汉语文言英译在词字比上存在较大的区别。本章第2.1节提到，汉语文言英译的词字比普遍大于1。相反，现代汉语英译的词字比则普遍小于1。在一定程度上，词字比的区别反映了现代汉语和汉语文言在词汇上的区别。以下［3a］是现代汉语原文，［3b］是其现代英语译文。

> ［3a］认知的本质是利用知识来指导当前的注意和行为，它涉及信息的获取、表征并转化为知识，知识的记忆（存贮和提取）和调用知识进行推理等心理过程。对于语言理解来说，认知过程的主要环节是语义的提取和利用知识进行语义推导。在本文中，我们尝试用扩散激活的语义记忆模型和缺省推理的非单调逻辑机制，来分析与一价名词相关的若干句式，借以展示语言的认知研究的一种新的途径。（袁毓林，1994：241）

> ［3b］The nature of cognition is the use of knowledge to guide one's attention and behaviour as a whole. There are various features involved in this, including: mental processes in terms of acquisition, representation and transformation of information into knowledge, knowledge memorisation (i.e., storage and retrieval), and the utilisation of knowledge for purposive reasoning. As far as natural language understanding is concerned, the major events during a cognitive process are semantic extraction and semantic inference through the use of knowledge. This chapter adopts a semantic memory model, i.e., spreading-activation theory, and a non-monotonic logic mechanism, or reasoning by default. A set of sentence patterns related to mono-valent nouns are analyzed, with the view to demonstrating a novel approach to cognitive studies on language. (Yuan & Wu, 2017: 38)

汉语原文［3a］包含161个汉字，英语译文［3b］包含122个单词，其词字比计算如下：$RWC_{3b} = 122/161 \approx 0.76$。现代汉语英译的总体词字比小于1，明显低于汉语文言英译的总体词字比。词字比因翻译语境不同而形成的波动性特征直接影响其在翻译实践中的应用。字词比的应用首先需要解决参照译文的选择问题。

3. 词字比在译文分析中的应用

词字比可用以分析习作译文，反映习作译文与参照译文之间在词汇数量上的差距。本节以词字比为切面在 Watson 的《汉书》节选译文的参照框架中分析一段《新五代史》的习作译文。一方面，欧阳修的《新五代史》和班固的《汉书》均为"二十四史"之一，二者保持大体一致的文辞风格；另一方面，Watson 的《汉书》译文具有较强的代表性，适合充当参照译文。另外，Watson 本人深入探索中国的文史哲，大量翻译汉语典籍，在翻译理论与实践上的积累丰硕。

3.1 习作原文及其译文

习作原文选自欧阳修的《新五代史·闽世家第八》。该篇包含 4 095 个汉字，721 个句读，其汉字密度约为 5.68，即单位句读平均包含 5.68 个汉字。习作原文叙述延翰建国称王、为人不孝，崔氏性陋、暴虐无度等具体事项。其原文如下：

> 审知同光三年卒，年六十四，谥曰忠懿。子延翰立。
>
> 延翰字子逸，审知长子也。同光四年，唐拜延翰节度使。是岁，庄宗遇弑，中国多故，延翰乃取司马迁《史记》闽越王无诸传示其将吏曰："闽，自古王国也，吾今不王，何待之有？"于是军府将吏上书劝进。十月，延翰建国称王，而犹禀唐正朔。
>
> 延翰为人长大，美皙如玉，其妻崔氏陋而淫，延翰不能制。审知丧未期，彻其几筵，又多选良家子为妾。崔氏性妒，良家子之美者，辄幽之别室，系以大械，刻木为人手以击颊，又以铁锥刺之，一岁中死者八十四人。崔氏后病，见以为祟而卒。

该文包含 199 个汉字，36 个句读，其汉字密度约为 5.53。该值略低于《新五代史·闽世家第八》的总体汉字密度。现将该文翻译如下：

> Shenzhi passed away in the third year of the Tongguang period (A. D. 925) when he was sixty-four years old and was honoured with the posthumous title of Zhongyi, i. e., the Loyal and Virtuous. His son Yanhan succeeded to the throne.
>
> Yanhan, with the courtesy name of Ziyi, was the eldest son of Shenzhi. In the fourth year of the Tongguang period (A. D. 926), the Tang dynastic court appointed Yanhan as provincial governor. In the same year, Emperor Zhuangzong was murdered, from which China

suffered very much. Yanhan then took out the *Historical Records* of Sima Qian and showed the "Biography of Wuzhu the King" to his generals and officials, declaring, "Min has been a kingdom since ancient times. If I do not claim the kingship now, what should I wait for?"

So the generals and officials in the military administration submitted written statements, advising him to proceed. In October, Yanhan founded the kingdom and claimed the kingship, though still observing the calendar of the Tang dynasty.

Yanhan had a tall and large figure, as beautiful and fair as a jade. His wife Madame Cui was ugly and dissolute, which Yanhan was not able to restrict. Before the mourning period for Shenzhi came to an end, Yanhan removed the sacrificial offerings, and once again selected girls of good breeding to be his concubines. Madame Cui was jealous-tempered. Those well-bred girls who were beautiful tended to be imprisoned in a special room, fastened to a punishment device, hit in the face with a hand-like bat carved out of wood, and then stabbed with an iron spike. Within one single year 84 of them were killed. Madame Cui later got sick and dead of being reported to have seen their ghosts.

习作译文包含289个英语单词，对应199个汉字，其词字比约为1.45，即翻译单位汉字平均使用约1.45个英语单词。习作译文的词字比自然引出两个相关的问题。

第一，词字比为1.45是否充分？在本章第2.1小节中，具有最大和最小的词字比值的《论语·学而第一》两种译文确立一种粗略的词字比区间[1.29-2.05]。习作译文的词字比值1.45处于该区间的较低位置。显然，该区间只能说明习作译文的词字比合理，无法说明其是否充分。

第二，词字比1.45是否标准？词字比所具有的波动性特征体现译文灵活多变。至今为止，翻译实践在词字比上还缺少可供参照的翔实数据。就第2.1小节提到的2.05、1.87、1.79和1.29四种词字比值来说，是要以最大的2.05为参照呢，还是要以最小的1.29为参照？或是要以中间数值为参照？即使要以中间数值为标准，也存在大小不等的数值选项：是要以较大的1.87为标准呢，还是要以较小的1.79为标准？如此种种，根本无法明确某种"标准"的词字比。词字比的较大波幅使其在实际应用中存在难以操作的问题。尽管如此，只要按实际的翻译需要为具体的原文选定某种合适的波动区间，那么词字比依然不失为一种行之有效的译文指标。

3.2 参照原文和参照译文

参照译文的词字比主要用以指导习作译文的修订。具体操作是，先取得习作译文之于参照译文在词字比上的差距，然后通过缩小词字比差以修订译文。本章所选的如下参照原文来自班固的《汉书·李广苏建传》，涉及李广不得侯爵的叙述：

> 初，广与从弟李蔡俱为郎，事文帝。景帝时，蔡积功至二千石。武帝元朔中，为轻车将军，从大将军击右贤王，有功中率，封为乐安侯。元狩二年，代公孙弘为丞相。蔡为人在下中，名声出广下远甚，然广不得爵邑，官不过九卿。广之军吏及士卒或取封侯。
>
> 广与望气王朔语云："自汉击匈奴，广未尝不在其中，而诸妄校尉已下，材能不及中，以军功取侯者数十人。广不为后人，然终无尺寸功以得封邑者，何也？岂吾相不当侯邪？"朔曰："将军自念，岂尝有恨者乎？"广曰："吾为陇西守，羌尝反，吾诱降者八百余人，诈而同日杀之，至今恨独此耳。"朔曰："祸莫大于杀已降，此乃将军所以不得侯者也。"

参照原文包含 224 个汉字，39 个句读，其汉字密度约为 5.74。该值略高于习作译文的汉字密度 5.53。相近的汉字密度表明，参照原文在字词特征上接近习作原文，适合用作参照基础。Watson 的《汉书》译本对上述参照原文的英译如下：

> Li Kuang and his cousin Li Ts'ai had begun their careers as attendants at the court of Emperor Wen. During the reign of Emperor Ching, Li Ts'ai managed to accumulate sufficient merit to advance to the position of a two thousand picul official. During the *yüan-so* era of Emperor Wu's reign, he was appointed a general of light carriage and accompanied the general-in-chief Wei Ch'ing in an attack on the Hsiung-nu Wise King of the Right. His achievements in this campaign placed him in the middle group of those who were to receive rewards and he was accordingly enfeoffed as marquis of Lo-an. In the second year of *yüan-shou* (121 B.C.) he replaced Kung-sun Hung as chancellor of the central court. In ability one would be obliged to rank Li Ts'ai very close to the bottom, and his reputation came nowhere near to equaling

that of Li Kuang. And yet Li Kuang never managed to obtain a fief and never rose higher than one of the nine lower offices of the government, that of colonel of the guard, while even some of Li Kuang's own officers and men succeeded in becoming marquises.

Li Kuang was once chatting with Wang So, a diviner who told men's fortunes by the configurations in the sky, and remarked on this fact. "Ever since the Han started attacking the Hsiung-nu, I have never failed to be in the fight. I've had men in my command who were mere company commanders or even lower and who didn't even have the ability of average men, and yet twenty or thirty of them have won marquisates. I have never been behind anyone else in doing my duty. Why is it I have never won an ounce of distinction so that I could be enfeoffed like the others? Is it that I just don't have the kind of face to become a marquis?"

"Think carefully, general," replied Wang So. "Isn't there something in the past that you regret having done?"

"Once, when I was governor of Lung-hsi, the Ch'iang tribes in the west started a revolt. I tried to talk them into surrendering, and in fact persuaded over eight hundred of them to give themselves up. But then I went back on my word and killed them all the very same day. I have never ceased to regret what I did. But that's the only thing I can think of."

"Nothing brings greater misfortune than killing those who have already surrendered to you," said Wang So. "This is the reason, general, that you have never gotten to be a marquis!" (Watson, 1974: 19)

参照译文包含 432 个英语单词，对应 224 个汉字，其词字比约为 1.93，即翻译单位汉字平均使用约 1.93 个英语单词。

只有确定参照译文，词字比才能有效地用来评价习作译文。此时，译文修订不再需要纠缠"习作译文的词字比是否符合某种数据标准"的问题，而只需要回答"习作译文在词字比上是否接近参照译文"的问题。词字比的应用自然也变得简便。

4. 词字比在译文修订中的作用

参照译文的词字比直接为习作译文提供修订依据。习作译文的词字比为 1.45，参照译文的词字比为 1.93，词字比差 0.48，即翻译 100 个汉字所用的单词数量平均相差 48。对于包含 199 个汉字的习作原文，如果把词字比从 1.45 提高到 1.93，那么习作译文需要添加 96 个单词。习作译文现有 289 个单词，添加 96 个单词意味着把篇幅加长 1/3，使其单词总数达到 385。显然，译文修订要求高，难度大。

诚然，参照译文的词字比不是一种译文修订的目标，即不是简单地把词字比从 1.45 提高到 1.93，而是一种为译文修订指明方向的"灯塔"，即在 1.45 和 1.93 所确定的方向上继续推敲和探索，直至译文趋于完美。事实上，相较于第 2.1 小节提到的 2.01、1.87、1.79 和 1.29 四种词字比，习作译文的词字比 1.45 也是处于中等偏下的位置。现朝着提高词字比的方向主要在以下 12 处修订习作译文。

[4a] 审知同光三年卒，年六十四，谥曰忠懿。

[4b] Shenzhi passed away in the third year of the Tongguang period (A. D. 925) when he was sixty-four years old and was honoured with the posthumous title of Zhongyi, i. e., the Loyal and Virtuous.

[4c] In the third year of the Tongguang period (A. D. 925), Shenzhi passed away at the age of sixty-four and was accordingly honoured with the posthumous title of "Zhongyi", that is, the "Loyal Virtuous".

此处对应 3 个句读。第 1 句和第 2 句"审知同光三年卒，年六十四"的习作译文为 Shenzhi passed away in the third year of the Tongguang period (A. D. 925) when he was sixty-four years old，修改为 In the third year of the Tongguang period (A. D. 925), Shenzhi passed away at the age of sixty-four。该修订把时间状语 in the third year of the Tongguang period (A. D. 925) 提前到句首，把状语从句 when he was sixty-four years old 改为介词短语 at the age of sixty-four。其他修订包括：添加一个副词 accordingly，改 i. e. 为 that is，并把 the Loyal and Virtuous 改为 the "Loyal Virtuous"。此处修订未增减单词数量和小句数量。

[5a] 子延翰立。

[5b] His son Yanhan succeeded to the throne.

［5c］His eldest son Yanhan succeeded him in order of seniority.

该修订把 his son 改为 his eldest son，把 succeeded to the throne 改为 succeeded him in order of seniority。由于"称王建国"在后，此时使用 throne（王位）不合时宜，所以改为 to succeeded him（继承他的位置）。修订译文明确了王延翰是王审知的长子，并说明前者因此而继承后者的位置。该修订增加3个单词。

［6a］是岁，庄宗遇弑，中国多故。

［6b］In the same year, Emperor Zhuangzong was murdered, from which China suffered very much.

［6c］In the same year, Emperor Zhuangzong was murdered, and the nation suffered from many misfortunes.

此处对应3个句读。第3句"中国多故"的习作译文为 from which China suffered very much，修改为 and the nation suffered from many misfortunes。该修订把从属结构改为并列结构，把"中国"的翻译 China 改为 the nation，把 suffered very much 改为 suffered from many misfortunes，使句意更清晰。译文修订增加1个单词。

［7a］延翰乃取司马迁《史记》闽越王无诸传示其将吏曰：……

［7b］Yanhan then took out the *Historical Records* of Sima Qian and showed the "Biography of Wuzhu the Minyue King" to his generals and officials, declaring …

［7c］Yanhan then took *Historical Records* by the grand historian Sima Qian of the Han dynasty and showed the "Biography of Wuzhu the King of Min and Yue" to his generals and officials, declaring …

该句"司马迁《史记》"的习作译文为 *Historical Records* of Sima Qian，其中的介词短语 of Sima Qian 被进一步解释为 by the grand historian Sima Qian of the Han dynasty，分别添加官职名称 the grand historian 和朝代名称 the Han dynasty，得到的修订版本为 *Historical Records* by the grand historian Sima Qian of the Han dynasty。此处修订增加7个单词。

［8a］闽，自古王国也，吾今不王，何待之有？

［8b］Min has been a kingdom since ancient times. If I do not claim the kingship now, what should I wait for?

[8c] Min has been a kingdom since ancient times. If I do not claim the kingship now, what then should I be waiting for?

此处对应 4 个句读。第 4 句"何待之有"的习作译文为 what should I wait for,修改为 what then should I be waiting for。该修订把一般现在时改为现在进行时,增加 2 个单词。此外,[7c] 和 [8c] 还可整合为如下 [4d+5d]:

[7d+8d] Yanhan then took out *Historical Records* by the grand historian Sima Qian of the Han dynasty and showed the "Biography of Wuzhu the Minyue King" to his generals and officials. "Min," he declared, "has been a kingdom since ancient times. If I do not claim the kingship now, what then should I be waiting for?"

该修订把 [8c] 的单词 Min 提前,把 [7c] 的 declaring(he declared)置于 [5c] 的句中,使译文语句之间的联结更为紧密。

[9a] 于是军府将吏上书劝进。十月,延翰建国称王,而犹禀唐正朔。

[9b] So the generals and officials in the military administration submitted written statements, advising him to proceed. In October, Yanhan founded the kingdom and claimed the kingship, though still observing the calendar of the Tang dynasty.

[9c] So the generals and officials in the military administration submitted written statements, advising him to commence the establishment of the kingdom of Min. In October (November, A. D. 926), Yanhan founded the kingdom and claimed the kingship, though still observing the calendar of the Tang dynasty.

此处对应 4 个句读。第 1 句"于是军府将吏上书劝进"的习作译文为 so the generals and officials in the military administration submitted written statements, advising him to proceed,其后半句修改为 advising him to commence the establishment of the kingdom of Min。该修订把 to proceed 改为 to commence,并把原文"劝进"之后省略的详细内容补充为 the establishment of the kingdom of Min。另外,在 October 后面添加公元纪年对应的实际年月 November, A. D. 926。该修订增加 10 个单词。

[10a] 延翰为人长大,美皙如玉。

[10b] Yanhan had a tall and large figure, as beautiful and fair as a jade.

[10c] Yanhan had a tall and large figure and he looked as beautiful and fair as a jade.

此处对应 2 个句读。第 2 句"美皙如玉"的习作译文为非限定分句 as beautiful and fair as a jade，修改为限定分句 and he looked as beautiful and fair as a jade。该修订增加 3 个单词。

[11a] 其妻崔氏陋而淫，延翰不能制。

[11b] His wife Madame Cui was ugly and dissolute, which Yanhan was not able to restrict.

[11c] His wife Madame Cui was ugly and dissolute, from which Yanhan was not able to restrain himself.

此处对应 2 个句读。第 2 句"延翰不能制"的习作译文为 which Yanhan was not able to restrict，修改为 from which Yanhan was not able to restrain himself。从上下文来看，王延翰既不能制止其妻，又无法制止自己。该修订增加 2 个单词，把简单的 to restrict 改为 to restrain himself (from)，保留了原文的双关。

[12a] 审知丧未期，彻其几筵，又多选良家子为妾。

[12b] Before the mourning period for Shenzhi came to an end, Yanhan removed the sacrificial offerings, and once again selected girls of good breeding to be his concubines.

[12c] Before the mourning period for Shenzhi came to an end, Yanhan removed the sacrificial offerings, and soon afterwards began to select numerous girls of good breeding to be his concubines.

此处对应 3 个句读。第 3 句"又多选良家子为妾"的习作译文为 and once again selected girls of good breeding to be his concubines，修改为 and soon afterwards began to select numerous girls of good breeding to be his concubines。该修订添加 began to（已开始），与前文的 before … came to an end（丧未期）相互对应，上下衔接。另外，把原文的"多"字补译为 numerous，把"又"字的翻译 once again 改为 soon afterwards。once again 有"又一次"的意思，soon afterwards 仅仅表示时间关联。由于上文并未提到此前还有"选良家子"事件，所以把它理解为 soon afterwards 较为妥当。该修订增加 3

个单词。

［13a］ 崔氏性妒。

［13b］ Madame Cui was jealous-tempered.

［13c］ Madame Cui was jealous-tempered in nature.

该句"性妒"的习作译文为 jealous-tempered，修改为 jealous-tempered in nature。修订译文把"性"字补译为 in nature。此处修订添加 2 个单词。

［14a］ 良家子之美者，辄幽之别室，系以大械，刻木为人手以击颊，又以铁锥刺之

［14b］ Those well-bred girls who were beautiful tended to be imprisoned in a special room, fastened to a punishment device, hit in the face with a hand-like bat carved out of wood, and then stabbed with an iron spike.

［14c］ Those well-bred girls who were beautiful tended to be imprisoned in a special room, fastened to a punishment device, hit in the face with a bat which was made out of wood and carved into a hand-like shape, and then stabbed with an iron spike.

此处对应 5 个句读。第 4 句"刻木为人手以击颊"的习作译文为 hit in the face with a hand-like bat carved out of wood，修改为 hit in the face with a bat which was made out of wood and carved into a hand-like shape，把 a hand-like bat 进一步解释为 a bat … into a hand-like shape。该修订增加 7 个单词。

［15a］ 一岁中死者八十四人。

［15b］ Within one single year 84 of them were killed.

［15c］ Eighty-four of them were killed within one single year.

该修订主要把时间状语 within one single year 后置。上述 12 处修订遵循三条"有利于"原则：第一，译文修订必须有利于概念功能的表达；第二，译文修订必须有利于人际功能的表达；第三，译文修订必须有利于语篇功能的表达。三条原则涉及的内容符合系统功能语言学的三种元功能，即概念功能、人际功能、语篇功能（Halliday, 1994/2000; Halliday & Matthiessen, 1999）。如果译文修订有利于任何一种功能的表达，那么该修订为合理；否则，译文不做修改。多数修订涉及概念功能，如第 2 处、第 6 处、第 11 处的修订。少数修订涉及人际功能，如第 5 处的修订。涉及语

篇功能的修订主要体现为语序的调整，如第1处和第12处的修订。现将修订译文整理如下：

In the third year of the Tongguang period (A.D. 925), Shenzhi passed away at the age of sixty-four and was accordingly honoured with the posthumous title of "Zhongyi", that is, the "Loyal Virtuous". His eldest son Yanhan succeeded him in order of seniority.

Yanhan, with the courtesy name of Ziyi, was the eldest son of Shenzhi. In the fourth year of the Tongguang period (A.D. 926), the Tang dynastic court appointed Yanhan as military commissioner. In the same year, Emperor Zhuangzong was murdered, and the nation suffered from many misfortunes. Yanhan then took out *Historical Records* by the grand historian Sima Qian of the Han dynasty and showed the "Biography of Wuzhu the King of Min and Yue" to his generals and officials. "Min," he declared, "has been a kingdom since ancient times. If I do not claim the kingship now, what then should I be waiting for?"

So the generals and officials in the military administration submitted written statements, advising him to commence the establishment of the kingdom of Min. In October (November, A.D. 926), Yanhan founded the kingdom and claimed the kingship, though still observing the calendar of the Tang dynasty.

Yanhan had a tall and large figure and he looked as beautiful and fair as a jade. His wife Madame Cui was ugly and dissolute, from which Yanhan was not able to restrain himself. Before the mourning period for Shenzhi came to an end, Yanhan removed the sacrificial offerings, and soon afterwards began to select numerous girls of good breeding to be his concubines. Madame Cui was jealous-tempered in nature. Those well-bred girls who were beautiful tended to be imprisoned in a special room, fastened to a punishment device, hit in the face with a bat which was made out of wood and carved into a hand-like shape, and then stabbed with an iron spike. Eighty-four of them were killed within one single year. Madame Cui later got sick and dead of being reported to have seen their ghosts.

修订译文一共增加 44 个单词，单词总数由 289 个增加到 333 个，其词字比为（333/199≈）1.67。现将习作译文、修订译文和参照译文的词字比对照如下（表 9-2）：

表 9-2　习作译文、修订译文和参照译文的词字比对照表

序号	译文	原文汉字/个	译文单词/个	词字比
1	习作译文	199	289	1.45
2	修订译文	199	333	1.67
3	参照译文	224	432	1.93

习作译文的词字比为 1.45，修订译文的词字比为 1.67，前后提高 0.19。该词字比差反映修订单位汉字所对应的译文平均增加 0.22 个单词，即每修订 5 个汉字所对应的译文约增加 1 个单词。尽管修订译文和参照译文的词字比差还有（1.93－1.67＝）0.26，习作译文总体上已经朝着靠近参照译文的方向优化，其在后续的修订中将进一步完善。

5. 从词字比到译文词汇密度

词字比直接关联译文词汇密度（lexical density，LD）。在汉语文言英译中，译文单词与原文句读在数量上的比例关系称为译文 LD，可简便地理解为翻译单位原文句读平均使用的译文单词数量（吴国向，2020：25）。词字比是以汉字为参照单位，而译文 LD 则是以句读为参照单位。就二者的数值关系来说，译文 LD 的值就是词字比和汉字密度的积。例如，本章第 3.1 小节的习作原文包含 199 个汉字，36 个句读，其汉字密度约为 5.53。对应的习作译文包含 289 个英语单词，其词字比约为 1.45。译文 LD 的值就是单词总数（289）和句读总数（36）的商（8.03），亦即其词字比（1.45）和汉字密度（5.53）的积（8.03）。

与词字比类似，译文 LD 也可用于指导译文修订。第 3.2 小节使用的参照原文包含 224 个汉字，39 个句读。Watson 的参照译文包含 432 个英语单词，其译文 LD 为（432/39≈）11.08，即翻译单位原文句读平均使用 11.08 个英语单词。参照译文 LD 和习作译文 LD 在数值上相差 3.05。显然，译文 LD 同样能够呈现习作译文之于参照译文在词汇特征上的差距。

经过第 4 节的修订，习作译文的单词总数由 289 个增加到 333 个，其译文 LD 约为（333/36≈）9.25。习作译文、修订译文和参照译文的译文 LD 对照如表 9-3 所示。

表 9-3　习作译文、修订译文和参照译文的译文 LD 对照表

序号	译文	原文句读/个	译文单词/个	译文 LD
1	习作译文	36	289	8.03
2	修订译文	36	333	9.25
3	参照译文	39	432	11.08

在参照译文的引领下，习作译文 LD 的值从 8.03 提升至 9.25，共提高 1.22。这表明修订每个句读平均增加 1.22 个单词。该译文 LD 的增值折合成词字比的增值约为（1.22/5.53≈）0.22，其中的 5.53 为习作译文的汉字密度。显然，译文 LD 和词字比在评价译文上具有异曲同工之处。

由于不同的文本具有不同的汉字密度，汉字密度的大小往往会对译文 LD 的大小产生或多或少的影响。在词字比相近的条件下，汉字密度越大，译文 LD 就越大；反之，译文 LD 则越小。然而，由于句读本身属于一种语法结构，以句读为参照单位的译文 LD 既是字词之间的比例关系，也是词句之间的比较关系。尽管译文 LD 在具体的数值上可能不如词字比准确，但具有很强的语法理论意义。因此，译文 LD 在译文修订和译文分析中也是一种有效的评估维度。

6. 小结

汉译英的词字比直接反映习作译文之于参照译文在词汇特征上的总体差距，为译文修订提供明确的方向。词字比在数值上所具有的波动性特征表明，并不存在某种绝对标准的数值区间，只有相对合适的参考范围。参照译文与习作译文是否匹配，又取决于二者的原文在词汇特征上的相似程度。本章所选的习作原文和参照原文在篇幅上尽管都比较短小，二者在汉字构成上却相近：前者的汉字密度是 5.53，后者的汉字密度是 5.74。至于参照译文，我们从 Watson 的《汉书》译文中选取三个篇幅相近的片段，其词字比分别为 1.93、1.88 和 1.75。相较于第 1.2 节提到的 2.05（Ku 的译文）、1.87（Waley 的译文）、1.79（Legge 的译文）和 1.29（Pound 的译文）4 种词字比值，三段参照译文的词字比值都处于中等或偏上的位置，且均高于修订译文的词字比 1.64。Pound 的译文的语言极其简练，有别于多数译本，因而并不适合在普通的文言英译中用作参照译文。由于本章以其词字比为 1.93 的片段为参照译文，所以译文修订的明确方向是，使习作译文的词字比朝着 1.93 的方向提高，进而在单词、词组、短语或小句等语法级阶上优化习作译文。

词字比不仅具有普遍的波动性特征，也存在明显的领域性区别。总体上，汉语文言英译的词字比普遍大于 1.60，而现代汉语英译的词字比往往小于 1.00。两种翻译领域的词字比在波动区间上并不存在明显的重合。只有在相近的领域中才能确保不同的原文具有相近的文辞特征，其译文的词字比才会有重合的波动区间。否则，单纯的词字比讨论没有多少实际意义，其具体的数值也不存在相互参照的价值。因此，只有选定合适的参照原文及其译文，才能在译文修订中充分发挥词字比的作用。由于包括《论语》在内的经典文本存在多重译文，所以不仅能够便利地从中选出代表性的译文，也能够按需选择具有某种词字比的参照译文。相反，包括"二十四史"在内的普通文言文本的英译程度较低，因而参照译文的选择受到较大的条件制约，往往只能在同类的文本及其译文中挑选。总之，确定合适的参照译文，少不了必要的调研工作。

译者在翻译实践中落实词字比的意识观念有利于促成良好的评价机制，提高自主的修订能力，提高翻译效率，确保译文质量。尽管词字比需要等到习作译文完成之后才能用于分析和比较，但这并不是说译者一定要等到那时才能引入词字比。相反，译者完全可以在翻译过程中有意识地强化词字比的观念。例如，普通的中国史籍英译按 1.70 以上为参照基点或以 1.90±0.20 为参照区间。通过适当地增加词汇数量，译者可以把习作译文的词字比控制在参照基点附近或参照区间之内。这也意味着参照译文的实际应用受制于习作译文的词字比。如果习作译文的词字比已经处于参照区间之内，那么词字比在译文修订中的指导作用明显弱化。尽管如此，合适的参照译文总是在遣词造句和译文风格上为译文的雕琢提供参考价值。

第 10 章

译文语法难度与译文修订

译文语法难度反映译文与原文在语法上的对等关系，其值为译文小句数量与原文句读数量的商。译文语法难度有别于第 9 章提到的词字比。词字比反映译文与原文在词汇上的对等关系，其值为译文单词数量与原文汉字数量的商。词字比可用以分析单词和汉字在量上的关系，译文语法难度可用于分析汉语文言句读与现代英语小句在量上的关系。

句读和小句属于不同的语法单位：汉语文言句读以阅读体验为依据，因而具有体验性特征，现代英语小句以主谓结构为基础，因而具有技术性特征。句读可类比现代语言的逗号（及句号）所界定的语法单位，并不完全对应小句（即主谓结构）。例如，前置的介词短语作状语时通常后接逗号，但不是小句。又如，在给定的逗号所界定的范围内时常存在多个主谓结构（即多个小句）。无论英语还是汉语，现代的逗号所界定的结构普遍大于小句。

在中国史籍英译中，从汉语句读到英语小句的转换其实就是体验单位到技术单位的转换。因此，翻译本质上是阅读体验在写作技术上的重构。译文语法难度能够展示作为体验单位的句读和作为技术单位的小句之间的转换关系。

1. 引论

语法难度（grammatical intricacy，GI）在功能语法中是指单位语句（clause complex）所包含的小句数量。语句的语法难度越大，语句内部的逻辑语义关系就越繁杂；相反，语法难度越小，其逻辑语义关系就越简易。例如，以下语句 in bridging river valleys, the early engineers built many notable masonry viaducts of numerous arches（Halliday，1994/2000：350 - 351）共有 2 个小句，其语法难度为 2。显然，语法难度其实就是语句的

"语法密度"或"小句密度",对应第9章的译文词汇密度。

在语法难度的基础上,笔者在《论语》英译研究中把汉语文言句读数量与英语译文小句数量之间的比例关系称为译文语法难度。译文语法难度的具体数值直接反映英语小句与汉语句读在数量上的对等关系。对于相同的如下 2 个句读:君子不重则不威。学则不固,Pound(1950/1969)的英语译文共有 2 个英语小句:a gentleman with no weight will not be revered, his style of study lacks vigour,其译文语法难度为 1。Waley(1938: 85)的英语译文共有 4 个小句:if a gentleman is frivolous, he will lose the respect of his inferiors and lack firm ground upon which to build up his education,其译文语法难度为 2。Pound 的译文语法难度为 1,表明翻译单位句读平均使用 1 个英语小句;Waley 的译文语法难度为 2,表明翻译单位句读平均使用 2 个英语小句。显然,前者在内部逻辑语义关系上较后者简易;后者具有较为繁杂的内部逻辑语义关系。

显然,有别于 Halliday 的英语单语的语法难度,译文语法难度是一种汉英双语的概念,能够反映译文的语法特征。在翻译实践中,译文语法难度能够有效地展示习作译文之于参照译文在语法特征上的差距,从而明确习作译文的修订方向。本章以 Watson 的《汉书》英译选段为参照译文,以《新五代史》节选片段的英语翻译为习作译文,探讨译文语法难度在译文修订中的作用。

2. 译文语法难度

译文语法难度的波动性特征取决于具体的翻译领域。跟词字比和译文词汇密度类似,译文语法难度也在特定的区间内波动。在汉语文言英译的语境中对多重译文的调研能够大致地取得译文语法难度在该领域的波动区间及其幅度范围。该区间及范围反过来又能够用以遴选参照译文。

2.1 多重《论语》英译的译文语法难度

包括《论语》在内的汉语典籍通常具有多重英语翻译,因而适合用来展示译文语法难度的波动性特征。例如,《论语·为政》全篇原文包含 143 个句读。如表 10-1 所示,Pound(1950/1969)、Legge(1893/1971)、Waley(1938)、Ku(1898)的四种译文的小句总数分别为 173 个、196 个、201 个、215 个。

表 10-1　四种《论语·为政》全篇的译文语法难度

序号	译者	原文句读/个	译文小句/个	译文语法难度
1	Pound	143	173	1.21
2	Legge	143	196	1.37
3	Waley	143	201	1.41
4	Ku	143	215	1.50

其中，Pound 的译文语法难度的值最小，仅有 1.21；Ku 的译文语法难度的值最大，达到 1.50。前后两种数值相差 0.29。该差值表明，每翻译 1 个汉语句读，前者比后者平均多出 0.29 个英语小句。Legge 的译文语法难度（1.37）和 Waley 的译文语法难度（1.41）处于上述两种译本所界定的数量区间之内。译文语法难度普遍大于 1 的事实表明，汉语句读总体上大于英语小句。

不同的译文语法难度在一定程度上体现分化的翻译措辞策略。对于同样的 2 个句读：君子不重则不威。学则不固，Legge（1893/1971）的英语翻译共有 3 个小句：if the scholar be not grave, he will not call forth any veneration, and his learning will not be solid，其译文语法难度为 1.50；Ku（1898）的英语翻译共有 4 个小句：a wise man who is not serious will not inspire respect, what he learns will not remain permanent，其译文语法难度为 2.00。两种译文的措辞在"学"字的翻译上出现明显的分化：前者选用词组 his learning，倾向于词汇策略；后者选用小句 what he learns，倾向于语法策略。不同的措辞策略最终促成不同的译文风格。

译文语法难度直接指示各种翻译措辞策略在译文中的总体使用情况。反过来说，在翻译实践中对译文语法难度的具体规定可用于调节翻译措辞策略。调高译文语法难度的数值要求，可使习作译文在措辞上的选择倾向于小句结构；相反，调低译文语法难度的数值要求，可使习作译文在措辞上的选择倾向于短语。正因为如此，在译文修订时使习作译文在语法难度的具体数值上尽量靠近参照译文，有利于形成跟参照译文近似的译文风格。

2.2　中国史籍英译的译文语法难度

相较于《论语》，中国史籍的英语翻译程度较低，多重翻译现象更为少见，因而参照译文的选择范围受到较大的限制。尽管如此，中国史籍文本与《论语》原文同属汉语文言文本，二者具有相近的词汇语法特征，因而二者的英语译文具有一定的可比性。例如，《汉书·李广苏建传》有关李广部分的原文包含 2 556 个汉字，495 个句读，其汉字密度约为 5.16。Watson 的译文包含 627 个小句，其译文语法难度约为（627/495≈）1.27。该值表明，Watson 翻译单位句读平均使用 1.27 个小句，即每译 4 个句读就会至少产生 5 个小句。从《论语·为政》的 4 组译文语法难度和《汉书·李广苏建传》的 1 组译文语法难度来看，汉语文言句读比现代英语小句在难度或长度上大 20%～50%。

当然，存在不少反例。在原文句读的数量统计中，置于句首充当时间状语的名词词组因有句读符号而被看作一种句读单位，增加了句读数量。然而，此类句读通常被译为介词短语，并未增加小句数量。例如，初°广与从弟李蔡俱为郎，其中的"初"字因有句读符号而被算作 1 个句读，因而原文语句涉及 2 个句读。Watson 把"初"字译为动宾结构 had begun their careers，与"为郎"的翻译 as attendants 组成复杂的谓语结构 had begun their careers as attendants。两个原文句读经翻译后在整体上变成 1 个英语小句：Li Kuang and his cousin Li Ts'ai had begun their careers as attendants。又如，孝文十四年°匈奴大入萧关，其中的名词词组"孝文十四年"也因有句读符号而被算作 1 个句读，因而原文语句涉及 2 个句读。Watson 把"孝文十四年"译为介词短语 in the fourteenth year of Emperor Wen's reign（166 B.C.），充当后句的状语。两个原文句读经翻译后在整体上变成 1 个英语小句：in the fourteenth year of Emperor Wen's reign（166 B.C.）the Hsiungnu entered the Hsiao Pass in great numbers。

同样常见的是，1 个文言句读整合 2 个或 2 个以上主谓结构或连动结构。此类结构在译文中通常相应地形成 2 个或 2 个以上主谓结构，从而增加小句数量。在《汉书·李广苏建传》中有关李广的叙述文本有以下 11 个例子包含"而"字，用以把前后两部分连接成 1 个复合的句读单元。

　　[1] 络而盛卧 they strung a litter between two horses and, laying him on it

　　[2] 暂腾而上胡儿马 suddenly he leaped out of the litter and onto the boy's horse

　　[3] 至军而斩之 and as soon as the man reported for duty, Li Kuang had him executed

　　[4] 以为虎而射之 which he mistook for a tiger. He shot an arrow at the rock

　　[5] 出其左右而还 scattering them to left and right, and then returned to his father's side

［6］诈而同日杀之 but then I went back on my word and killed them all the very same day

［7］发即应弦而倒 when he did discharge an arrow, however, the bowstring had no sooner sounded than his victim would fall to the ground

［8］且臣结发而与匈奴战 I have been fighting the Hsiungnu ever since I was old enough to wear my hair bound up

［9+10］广不谢大将军而起行。意象愠怒而就部 Li Kuang did not even bother to take leave of Wei Ch'ing but got up and went straight to his division, burning with obvious rage and indignation

［11］弗能得而还 being unable to capture him, was forced to turn back south again

除了第［2］句和第［7］句外，其余9个句读的翻译均包含2个小句。第［2］句"暂腾而上胡儿马"的"上［胡儿马］"字被译为介词 onto (the boy's horse)，消解1个原文动宾结构，从而使译文仅有1个小句：suddenly he leaped out of the litter and onto the boy's horse。第［7］句"发即应弦而倒"既有"而"字，又有"即"字："即"字用以连接"发"和"应弦"两个动作，译为以 when 引导的状语从句；"而"字用以连接"应弦"和"倒"两个动作，译为以 no sooner than 引导的状语从句。该句的译文最终包含3个小句 when he did discharge an arrow, however, the bowstring had no sooner sounded than his victim would fall to the ground。在其余9个句读的翻译中，第［1］句、第［3］句、第［5］句、第［8］句、第［10］句和第［11］句被译为从属关系，第［6］句和第［9］句被译为并列关系，而第［4］句的前后两部分则被分散到两个不同的句子中。被译为从属关系的句读在数量上明显超过被译为并列关系的句读。显然，译文语法难度虽然不能反映逻辑语义关系在译文中的分化现象，但能够有效地反映译文在逻辑语义关系上的繁难程度。

3. 译文语法难度在译文分析中的应用

译文语法难度的波幅明显受到样本大小的影响。如果原文样本仅有少量句读，那么译文语法难度的值可能为0或1，常常超过2，达到3或4，甚至更高。随着样本规模增大，译文语法难度的值将会逐渐地稳定在某个数值区间内。在本章第2.1小节中，四种《论语·为政》的译文语法难度确立的波幅区间是［1.21，1.50］，而第 2.2 小节引用的《汉书》的译文语法难度就处于该区间内。译文语法难度的上限、下限和波幅为参照译文的遴选提供相对的依据。

3.1 习作译文的语法难度

本小节从《新五代史·闽世家第八》中选取以下涉及王审知和王潮二人接管福建的叙述片段作为习作原文，其中涉及推潮为主、攻克彦若、攻破范晖、审知代立等事项。原文如下：

绪已见废，前锋将曰："生我者潮也。"乃推潮为主。是时，泉州刺史廖彦若为政贪暴，泉人苦之，闻潮略地至其境，而军行整肃，其耆老相率遮道留之，潮即引兵围彦若，逾年克之。

光启二年，福建观察使陈岩表潮泉州刺史。景福元年岩卒，其婿范晖自称留后。潮遣审知攻晖，久不克，士卒伤死甚众，审知请班师，潮不许。又请潮自临军，且益兵，潮报曰："兵与将俱尽，吾当自往。"审知乃亲督士卒攻破之，晖见杀。

唐即以潮为福建观察使，潮以审知为副使。审知为人状儿雄伟，隆准方口，常乘白马，军中号"白马三郎"。乾宁四年，潮卒，审知代立。

习作原文包含 205 个汉字，37 个句读，其汉字密度约为 5.54，略小于《新五代史·闽世家第八》全文的汉字密度 5.64。现将其翻译如下：

> Now that Xu had been deposed, the forward commander said, "It is Chao who has given us a second life." So Chao was recommended as the lord. At that time, Liao Yanruo, magistrate of Quanzhou, led a corruptive and atrocious government, from which the people of Quanzhou suffered very much. When it was heard that Chao had invaded across territories to the border and that the army was disciplined, the elder people leading their youngsters blocked the way with the hope that Chao and his troops would stay. Chao then led his troops to outflank Yanruo and conquered Quanzhou the next year.
>
> In the second year of the Guangqi period (A.D. 886), Chen Yan, the surveillance commissioner of Fujian Province, nominated Chao as magistrate of Quanzhou. Yan passed away in the first year of the Jingfu period (A.D. 892). His son-in-law Fan Hui pronounced himself as the successor. Chao sent Shenzhi to attack Hui, but the war

turned out to be a long stalemate, which caused numerous casualties. Shenzhi asked to withdraw the troops, but Chao disapproved, so Shenzhi requested Chao to lead the troops in person and to send more soldiers. Chao replied, "If both soldiers and generals have died out, I should surely go fighting myself." Shenzhi then launched another campaign and led the commanders and soldiers in person. Hui's troops were defeated and Hui himself was killed.

The Tang dynasty soon afterwards appointed Chao as surveillance commissioner of Fujian Province and Chao in turn nominated Shenzhi as assistant. Shenzhi was tall and strong with a high nose and a square mouth. Since he often rode a white horse, he earned himself the name of "White Horse Cavalry the Third" in the army. In the fourth year of the Qianning period (A.D. 897), Chao passed away and Shenzhi succeeded to the position of Chao.

习作译文包含306个单词,40个小句,其译文语法难度为1.08,反映1个汉语句读大体上对应1个英语小句。该值明显低于《论语》或《汉书》选段的译文语法难度。相较而言,习作译文的小句数量有待提高。

3.2 参照译文的语法难度

本小节选用《汉书·李广苏建传第二十四》中司马迁为李陵盛言的叙述片段作为参照原文,其中涉及陵降上怒、步乐自杀、群臣罪陵、迁为盛言等事项。该段原文如下:

> 陵败处去塞百余里,边塞以闻。上欲陵死战,召陵母及妇,使相者视之,无死丧色。后闻陵降,上怒甚,责问陈步乐,步乐自杀。群臣皆罪陵,上以问太史令司马迁,迁盛言:
>
> "陵事亲孝,与士信,常奋不顾身以殉国家之急。其素所畜积也,有国士之风。今举事一不幸,全躯保妻子之臣随而媒蘖其短,诚可痛也! 且陵提步卒不满五千,深轺戎马之地,抑数万之师,虏救死扶伤不暇,悉举引弓之民共攻围之。转斗千里,矢尽道穷,士张空拳,冒白刃,北首争死敌,得人之死力,虽古名将不过也。身虽陷败,然其所摧败亦足暴于天下。彼之不死,宜欲得当以报汉也。"

参照原文包含212个汉字,37个句读,其汉字密度约为5.73,略大于习作原文的汉字密度5.54。相较于习作原文,此段的句读总数相同,而汉

第 10 章　译文语法难度与译文修订

字总数多 7 个。Watson（1974：29-30）的译文如下：

　　When reports first came from the border, the emperor hoped that Li Ling had died fighting, but when he summoned Li Ling's mother and wife and had them examined by a physiognomizer, the latter could discern no sign of a death in the family. Later, when word came that Li Ling had surrendered, the emperor was enraged. He began to question and berated Ch'en Pu-lo, whereupon Ch'en Pu-lo committed suicide.

　　The mass of court officials all blamed Li Ling, but when the emperor questioned the grand historian Ssu-ma Ch'ien, he spoke enthusiastically on Li Ling's behalf, declaring that "he is filial to his parents and trustworthy with his associates; constantly he has hastened forward in time of need to sacrifice himself for his country without thought for his own safety. This was always in his mind—his ways marked him as one of the finest men of the nation. Now he has committed one unfortunate act, and the officials who think only to save themselves and protect their own wives and children vie with each other in magnifying his shortcomings. Truly it makes one sick! The infantry that Li Ling commanded did not come up to five thousand. They marched deep into nomad territory, fending off the numberless hosts, so that the enemy did not have time even to rescue their dead or aid their wounded. They called up all their men who could use a bow and together they surrounded and attacked Li Ling's army, which fought its way along for a thousand li, until its arrows were gone and the road was blocked. Then the men stretched out their empty bows and warded off the bare blades of the attackers, facing north and fighting to the death with the foe. Li Ling was able to command the loyalty of his troops in the face of death—even the famous generals of old could do no more! And though he fell into captivity, yet the losses and injury which he has inflicted upon the enemy are worthy to be proclaimed throughout the world. The fact that he did not choose to die must mean that he hopes sometime to find a way to repay his debt to the Han."

　　参照译文包含 370 个单词，49 个小句，其译文语法难度为 1.32，略高于 Watson 的《汉书》译文有关李广部分的译文语法难度 1.27。参照译文的语法难度处于正常范围，可用以指导译文修订。

4. 译文修订

习作译文与参照译文在译文语法难度上差距明显：前者的译文语法难度为 1.03，后者的译文语法难度为 1.32。两种数值相差 0.29，即每翻译 4 个句读参照译文平均比习作译文至少多出 1 个小句。如果习作译文在语法难度上与参照译文保持一致，那么每翻译 1 个句读平均需要增加 0.29 个小句。习作原文共有 37 个句读，一共需要增加至少 11 个小句。当然，参照译文的语法难度不是译文修订的目标，而是一种用以确定修订方向的基点。译文修订在总体上是朝着增加小句的方向来进行的。现将译文的修订过程逐节分析如下：

[1a] 绪已见废°前锋将曰°生我者潮也

[1b] Now that Xu had been deposed, the forward commander said, "It is Chao who has given us a second life."

[1c] Now that Xu had been deposed, the forward commander persuaded the generals and officials to uphold Chao as their new chief. "It is Chao," he said, "who has given us a second life."

该节包含 3 个句读。第 2 句和第 3 句"前锋将曰°生我者潮也"的习作译文 the forward commander said, "It is Chao who has given us a second life." 改为 the forward commander persuaded the generals and officials to uphold Chao as their new chief. "It is Chao," he said, "who has given us a second life." 该修订按下文的语义线索添加 1 个小句 persuaded the generals and officials to uphold Chao as their new chief，一共增加 12 个单词。增补的内容在原文中没有直接对应的词语。另外，引语中间插入 he said，使行文更加符合英语的表达习惯。

[2a] 是时°泉州刺史廖彦若为政贪暴°泉人苦之°闻潮略地至其境°而军行整肃°其耆老相率遮道留之°潮即引兵围彦若°逾年克之

[2b] At that time, Liao Yanruo, magistrate of Quanzhou, led a corruptive and atrocious government, from which the people of Quanzhou suffered very much. When it was heard that Chao had invaded across territories to the border and that the army was disciplined, the elder people leading their youngsters blocked the way

with the hope that Chao and his troops would stay. Chao then led his troops to outflank Yanruo and conquered Quanzhou the next year.

[2c] At that time, Liao Yanruo, magistrate of Quanzhou, led a corruptive and atrocious government, from which the people of Quanzhou suffered very much. When it was heard that Chao had invaded across territories to the border and that the army paraded in a disciplined order, the elder people leading their youngsters blocked the way with the hope that Chao and his troops would stay so as to replace the government by Yanruo. Chao then led his troops to outflank Yanruo and occupied Quanzhou the next year.

该节语句较长，包含 8 个句读，其译文被分为 3 个句子。前 3 句"是时°泉州刺史廖彦若为政贪暴°泉人苦之"和后 2 句"潮即引兵围彦若°逾年克之"分别译为 1 个句子，均未修改。第 4 句、第 5 句和第 6 句"闻潮略地至其境°而军行整肃°其耆老相率遮道留之"的习作译文为 when it was heard that Chao had invaded across territories to the border and that the army was disciplined, the elder people leading their youngsters blocked the way with the hope that Chao and his troops would stay, 修改为 when it was heard that Chao had invaded across territories to the border and that the army paraded in a disciplined order, the elder people leading their youngsters blocked the way with the hope that Chao and his troops would stay so as to replace the government by Yanruo。该修订按下文的语义发展添加 1 个小句 so as to replace the government by Yanruo, 一共增加 8 个单词。增补的内容在原文中没有直接对应的词语。

[3a] 景福元年岩卒°其婿范晖自称留后

[3b] Yan passed away in the first year of the Jingfu period (A.D. 892). His son-in-law Fan Hui pronounced himself as the successor.

[3c] Yan passed away in the first year of the Jingfu period (A.D. 892). His son-in-law Fan Hui announced that he himself succeed to the title of surveillance commissioner.

该节包含 2 个句读。第 2 句"其婿范晖自称留后"的习作译文 his son-in-law Fan Hui pronounced himself as the successor 改为 his son-in-law Fan Hui announced that he himself succeed to the title of surveillance commissioner。

该修订添加 1 个小句 that he himself succeed to the title of surveillance commissioner, 一共增加 6 个单词。增补的小句对原文"留后"添加详细的说明。

[4a] 潮遣审知攻晖。久不克。士卒伤死甚众。审知请班师。潮不许

[4b] Chao sent Shenzhi to attack Hui, but the war turned out to be a long stalemate, which caused numerous casualties. Shenzhi asked to withdraw the troops, but Chao disapproved ...

[4c] Dissatisfied with Hui's claim of the title, Chao sent Shenzhi to attack Hui, but the war turned out to be a long stalemate and resulted in a large number of injuries and casualties. Shenzhi first requested to withdraw the troops, but it was disapproved of by Chao ...

该节包含 5 个句读。第 1 句"潮遣审知攻晖"的习作译文 Chao sent Shenzhi to attack Hui 改为 dissatisfied with Hui's claim of the title, Chao sent Shenzhi to attack Hui。该修订根据上下文的语义关系添加 1 个小句 dissatisfied with Hui's claim of the title, 一共增加 7 个单词。增补的内容在原文中没有直接对应的词语。第 3 句"士卒伤死甚众"的习作译文 which caused numerous casualties 改为 and resulted in a large number of injuries and casualties。该修订把从属结构变为并列结构，并且把原文"伤死"明确为 injuries and casualties。第 5 句"潮不许"的习作译文为主动态的小句 but Chao disapproved，修改为被动态的小句 but it was disapproved of by Chao。

[5a] 又请潮自临军。且益兵。潮报曰。兵与将俱尽。吾当自往

[5b] ... so Shenzhi requested Chao to lead the troops in person and to send more soldiers. Chao replied, "If both soldiers and generals have died out, I should surely go fighting myself."

[5c] ... so he further requested that Chao lead the troop in person and that more soldiers be summoned and sent. Chao sent nothing but a report. "If both soldiers and generals have died out," he stated, "I shall surely go fighting myself."

该节包含 5 个句读。第 1 句和第 2 句"又请潮自临军。且益兵"的习作译文 so Shenzhi requested Chao to lead the troops in person and to send more soldiers 改为 so he further requested that Chao lead the troop in person and that more soldiers be summoned and sent。该修订添加两个小句，即 that Chao lead the troop in person 和 that more soldiers be summoned and sent。第 3 句"潮报曰"的习作译文为 Chao replied，修改为 Chao sent nothing but a report ... he stated，其中的后部插入引语内部。该修订补充"曰"字的翻译，还把 replied 更换为 sent nothing but a report，一共添加 1 个小句和 3 个单词。

[6a] 审知为人状儿雄伟。隆准方口。常乘白马。军中号白马三郎

[6b] Shenzhi was tall and strong with a high nose and a square mouth. Since he often rode a white horse, he earned himself the name of "White Horse Cavalry the Third" in the army.

[6c] Shenzhi was a big, burly man, with his nose bridge highly upright and mouth widely square. He often rode a white horse, so he earned himself the name of "White Knight the Third" in the army.

该节包含 4 个句读。第 2 句"隆准方口"的习作译文是 1 个复杂的介词短语 with a high nose and a square mouth，修改为 2 个非限定小句 with his nose bridge highly upright and his mouth widely square。该修订一共添加 2 个小句和 5 个单词。现将修订译文整理如下：

Now that Xu had been deposed, his forward commander persuaded other generals and officials to uphold Chao as the new chief. "It is Chao," he said, "who has given us a second life." So Chao was promoted to be the lord. At that time, Liao Yanruo, magistrate of Quanzhou, led a corruptive and atrocious government, from which the people of Quanzhou suffered very much. When it was heard that Chao had invaded across territories to the border and that the army paraded in a disciplined order, the elder people leading their youngsters blocked the road with the hope that Chao and his troops would stay so as to replace the government by Yanruo. Chao then led his troops to outflank Yanruo and occupied Quanzhou the next year.

In the second year of the Guangqi period (A.D. 886), Chen Yan, surveillance commissioner of Fujian, nominated Chao as magistrate of Quanzhou. Yan passed away in the first year of the Jingfu period (A.D. 892). His son-in-law Fan Hui announced that he himself succeed to the title of surveillance commissioner. Dissatisfied with Hui's claim of the title, Chao sent Shenzhi to attack Hui, but the war turned out to be a long stalemate and resulted in a large number of injuries and casualties. Shenzhi first requested to withdraw the troops, but it was disapproved of by Chao, so he further requested that Chao lead the troops in person and that more soldiers be summoned and sent. Chao sent nothing but a report. "If both soldiers and generals have died out," he stated, "I shall surely go fighting myself." Shenzhi had no choice but to launch another campaign, leading commanders and soldiers in person. Hui's troops were eventually defeated and Hui himself was killed.

Later, the Tang dynastic court appointed Chao as surveillance commissioner of Fujian and Chao in turn nominated Shenzhi as assistant. Shenzhi was a big, burly man, with his nose bridge highly upright and mouth widely square. He often rode a white horse, so he earned himself the name of "White Knight the Third" in the army. In the fourth year of the Qianning period (A.D. 897), Chao passed away and Shenzhi succeeded to his position.

修订译文从整体上改变了习作译文的语法特征：一共增加7个小句，小句总数由40个增加到47个，其译文语法难度由1.08提高到1.27。该值与参照译文的语法难度1.32仅有0.05的差距，即总体上只有4个小句的差距。当然，参照译文的译文语法难度本身不是具体的修订目标，而是一种用以确定修订方向的参照基点，因而并不存在补足现有差距的硬性要求。

值得注意的是，上述修订不仅提高译文语法难度，也提高词字比和译文词汇密度。修订译文的单词总数从307个升至364个，一共增加57个单词。对应的习作原文包含212个汉字，37个句读。词字比的值从原来的约（307/212≈）1.45增加到当前的约（364/212≈）1.72；译文词汇密度从原来的约（307/37≈）8.30增加到当前的约（364/37≈）9.84。词字比和译文词汇密度的具体数值都有显著的提高。由此可见，译文语法难度、译文词汇密度和词字比存在相通的地方。

另外，除了核实少数此前漏译的原文词语并加以补译之外（如[5c]），多数修订都是出于贯通文意这一目的，使上下文在逻辑语义上的衔接更为紧密。

5. 译不厌修

既然提高译文语法难度能够同时提高词字比和译文词汇密度，提高词字比和译文词汇密度也能同时提高译文语法难度，那么是不是只需使用一种方案就可以达到预期的修订效果呢？从现有的《论语》英译来看，要么不断地修订译文，要么不断地复译原文。出版的复译文本追溯起来相对容易。现有的 60 余种《论语》英译版本就是 200 多年来复译的结果。然而，由于译文修订往往在出版之前就已经完成，所以修订过程很难追溯。只有少量再版译本存在较大的修订痕迹，可为译文修订和研究提供直接的证据。例如，Legge 的 1893 年译本和 1861 年译本存在明显的区别。可以说，复译是一种永无止境的活动，而译文修订则受个体译者的条件限制。尽管如此，译文修订是一个精益求精的过程，因而译不厌修。包括词字比、译文词汇密度、译文语法难度等在内的数值指标能够把这种有限的修订行为转换为包含有限步骤的修订流程。该流程设立具体的修订目标，明确足够的修订次数，确保较高的翻译质量。

译文语法难度的波动性特征表明，只存在相对的波动区间，不存在绝对的数值标准。使用译文语法难度来指导中国史籍英译，需要在调研的基础上选择合适的参照译文，借以确定译文修订的具体方向。由于译文语法难度偏低是习作译文普遍存在的问题，所以译文修订的主要任务是添加特定的小句以补充语句内部的语义内容，或者明确语句之间的逻辑关系。特别是调整语句之间的逻辑关系涉及对习作原文、习作译文和修订译文的重新审视，既要考虑源语言的语境因素，又要考虑译入语的语境因素。

译文修订需要吸收各类参照文本的优点。参照译文是习作译文的共时参照，而此前的修订译文则是当前的修订译文的历时参照。不同的修订译文围绕相同的原文形成互文关系。新的版本脱胎于旧的版本，但总是继承后者的主体特征，并且成为后续修订的基础。换言之，由于所有修订译文都可能是参照，所以"最终的译文"其实是从各种参照样本中挑选出来的代表译文。显然，译文语法难度的研究不仅能够反映各种版本之间的关系，而且能够揭示复译现象的本质。

6. 小结

译文语法难度有利于在翻译中形成自我完善的意识，提高译文修订的主观能动性。合适的译文语法难度数值既可提高翻译的效率，又可提高译文的质量，还可促成特定的风格。译文语法难度的大小在一定程度上体现口头和书面两种风格。一般来说，译文语法难度越大，译文的口头风格就越强，越适合口语场景。相反，译文语法难度越小，译文的书面风格就越强，越适合书面场景。同理，具有中等语法难度的译文则具有中性的风格。换言之，在翻译中确定高、中、低等译文语法难度的区间范围能够在总体上获得具有口头、中性、书面等风格的译文。

译文语法难度体现句读和小句在数量上的对等关系。前者是阅读中的体验单位，后者是语法中的技术单位。翻译过程就是以语法的技术单位来转换阅读的体验单位，即原文句读如何转化为译文小句。译文语法难度直接反映体验单位和技术单位之间的这种转换关系，能够从侧面反映翻译的本质。

译文语法难度对文言英译研究具有较强的理论意义。以译文语法难度来比较汉语文言和现代英语两种语言，其实是用英语的语法结构来衡量汉语的语法结构，为汉语文言的语法结构研究提供一种行之有效的量化方案。对现有文言英译的调研能够获得汉语文言和现代英语在语法上的比例关系。此外，由于现代英语是一种现代语言，而汉语文言则是一种古代语言，所以译文语法难度分析其实也为现代语言和古代语言之间的比较研究提供一种思路。

第11章

单语视角的语法复杂性

译文词汇密度和译文语法难度都是在双语语境中形成的对等概念，能够呈现双语的语法复杂性特征：前者反映译文和原文在字词数量上的对等关系，后者反映译文和原文在小句数量上的对等关系。除了双语视角的语法复杂性外，译文内部还存在单语视角的语法复杂性。与双语语法复杂性类似，单语语法复杂性主要包含单语词汇密度和单语语法难度两个方面：单语词汇密度是指单位小句包含的词汇数量，单语语法难度是指单位语句包含的小句数量。显然，两种单语的语法复杂性指标不是反映译文与原文之间在词汇语法上的互文关系，而是反映译文本身在词汇语法上的数量构成。就英语来说，单语视角的文本包括英语原生文本、汉译英文本，以及非汉译英文本。就汉译英文本来说，由于不考虑汉语原文，也就不讲译文词汇密度和译文语法难度，只讲单语词汇密度和单语语法难度。

单语词汇密度和单语语法难度能够用以分析译文和译入语中的其他文本之间在词汇语法上的互文关系。例如，在中国史籍英译中，两种单语的语法复杂性指标能够反映汉译英的习作译文和英语原生文本之间的区别，进而明确译文修订的具体策略，使习作译文在词汇语法上靠近原生文本。

1. 引论

在翻译互文性的理论框架中，第9章和第10章分别以词字比、译文词汇密度和译文语法难度三种双语的语法复杂性指标来比较习作译文和参照译文，反映习作译文的词汇语法现状，从而确定译文修订的具体方向。一种汉译英文本一旦形成，就会在英语语境中独立存在，并与英语原生文本、非汉译英文本或其他汉译英文本形成互文关系。在此类参照文本的基础上评价习作译文，通常需要借助单语词汇密度和单语语法难度。

单语词汇密度和单语语法难度最早用以测量英语文本或英语语句的语

法复杂性特征。Halliday（1994/2000：350-351）把词汇密度定义为单位小句平均包含的实义词（content word）数量、把语法难度定义为单位语句平均包含的句级小句（ranking clause）数量。其中，语句对应的英语术语是 clause complex，通常译为"小句复合体"（方琰，2001），其在本书中被简化为"语句"。简言之，词汇密度反映文本内部的单词数量和小句数量之间的比例关系，即小句在单词上的数量构成；语法难度反映文本内部的小句数量和语句数量的比例关系，即语句在小句上的数量构成。如：

(a) In bridging river valleys, the early engineers built many notable masonry viaducts of numerous arches. (Halliday, 1994/2000: 350)

(b) In the early days when engineers had to make a bridge across a valley and the valley has a river flowing through it, they often built viaducts, which were constructed of masonry and has numerous arches in them; and many of these viaducts became notable. (Halliday, 1994/2000: 351)

前句包含 11 个实义词、2 个句级小句，其词汇密度为 5.50，语法难度为 2.00。后句包含 20 个实义词、6 个句级小句，其词汇密度约为 3.33，语法难度为 6.00。词汇密度和语法难度涉及语句的词项构成和语法特征，是语句的语法复杂性的主要方面。

本章以单语词汇密度和单语语法难度为指标、以汉译英文本及英语原生文本为参照来分析习作译文的词汇语法特征，进而为习作译文的最后修订提供方向性的指导。

2. 单语语法复杂性

译文最终会脱胎于原文，离开源语言语境进入译入语语境，变成一种独立的文本，与译入语中的其他文本形成互文关系。单语词汇密度和单语语法难度能够分别呈现习作译文和译入语中的其他文本之间的区别性特征，进而为习作译文提供译入语角度的修订方案。出于方便，本章在讨论单语词汇密度时不区分实义词和功能词，在讨论单语语法难度时不区分句级小句和降级小句，因而词汇数量就是全部单词的数量，小句数量就是全部主谓结构的数量。

2.1 习作原文与习作译文

本节所选的习作原文主要讲述审知德政，其中涉及封琅琊王、拜中书令、朝贡于梁、好礼下士、建学四门、招商开港等具体事项。选段原文如下：

唐以福州为威武军。拜审知节度使。累迁同中书门下平章事。封琅琊王。唐亡。梁太祖加拜审知中书令。封闽王。升福州为大都督府。是时。杨行密据有江淮。审知岁遣使泛海。自登莱朝贡于梁。使者入海。覆溺常十三四。

审知虽起盗贼。而为人俭约。好礼下士。王淡。唐相溥之子。杨沂。唐相涉从弟。徐寅。唐时知名进士。皆依审知仕宦。又建学四门。以教闽士之秀者。招来海中蛮夷商贾。海上黄崎。波涛为阻。一夕风雨雷电震击。开以为港。闽人以为审知德政所致。号为甘棠港。

习作原文包含 182 个汉字、33 个句读，其汉字密度约为 5.52。该值略低于《新五代史·闽世家第八》全文的汉字密度 5.64。现将习作原文翻译如下：

  The Tang dynastic court established a military government in Fuzhou, that is, "Weiwu Military Government", and accordingly appointed Shenzhi as governor. He was then promoted several times until he was eventually nominated as prime minister and was granted with the title of "King of Langya". After the fall of the Tang dynasty, the Founding Emperor of the Liang dynasty nominated Shenzhi as general secretary of the imperial secretariat, entitled him with "King of Min", and accordingly promoted Fuzhou as Metropolitan Government. At this time, Yang Xingmi occupies the Jianghuai area, blocking the region between the Yangtze River and the Huai River, so Shenzhi yearly dispatched envoys by seaway to pay loyal tribute to the Liang dynasty via Dengzhou or Laizhou. Among the envoys sailing into the sea, often three or four out of ten got drowned.

  Though Shenzhi had risen up among the bandits, he kept a thrifty way of life and treated his subordinates with courtesy. Wang Dan was the son of Wang Pu, former prime minister of the Tang dynasty; Yang Yi was the younger brother of Yang She, former prime minister of the Tang dynasty; Xu Ying was a well-known scholar of the Tang dynasty. They all took office in Shenzhi's government. Shenzhi also opened a national academy to teach those talented people in the region of Min. He then attracted overseas and foreign merchants, but the Huangqi

Island across the sea was obstructed by the waves. One evening, a fearful tempest arose with thunder and lightning; the Huangqi Island became a seaport overnight. The Min people thought that this was what the virtue of Shenzhi and his government had brought about, so they called it "Gantang Port", that is, the Sweet-Pear Port.

习作译文包含 287 个单词、30 个小句、12 个句子。从双语语法复杂性来看，习作译文的词字比约为（287/182≈）1.58，其译文语法难度约为（30/33≈）0.91。相较于第 9 章和第 10 章分别论涉的词字比和译文语法难度的参照数值区间，习作译文在词字比及译文语法难度两个维度上均有较大的提升空间。从单语语法复杂性来看，习作译文的单语词汇密度约为（287/30≈）9.57，其单语语法难度为（30/12＝）2.50。下文将在 1 篇汉译英文本和 1 篇非汉译英文本的基础上，从单语词汇密度和单语语法难度两个维度来分析习作译文的词汇语法特征。

2.2 汉译英的参照文本

本节选取的参照原文来自《汉书·李广苏建传》。该节主要叙述李陵恭送苏武回汉朝，其中涉及置酒贺武、陵起歌舞、泣与武决、苏武归还等具体事项。选段原文如下：

于是李陵置酒贺武曰。今足下还归。扬名于匈奴。功显于汉室。虽古竹帛所载。丹青所画。何以过子卿。陵虽驽怯。令汉且贳陵罪。全其老母。使得奋大辱之积志。庶几乎曹柯之盟。此陵宿昔之所不忘也。收族陵家。为世大戮。陵尚复何顾乎。已矣。令子卿知吾心耳。异域之人。壹别长绝。

陵起舞。歌曰。径万里兮度沙幕。为君将兮奋匈奴。路穷绝兮矢刃摧。士众灭兮名已隤。老母已死。虽欲报恩将安归。

陵泣下数行。因与武决。单于召会武官属。前以降及物故。凡随武还者九人。

参照原文包含 181 个汉字、33 个句读，其汉字密度约为 5.48。该值接近习作原文的汉字密度 5.52。本节把 Watson（1974：40-41）对该文的英语翻译作为参照译文，记为"参照译文 A"，其文如下：

Li Ling then set out wine and offered a toast of congratulation to Su Wu. "Now you will be going home," he said. "Your fame has spread abroad among the Hsiung-nu, your achievements reflect glory on the house of Han; those heroes of old whose stories are recorded in books on bamboo and silk, whose portraits are limned in pigments of red and green—even they could not surpass you, Tzu-Ch'ing! As for myself, though I may be a tired old horse, and a cowardly one at that, if the Han had been willing to overlook my offense, had left my old mother unharmed, and had given me a chance to fulfill those long-nurtured hopes I had of wiping out the terrible shame I had incurred—then I would have become a veritable Ts'ao Mei at the altar of K'o!① All those days the thought of it never left my mind. But they arrested my family and wiped them out—one of the most terrible slaughters of the age! Now who is there left for me to care about? Well, let it be. I wanted you to know what is in my heart, that was all. We are men of different lands—once we part, it must be forever." Then Li Ling rose and danced, singing this song:

Trekking ten thousand li,

crossing desert sands,

marching in the sovereign's name,

I challenged the Hsiung-nu.

But roads ran out, cut off,

arrows and blades were broken;

armies of men wiped out—

my good name perished with them.

Now that my old mother is dead and gone,

though I might wish to repay kindness,

where could I turn?

Tears streamed down Li Ling's face as he said farewell to Su Wu.

The Shan-*yü* called together the officials who had been in Su Wu's party, but since some had long ago surrendered to the Hsiung-nu and others had died, only nine men in all were left to accompany Su Wu home.

---

① Ts'ao Mei, a general of Lu, participated in a diplomatic meeting at K'o between his sovereign, Duke Chuang of Lu (r. 693–662), and Duke Huan of Ch'i. There he mounted the altar that had been set up for the oath of agreement, seized Duke Huan, and threatened him with a dagger until he agreed to return the lands he had earlier taken away from Lu. Li Ling is suggesting that he might have seized and threatened the *Shan-yü* in the same way.

参照译文 A 包含 328 个单词、48 个小句、15 个句子。参照译文 A 的单词数量和小句数量都远超习作译文。从双语语法复杂性来看,参照译文 A 的词字比约为(328/181≈)1.81,其译文语法难度约为(48/33≈)1.45。两种数值均明显高于习作译文的对应数值,因而能够充当译文修订参照的基础。

从单语语法复杂性来看,参照译文 A 的译文词汇密度约为(328/48≈)6.83,其译文语法难度为(48/15=)3.20。由于参照译文 A 在小句数量上比习作译文多 60.0%,远远大于其在单词数量上比习作译文多出的百分比值 17.1%,所以参照译文 A 的单语词汇密度(6.83)反而低于习作译文的单语词汇密度(9.57)。第 2.1 小节已经提到,习作译文的译文语法难度只有 0.91。后续的修订将会增加小句数量,以修正关联的数据指标。

2.3 非汉译英的参照文本

在单语条件下分析习作译文所需的参照文本不仅包括其他汉译英文本,也包括非汉译英文本。非汉译英文本包括以非汉语文本为原文的其他译文及英语原生文本。本节从 Tacitus(2009:52-53)的《塔西佗编年史》(*The Annals of Tacitus*)中节选如下非汉译英文本为参照,记为"参照译文 B"。参照译文 B 并非英语原生文本,而是由拉丁语转译而成的英语文本。在此前两章的讨论中,词字比和译文语法难度分别是在汉语原文的基础上定义的词汇和语法指标。对于以下参照译文 B,由于没有对应的汉语原文,自然就缺少双语的词字比和译文语法难度,只有单语的词汇密度和语法难度。

> To this accordingly he gave his mind, and sent Publius Vitellius and Caius Antius to collect the taxes of Gaul. Silius, Anteius, and Caecina had the charge of building a fleet. It seemed that a thousand vessels were required, and they were speedily constructed, some of small draught with a narrow stem and stern and a broad centre, that they might bear the waves more easily; some flat-bottomed, that they might ground without being injured; several, furnished with a rudder at each end, so that by a sudden shifting of the oars they might be run into shore either way. Many were covered in with decks, on which engines for missiles might be conveyed, and were also fit for the carrying of horses or supplies, and being equipped with sails as well as rapidly moved by oars, they assumed, through the enthusiasm of our

soldiers, an imposing and formidable aspect. The island of the Batavi was the appointed rendezvous, because of its easy landing-places, and its convenience for receiving the army and carrying the war across the river. For the Rhine after flowing continuously in a single channel or encircling merely insignificant islands, divides itself, so to say, where the Batavian territory begins, into two rivers, retaining its name and the rapidity of its course in the stream which washes Germany, till it mingles with the ocean. On the Gallic bank, its flow is broader and gentler; it is called by an altered name, the Vahal, by the inhabitants of its shore. Soon that name too is changed for the Mosa river, through whose vast mouth it empties itself into the same ocean.

参照译文 B 包含 273 个单词、33 个小句、11 个句子。由于缺少汉语原文，参照译文 B 只有单语的语法复杂性特征：单语词汇密度约为（273/33≈）8.27，该值略低于参照译文 A 的相应数值（8.54）；单语语法难度为（33/11＝）3.00，该值略低于参照译文 A 的相应数值 3.20。显然，单语词汇密度和单语语法难度能够用以比较汉译英文本和包括英语原生文本在内的非汉译英文本。

3. 单语语法复杂性与译文修订

对于习作译文，现有汉译英的参照译文 A 和非汉译英的参照译文 B。前者具有汉英双语的基础，后者只有英语单语的语境。一般来说，译文修订最好还是先参照汉译英文本，而后才参照非汉译英文本。换言之，非汉译英文本通常充当译文修订的后期参照。本章第 2 节的分析表明，习作译文的译文语法难度只有 0.91，而参照译文 A 的译文语法难度为 1.45。显然，习作译文在译文语法难度上存在较大的修订空间。现按提高译文语法难度的方向来修订习作译文，其具体的修订记录分节详述如下：

[1a] 唐以福州为威武军。拜审知节度使。累迁同中书门下平章事。封琅琊王。

[1b] The Tang dynastic court established a military government in Fuzhou, that is, "Weiwu Military Government", and accordingly appointed Shenzhi as governor. He was then promoted several times until he was eventually nominated as prime minister and was granted with the title of "King of Langya".

[1c] The Tang dynastic court established a military institution entitled as "Weiwu Military Government" in Fuzhou and accordingly appointed Shenzhi as commissioner. He was then promoted several times until he was eventually nominated as the manager of affairs with the secretariat chancellery and was granted with the title of "King of Langya".

该节包含 4 个句读。第 1 句"唐以福州为威武军"的习作译文 the Tang dynastic court established a military government in Fuzhou, that is, "Weiwu Military Government" 改为 the Tang dynastic court established a military institution entitled as "Weiwu Military Government" in Fuzhou。该修订调整部分字词, 明确 1 个非限定小句。第 2 句"拜审知节度使"的习作译文 and accordingly appointed Shenzhi as governor 改为 and accordingly appointed Shenzhi as commissioner。该修订调整了"节度使"的翻译, 强调军政府的职能。第 3 句和第 4 句"累迁同中书门下平章事。封琅琊王"在习作译文中被整合并译为复杂句 he was then promoted several times until he was eventually nominated as prime minister and was granted with the title of "King of Langya"; 该译文改为 he was then promoted several times until he was eventually nominated as the manager of affairs with the secretariat chancellery and was granted with the title of "King of Langya"。该修订调整了专有名词"同中书门下平章事"的翻译, 使译文更准确。该节修订一共添加 6 个单词、1 个小句。

[2a] 唐亡。梁太祖加拜审知中书令。封闽王。升福州为大都督府

[2b] After the fall of the Tang dynasty, the Founding Emperor of the Liang dynasty nominated Shenzhi as general secretary of the imperial secretariat, entitled him with "King of Min", and Fuzhou was accordingly promoted as Metropolitan Government.

[2c] After the fall of the Tang dynasty, the Founding Emperor Taizu of the Liang dynasty nominated Shenzhi as general secretary of the imperial secretariat, entitled him with "King of Min", and accordingly promoted Fuzhou as Metropolitan Government.

该节包含 4 个句读。译文修订只调整个别词汇, 包括补上"太祖"的音译 Taizu, 把最后的被动语态 Fuzhou was accordingly promoted as

Metropolitan Government 改为主动语态 and accordingly promoted Fuzhou as Metropolitan Government。实际上，如果把第 1 句的译文 after the fall of the Tang dynasty 改为 after the Tang dynasty fell，虽然会减少 2 个单词，却可以直接添加 1 个小句。

[3a] 是时°杨行密据有江淮°审知岁遣使泛海°自登莱朝贡于梁°使者入海°覆溺常十三四

[3b] At this time, Yang Xingmi occupies the Jianghuai area, blocking the region between the Yangtze River and the Huai River, so Shenzhi yearly dispatched envoys by seaway to pay loyal tribute to the Liang dynasty via Dengzhou or Laizhou. Among the envoys sailing into the sea, often three or four out of ten got drowned.

[3c] At that time, Yang Xingmi occupied the Jianghuai area, blocking the land route in the region between the Yangtze River and the Huai River. Nevertheless, Shenzhi still contrived to pay loyal tribute to the Liang dynasty every year by dispatching envoys to go by seaway via the seaport commanderies of Dengzhou and Laizhou. Before they reached the port of destination, however, their boats often capsized, and, among the envoys sailing into the sea, as many as three or four out of ten got drowned.

该节包含 6 个句读。第 1 句"是时"为时间句读，在译文中充当第 2 句译文的时间状语。第 1 句和第 2 句"是时°杨行密据有江淮"的习作译文 At this time, Yang Xingmi occupies the Jianghuai area, blocking the region between the Yangtze River and the Huai River 改为 At that time, Yang Xingmi occupied the Jianghuai area, blocking the land route in the region between the Yangtze River and the Huai River。该修订保留原有的句式，调整个别词语：把 blocking the region 改为 blocking the land route in the region。修改后的句意变得清晰、直接。第 3 句和第 4 句"审知岁遣使泛海°自登莱朝贡于梁"习作译文 so Shenzhi yearly dispatched envoys by seaway to pay loyal tribute to the Liang dynasty via Dengzhou or Laizhou 改为 Nevertheless, Shenzhi still contrived to pay loyal tribute to the Liang dynasty every year by dispatching envoys to go by seaway via the seaport commanderies of Dengzhou and Laizhou。该修订确立 2 个小句，添加连接副词 nevertheless，同时明确登州和莱州均为港口城市。第 5 句和第 6 句"使者入海°覆溺常十三四"的习作译文

Among the envoys sailing into the sea, often three or four out of ten got drowned 改为 Before they reached the port of destination, however, their boats often capsized, and, among the envoys sailing into the sea, as many as three or four out of ten got drowned。该修订相对较大,直接添加 2 个小句 before they reached the port of destination, however, their boats often capsized, 用以衔接上下文。该节修订一共添加 29 个单词、3 个小句。

[4a] 审知虽起盗贼。而为人俭约。好礼下士

[4b] Though Shenzhi had risen up among the bandits, he kept a thrifty way of life and treated his subordinates with courtesy.

[4c] Shenzhi, though having risen up among the bandits, led a thrifty life, treated his subordinates with courtesy, and also received or recruited scholars or officials who had been dismissed from the central court after the downfall of the Tang dynasty.

该节包含 3 个句读。第 1 句"审知虽起盗贼"的习作译文 Though Shenzhi had risen up among the bandits 改为 Shenzhi, though having risen up among the bandits。该修订仅调整从句的位置。第 2 句和第 3 句"而为人俭约。好礼下士"的习作译文 he kept a thrifty way of life and treated his subordinates with courtesy 改为 [Shenzhi] led a thrifty life, treated his subordinates with courtesy, and also received or recruited scholars or officials who had been dismissed from the central court after the downfall of the Tang dynasty。该修订的前半部分变化不大,后半部分直接添加 2 个承上启下的小句。该节修订一共添加 19 个单词、2 个小句。

[5a] 王淡。唐相溥之子。杨沂。唐相涉从弟。徐寅。唐时知名进士。皆依审知仕宦

[5b] Wang Dan was the son of Wang Pu, former prime minister of the Tang dynasty; Yang Yi was the younger brother of Yang She, former prime minister of the Tang dynasty; Xu Ying was a well-known scholar of the Tang dynasty. They all took office in Shenzhi's government.

[5c] Those who took official positions in Shenzhi's government included Wang Dan, whose father was Wang Pu, the former prime minister of the Tang dynasty, Yang Yi, whose elder brother was Yang She, the former prime minister of the Tang dynasty, and Xu Ying, who

was a well-known scholar of the Tang dynasty.

该节包含 7 个句读，其中的前 6 个句读两两构成三组。第 1 句和第 2 句"王淡°唐相溥之子"的习作译文 Wang Dan was the son of Wang Pu, former prime minister of the Tang dynasty 改为 Wang Dan, whose father was Wang Pu, the former prime minister of the Tang dynasty。该修订把"儿子"（son）改为"父亲"（father）以使语句的表达更为顺畅。第 3 句和第 4 句"杨沂°唐相涉从弟"习作译文 Yang Yi was the younger brother of Yang She, former prime minister of the Tang dynasty 改为 Yang Yi, whose elder brother was Yang She, the former prime minister of the Tang dynasty。该修订把"弟"（younger brother）改为"兄"（elder brother）以理顺语句的表达次序。第 5 句和第 6 句"徐寅°唐时知名进士"习作译文为 Xu Ying was a well-known scholar of the Tang dynasty 改为 Xu Ying, who was a well-known scholar of the Tang dynasty。该修订仅按语句的结构需要调整个别词语，以使句意变得更加准确。第 7 句"皆依审知仕宦"的习作译文 They all took office in Shenzhi's government 改为 those who took official positions in Shenzhi's government included，并将语句提到句首，以使译文符合英语的惯常表达。该修订添加 1 个小句。该节修订一共添加 4 个单词、1 个小句。

［6a］又建学四门°以教闽士之秀者

［6b］Shenzhi also opened a national academy to teach those talented people in the region of Min.

［6c］In addition, a national academy was established to educate talented people in the region of Min.

该节包含 2 个句读。在习作译文中，"又"字译为 also，其在修订中改为前置的介词短语 in addition。另外，译文语句由主动语态 Shenzhi also opened a national academy 变为被动语态 a national academy was established。

［7a］招来海中蛮夷商贾°海上黄崎°波涛为阻

［7b］He then attracted overseas and foreign merchants, but the Huangqi Island across the sea was obstructed by the waves.

［7c］and policies were implemented to invite overseas and foreign merchants to boost the local economy. The merchant ships, however, could only berth across the sea at the Huangqi Island, between which and the mainland the mighty waves remained the last obstacle.

该节包含 3 个句读，与上节 2 句关联密切。第 1 句 "招来海中蛮夷商贾" 的习作译文 He then attracted overseas and foreign merchants 改为 and policies were implemented to invite overseas and foreign merchants to boost the local economy。该修订把主动句变为被动句，同时更换主语并添加不定式结构 to boost the local economy，以表示目的。第 2 句和第 3 句 "海上黄崎。波涛为阻" 的习作译文 but the Huangqi Island across the sea was obstructed by the waves 改为 The merchant ships, however, could only berth across the sea at the Huangqi Island, between which and the mainland the mighty waves remained the last obstacle。该修订添加 1 个小句，用来衔接上下文的语义。该节修订添加 22 个单词、2 个小句。

[8a] 一夕风雨雷电震击。开以为港。闽人以为审知德政所致。号为甘棠港

[8b] One evening, a fearful tempest arose with thunder and lightning; the Huangqi Island became a seaport overnight. The Min people thought that this was what the virtue of Shenzhi and his government had brought about, so they called it "Gantang Port", that is, the Sweet-Pear Port.

[8c] One evening, after a fearful tempest had arisen with thunder and lightning, the sea was then split into two parts by a road leading to the island, which thus became a seaport overnight. The Min people believed that this was what the virtue of Shenzhi and his government had brought about, so they called it "Gantang Port", that is, the Sweet-Pear Port.

该节包含 4 个句读。第 1 句和第 2 句 "一夕风雨雷电震击。开以为港" 的习作译文 One evening, a fearful tempest arose with thunder and lightning; the Huangqi Island became a seaport overnight 改为 One evening, after a fearful tempest had arisen with thunder and lightning, the sea was then split into two parts by a road leading to the island, which thus became a seaport overnight。该修订把并列结构变为从属结构。习作译文对 "开以为港" 的翻译 the Huangqi Island became a seaport overnight 过于简单，其在修订中明确为 the sea was then split into two parts by a road（大海被道路一分为二），并且详细地说明海港形成的过程：(a road) leading to the island, which thus became a seaport overnight。第 3 句和第 4 句 "闽人以为审知德政所致。号为甘棠港" 的习作

译文不做修改，保留原有译文 the Min people thought that this was what the virtue of Shenzhi and his government had brought about, so they called it "Gantang Port", that is, the Sweet-Pear Port。该节修订添加 16 个单词。现将修订译文整理如下，在整理中又对个别字词做了调整：

> The Tang dynasty established a military institution entitled "Weiwu Military Government" in Fuzhou and accordingly appointed Shenzhi as military commissioner. Since then, he had been promoted several times until he was eventually nominated as the joint manager of affairs with the secretariat chancellery and was granted with the title of "King of Langya". After the fall of the Tang dynasty, the Founding Emperor Taizu of the Liang dynasty nominated Shenzhi as general secretary of the imperial secretariat, granted him with "King of Min", and promoted Fuzhou as Metropolitan Government. At that time, Yang Xingmi occupied the Jianghuai area, blocking the land route in the region between the Yangtze River and the Huai River. Nevertheless, dispatching envoys to go by seaway via the seaport commanderies of Dengzhou and Laizhou, Shenzhi still contrived to pay loyal tribute to the Liang dynasty every year. Before his envoys reached the ports of destination, however, their boats often capsized, and, among the envoys sailing into the sea, as many as three or four out of ten got drowned.
>
> Shenzhi, though having risen up among the bandits, led a thrifty life, treated his subordinates with courtesy, and also received or recruited scholars or officials who had been dismissed from the central court after the downfall of the Tang dynasty. Those who took official positions in Shenzhi's government included Wang Dan, whose father was Wang Pu, the former prime minister of the Tang dynasty, Yang Yi, whose elder brother was Yang She, the former prime minister of the Tang dynasty, and Xu Ying, who was a well-known scholar of the Tang dynasty. In addition, a national academy was established to educate talented people in the region of Min, and policies were carried out to invite overseas and foreign merchants to boost the local economy. The merchant ships, however, could only berth across the sea at the Huangqi Island, between which and the mainland the mighty waves

remained the last obstacle. One evening, after a fearful tempest had arisen with thunder and lightning, the sea was then split into two parts by a road leading to the island, which thus became a seaport overnight. The Min people believed that this was what the virtue of Shenzhi and his government had brought about, so they called it "Gantang Port", that is, the Sweet-Pear Port.

修订译文 B 在风貌上已经明显有别于习作译文 A。修订译文 B 一共增加 98 个单词、10 个小句，单词总数由 287 个增加到 385 个、小句数量由 30 个增加到 40 个，其词字比从约（287/182≈）1.58 提高到约（385/182≈）2.12，译文词汇密度从约（287/33≈）8.70 提高到约（385/33≈）11.67，译文语法难度从约（30/33≈）0.91 提高到约（40/33≈）1.21。现将习作译文 A、修订译文 B、参照译文 A 和参照译文 B 的各项数值列入表 11-1。

表 11-1 习作译文、修订译文及其两种参照译文的语法复杂性对照表

译文	原文汉字/个	原文句读/个	译文单词/个	译文小句/个	译文句子/个	RWC	bi-LD	bi-GI	mono-LD	mono-GI
习作译文 A	182	33	280	30	11	1.54	8.48	0.91	9.33	2.73
修订译文 B	182	33	385	40	12	2.12	11.67	1.21	9.48	3.33
参照译文 A	181	33	328	48	15	1.87	9.94	1.45	6.83	3.20
参照译文 B	—	—	273	33	11	—	—	—	8.27	3.00

修订译文 B 的词字比（2.12）及其译文词汇密度（11.67）分别大幅反超参照译文 A 的词字比（1.87）及其译文词汇密度（9.94）。修订译文 B 的译文语法难度提高 0.3，达到 1.21，但该值依然小于参照译文 A 的译文语法难度 1.45。

单语词汇密度与译文语法难度存在一定的反比关系。就习作译文 A 来说，其译文语法难度较低（0.91），因而其单语词汇密度较高（9.33）。同理，对于修订译文 B 来说，其译文词汇密度较高（11.67），但其译文语法难度不高（1.21），因而其单语词汇密度明显超过参照译文 A 的 6.83 和参照译文 B 的 8.27，甚至超过习作译文 A 的 9.33，达到 9.48。此外，修订译文 B 的单语语法难度（3.33）超过参照译文 A 的单语语法难度（3.20）和参照译文 B 的单语语法难度（3.00）。由此可见，习作译文已经得到较为深入的修订。

4. 习作译文、修订译文与参照译文之间的互文关系

翻译需要达到的目标是对等。Halliday（1966/2007：31）为人工翻译建立一种对等模型，包含三个阶段：第一，按照源语言和译入语在翻译对等上的普遍关系，为原文的词项及语法结构匹配译文的词项及语法结构，使译文和原文在词汇语法上的匹配体现最高的对等概率。第二，按照原文内部的上下文语境对词项及语法结构所施加的语义限制与要求，调整第一步所确定的匹配关系，使译文和原文在词汇语法上符合语境要求。第三，按照译入语的词汇体系和语法体系对译文词项及语法结构所形成的特殊要求，校正第二步的调整，使译文在词汇语法上符合译入语的要求。

经过上述三个阶段，原文转换为译文，最终译文完全脱离原文和源语言，成为译入语中的一个独立文本。就译文来说，原文首先必不可少，然后仅供参考，最后不再需要。在第一阶段中，翻译主要参照原文来形成译文，因而原文不可缺少；在第二阶段中，翻译主要参照源语言的语境因素和结构体系来修订译文，因而原文充当一种辅助的参考资料；在第三阶段中，翻译主要参照译入语的语境因素和结构体系来完善译文，此时的译文已经脱离原文而独立存在。

当然，这并不是说译文与原文解除任何关联。相反，只有在相互独立后二者之间的翻译互文性才完全确立。翻译互文性可反映为语法复杂性：词字比的分析大致处于第一阶段；译文词汇密度和译文语法难度的分析大致处于第二阶段；单语词汇密度和单语语法难度的分析大致处于第三阶段。第一阶段和第二阶段属于双语语境，引入汉译英的参照译文 A，形成早期的修订译文 B。第三阶段属于单语语境，引入非汉译英的参照译文 B，形成后期的修订译文 C。各类习作译文、修订译文和参照译文的关系如图 11-1 所示。

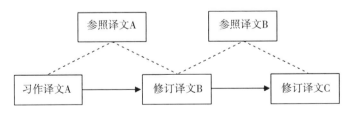

图 11-1　习作译文、修订译文和参照译文的关系示意图

习作译文 A 借助参照译文 A 而转变为修订译文 B；修订译文 B 借助参照译文 B 而转变为修订译文 C。以此类推，直至修订结束。由于本章提到

的修订译文 B 在词汇密度和语法难度上都已超过或接近参照译文 B，所以后者已经无法在这两个方面上为前者提供进一步的修订指导。当然，这既不是说修订译文 B 在质量上已经超越参照译文 B，也不是说参照译文 B 已经失去任何参考价值。相反，除了词字比、译文词汇密度、译文语法难度、单语语法复杂性等指标外，还有其他指标，如实义词比例。在修订译文 B 的全部 385 个单词中，包括动词、名词和形容词在内的实义词总数为 215 个，其百分比值为 55.8%。在参照译文 B 的全部 273 个单词中，实义词总数为 125 个，其百分比值为 45.8%。两种百分比值之差多达 10.0%。显然，此类分析和比较也很值得关注。总之，多维的分析与比较为译文修订提供坚实的理论依据。

5. 小结

中国史籍英译既要考虑双语的语法复杂性指标，也要考虑单语的语法复杂性指标。译文词汇密度和译文语法难度是双语语法复杂性的两个主要方面，体现英语译文和汉语原文之间在词汇语法上的互文关系。单语词汇密度和单语语法难度是单语语法复杂性的两个方面，体现汉译英文本和其他非汉译英文本或英语原生文本之间在词汇语法上的互文关系。尽管单语语法复杂性只在翻译的后期才形成，但直接涉及译文在译入语中的适应问题。因此，对于后期的译文修订具有较强的参考价值。

第 12 章

译文的成长过程

译文从当前译稿到后一译稿、从前期译稿到后期译稿的转变能够体现译文自身在词汇、语法、语义、功能等方面上的成长过程。在此过程中，译文的词项数目不断增加，语法结构逐渐丰富，语义内容趋于完整，功能维度接近对等。本章选取 4 段译文及其中间译稿，分别从三种双语的参考指标和两种单语的参考指标来反映中间译稿的分时状态，其目的是追溯译文成长的全过程。其中，三种双语的参考指标包括词字比 RWC、译文词汇密度 bi-LD、译文语法难度 bi-GI，其具体的数值要求分别是：RWC$\geqslant$1.80；bi-LD＝11.50±1.00；bi-GI$\geqslant$1.30。两种单语的参考指标包括单语词汇密度 mono-LD 和单语语法难度 mono-GI，其具体的数值要求分别是：mono-LD＝8.80±0.80；mono-GI$\geqslant$3.00。

1. 案例一

第一个案例的原文描述王曦为政贪暴，其中涉及廷英献钱、释赞不答、贬黄峻昇、鞭陈光逸、剖棺断尸等具体事项。其原文如下：

泉州刺史余廷英尝矫曦命掠取良家子。曦怒。召下御史劾之。廷英进买宴钱千万。曦曰。皇后土贡何在。廷英又献皇后钱千万。乃得不劾。曦尝嫁女。朝士有不贺者笞之。御史中丞刘赞坐不纠举。将加笞。谏议大夫郑元弼切谏。曦谓元弼曰。卿何如魏郑公。乃敢强谏。元弼曰。陛下似唐太宗。臣为魏郑公可矣。曦喜。乃释赞不笞。

曦弟延政为建州节度使。封富沙王。自曦立。不叶。数举兵相攻。曦由此恶其宗室。多以事诛之。谏议大夫黄峻昇樏诣朝堂极谏。曦怒。贬峻漳州司户参军。校书郎陈光逸上书疏曦过恶五十余事。曦命卫士鞭之百而不死。以绳系颈。挂于木。久而乃绝。国计使陈匡范增算商之法以献。曦曰。匡范人中宝也。已而岁入不登其数。乃借于民以足之。匡范以忧死。其后知其借于民也。剖棺断尸。弃之水中。

原文全文包含278个汉字、45个句读，其汉字密度为6.32。其中，前段包括125个汉字、21个句读，其汉字密度为6.25；后段包含153个汉字、24个句读，其汉字密度为6.38。汉字密度较大。

1.1 第1稿及其词字比

第1稿（即初稿）是在群组翻译的基础上调整语序、添加标点及引入连词而获得的译稿，其全文如下：

> Magistrate of Quanzhou Yu Tingying once took a false command from Xi and seized girls of good breeding. Xi flew into a rage and ordered censors to impeach him. Tingying handed in ten thousand grands of money for banquet expenditure to Xi. "What have you presented to the queen?" asked Xi. Tingying presented another ten million grands of money to the queen, so he was not impeached. Xi once married his daughter and those court officials who failed to congratulate were whipped. Vice censor-in-chief Liu Zan was to be punished and whipped for his unwillingness to impeach other ministers. Grand master of remonstrance Zheng Yuanbi tried his best to dissuade the punishment, so Xi turned to Yuanbi and compared him with Duke Zheng of the Wei state. "How can you compare yourself to Duke Zheng of Wei?" he asked. "And how dare you have dissuaded me so far?" Yuanbi answered, "If Your Majesty compare yourself to the founding emperor Taizong of Tang, I can humbly compare myself to Duke Zheng of Wei." Xi was so pleased that Zan was released and exempted from the punishment.
>
> Wang Xi's yonger brother Wang Yanzheng had been appointed as military commissioner and granted with the title of "King of Fusha". Since Wang Xi came to the throne, they had not been in a good term and had dispatched their troops to attack each other several times. Therefore, Xi hated his clan and family and even killed some of them for one or another reason. Grand master of remonstrance Huang Jun carried a coffin to the court and tried his best to remonstrate. Xi flew into a rage and demoted Jun to an adjutant fiscal officer. The editor Chen Guangyi presented a written document to explain more than fifty

faults and misdeeds that he had done. Xi ordered his guards to whip Guangyi a hundred times but he was still alive, so he was hung in the neck with a rope under a tree only to die after a long while. Minister of finance Chen Kuangfan presented a method to increase taxes on merchants. Xi said, "Kuangfan is rare and precious among men." The annual revenue, however, failed to reach to the expected amount, so Kuangfan made use of private borrowing to make it up. He soon died of worries for this. Later, Xi discovered that Kuangfan had used private borrowing, so he split up Kuangfan's coffin and dismembered the body and discarded those pieces into the water.

第 1 稿全文包含 414 个单词，其词字比 RWC1 约为（414/278≈）1.49。其中，前段译稿包含 185 个单词，其词字比 RWC_a1 为（185/125=）1.48；后段译稿包含 229 个单词，其词字比 RWC_b1 约为（229/153≈）1.50。

1.2　第 2 稿及其词字比

第 2 稿是在第 1 稿的基础上修订而成的译稿。第 1 稿的词字比为 1.49，远低于参照词字比值（≥1.80），因而具有较大的修改空间。从第 1 稿到第 2 稿的修订主要增加词汇数量，以提高词字比。修订后的译稿（第 2 稿）全文如下：

Magistrate of Quanzhou Yu Tingying once robbed girls of good breeding from the civilian with a false command which was said to have been issued by Xi. For this reason, Xi flew into a rage and ordered censors to impeach and punish him. Tingying handed in ten thousand grands of money for banquet expenditure to Xi. "What have you presented to the queen?" asked Xi. Accordingly, Tingying presented another ten million grands of money to the queen. As a result, he was not impeached. Xi once married one of his daughters and those dynastic officials who failed to congratulate or present gifts were whipped. Vice censor-in-chief Liu Zan was to be punished for his unwillingness to impeach other ministers, and, as he was about to be whipped, grand master of remonstrance Zheng Yuanbi tried his best to dissuade the punishment, so Xi turned to Yuanbi and compared him to Duke Zheng of the Wei state in the Spring-Autumn period. "How can you compare yourself to Duke Zheng of Wei?" he asked. "And how dare you have dissuaded so far?" Yuanbi in return compared Xi to the founding emperor Taizong of the Tang dynasty. "If Your Majesty compare yourself to Taizong of Tang," he answered, "I can humbly compare myself to Duke Zheng of Wei." Xi was so pleased that he released Zan and exempted him from the punishment of whipping.

Wang Yanzheng, one of Xi's elder brothers, had been appointed as military commissioner of Jianzhou Commandery and granted with the title of "King of Fusha". Since Xi came to the throne, they had been in such a bad term with each other that they had even dispatched their troops to fight back and forth several times. Xi therefore vented his hatred on Yanzheng's clan and family and killed some of them for one or another reason. Grand master of remonstrance Huang Jun carried a coffin to the court and tried his best to remonstrate him from committing misdeeds, but Xi was deeply enraged by his remonstrance, so he demoted Jun to an adjutant fiscal officer. The editor Chen Guangyi presented a written document to explain more than fifty faults that Xi had or misdeeds that he committed. Xi ordered his guards to whip Guangyi a hundred times but failed to kill him, so Guangyi was then hung in the neck by them with a rope under a tree only to be found dead after a long while. Minister of finance Chen Kuangfan presented a method to increase taxes on business and commerce. Xi was at first pleased with him and praised, "Kuangfan is rare and precious among men." When it came to the end of the year, however, the annual revenue failed to reach to the expected amount, so Kuangfan had to make use of private borrowing to make it up. Kuangfan soon died of worries for his faults. Later, Xi discovered that Kuangfan had used private borrowing, so he ordered his men to split up Kuangfan's coffin, dismembered the body into pieces and discarded them into the water.

此次修订一共添加 95 个单词。第 2 稿现有 509 个单词，其词字比 RCW2 约为（509/278≈）1.83。其中，前段译稿包含 230 个单词，其词字比 RWC_a2 为（230/125 =）1.84；后段译稿包含 279 个单词，其词字比 RWC_b2 约为（279/153≈）1.82。词字比由第 1 稿的 1.49 增加到第 2 稿的 1.83，增幅为 0.34，已经高于参照数值 1.80。

1.3 第 3 稿及其译文词汇密度

第 2 稿共有 509 个单词，其译文词汇密度 bi-LD2 约为（509/45≈）11.31。其中，前段译稿包含 230 个单词，其译文词汇密度 bi-LD_a2 约为（230/21≈）10.95；后段译稿包含 279 个单词，其译文词汇密度 bi-LD_b2 约为（279/24≈）11.63。由于前后两段的译文词汇密度均已高于参照范围的下限数值 10.50，所以只需对第 2 稿稍做修订便可形成第 3 稿。第 3 稿的译文词汇密度 bi-LD3 与第 2 稿的译文词汇密度相同，均约为（509/45≈）11.31。其中，前段的译文词汇密度 bi-LD_a3 和 bi-LD_a2 均约为（230/21≈）10.95；后段的译文词汇密度 bi-LD_b3 和 bi-LD_b2 均为（279/24=）11.625。

1.4 第 4 稿及其译文语法难度

第 3 稿包含 54 个小句，其译文语法难度 bi-GI3 为（54/45=）1.20。其中，前段的译文语法难度 bi-GI_a3 约为（27/21≈）1.29，基本达到参照数值（≥1.30）；后段的译文语法难度 bi-GI_b3 为（27/24=）1.125，明显低于参照数值。下一步的主要修订任务是提高后段译稿的小句数量。现将经修订而得到的第 4 稿逐句分析并标示如下：

> Magistrate of Quanzhou Yu Tingying once robbed girls of good breeding from the civilian with a false command | which was said to have been issued by Xi. | For this reason, Xi flew into a rage and | ordered censors to impeach and punish him. | Tingying handed in ten thousand grands of money for banquet expenditure to Xi. | "What have you presented to the queen?" | asked Xi. | Accordingly, Tingying presented another ten million grands of money to the queen. | As a result, he was not impeached. | Xi once married <u>his daughter to someone</u> and | those dynastic officials who failed to congratulate or present gifts | were whipped. | Vice censor-in-chief Liu Zan was to be punished for his unwillingness to impeach other ministers, | and, as he was about to be whipped, | grand master of remonstrance Zheng Yuanbi tried his best to dissuade the punishment, | so Xi turned to Yuanbi and | compared him to Duke Zheng of the Wei state in the Spring-Autumn period. | "How can you compare yourself to Duke Zheng of Wei?" | he asked. | "And how dare you have dissuaded so far?" | Yuanbi in return compared Xi to the founding emperor Taizong of the Tang dynasty. | "If Your Majesty compare yourself to Taizong of Tang," | he answered, | "I can humbly compare myself to Duke Zheng

of Wei. " | Xi was so pleased | that he released Zan and | exempted him from the punishment of whipping. |

Wang Yanzheng was one of Xi's elder brothers. | He had been appointed as military commissioner of Jianzhou Commandery and | granted with the title of "King of Fusha" before the reign of Xi. | Since Xi came to the throne, | they had been in such a bad term with each other | that they had even dispatched their troops to fight back and forth several times. | Xi therefore vented his hatred on Yanzheng's clan and house and | killed some of them for one or another reason. | Grand master of remonstrance Huang Jun carried a coffin to the court and | tried his best to remonstrate him | from committing misdeeds, | but Xi was deeply enraged by his remonstrance, | so he demoted Jun to an adjutant fiscal officer. | The editor Chen Guangyi presented a written document | in which more than fifty faults that Xi had or | misdeeds that he committed | were sorted out. | Xi ordered his guards to put Guangyi to death. | Guangyi was first whipped a hundred times | but he was still alive and | then he was hung in the neck by the guards with a rope under a tree | only to be found dead after a long while. | Minister of finance Chen Kuangfan presented a method to increase taxes on business and commerce. | Xi was at first pleased with him and | thought highly of him. | "Kuangfan is rare and precious among men," | said Xi. | When it came to the end of the year, | however, the annual revenue failed to reach to the expected amount, | so Kuangfan had to make use of private borrowing to make it up. | Kuangfan soon died of worries for his faults. | Later, Xi discovered that Kuangfan had used private borrowing, | so he ordered his men to split up Kuangfan's coffin, | dismembered the body into pieces and | discarded them into the water. |

第 4 稿现有 62 个小句，其译文语法难度 bi-GI4 约为（62/45 ≈）1.38。其中，前段译稿包含 27 个小句，其译文语法难度 bi-GI$_a$4 与第 3 稿的译文语法难度 bi-GI$_a$3 同约为（27/21 ≈）1.29；后段译稿包含 35 个小句，其译文语法难度 bi-GI$_b$4 约为（35/24 ≈）1.46。第 4 稿的译文语法难度已经高于参照数值 1.30。此外，经过上述从第 3 稿到第 4 稿的修订，译稿的单词总数由 509 个增加到 531 个，一共增加了 22 个单词，因而词字比和译文词汇密度的数值也相应地得到了提高。第 4 稿的词字比 RWC4 约为 （531/278≈）1.91，其译文词汇密度 LD4 为（531/45=）11.80。

1.5 第 5 稿及其单语词汇密度

第 4 稿共有 531 个单词、62 个小句，其单语词汇密度 mono-LD4 约为 （531/62≈）8.56。其中，前段译稿包含 230 个单词、27 个小句，其单语词汇密度 mono-LD_a4 约为（230/27≈）8.52；后段译稿包含 301 个单词、35 个小句，其单语词汇密度 mono-LD_b4 为（301/35=）8.60。由于前后两段译稿的单语词汇密度均已高于参照范围的下限数值 8.00，所以对第 4 稿仅做少量修订就可得到第 5 稿。

1.6 第 6 稿及其单语语法复杂性

第 5 稿包含 529 个单词、62 个小句、25 个句子，其单语语法复杂性的两个指标分别为：单语词汇密度 mono-LD5 约为（529/62≈）8.53；单语语法难度 mono-GI5 为（62/25=）2.48。其中，前段译稿包含 230 个单词、27 个小句、12 个句子，其单语词汇密度 mono-LD_a5 约为（230/27≈）8.52，单语语法难度 mono-GI_a5 为（27/12=）2.25；后段译稿包含 299 个单词、35 个小句、13 个句子，其单语词汇密度 mono-LD_b5 约为（299/35≈）8.54，单语语法难度 mono-GI_b5 约为（35/13≈）2.69。两段译稿的单语词汇密度均在参照范围之内（8.80±0.80），而其单语语法难度均小于参照数值（3.00）。下一步的主要修订任务是重新整合小句以减少整个译文的句子总数，其目的是提高其单语语法难度。在第 5 稿的基础上可做如下修订（其中的"｜"为小句标记；"‖"为句子标记）：

> Magistrate of Quanzhou Yu Tingying once robbed girls of good breeding from the civilian with a false command | which was said to have been issued by Xi. ‖ For this reason, Xi flew into a rage and ordered censors to impeach and punish him, | but Tingying tried to smooth this critical situation | by handing in ten thousand grands of money for banquet expenditure to Xi. ‖ "What have you presented to the queen?" | asked Xi. ‖ Accordingly, Tingying presented another ten million grands of money to the queen, | and, as a result, he was not impeached. ‖ Xi once married his daughter to someone and | those dynastic officials who failed to congratulate or present gifts | were whipped. ‖ Vice censor-in-chief Liu Zan was to be punished | for his unwillingness to impeach other ministers, | and, as he was about to be whipped, | grand master of remonstrance Zheng Yuanbi tried his best to

dissuade the punishment, | so Xi turned to Yuanbi and | compared him to Duke Zheng of the Wei state in the Spring-Autumn period. || "How can you compare yourself to Duke Zheng of Wei?" | he asked, | "and how dare you have dissuaded so far?" || Yuanbi in return compared Xi to the founding emperor Taizong of the Tang dynasty, | and answered, | "If Your Majesty compare yourself to Taizong of Tang, | I can humbly compare myself to Duke Zheng of Wei." || Xi was so pleased | that he released Zan and exempted him from the punishment of whipping. ||

Wang Yanzheng, who was one of Xi's elder brothers, | had been appointed as military commissioner of Jianzhou and | granted with the title of "King of Fusha" before the reign of Xi. || Since Xi came to the throne, | they had been in such a bad term with each other | that they had even dispatched their troops to fight back and forth several times. | Xi therefore vented his hatred on Yanzheng's clan and house and | killed some of them for one or another reason. || Grand master of remonstrance Huang Jun carried a coffin to the court and | tried his best to remonstrate him | from committing further misdeeds, | but Xi was deeply enraged by his remonstrance, | so he demoted Jun to an adjutant fiscal officer. || The editor Chen Guangyi presented a written document | in which more than fifty faults that Xi had or | misdeeds that he committed | were sorted out. || Xi ordered his guards to put Guangyi to death: | Guangyi was first whipped a hundred times | but he was still alive, | so he was hung in the neck by the guards with a rope under a tree | only to be found dead after a long while. || Minister of finance Chen Kuangfan presented a method to increase taxes on business and commerce. || Xi was at first pleased with him and | thought highly of him. || "Kuangfan is rare and precious among men," | said Xi. || When it came to the end of the year, | however, the annual revenue failed to reach to the expected amount, | so Kuangfan had to make use of private borrowing to make it up. || Kuangfan soon died of worries for this fault. || Later, Xi discovered that Kuangfan had used private borrowing, | so he ordered his men to split up Kuangfan's coffin, | dismembered the body into pieces and | discarded them into the water. ||

经修改得到的第 6 稿共有 539 个单词、63 个小句、20 个句子，其单语语法复杂性的两个指标分别为：单语词汇密度 mono-LD6 约为（539/63≈）8.56；单语语法难度 mono-GI6 为（63/20=）3.15。其中，前段译稿包含 239 个单词、28 个小句、9 个句子，其单语词汇密度 mono-LD$_a$6 约为（239/28≈）8.54，单语语法难度 mono-GI$_a$6 约为（28/9≈）3.11；后段译稿包含 300 个单词、35 个小句、11 个句子，其单语词汇密度 mono-LD$_b$6 约为（300/35≈）8.57，单语语法难度 mono-GI$_b$6 约为（35/11≈）3.18。总体上，单语语法难度数值已经达到参照范围（≥3.00）。

2. 案例二

第二个案例的原文描述曦性淫虐，其中涉及以色取人、常为牛饮、杀弃酒者、醉归见杀、延政建国等具体事项。其原文如下：

曦性既淫虐°而妻李氏悍而酗酒°贤妃尚氏有色而宠°李仁遇°曦甥也°以色嬖之°用以为相°曦常为牛饮°群臣侍酒°醉而不胜°有诉及私弃酒者辄杀之°诸子继柔弃酒°并杀其赞者一人°连重遇杀昶°惧为国人所讨°与朱文进连姻以自固°曦心疑之°常以语诮重遇等°重遇等流涕自辨°李氏妒尚妃之宠°欲图曦而立其子亚澄°乃使人谓重遇等曰°上心不平于二公°奈何°重遇等惧°六年三月°曦出游°醉归°重遇等遣壮士拉于马上而杀之°谥曰景宗°

延政°审知子也°曦立°为淫虐°延政数贻书谏之°曦怒°遣杜建崇监其军°延政逐之°曦乃举兵攻延政°为延政所败°延政乃以建州建国称殷°改元天德°

原文全文包含 229 个汉字、42 个句读，其汉字密度约为 5.45。其中，前段包括 172 个汉字、30 个句读，其汉字密度约为 5.73；后段包含 57 个汉字、12 个句读，其汉字密度为 4.75。

2.1 第 1 稿及其词字比

在群组翻译的基础上添加标点符号、少量连接词语或语句后整理而成的第 1 稿包含如下两段译文：

> Xi was dissolute and tyrannical in nature, and his wife Mrs Li was ferocious and indulged in drinking. His concubine Mrs Shang was favoured for her good appearance. Li Renyu was one of Xi's nephews. He was favoured by Xi for his good appearance, so he was appointed as prime minister. Xi often boozed. The ministers also served by his side

and catered for the drinking, but they often failed to sustain the excessive drinking and got heavily drunk. Those who refused to drink or discarded any wine in private were often killed. On one occasion, his son Jirou, after discarding some wine, was killed together with one of his emcees. Since Lian Chongyu killed Chang, he had been frightened that he would be sanctioned by the nationals, so he made use of a marriage with Zhu Wenjin's family to strengthen his position and ensure his safety. Xi was suspicious with Chongyu and those who were concerned, so he often blamed them for the guilt and they could do nothing but defend themselves with a running nose. Mrs Li envied Princess Shang for being favoured, so she conspired against Xi and intended to enthrone her son Yacheng. She sent a man to take words to Chongyu and his colleagues. "His Majesty does not treat you in a fair manner," he said, "and how can this situation be coped with?" They were panicked. In March of the sixth year of the Yonglong period (April or May, A.D. 944), after Xi took an excursion, he drank and returned. Chongyu and his colleagues dispatched soldiers to drag him down from the horse and killed him. Xi was honoured with the posthumous title of "Jingzong", that is, the Grand Emperor.

Wang Yanzheng is one of Wang Shenzhi's sons. Xi succeeded to the throne. He was dissolute and tyrannical. Yanzheng submitted several written statements to remonstrate him. Xi flew into a rage, so he sent Du Jiancong to supervise his army. Yanzheng expelled them and then Xi raised troops to attack Yanzheng only to be defeated by Yanzheng. Yanzheng founded a new state called "Yin" on the basis of Jianzhou Commandery. The reigning designation was changed into "Tiande", that is, "Heavenly Virtue".

第1稿全文包含367个单词，其词字比 RWC1 为（367/229＝）1.60。其中，前段包含286个单词，其词字比 RWC_a1 约为（286/172≈）1.66；后段包含81个单词，其词字比 RWC_b1 约为（81/57≈）1.42。

2.2　第2稿及其词字比

第1稿的总体词字比为1.60，低于参照词字比值（≥1.80），因而存在修改的空间。通过增加单词数量得到如下第2稿：

第 12 章 译文的成长过程

Xi was dissolute and tyrannical in nature, whereas his wife Mrs Li was ferocious and indulged in drinking. Xi employed people according to their appearance: Mrs Shang looked fairly nice, so she became the favourite princess; Xi's nephew Li Renyu also had good appearance, so he was favoured and appointed by Xi as prime minister. Xi also indulged in drinking and always boozed. He requested his ministers to serve by his side and cater for the drinking, but they often failed to sustain the excessive amount and got heavily drunk. Those who refused to drink or discarded any wine in private were often killed. On one occasion, his son Jirou discarded some drink, so he was killed together with a master of ceremonies. Meanwhile, since Lian Chongyu killed Chang, he had been frightened that he would be sanctioned by the nationals, so he made use of a marriage with Zhu Wenjin's family to strengthen his position and ensure his own safety. Xi was suspicious with Chongyu and his colleagues and often blamed them for the guilt, but what they could do was to defend themselves with a running nose. Mrs Li envied Princess Shang for being favoured, so she conspired against Xi and intended to enthrone her son Yacheng. She sent someone to take words to Chongyu and his colleagues. "His Majesty does not treat you in a fair manner," the man said, "and how can this situation be coped with?" Chongyu and his colleagues were all panicked, so they planned to take a measure. In March of the sixth year of the Yonglong period (April or May, A. D. 944), after Xi took an excursion, he drank and returned to the palace. Chongyu and his colleagues dispatched soldiers to drag him down from the horse and then killed him. Xi was honoured with the posthumous title of "Jingzong", that is, "the Grand Emperor".

Yanzheng, another son of Shenzhi, had submitted several written statements to remonstrate his brother Xi from committing misdeeds, because he had been dissolute and tyrannical ever since he succeeded to the throne. These remonstrations only irritated Xi to such an extent that he sent Du Jiancong to supervise Yanzheng's army. Yanzheng did not accept this, so he expelled Jiancong. This eventually led to a war between them. Xi raised troops to attack Yanzheng, but he was defeated by Yanzheng. Yanzheng soon afterwards founded a new state called "Yin" on the basis of Jianzhou Commandery and changed the designation of the reign into "Tiande", that is, Heavenly Virtue.

对第 1 稿的修订一共添加 53 个单词。经修改后得到的第 2 稿全文包含 420 个单词，其词字比 RWC2 约为（420/229≈）1.83。其中，前段译稿包含 313 个单词，其词字比 RWC$_a$2 约为（313/172≈）1.82；后段译稿包含 107 个单词，其词字比 RWC$_b$2 约为（107/57≈）1.88。

2.3 第 3 稿及其译文词汇密度

第 2 稿共有 420 个单词，其译文词汇密度 bi-LD2 为（420/42＝）10.00。其中，前段译稿包含 313 个单词，其译文词汇密度 bi-LD$_a$2 约为（313/30≈）10.43，基本处于参照区间（11.50±1.00）之内；后段译稿包含 107 个单词，其译文词汇密度 bi-LD$_b$2 约为（107/12≈）8.92，明显低于上述参照数值的下限，存在较大的修改空间。现对后段第 2 稿修订如下：

Earlier, Yanzheng, who was another son of Shenzhi, had submitted several written statements in which he remonstrated his brother Xi from further committing misdeeds, for Xi had been dissolute and tyrannical ever since he succeeded to the throne. These remonstrations only irritated Xi to such an extent that he in return sent Du Jiancong as commissioner to supervise Yanzheng's army. Yanzheng did not accept such military supervision, so he expelled Jiancong and sent him back to Fuzhou. This eventually led to a war between them. Xi first dispatched his troops to attack Yanzheng, but his troops were defeated by Yanzheng. Yanzheng soon afterwards founded a new state called "Yin" on the basis of Jianzhou Commandery and changed the designation of the reign into "Tiande", that is, Heavenly Virtue.

对后段第 2 稿的修改一共添加 23 个单词。经修订得到的后段第 3 稿现有 128 个单词，其译文词汇密度 bi-LD$_b$3 约为（128/12≈）10.67。第 3 稿全文现有 441 个单词，其总体的译文词汇密度 bi-LD3 为（441/42＝）10.50。

2.4 第 4 稿及其译文语法难度

第 3 稿全文包含 61 个小句，其译文语法难度 bi-GI3 约为（61/42≈）1.45。其中，前段包含 43 个小句，其译文语法难度 bi-GI$_a$3 约为（43/30≈）1.43；后段包含 18 个小句，其译文语法难度 bi-GI$_b$3 为（18/12＝）1.50。第 3 稿的译文语法难度的数值已经较高，因而只须对其稍做调整就可得到第 4 稿。第 4 稿的译文语法难度 bi-GI4 与第 3 稿的译文语法难度 bi-GI3 同约为（61/42≈）1.45。其中，前段第 4 稿的译文语法难度 bi-GI$_a$4 与其第 3 稿的译文语法难度 bi-GI$_a$3 同约为（43/30≈）1.43；后段第 4 稿的译文语法难度 bi-GI$_b$4 与其第 3 稿的译文语法难度 bi-GI$_b$3 同为（18/12＝）1.50。

2.5　第 5 稿及其单语词汇密度

第 4 稿共有 442 个单词、61 个小句，其单语词汇密度 mono-LD4 约为（442/61≈）7.25。其中，前段译稿包含 314 个单词、43 个小句，其单语词汇密度 mono-LD$_a$4 约为（314/43≈）7.30；后段译稿包含 128 个单词、18 个小句，其单语词汇密度 mono-LD$_b$4 约为（128/18≈）7.11。相较于单语词汇密度的参照数值区间（8.80±0.80），第 4 稿还有一定的修改空间。由于第 4 稿的译文语法难度为 1.45，明显高于参照数值的下限 1.30，所以从第 4 稿到第 5 稿的修订可适当增加单词数量或减少小句数量，以提高单语词汇密度。经修改得到的第 5 稿按小句分析并标注如下：

Xi was dissolute and tyrannical in nature, | whereas his wife Mrs Li was ferocious and indulged in drinking. | Xi employed people <u>according to their appearance</u>: | Mrs Shang became the favourite princess | simply because she looked fairly nice; | Xi's nephew Li Renyu also had good appearance, | so he was favoured and appointed by Xi as prime minister. | Xi also indulged in drinking and always boozed. | <u>In addition</u>, he requested his ministers to serve by his side and cater for the drinking, | but they often failed to sustain the excessive amount and | got heavily drunk. | Those who refused to drink or | discarded any wine in private | <u>were often</u> <u>punished or even</u> <u>put to death</u>. | On one occasion, his son Jirou discarded some drink, | so he was killed together with a master of ceremonies. | Meanwhile, since Lian Chongyu killed Chang, | he had been frightened | that he would be sanctioned by the nationals, | so he made use of a marriage with Zhu Wenjin's family to strengthen his position and | ensure his own safety. | Xi was suspicious with Chongyu and his colleagues and | often blamed them for one or another offence, | but what they could do | was to defend themselves with a running nose. | Mrs Li herself envied Princess Shang | for being favoured by Xi, | <u>so she joined a conspiracy against Xi and</u> | intended to enthrone her son Yacheng. | She sent someone to take words to Chongyu and his colleagues. | <u>The man came to Chongyu</u>

and Wenjin and referred them as dukes. | "His Majesty treats you both in an unfair manner," | the man said, | "and how can this situation be coped with?" | Chongyu and his colleagues were all panicked, | so they planned to take a measure. | In March of the sixth year of the Yonglong period (April or May, A.D. 944), after Xi took an excursion, | he drank and returned to the palace. | Chongyu and his colleagues dispatched soldiers to drag him down from the horse | and then killed him. | Xi was honoured with the posthumous title of "Jingzong", | that is, the Grand Emperor. |

Earlier, Yanzheng, who was also son of Shenzhi, | had submitted several written statements of <u>remonstrance to Xi</u>, | because Xi was dissolute in nature and tyrannical in government | since he had succeeded to the throne. | These remonstrations, however, irritated Xi to such an extent | that he in return sent Du Jiancong as commissioner to supervise Yanzheng's army. | Yanzheng <u>rejected</u> Xi's military supervision, | so he expelled and sent Jiancong back to Fuzhou. | This eventually led to a war between <u>these two brothers</u>. | Xi first dispatched his troops to attack Yanzheng, | but his troops were defeated by Yanzheng's. | Soon afterwards, Yanzheng founded a new kingdom with "Yin" as the name on the basis of Jianzhou Commandery and | changed the designation of the reign into "Tiande", | that is, "Heavenly Virtue". |

相较于第 4 稿，第 5 稿增加 23 个单词，减少 5 个小句，全文现有 465 个单词、56 个小句，其单语词汇密度 mono-LD5 约为（465/56≈）8.30。其中，前段译稿包含 340 个单词、42 个小句，其单语词汇密度 mono-LD_a5 约为（340/42≈）8.10；后段译稿包含 125 个单词、14 个小句，其单语词汇密度 mono-LD_b5 约为（125/14≈）8.93。

2.6　第 6 稿及其单语语法复杂性

第 5 稿全文包含 465 个单词、56 个小句、21 个句子，其单语语法复杂性的两个指标分别为：单语词汇密度 mono-LD5 约为（465/56≈）8.30；单语语法难度 mono-GI5 约为（56/21≈）2.67。其中，前段译稿包含 340 个单词、42 个小句、15 个句子，其单语词汇密度 mono-LD_a5 约为（340/42≈）8.10；单语语法难度 mono-GI_a5 为（42/15＝）2.80；后段译稿包含 125 个单词、14 个小句、6 个句子，其单语词汇密度 mono-LD_b5 约为

$(125/14 \approx)$ 8.93；单语语法难度 mono-GI_b5 约为 $(14/6 \approx)$ 2.33。总体上，第5稿的单语词汇密度 mono-LD5 已经处于参照范围之内（8.80±0.80），但其单语语法难度 mono-GI5 还低于参照范围的下限数值 3.00。为了提高第5稿的单语语法难度，可把部分小句相互归并，形成较长的语句。现将第5稿修改并按小句（|）和句子（||）分析如下：

Xi was dissolute and tyrannical in nature, | whereas his wife Mrs Li was ferocious and indulged in drinking. || Xi employed people according to their appearance: | Mrs Shang became the favourite princess | simply because she looked fairly nice; | Xi's nephew Li Renyu also had good appearance, | so he was favoured and appointed by Xi as prime minister. || <u>Xi also indulged in drinking and always boozed;</u> | in addition, <u>he requested his ministers to serve by his side and cater for the drinking,</u> | but most of them failed to sustain the excessive amount and | often got heavily drunk. || Those who refused to drink or discarded any wine in private | were often punished or even got killed. || On one occasion, his son Jirou discarded some drink, | so he was killed together with a master of ceremonies. || Meanwhile, since Lian Chongyu killed Chang, | he had been frightened | that he would be sanctioned by the nationals, | so he made use of a marriage with Zhu Wenjin's family | in order to strengthen his position and ensure his own safety. || Xi later became suspicious with Chongyu and his colleagues and | often blamed them for the guilt | that they had committed to the loyal clan, | but what they could do was | simply to defend themselves with their running noses. || <u>This was well noticed of by Mrs Li,</u> | who had been envious of Princess Shang | <u>since the latter was favoured by Xi.</u> || Mrs Li worked out a conspiracy against Xi and | <u>intended to enthrone her son Yacheng,</u> | <u>so she sent someone to take words to Chongyu and his colleagues.</u> || The man came to Chongyu and Wenjin and referred them as dukes. || "His Majesty treats you both in an unfair manner," | he said, | "and how can this situation be coped with?" || Chongyu and his colleagues were all panicked, | <u>so they planned to take an action to solve this problem.</u> || In March of the sixth year of the Yonglong period (April or May, A.D. 944), | <u>after Xi took an excursion,</u> | <u>he drank as usual and returned to the palace,</u> | <u>but he was</u>

dragged down from the horse on mid-way and | then killed by soldiers | who had been dispatched by Chongyu and his colleagues. ‖ Xi was honoured with the posthumous title of "Jingzong", | that is, the Grand Emperor. ‖

Earlier, Yanzheng, who was also son of Shenzhi, | had submitted several written statements of remonstrance to Xi | because Xi was dissolute in nature and tyrannical in government | since Xi had succeeded to the throne. ‖ These remonstrations, however, irritated Xi to such an extent | that he in return sent Du Jiancong as commissioner to supervise Yanzheng's army. ‖ Yanzheng rejected Xi's military supervision | by expelling and sending Jiancong back to Fuzhou, | and, as a result, a war was brought about between these two brothers. ‖ Xi first dispatched his troops to attack Yanzheng, | but his troops were defeated. ‖ Soon afterwards, Yanzheng founded a new kingdom with "Yin" as the name on the basis of Jianzhou Commandery and | changed the designation of the reign into "Tiande", | that is, "Heavenly Virtue". ‖

以上修订一共增加 36 个单词，减少 2 个小句及 3 个句子。经修改得到的第 6 稿现有 501 个单词、58 个小句、19 个句子，其单语语法复杂性的两个指标分别为：单语词汇密度 mono-LD6 约为（501/58≈）8.64；单语语法难度 mono-GI6 约为（58/19≈）3.05。其中，前段译稿包含 375 个单词、44 个小句、14 个句子，其单语词汇密度 mono-LD_a6 约为（375/44≈）8.52；单语语法难度 mono-GI_a6 约为（44/14≈）3.14。后段译稿包含 126 个单词、14 个小句、5 个句子，其单语词汇密度 mono-LD_b6 为（126/14=）9.00；单语语法难度 mono-GI_b6 为（14/5=）2.80。总体上，单语语法难度的数值已经高于 3.00。

3. 案例三

第三个案例的原文详细描述延政得闽的过程，其中涉及文进篡闽、称晋年号、诸州复辟、迁都福州等具体事项。其原文如下：

明年。连重遇已杀曦。集闽群臣告曰。昔太祖武皇帝亲冒矢石。遂启有闽。及其子孙。淫虐不道。今天厌王氏。百姓与能。当求有德。以安此土。群臣皆莫敢议。乃掖朱文进升殿。率百官北面而臣之。文进以重遇判六军诸卫事。王氏子弟在福州者无少长皆杀之。以黄绍颇守泉州。程赟守漳州。许文缜守汀州。称晋年号。时开运元年也。

泉州军将留从效诈其州人曰。富沙王兵收福州矣。吾属世为王氏臣。安能交臂而事贼乎。州人共杀绍颇。迎王继勋为刺史。漳州闻之。亦杀赟。迎王继成为刺史。皆王氏之诸子也。文缜惧。以汀州降于延政。延政已得三州。重遇亦杀文进。传首建州以自归。福州裨将林仁翰又杀重遇。谋迎延政都福州。

原文全文包含 243 个汉字、38 个句读，其汉字密度约为 6.39。其中，前段包括 127 个汉字、21 个句读，其汉字密度约为 6.05；后段包含 116 个汉字、17 个句读，其汉字密度约为 6.82。汉字密度较大。

3.1 第 1 稿及其词字比

在添加标点符号、少量连接词语或附加语句后，由群组翻译所得的语句整理而成的第 1 稿包含如下两段译文：

  One year after Lian Chongyu killed Chang, he summoned all ministers in the state of Min and persuaded them to establish a new government. "In the past," he said, "the Founding Emperor Wu went through the battlefield in spite of arrows and stones. Since then the state of Min has been established. His sons and grandsons, however, were dissolute and tyrannical and not on the right way, and now the heaven hates the Wang's house and the common people recommended men of talent. We should accept those who are virtuous so as to make this land peaceful." No ministers dared to raise any further suggestions, so he supported Zhu Wenjin into the palace and led all the officials to face north and submit to him. Wenjin in turn appointed Chongyu to take charge of the six legions of armed forces and all security affairs. Those brothers and sons of the Wang family who resided in Fuzhou were mostly killed regardless of their ages. Huang Shaopo was sent to defend Quanzhou, Chen Yun was sent to defend Quanzhou, and Xu Wenzhen was sent to defend Tingzhou. The designation of the Jin dynasty was adopted. It was the first year of the Kaiyun period (A. D. 944).

  The general commander of Quanzhou Liu Congxiao deceived the people of Quanzhou and said, "Fusha King is recapturing Fuzhou with armed forces. We have been ministers at the service in the Wang's house for all our life. How can we surrender to and serve for these traitors?" People in Quanzhou rose up together to kill Shaopo and received Wang Jixun as magistrate. On hearing this, people in Zhangzhou also killed Yun and received Wang Jicheng as magistrate. Both of them are princes of the Wang's house. Wenzhen was so frightened that he surrendered Tingzhou to Yanzheng. Yanzheng now took control of three military commanderies. Chongyu also killed Wenjin and transferred his head to Jianzhou to show his submission, but assistant general of Fuzhou Lin Renhan in turn killed Chongyu and planned to receive Yanzheng to move the capital to Fuzhou.

第 1 稿包含 345 个单词，其词字比 RCW1 约为（345/243≈）1.42。其中，前段译稿包含 205 个单词，其词字比 RCW_a1 约为（205/127≈）1.61；后段译稿包含 140 个单词，其词字比 RCW_b1 约为（140/116≈）1.21。

3.2 第 2 稿及其词字比

第 1 稿的总体词字比为 1.42。其中，前段的词字比已达 1.61，存在一定的修订空间；后段的词字比仅有 1.21，存在较大的修订空间。通过增加词汇得到如下第 2 稿：

It had been one year also since Lian Chongyu killed Chang. On one occasion, Chongyu summoned all ministers in the Min government and declared that they were to break away from the reign of the Wang's clan. "In the past," he said, "the Founding Emperor Wu went through battlefields in spite of arrows and stones. Since then the state of Min has been established. His sons and grandsons, however, are dissolute and tyrannical. They have gone too far away from the right path so that the heaven has begun to hate the Wang's clan. Now the common people begin to recommend men of talent to replace them. We should accept those who are virtuous so as to make this land peaceful." Seeing that none of the ministers dared to have any further discussion on this topic, Chongyu supported Zhu Wenjin in person to ascend into the palace, seated him on the throne, and led all the officials to face north and submit to Wenjin. Wenjin in turn appointed Chongyu to take charge of the six legions of armed forces and all security affairs. Most of those brothers and sons from the Wang's clan who resided in Fuzhou were killed, regardless of their ages. Huang Shaopo, Chen Yun and Xu Wenzhen were sent to defend Quanzhou, Zhangzhou and Tingzhou, respectively. The new government adopted the designation of the Jin dynasty. It was the first year of the Kaiyun period (A. D. 944).

The general commander of Quanzhou Liu Congxiao deceived the men in Quanzhou in the belief that Yanzheng, King of Fusha, was dispatching armed forces to capture Fuzhou. "King of Fusha," he said, "is now leading troops to occupy Fuzhou and all traitors in Fuzhou are sure to be sanctioned. We have served as ministers in Wang's government for all our life. How can we submit to those traitors and even serve them as accomplices?" The men of Quanzhou were fully convinced of this unreal situation, so they rose up together against Shaopo and put him to death. Wang Jixun was received and nominated as magistrate. After the news from Quanzhou arrived, the men of Zhangzhou also killed Yun and then received Wang Jicheng as magistrate. Both Jixun and Jicheng were princes of the Wang's clan. When the news came to Tingzhou, Wenzhen was so frightened that he surrendered Tingzhou to Yanzheng directly. At this time, Yanzheng had taken control of three military commanderies, including Quanzhou, Zhangzhou and Tingzhou. In this situation, Chongyu also killed Wenjin and transferred his head to Jianzhou, showing his willingness to surrender Fuzhou to Yanzheng, but he was in turn killed by Lin Renhan, assistant general of Fuzhou. Renhan planned to receive Yanzheng to move the capital to Fuzhou.

对第 1 稿的修订一共添加 109 个单词。经过修改得到的第 2 稿包含 454 个单词，其词字比 RCW2 约为 （454/243≈） 1.87。其中，前段译稿包含 241 个单词，其词字比 $RCW_a 2$ 约为 （241/127≈） 1.90；后段译稿包含 213 个单词，其词字比 $RCW_b 2$ 约为 （213/116≈） 1.84。

3.3　第 3 稿及其译文词汇密度

第 2 稿共有 454 个单词，其译文词汇密度 bi-LD2 约为 （454/38≈） 11.95。其中，前段译稿包含 241 个单词，其译文词汇密度 $bi\text{-}LD_a 2$ 约为 （241/21≈） 11.48；后段译稿包含 213 个单词，其译文词汇密度 $bi\text{-}LD_b 2$

约为（213/17≈）12.53。前后两段译稿的译文词汇密度大体处于 10.50 与 12.50 之间。因此，只须对第 2 稿做少量修改便可获得第 3 稿。第 3 稿的译文词汇密度 bi-LD3 与第 2 稿的译文词汇密度 bi-LD2 同为 11.95。其中，第 3 稿前段的译文词汇密度 bi-LD_a3 与第 2 稿前段的译文词汇密度 bi-LD_a2 同为 11.48；第 3 稿后段的译文词汇密度 bi-LD_b3 与第 2 稿后段的译文词汇密度 bi-LD_b2 同为 12.53。

3.4　第 4 稿及其译文语法难度

第 3 稿全文包含 52 个小句，其译文语法难度 bi-GI3 约为（51/38≈）1.34，高于参照数值 1.30。其中，前段译稿包含 24 个小句，其译文语法难度 bi-GI_a3 约为（26/21≈）1.24，低于参照数值 1.30，还有一些修改空间；后段译稿包含 26 个小句，其译文语法难度 bi-GI_b3 约为（26/17≈）1.53，明显高于参照数值 1.30。以下是第 3 稿的句读分析情况：

> It had been one year also | since Lian Chongyu killed Chang. | On one occasion, Chongyu summoned all ministers in the Min government | and declared | that they were to break away from the reign of the Wang's clan. | "In the past," he said, | "the Founding Emperor Wu went through battlefields in spite of arrows and stones. | Since then the state of Min has been established. | His sons and grandsons, however, are dissolute and tyrannical. | They have gone too far away from the right path | so that the heaven has begun to hate the Wang's clan. | Now the common people begin to recommend men of talent to replace them. | We should accept those | who are virtuous | so as to make this land peaceful." | Seeing that | none of the ministers dared to have any further discussion on this topic, | Chongyu supported Zhu Wenjin in person to ascend into the palace, | seated him on the throne, | and led all the officials to face north and submit to Wenjin. | Wenjin in turn appointed Chongyu to take charge of the six legions of armed forces and all security affairs. | Most of those brothers and sons from the Wang's clan who resided in Fuzhou | were killed, regardless of their ages. | Huang Shaopo, Chen Yun and Xu Wenzhen were sent to defend Quanzhou, Zhangzhou and Tingzhou, respectively. | The new government adopted the designation of the Jin dynasty. | It was the first year of the Kaiyun period (A.D. 944).
>
> 　　The general commander of Quanzhou Liu Congxiao deceived the

第 12 章 译文的成长过程

men in Quanzhou in the belief | that Yanzheng, King of Fusha, was dispatching armed forces to capture Fuzhou. | "King of Fusha," he said, | "is now leading troops to occupy Fuzhou and | all traitors in Fuzhou are sure to be sanctioned. | We have served as ministers for the Wang's house for all our life. | How can we submit to those traitors and | even serve them as accomplices?" | The men of Quanzhou were fully convinced of this unreal situation, | so they rose up together against Shaopo and | put him to death. | Wang Jixun was received and nominated as magistrate. | After the news from Quanzhou arrived, | the men of Zhangzhou also killed Yun | and then received Wang Jicheng as magistrate. | Both Jixun and Jicheng were princes of the Wang's clan. | When the news came to Tingzhou, | Wenzhen was so frightened | that he surrendered Tingzhou to Yanzheng directly. | At this time, Yanzheng had taken control of three military commanderies, | including Quanzhou, Zhangzhou and Tingzhou. | In this situation, Chongyu also killed Wenjin and | transferred his head to Jianzhou, | showing his willingness to surrender Fuzhou to Yanzheng, | but he was in turn killed by Lin Renhan, assistant general of Fuzhou. | Renhan planned to receive Yanzheng to move the capital to Fuzhou. |

现对上述译稿的前段修改如下：

It had been one year also | since Lian Chongyu killed Chang. | One day, Chongyu summoned all ministers in the Min government | and declared | that they should break away from the reign of the Wang's clan. | "In the past," he said, | "the Founding Emperor Wu went through battlefields in spite of arrows and stones. | Since then the state of Min has been established. | His sons and grandsons, however, are dissolute and tyrannical. | They have gone too far away from the right path | so that the heaven has begun to hate the Wang's clan. | Now the common people begin to recommend men of talent to replace them. | We should accept those | who are virtuous | so as to make this land peaceful." | Seeing that | none of the ministers dared to have any further discussion on this topic, | Chongyu supported Zhu Wenjin in person to ascend into the palace, | seated him on the throne, | and led hundreds of officials to face north and submit to Wenjin. | Wenjin in turn appointed Chongyu to take charge of the six legions of armed forces and all security affairs. | Most of those brothers and sons from the Wang's clan who resided in Fuzhou | were killed, regardless of their ages. | Huang Shaopo was sent to defend Quanzhou, | Chen Yun was to defend Zhangzhou, and | Xu Wenzhen was to defend Tingzhou. | The new government adopted the designation of the Jin dynasty. | It was the first year of the Kaiyun period (A.D.944). |

在第 3 稿的基础上主要添加 2 个小句后所得到的第 4 稿现有 54 个小句,其译文语法难度 bi-GI4 约为 (54/38≈) 1.42。其中,前段译稿包含 28 个小句,其译文语法难度 bi-GI$_a$4 约为 (28/21≈) 1.33;后段译稿包含 26 个小句,其译文语法难度 bi-GI$_b$4 约为 (26/17≈) 1.53。

3.5 第 5 稿及其单语词汇密度

第 4 稿共有 457 个单词、54 个小句,其单语词汇密度 mono-LD4 约为 (457/53≈) 8.62。其中,前段译稿包含 243 个单词、28 个小句,其单语词汇密度 mono-LD$_a$4 约为 (243/28≈) 8.68;后段译稿包含 214 个单词、26 个小句,其单语词汇密度 mono-LD$_b$4 约为 (214/26≈) 8.23。总体上,单语词汇密度已经高于 8.00,处于参照区间之内 [8.80±0.80]。现对第 4 稿的后段调整如下:

The general commander of Quanzhou Liu Congxiao deceived the men in Quanzhou in the belief | that Yanzheng, King of Fusha, was dispatching armed forces to capture Fuzhou. | "King of Fusha," he said, | "is now leading troops to occupy Fuzhou and | all traitors in Fuzhou are sure to be sanctioned. | We have served as ministers for the Wang's house for all our life. | How can we submit to those traitors and | even serve them as accomplices?" | The men of Quanzhou were fully convinced of this unreal situation, | so they rose up together against Shaopo, | put him to death, | and then received and nominated Wang Jixun as magistrate. | After the news from Quanzhou arrived, | the men of Zhangzhou also killed Yun | and then received Wang Jicheng as magistrate. | Both Jixun and Jicheng were princes of the Wang's clan. | When the news came to Tingzhou, | Wenzhen was so frightened | that he surrendered Tingzhou to Yanzheng directly. | At this time, Yanzheng had taken control of the commanderies of Quanzhou, Zhangzhou, and Tingzhou. | In this situation, Chongyu also killed Wenjin and | transferred his head to Jianzhou, | showing his willingness to surrender Fuzhou to Yanzheng, | but he was in turn killed by Lin Renhan, assistant general of Fuzhou. | Renhan planned to receive Yanzheng to move the capital to Fuzhou. |

经调整得到的第 5 稿共有 456 个单词、53 个小句，其单语词汇密度 mono-LD5 约为（456/53≈）8.60。其中，前段译稿包含 243 个单词、28 个小句，其单语词汇密度 mono-LD_a5 约为（243/28≈）8.68；后段译稿包含 213 个单词、25 个小句，其单语词汇密度 mono-LD_b5 为（213/25=）8.52。

3.6　第 6 稿及其单语语法复杂性

第 5 稿全文包含 456 个单词、53 个小句、25 个句子，其单语语法复杂性的两个指标分别为：单语词汇密度 mono-LD5 约为（456/53≈）8.60；单语语法难度 mono-GI5 为（53/25=）2.12。其中，前段译稿包含 243 个单词、28 个小句、14 个句子，其单语词汇密度 mono-LD_a5 约为（243/28≈）8.68；单语语法难度 mono-GI_a5 为（28/14=）2.00；后段译稿包含 213 个单词、25 个小句、11 个句子，其单语词汇密度 mono-LD_a5 为（213/25=）8.52；单语语法难度 mono-GI_a5 约为（25/11≈）2.27。总体上，第 5 稿的单语词汇密度 mono-LD5 已经高于 8.00，处于参照范围之内（≈8.80±0.80），但其单语语法难度 mono-GI5 还远低于参照数值（≥3.00），存在较大的修改空间。修改所得的第 6 稿全文按小句（|）和句子（‖）分析如下：

It had been one year also | since Lian Chongyu killed Chang and, | one day, Chongyu summoned all of the ministers in the Min government | and declared | that they were to break away from the ruling of the Wang's clan. ‖ "In the past," he said, | "the Founding Emperor Wu went through battlefields in spite of arrows and stones, | and since then the state of Min has been established. ‖ His sons and grandsons, however, are dissolute and tyrannical and | they have gone too far away from the right path | so that the heaven has begun to hate the Wang's clan. ‖ Now that the common people begin to recommend men of talent to replace them, | we should accept those | who are virtuous | so as to make this land peaceful." ‖ None of the ministers dared to have any further discussion | as to whether it is justifiable or not, and, | seeing | that there was no explicit protest, | Chongyu in person supported Zhu Wenjin to ascend into the palace, | seated him on the throne, | and led all the officials to face north and submit to Wenjin. ‖ Wenjin in turn appointed Chongyu to take charge of the six legions of armed forces and all security affairs. ‖ Those brothers and sons from the Wang's clan who resided in Fuzhou | were mostly killed, regardless of their ages. ‖ Huang Shaopo was sent to defend Quanzhou, | Chen Yun was to defend Zhangzhou, and | Xu Wenzhen was to defend Tingzhou. ‖ <u>The new government adopted the designation of the Jin dynasty;</u> | <u>it was the first year of the Kaiyun period (A. D. 944)</u>. ‖

The general commander of Quanzhou Liu Congxiao deceived the men of Quanzhou | in the belief that Yanzheng, King of Fusha, was dispatching armed forces to capture Fuzhou. ‖ "King of Fusha," he said, | "is now leading troops to occupy Fuzhou and | all traitors in Fuzhou are sure to be sanctioned. ‖ We have served as ministers for the Wang's house for all our life, | and how can we submit to those traitors and | even serve them as accomplices?" ‖ The men of Quanzhou were fully convinced of this unreal situation, | so they rose up together against Shaopo, | put him to death and | then received and nominated Wang Jixun as magistrate. ‖ After the news from Quanzhou arrived, | the men of Zhangzhou also killed Yun and | then received Wang Jicheng as magistrate. ‖ Both Jixun and Jicheng were princes of the Wang's clan. ‖ When the news came to Tingzhou, | Wenzhen was so frightened | that he surrendered Tingzhou to Yanzheng directly. ‖ <u>Seeing that</u> | <u>Yanzheng had taken control of the three commanderies of Quanzhou, Zhangzhou and Tingzhou,</u> | Chongyu had to kill Wenjin and | transferred his head to Jianzhou, | <u>showing his willingness to surrender Fuzhou to Yanzheng,</u> | <u>but he was in turn killed by Lin Renhan, assistant general of Fuzhou;</u> | Renhan planned to receive Yanzheng to move the capital from Jianzhou to Fuzhou. ‖

第 6 稿全文包含 474 个单词、56 个小句,17 个句子,其单语语法复杂性的两个指标分别为:单语词汇密度 mono-LD6 约为 (474/56 ≈) 8.46;

单语语法难度 mono-GI6 约为（56/17≈）3.29。其中，前段译稿包含 260 个单词、30 个小句、9 个句子，其单语词汇密度 mono-LD$_a$6 约为（260/30≈）8.67；单语语法难度 mono-GI$_b$6 约为（30/9≈）3.33。后段译稿包含 214 个单词、26 个小句、8 个句子，其单语词汇密度 mono-LD$_a$6 约为（214/26≈）8.23；单语语法难度 mono-GI$_b$6 为（26/8＝）3.25。总体上，单语语法难度的数值已经高于 3.00。

4. 案例四

第四个案例的原文主要描述李景攻闽的详细过程，其中涉及延政反攻、仁达自立、延政降唐、仁达降于吴越、从效臣于南唐等具体事项。其原文如下：

> 是时°南唐李景闻闽乱°发兵攻之°延政遣其从子继昌守福州°而南唐兵方急攻延政°福州将李仁达谓其徒曰°唐兵攻建州°富沙王不能自保°其能有此土也°乃擒继昌杀之°欲自立°惧众不附°以雪峰寺僧卓俨明示众曰°此非常人也°被以衮冕°率诸将吏北面而臣之°已而又杀俨明°乃自立°送款于李景°景以仁达为威武军节度使°更其名曰弘义°而景兵攻破建州°迁延政族于金陵°封鄱阳王°是岁°景保大四年也°
>
> 留从效闻延政降唐°执王继勋送于金陵°李景以泉州为清源军°以从效为节度使°景已破延政°遣人召李仁达入朝°仁达不从°遂降于吴越°而留从效亦逐景守兵°据泉漳二州°景犹封从效晋江王°周世宗时°从效遣牙将蔡仲兴为商人°间道至京师°求置邸内属°是时°世宗与李景画江为界°遂不纳°从效仍臣于南唐°其后事具国史°

原文全文包含 288 个汉字、46 个句读，其汉字密度约为 6.26。其中，前段包含 160 个汉字、26 个句读，其汉字密度约为 6.15；后段包含 128 个汉字、20 个句读，其汉字密度为 6.40。

4.1 第 1 稿及其词字比

在群组翻译的基础上添加标点符号、少量连接词语或附加语句后整理而成的第 1 稿包含如下两段译文：

> At that time, Li Jing of Southern Tang heard that the state of Min was in disorder, so he dispatched his soldiers to attack it. Yanzheng sent his nephew Jichang to defend Fuzhou. When the troops of Southern Tang were launching a quick attack on Yanzheng, the general

commander of Fuzhou Li Renda persuaded his followers and said, "The troops of Southern Tang were now attacking Jianzhou, and King of Fusha is not able to survive. How can he possess the land?" So he arrested Jichang and killed him. He wanted to claim the kingship, but he was afraid that no one supported him, so he showed Monk Zhuo Yanming from the Snow Peak Temple to the public and said, "This is not a common person." He wore him with the dragon crown and guided generals and officials to face north and submit to him as ministers. Later, he killed Yanming and then he claimed the kingship and sent his sincerity to Li Jing. Li Jing in turn appointed Li Renda as military commissioner of Weiwu Military Government and changed his name into "Hongyi". After the troops of Li Jing conquered Jianzhou, Yanzheng's clan and family were migrated to Jinling, the capital of Southern Tang, and Yanzheng was granted with the title of "King of Boyang". It was the fourth year of the Baoda period during the reign of Li Jing (A. D. 946).

Liu Congxiao heard that Yanzheng surrendered to Southern Tang, so he arrested Wang Jixun and escorted him to Jinling. Li Jing established a military institution entitled "Qingyuan Military Government" in Quanzhou and appointed Congxiao as commissioner. After Jing had destroyed the defence of Yanzheng, he sent someone to summon Li Renda to the court. Renda was unwilling to submit to Southern Tang, so he surrendered to the state of Wu and Yue. Meanwhile, Liu Congxiao also expelled the garrison soldiers of Li Jing and occupied the two commanderies of Quanzhou and Zhangzhou. Jing still granted Congxiao with the title of "King of Jinjiang". During the reign of Emperor Shizong of the Zhou dynasty (A. D. 954 – 959), Congxiao dispatched his company commander Cai Zhongxing in the guise of a merchant, went through some bypaths to the capital, managed to establish a representative office and submitted to the Zhou dynasty as a dependent state. At this time, since Shizong and Li Jing took the river as the border, loyal tribute was no longer paid to the Zhou dynasty and Congxiao was still subject to Southern Tang. What came after was documented in the state history.

第 1 稿全文包含 426 个单词，其词字比 RWC1 约为（426/288≈）1.48。其中，前段译稿包含 233 个单词，其词字比 RWC_a1 约为（233/160≈）1.46；后段译稿包含 193 个单词，其词字比 RWC_b1 约为（193/128≈）1.51。

4.2 第 2 稿及其词字比

第 1 稿的总体词字比为 1.48，其前段译稿的词字比值为 1.46，后段译稿的词字比值为 1.51。前后两段都有较大的修改空间。通过增加词汇得到如下第 2 稿：

> At this time, Li Jing, King of Southern Tang, heard that the state of Min was in disorder, so he dispatched an army with the aim of taking it over. While he himself stayed in Jianzhou, Yanzheng sent his nephew Jichang to defend Fuzhou. As the troops of Southern Tang were launching a fierce attack on Yanzheng in Jianzhou, Li Renda, general commander of Fuzhou, took this opportunity and persuaded his followers to start a revolt against Jichang so as to separate Fuzhou from Jianzhou. "The troops of Southern Tang were now conquering Jianzhou," Renda said. "King of Fusha is not able to protect himself now. How can he possess this land?" Soon afterwards, Renda and his men arrested Jichang and killed him. Now Renda intended to claim the kingship, but he was afraid that no one would support him, so he invited a monk named Zhuo Yanming out of the Snow Peak Temple and showed him to the public. "This is not an ordinary man!" announced Renda to them. He then wore Yanming with the dragon crown and guided generals and officials to face north and submit themselves to Yanming as ministers, but Yanming was killed by Renda soon afterwards. Not until Yanming's death did Renda claim the kingship. After he came to the throne, Renda sent his sincerity to Li Jing and Jing in turn appointed Renda as commissioner of the Weiwu Military Government. Renda later renamed himself into "Hongyi". After the troops of Li Jing conquered Jianzhou, he migrated Yanzheng's family and clan to the capital city of Jinling and granted Yanzheng with the title of "King of Boyang". It was the fourth year of the Baoda period during the reign of Li Jing (A. D. 946).
>
> After Liu Congxiao heard that Yanzheng had surrendered to

Southern Tang, he arrested Wang Jixun and escorted him to Jinling. Li Jing in turn set up a military institution entitled "Qingyuan Military Government" in Quanzhou and Congxiao was accordingly appointed as commissioner. Now Li Jing had conquered Jianzhou and settled down Yanzheng in Jinling, so he sent someone to Fuzhou and summoned Li Renda to the central court. Renda was unwilling to submit to Southern Tang, so he surrendered to the state of Wu and Yue instead. Meanwhile, Liu Congxiao also expelled the garrison soldiers of Li Jing and occupied the two commanderies of Quanzhou and Zhangzhou, but Li Jing still granted Congxiao with the title of "King of Jinjiang". During the reign of Emperor Shizong of the Zhou dynasty (A. D. 954–959), Congxiao dispatched his company commander Cai Zhongxing in the guise of a merchant to the dynastic court. Zhongxing went through some bypaths to the capital city and managed to establish a representative office, seeking solutions to a possible submission to the Zhou dynasty as a dependent state. Except for this, since Emperor Shizong and Li Jing took Yangtze River as their border and no direct connection could be easily established, loyal tribute was no longer paid to the Zhou dynasty, so Congxiao was still subject to Southern Tang. What came after was documented in the history of the state of Southern Tang.

上述修订一共添加 98 个单词。经过修改得到的第 2 稿全文包含 524 个单词，其词字比 RWC2 约为（524/288≈）1.82。其中，前段译稿包含 289 个单词，其词字比 RWC_a2 约为（289/160≈）1.81；后段译稿包含 235 个单词，其词字比 RCW_b2 约为（235/128≈）1.84。

4.3 第 3 稿及其译文词汇密度

第 2 稿共有 524 个单词，其译文词汇密度 bi-LD2 约为（524/46≈）11.39。其中，前段译稿包含 289 个单词，其译文词汇密度 $bi\text{-}LD_a2$ 约为（289/26≈）11.12；后段译稿包含 235 个单词，其译文词汇密度 $bi\text{-}LD_b2$ 为（235/20=）11.75。前后两段译稿的译文词汇密度均处于 10.50 和 12.50 之间。只须对第 2 稿做少量修改就可得到第 3 稿，因而两种译稿的译文词汇密度基本保持一致。第 3 稿的译文词汇密度 bi-LD3 与第 2 稿的译文词汇密度同为 11.39。其中，第 3 稿前段的译文词汇密度 $bi\text{-}LD_a3$ 与第 2 稿前段的译文词汇密度 $bi\text{-}LD_a2$ 同为 11.12；第 3 稿后段的译文词汇密度 $bi\text{-}LD_b3$ 与第 2 稿后段的译文词汇密度 $bi\text{-}LD_b2$ 同为 11.75。

4.4 第4稿及其译文语法难度

第3稿全文包含58个小句,其译文语法难度 bi-GI3 约为(58/46≈) 1.26。其中,前段译文包含34个小句,其译文语法难度 bi-GI$_a$3 约为(34/ 26≈)1.31;后段译文包含24个小句,其译文语法难度 bi-GI$_b$3 为(24/ 20=)1.20。总体上,第3稿的译文语法难度略低于1.30,因而存在一定的修改空间。现把经过修改得到的第4稿按小句分析如下:

<u>At this point</u>, Li Jing, King of Southern Tang, heard that the state of Min was in disorder, | <u>so he dispatched his troops to invade the land with the aim to taking it over.</u> | While Yanzheng himself stayed in Jianzhou, | he sent his nephew Jichang to defend Fuzhou. | As the troops of Southern Tang were launching a fierce attack on Yanzheng in Jianzhou, | Li Renda, general commander of Fuzhou, took this opportunity and | persuaded his followers to start a revolt against Jichang | with the aim to separating Fuzhou from Jianzhou. | "The troops of Southern Tang were now conquering Jianzhou." | Renda said. | "King of Fusha is not able to protect even himself. | How can he possess this land?" | Soon afterwards, Renda and his colleagues captured and killed Jichang. | Now Renda intended to claim the kingship, | but he was afraid | that no one would support him, | so he invited a monk | named Zhuo Yanming out of the Snow Peak Temple, | showed him to the public, | and tried to pursuade them to accept the monk as king. | "This is not an ordinary man!" | announced Renda <u>before the public.</u> | He then wore Yanming with the dragon crown and | guided generals and officials to face north and submit themselves to Yanming as ministers, | but Yanming was killed by Renda soon afterwards. | <u>Renda took over the throne after the death of Yanming,</u> | <u>he sent his sincerity to Li Jing</u>, and | Li Jing in turn appointed Li Renda as commissioner of Weiwu Military Government. | <u>Renda later was renamed into "Hongyi".</u> | After Jianzhou was conquered and occupied by Li Jing's troops, | Li Jing migrated Yanzheng's family and clan to the capital city of Jinling, | and granted Yanzheng with the title of "King of Boyang". | It was the fourth year of the Baoda period during the reign of Li Jing (A. D. 946). |

<u>On hearing that</u> | Yanzheng had surrendered to the state of

Southern Tang, | Liu Congxiao arrested Wang Jixun and escorted him to Jinling, | showing his sincerity and submission to Li Jing. | Li Jing in turn set up a military institution | entitled "Qingyuan Military Government" in Quanzhou and | Congxiao was accordingly appointed as commissioner. | <u>After Li Jing conquered Jianzhou and</u> | settled Yanzheng's clan down in Jinling, | he sent someone to Fuzhou and | summoned Li Renda to the central court in Jinling. | <u>Instead of obeying Li Jing's instruction,</u> | <u>Renda directly surrendered to the state of Wu and Yue.</u> | Meanwhile, Liu Congxiao also expelled the garrison soldiers of Li Jing and | took control of the two commanderies of Quanzhou and Zhangzhou, | and Li Jing still granted Congxiao with the title of "King of Jinjiang" though. | During the reign of Emperor Shizong of the Zhou dynasty (A. D. 954-959), Congxiao dispatched his company commander Cai Zhongxing in the guise of a merchant to the dynastic court. | Zhongxing went through some bypaths to the capital city and | managed to establish a representative office, | seeking solutions to a possible submission to the Zhou dynasty as a dependent state. | Except for this, since Emperor Shizong and Li Jing took Yangtze River as their border and | no direct connection could be easily established, | loyal tribute was no longer paid to the Zhou dynasty, | so Congxiao was still subject to the state of Southern Tang. | What came after | was documented in the state history of Southern Tang. |

第 4 稿共有 60 个小句，其译文语法难度 bi-GI4 约为（60/46≈）1.30。其中，前段译稿包含 34 个小句，其译文语法难度 bi-GI_a4 约为（34/26≈）1.31；后段译稿包含 26 个小句，其译文语法难度 bi-GI_b4 为（26/20=）1.30。

4.5 第 5 稿及其单语词汇密度

第 4 稿共有 550 个单词、60 个小句，其单语词汇密度 mono-LD4 约为（550/60≈）9.17。其中，前段译稿包含 303 个单词、34 个小句，其单语词汇密度 mono-LD_a4 约为（303/34≈）8.91；后段译稿包含 247 个单词、26 个小句，其单语词汇密度 mono-LD_b4 为（247/26=）9.50。总体上，第 4 稿的单语词汇密度已经高于 8.00，因而只须在第 4 稿的基础上做少量的调整就可得到第 5 稿。前后两稿保持基本相同的单语词汇密度。第 5 稿的单语词汇密度 mono-LD5 与第 4 稿的单语词汇密度 mono-LD4 同为 9.17。其中，第 5 稿前段的单语词汇密度 mono-LD_a5 与第 4 稿前段的单语词汇密度

mono-LD$_a$4 同为 8.91；第 5 稿后段的单语词汇密度 mono-LD$_b$5 与第 4 稿后段的单语词汇密度 mono-LD$_b$4 同为 9.50。

4.6　第 6 稿及其单语语法复杂性

第 5 稿全文包含 550 个单词、60 个小句、22 个句子，其单语语法复杂性的两个指标分别为：单语词汇密度 mono-LD5 约为（550/60≈）9.17；单语语法难度 mono-GI5 约为（60/22≈）2.73。其中，前段译稿包含 303 个单词、34 个小句、14 个句子，其单语词汇密度 mono-LD$_a$5 约为（303/34≈）8.91，单语语法难度 mono-GI$_a$5 约为（34/14≈）2.43；后段译稿包含 247 个单词、26 个小句、8 个句子，其单语词汇密度 mono-LD$_b$5 为（247/26=）9.50，单语语法难度 mono-GI$_b$5 为（26/8=）3.25。就单语词汇密度的数值来看，第 5 稿前后两段的单语词汇密度均已处于参照范围之内（≈8.80±0.80）。就单语语法难度的数值来看，前段的数值处于参照范围之外，而后段的数值处于参照范围之内。因此，对第 5 稿的修订主要提高前段的单语语法难度。现将修改所得的第 6 稿按小句（｜）和句子（‖）分析如下：

> At this point, Li Jing, King of Southern Tang, heard that the state of Min was in disorder, | so he dispatched his troops to invade it | with the aim to taking over its land. ‖ While Yanzheng himself stayed in Jianzhou, | he sent his nephew Jichang to defend Fuzhou. ‖ As the troops of Southern Tang were launching a fierce attack on Yanzheng in Jianzhou, | Li Renda, general commander of Fuzhou, took this opportunity and | persuaded his followers to start a revolt against Jichang | so as to separate Fuzhou from Jianzhou. ‖ "The troops of Southern Tang were now conquering Jianzhou," | Renda said, | "<u>but King of Fusha cannot even protect himself,</u> | <u>so how can he possess this land?</u>" ‖ Soon afterwards, Renda and his men captured and killed Jichang. ‖ Now Renda intended to claim the kingship, | but he was afraid | that no one would support him, | so he invited a monk | named Zhuo Yanming out of the Snow Peak Temple, | showed him to the public, | and tried to pursuade them to accept the monk as king. ‖ "This is not an ordinary man!" | announced Renda before the public. | He then wore Yanming with the dragon crown and | guided generals and officials to face north and submit themselves to Yanming as ministers, | but Yanming was killed by Renda soon afterwards. ‖

Renda took over the throne | after Yanming died, | and he sent his sincerity to Li Jing; | Li Jing in turn appointed Li Renda, who was later renamed into "Hongyi", as commissioner of the Weiwu Military Government. ‖ After Jianzhou was conquered and occupied by Li Jing's troops, | Li Jing migrated Yanzheng's family and clan to the capital city of Jinling | and granted Yanzheng with the title of "King of Boyang". ‖ It was the fourth year of the Baoda period during the reign of Li Jing (A. D. 946). ‖

On hearing that | Yanzheng had surrendered to the state of Southern Tang, | Liu Congxiao arrested Wang Jixun and sent him to Jinling, | showing his sincerity and submission to Li Jing. ‖ Li Jing in turn set up a military institution | entitled "Qingyuan Military Government" in Quanzhou and | Congxiao was accordingly appointed as commissioner. ‖ After Li Jing conquered Jianzhou and | settled Yanzheng's clan down in Jinling, | he sent someone to Fuzhou and | summoned Li Renda to the central court in Jinling. ‖ Instead of obeying Li Jing's instruction, however, | Li Renda directly surrendered to the state of Wu and Yue. ‖ Meanwhile, Liu Congxiao also expelled the garrison soldiers of Li Jing and | took control of the two commanderies of Quanzhou and Zhangzhou, | and Li Jing still granted Congxiao with the title of "King of Jinjiang" though. ‖ During the reign of Emperor Shizong of the Zhou dynasty (A. D. 954 – 959), Congxiao dispatched his company commander Cai Zhongxing in the guise of a merchant to the dynastic court, | so Zhongxing went through some bypaths to the capital city and | managed to establish a representative office, | seeking solutions to a possible submission to the Zhou dynasty as a dependent state. ‖ Except for this, since Emperor Shizong and Li Jing took Yangtze River as their border and | no direct connection could be easily established, | loyal tribute was no longer paid to the Zhou dynasty, | so Congxiao was still subject to the state of Southern Tang. ‖ What came later | was documented in the state history of Southern Tang. ‖

第6稿全文包含550个单词、60个小句、18个句子，其单语语法复杂性的两个指标分别为：单语词汇密度 mono-LD6 约为（550/60≈）9.17；单语语法难度 mono-GI6 约为（60/18≈）3.33。其中，前段译稿包含300

个单词、34 个小句、10 个句子,其单语词汇密度 mono-LD_a6 约为(300/34≈)8.82;单语语法难度 mono-GI_a6 为(34/10=)3.40。后段译稿包含 250 个单词、26 个小句、8 个句子,其单语词汇密度 mono-LD_b6 约为(250/26≈)9.62;单语语法难度 mono-GI_b6 为(26/8=)3.25。总体上,单语语法难度的数值已经高于 3.00。

5. 译文语法复杂性的变化轨迹

本章所采集的四个翻译案例详细地呈现了译文语法复杂性的变化轨迹,展示了译文生成的完整过程。四段原文共有 1 038 个汉字、171 个句读,其汉字密度约为 6.07。四段译文的第 1 稿合计 1 552 个单词,其词字比为 1.50,较参照词字比的下限数值 1.80 少 0.30,存在明显的修订空间。在第 1 稿的基础上,通过提高词字比,得到第 2 稿。在第 2 稿的基础上,通过提高译文词汇密度,得到第 3 稿。在第 3 稿的基础上,通过提高译文语法难度,得到第 4 稿。在第 4 稿的基础上,通过调整单语词汇密度,得到第 5 稿。在第 5 稿的基础上,主要通过调整单语语法难度,最终得到第 6 稿。第 6 稿合计 2 064 个单词,其词字比为 1.99,较参照词字比的下限数值 1.80 多 0.19。另外,第 6 稿合计 237 个小句、74 个句子,其译文词汇密度为 12.07,译文语法难度为 1.39,单语词汇密度为 8.71,单语语法难度为 3.20。上述所有的指标均已处于参照区间的范围之内。具体数值详见表 12-1。

6. 信息冗余分析

习作译文是在添加大量单词和语句的基础上逐渐修订而成的,其词字比及单语或双语的词汇密度和语法难度等数值指标除了受到参照译文的约束之外,最后还需接受阅读理解的检验。阅读检验通常涉及信息冗余分析,即译文是否存在信息冗余及冗余程度如何。先节选以下译文片段为例:

> The general commander of Quanzhou Liu Congxiao deceived the men of Quanzhou in the belief that Yanzheng, King of Fusha, was dispatching armed forces to capture Fuzhou. "King of Fusha," he said, "is now leading troops to occupy Fuzhou and all traitors in Fuzhou are sure to be sanctioned. We have served as ministers for the

表 12-1 译文语法复杂性的具体指标变化汇总表

	案例一		案例二		案例三		案例四	
	片段 A	片段 B	片段 A	片段 B	片段 A	片段 B	片段 A	片段 B
第1稿（双语）	$RWC_a 1 = 1.48$	$RWC_b 1 = 1.50$	$RWC_a 1 = 1.66$	$RWC_b 1 = 1.42$	$RWC_a 1 = 1.61$	$RWC_b 1 = 1.21$	$RWC_a 1 = 1.46$	$RWC_b 1 = 1.51$
第2稿（双语）	总体：$RWC1 = 1.84$	总体：$RWC1 = 1.49$	总体：$RWC1 = 1.82$	总体：$RWC1 = 1.60$	总体：$RWC1 = 1.90$	总体：$RWC1 = 1.42$	总体：$RWC1 = 1.81$	总体：$RWC1 = 1.48$
	$RWC_a 2 = 1.84$	$RWC_b 2 = 1.82$	$RWC_a 2 = 1.82$	$RWC_b 2 = 1.88$	$RWC_a 2 = 1.90$	$RWC_b 2 = 1.83$	$RWC_a 2 = 1.81$	$RWC_b 2 = 1.82$
	总体：$RWC2 = 1.83$		总体：$RWC2 = 1.83$		总体：$RWC2 = 1.87$		总体：$RWC2 = 1.82$	
第3稿（双语）	$LD_a 3 = 10.95$	$LD_b 3 = 11.63$	$LD_a 3 = 10.43$	$LD_b 3 = 10.67$	$LD_a 3 = 11.48$	$LD_b 3 = 12.53$	$LD_a 3 = 11.12$	$LD_b 3 = 11.75$
	总体：$LD3 = 11.31$		总体：$LD3 = 10.50$		总体：$LD3 = 11.95$		总体：$LD3 = 11.39$	
第4稿（双语）	$GI_a 4 = 1.29$	$GI_b 4 = 1.46$	$GI_a 4 = 1.43$	$GI_b 4 = 1.50$	$GI_a 4 = 1.33$	$GI_b 4 = 1.53$	$GI_a 4 = 1.31$	$GI_b 4 = 1.30$
	总体：$GI4 = 1.38$		总体：$GI4 = 1.45$		总体：$GI4 = 1.42$		总体：$GI4 = 1.30$	
第5稿（单语）	$m\text{-}LD_a 5 = 8.52$	$m\text{-}LD_b 5 = 8.54$	$m\text{-}LD_a 5 = 8.10$	$m\text{-}LD_b 5 = 8.93$	$m\text{-}LD_a 5 = 8.68$	$m\text{-}LD_b 5 = 8.52$	$m\text{-}LD_a 5 = 8.91$	$m\text{-}LD_b 5 = 9.50$
	总体：$mono\text{-}LD5 = 8.53$		总体：$mono\text{-}LD5 = 8.30$		总体：$mono\text{-}LD5 = 8.60$		总体：$mono\text{-}LD5 = 9.17$	
	$m\text{-}LD_a 6 = 8.54$	$m\text{-}LD_b 6 = 8.57$	$m\text{-}LD_a 6 = 8.52$	$m\text{-}LD_b 6 = 9.00$	$m\text{-}LD_a 6 = 8.67$	$m\text{-}LD_b 6 = 8.23$	$m\text{-}LD_a 6 = 8.82$	$m\text{-}LD_b 6 = 9.62$
第6稿（单语）	总体：$mono\text{-}LD6 = 8.56$		总体：$mono\text{-}LD6 = 8.64$		总体：$mono\text{-}LD6 = 8.46$		总体：$mono\text{-}LD6 = 9.17$	
	$m\text{-}GI_a 6 = 3.11$	$m\text{-}GI_b 6 = 3.18$	$m\text{-}GI_a 6 = 3.14$	$m\text{-}GI_b 6 = 2.80$	$m\text{-}GI_a 6 = 3.33$	$m\text{-}GI_b 6 = 3.25$	$m\text{-}GI_a 6 = 3.40$	$m\text{-}GI_b 6 = 3.25$
	总体：$mono\text{-}GI6 = 3.15$		总体：$mono\text{-}GI6 = 3.07$		总体：$mono\text{-}GI6 = 3.29$		总体：$mono\text{-}GI6 = 3.33$	

说明：

1. 案例一的原文包含 278 个汉字，45 个句读。第 1 稿全译文包含 414 个单词，其词字比为 1.49。第 6 稿共有 539 个单词，单语词汇密度为 8.56，单语字比为 1.94。
2. 案例二的原文包含 229 个汉字，42 个句子，其译文包含 367 个单词，其词字比为 1.40。第 1 稿全译文包含 367 个单词，其词字比为 1.60。第 6 稿共有 501 个单词，单语词汇密度为 8.64，单语字比为 2.19。
3. 案例三的原文包含 243 个汉字，38 个句子，其译文包含 345 个单词，其词字比为 1.39。第 1 稿全译文包含 345 个单词，其词字比为 1.42。第 6 稿共有 474 个单词，单语词汇密度为 8.46，单语字比为 1.95。
4. 案例四的原文包含 288 个汉字，46 个句子，其译文包含 426 个单词，其词字比为 1.47。第 1 稿全译文包含 426 个单词，其词字比为 1.48。第 6 稿共有 550 个单词，单语词汇密度为 9.17，单语字比为 1.91。
5. 上述四个案例的原文共有 1 038 个汉字，171 个句读。第 1 稿共有 1 552 个单词，译文词汇密度为 11.96，其词字比为 1.30。第 6 稿共有 2 064 个单词，其译文词汇密度为 12.07，其词字比为 1.50。第 6 稿包含 237 个小句，74 个句子，其译文词汇密度为 1.39，单语词汇密度为 8.71，单语字比增至为 1.99。另外，第 6 稿包含 237 个小句，74 个句子，其译文词汇密度为 1.39，单语词汇密度为 8.71，单语法难度为 3.20。

Wang's house for all our life, and how can we submit to those traitors and even serve them as accomplices?" The men of Quanzhou were fully convinced of this unreal situation, so they rose up together against Shaopo, put him to death and then received and nominated Wang Jixun as magistrate. After the news from Quanzhou arrived, the men of Zhangzhou also killed Yun and then received Wang Jicheng as magistrate. Both Jixun and Jicheng were princes of the Wang's clan. When the news came to Tingzhou, Wenzhen was so frightened that he surrendered Tingzhou to Yanzheng directly. Seeing that Yanzheng had taken control of the three commanderies of Quanzhou, Zhangzhou and Tingzhou, Chongyu had to kill Wenjin and transferred his head to Jianzhou, showing his willingness to surrender Fuzhou to Yanzheng, but he was in turn killed by Lin Renhan, assistant general of Fuzhou; Renhan planned to receive Yanzheng to move the capital from Jianzhou to Fuzhou.

本章第 3 节已经涉及该段译文，其中包括 214 个单词、26 个小句、8 个句子。对应的原文如下：

> 泉州军将留从效诈其州人曰。富沙王兵收福州矣。吾属世为王氏臣。安能交臂而事贼乎。州人共杀绍颇。迎王继勋为刺史。漳州闻之。亦杀赟。迎王继成为刺史。皆王氏之诸子也。文缜惧。以汀州降于延政。延政已得三州。重遇亦杀文进。传首建州以自归。福州裨将林仁翰又杀重遇。谋迎延政都福州。

该段原文包含 116 个汉字、17 个句读。因此，上述译文选段的词字比、译文词汇密度、译文语法难度、单语词汇密度、单语语法难度五种数值计算如下：

词字比：214/116 ≈ 1.84

译文词汇密度：214/17 ≈ 12.59

译文语法难度：26/17 ≈ 1.53

单语词汇密度：214/26 ≈ 8.23

单语语法难度：26/8 = 3.25

除了译文词汇密度的值外，其余四种数值均处于参照范围之内。译文词汇密度的值约为 12.59，略微超过参照区间 [10.50, 12.50] 的上限

12.50。此外,译文语法难度的值也较高,达到 1.53。我们把上述译文分发给华侨大学 2019 级 16 名翻译硕士研究生阅读并分析其中的信息冗余情况。此次调研主要收到如下四项反馈:

第一,译文可能因人名和地名的重复而存在冗余的信息。例如,在 "King of Fusha," he said, "is now leading troops to occupy Fuzhou and all traitors in Fuzhou are sure to be sanctioned" 及 When the news came to Tingzhou, Wenzhen was so frightened that he surrendered Tingzhou to Yanzheng directly 两个句子中,同一地名重复出现了两次,分别换成副词 there 或代词 it 是不是更好?

第二,原文"漳州闻之。亦杀赟。迎王继成为刺史"对应的译文是:After the news from Quanzhou arrived, the men of Zhangzhou also killed Yun and then received Wang Jicheng as magistrate。在第 1 个分句 after the news from Quanzhou arrived 中是否需要明确泉州?读者根据上下文应该能知晓上述消息来自泉州。如果改为 After the men of Zhangzhou heard about it, they also killed Yun and then received Wang Jicheng as magistrate,使两个分句的主语保持一致,读起来是否更通顺? 当然,这样修订会减少 1 个单词。以上是个人的看法,不知是否合理?

第三,原文"富沙王兵收福州矣"的翻译 King of Fusha … is now leading troops to occupy Fuzhou 使用完成时是否更合适?例如,改为 King of Fusha has already captured Fuzhou with his armed forces。译文语句 all traitors in Fuzhou are sure to be sanctioned 属于增补的信息,在原文中没有对应的词项。另外,译文语句 deceived the men in Quanzhou in the belief that Yanzheng … 是否可以简化为 deceived Quanzhou people that Yanzheng … ?

第四,译文语句 we have served as ministers for the Wang's house for all our life 的介词 for 是否可以删除?

对于第 1 项反馈,把 in Fuzhou 换成 there 的确可以避免词汇重复。该反馈涉及的两项词语在原文中没有对应的词项。由于上述选段涉及的地名较多,添加具体的地名可以减少代词照应,直接说明它们之间的相应关系,方便阅读。对于第 2 项反馈的第 1 个疑问,虽然涉及的消息的确是从泉州传来的,但是前文提到泉州和福州两个地方,因而在译文中添加介词短语 from Quanzhou(泉州传来的)能使句意更明朗;对于第 2 个疑问,相同的主语阅读起来是要通顺一些的。因此，尽管可能会减少单词的数量，类似的修订还是需要鼓励的。现有的词字比 1.84 已经超过参考数值的下限，因而此类修订并不会对译文造成明显的影响。当然，如果此处从句的主语改为 the men of Zhangzhou，那么当前从句跟上句的从句在主语上又无法保持一致。在上句中，从句的主语是 the news。对于第 3 项反馈的第 1 个疑问，涉及的"矣"字有歧义，既有动作"完成"的意义，也有语气意义。如果是前者，那么就用完成体；如果是后者，则可用进行体。上述译文采用后者。对于第 3 项反馈的第 2 个疑问，简化的表达形式阅读起来的确简便一些。对于第 4 项反馈，把 for all our life 改为 all our life 在总体上保留相同的意思。

信息冗余分析的目的不是消除构成冗余的全部语句，而是用以说明各项数值指标对于中国历史典籍英译是否合适。毕竟，少量的冗余信息有利于译文的阅读理解。本节的调研显示，从阅读体验来看，本章开篇所明确的各项数值指标总体上适用于中国历史典籍英译，即词字比 $RWC \geqslant 1.80$，译文词汇密度 $bi\text{-}LD = 11.50 \pm 1.00$，译文语法难度 $bi\text{-}GI \geqslant 1.30$；单语词汇密度 $mono\text{-}LD = 8.80 \pm 0.80$，单语语法难度 $mono\text{-}GI \geqslant 3.00$。当然，这并不是说该组数值指标适合整个汉语文言英译。各项数值指标会因翻译场景的变动而有所调整。

结　论

本书在中国历史典籍英译中建立一种翻译案例资源，形成一种教学实践模式，提出一种翻译研究思路。案例、实践和研究的有机结合促成了译学研互长，有利于在案例中提高翻译效率，在实践中拓宽理论视野，在研究中改进教学模式。此外，从词汇语法的角度对译文形成过程的微观分析揭示了汉英语际转换和汉语文言英译的本质，为翻译教学、实践与研究提供一定的学术参考。

1. 翻译流程和群组翻译的意义

以群组翻译为基础的翻译实践流程包含四个步骤：第一步，以句读为单位使原文结构化，建立便于阅读理解的句读库；第二步，在句读库中分析句读的语法结构并逐句标注其结构类型，完善句读库的信息检索和信息组织功能；第三步，提取同类句读并实施群组翻译，建立翻译案例库；第四步，在比较分析的基础上充分修订中间译稿，形成译文。其中，第二步的语法分析用以检验阅读理解的完成情况，为准确的翻译提供语义保障。基于语法分析和类型标注的句读库便于检索并提取相同的句读群组。群组翻译从句读所共享的语法结构入手实施流水作业，创建翻译案例资源。

以天干地支为记时形式的名词性状语句读是一种特殊的句读群组，其在翻译中既要转换为公元纪年的记时形式，又要保留原有的文化符号。两种记时形式的转换离不开日历词典。对于文化符号，天干的翻译转化为阴阳五行的翻译；地支的翻译转化为十二生肖的翻译。阴阳五行和十二生肖都是贴近生活的文化符号，因而天干地支的英语翻译不仅保留了中国历法的科学性，也传递了中国文化的趣味性。

总之，本书所提出的翻译实践流程集理解、翻译和修订于一体，涉及准确理解原文、快速生成初稿、不断修订译稿，直至获得译文，能够充分发挥各种语言活动的边际效应，既提高翻译效率，又确保翻译质量。

2. 语法分析和翻译案例的意义

基于语法分析的翻译案例资源以句读类型为线索使原文语句和译文语句保持一种平行关系。语法分析明确 21 种主要的句读类型，可归入普通体词性句读、简单谓词性句读、特殊谓词性句读、复杂句读 4 种句读群组。其中，普通体词性句读包括完全体词性句读、名词性主语句读、名词性谓语句读、名词性状语句读、名词性列举句读 5 种类型。简单谓词性句读包括不及物动词谓语句读、单及物动词谓语句读、双及物动词谓语句读 3 种类型。特殊谓词性句读包括轻动词谓语句读、形容词谓语句读、形容词活用动词句读、名词活用动词句读、被动语态句读、能愿动词句读 6 种。复杂句读包括双扇句读、连动句读、并列谓语句读、主谓宾语句读、主谓主语句读、主副动宾句读 6 种类型。

就《新五代史·闽世家第八》来看，简单谓词性句读的数量在句读总数中所占的比例为 37.6%，复杂句读的占比为 34.4%，特殊谓词性句读的占比为 15.0%，普通体词性句读的占比为 13.0%。占比较大的简单谓词性句读和复杂句读不仅需要分别明确多种句读类型，而且各种句读类型还需进一步的细分。多数复杂句读在译文中转化为双重或多重主谓结构，得到两个或多个小句。这是造成中国史籍英译的译文语法难度大于 1 的主要语言因素。

翻译案例资源能够避免过度集中的词语选择，有利于实施多样化的措辞策略，使译项分布趋于合理，形成丰富的语法形式和活泼的行文风格。

3. 翻译互文性和文本的再生

因汉英两种语言的交往和互译而逐渐累积的翻译互文性为中国历史典籍英译提供坚实的基础。在翻译教学与实践中，翻译互文性的相关知识有助于提高翻译的效率，塑造译文的风格，凝练翻译实务技巧，以及提升语言表达能力。引用参照译文是利用翻译互文性的主要方式之一。在参照译文的引领下，词字比、译文词汇密度、译文语法难度 3 项双语的译文语法复杂性指标既可用以反映习作译文的中间形态，又可呈现习作译文之于参照译文的差距。其中，词字比和译文词汇密度用以反映词汇差距，而译文语法难度则用以反映语法差距。习作译文和参照译文在词汇和语法上的差距为译文修订指明方向，而进一步的修订能使习作译文在各项指标上靠近参照译文。

选定合适的参照译文离不开对现有的翻译互文生态做充分的调研。译文语法复杂性的各项指标只有相对的参考范围，没有绝对的数值标准。一方面，各项指标存在明显的领域性特征，只有在领域相近的翻译中相关的数据才具有参考价值；另一方面，各项指标会因原文的文辞特点而呈现不同的数值范围。只有在文辞相近的翻译中相关的数据才具有参考价值。因此，合适的参照译文既取决于其原文与习作原文在领域上的相似程度，又取决于其原文与习作原文在文辞上的相似程度。翻译互文性的调研能够明确某种参照译文是否适用于译文修订。同时，加强译文语法复杂性的意识培养能够促成良好的自主评价机制。尽管各项数值指标主要用以译文修订，但是在翻译开始时就强化译文语法复杂性的意识，适当地调整单词、词组、短语或小句的使用，也可把习作译文的相关指标控制在参照基点附近或参照区间之内。

译文语法复杂性的各项数值指标能够呈现特定的翻译风格。一般来说，数值指标越大，译文的口头特征和直解风格越强，其使用小句的倾向越明显；数值指标越小，译文的书面特征和直译风格越强，其使用单词的倾向越明显。具有中等数值指标的译文则体现调和的语式和意译的风格，倾向于使用词组或短语。因此，在翻译中落实高、中、低等译文语法难度的数值范围能够在语式、译解、措辞上获得不同风格的译文。

译文语法复杂性是一种重要的语际比较方法，能够呈现汉语文言和现代英语在词汇语法上的语际关系。以译文词汇密度和译文语法难度来分析汉语文言的英语翻译，其实是用英语的词汇系统和语法结构来测量汉语的词汇系统和语法结构。该方法为汉语文言研究提供一种外在的量化方案。

最后，翻译最终需要解决译文在译入语中的适应问题。中国历史典籍英译在本质上是汉语原文在英语语境中的再生，其过程可识别不同的译文形态，体现译文从旧版到新版在词汇、语法、语义、功能等方面上的转变。该转变过程呈现译文的词项数量不断增加，语法结构逐渐丰富，语义内容趋于完整，功能维度接近对等。在英语语境中，英语词汇密度和英语语法难度两种单语指标能够呈现汉译英文本和英语原生文本（或非汉译英文本）的互文关系，为译文的最后修订提供依据，使其更加适应英语语境。

4. 中国历史典籍英译在翻译教育中的作用

当代中国译界担负着向世人讲好中国故事的历史使命。中国具有独特的社会模式、独特的历史渊源、独特的文化传统、独特的基本国情。自古至今不断扬弃的社会历史文化要素都是我们讲述中国故事的基础原料。中国历史典籍是中国故事的主要线索，蕴含着深厚的中国哲学根源。载于本书附录的部分世家的英语翻译就是我们在翻译教学中讲述中国故事的实例。中国历史典籍既记录圣贤才智，又记录平庸愚劣；既有和平，又有战争。宋代陈师锡在《新五代史·五代史记序》中充分肯定欧阳修重新撰写历史的功绩，并且引用孟子的观点"三代之得天下也以仁，其失天下也以不仁"来说明"天人合一"的社会治理哲学。中国历史典籍在兴衰成败中佐证中国的哲学文化思想，其英语翻译有利于在翻译教育中强化中华民族的主体性特征。

参考文献

Bodde, D. (1940). *Statesman, Patriot, and General in Ancient China: Three Shih-chi Biographies of Chin Dynasty*. New Haven, Conn: American Oriental Society.

Bolby, W. and Scott, J. (1974). *Sima Qian and Warlords, Translated with Twelve Other Stories from His History Records*. Edinburgh: Southside.

Catford, J. C. (1965). *A Linguistic Theory of Translation*. Oxford: Oxford University Press.

Collie, D. (1828). *The Chinese Classical Works Commonly Called the Four Books*. Malacca: The Mission Press.

Davis, R. L. (2004). *Historical Records of the Five Dynasties*. New York/Chichester/West Sussex: Columbia University Press.

Halliday, M. A. K. (1966/2007). Linguistics and machine translation. In *Computational and Quantitative Studies*, edited by J. J. Webster. Beijing: Peking University Press.

Halliday, M. A. K. (1994/2000). *An Introduction to Functional Grammar* (second edition). Beijing: Foreign Language Teaching and Research Press.

Halliday, M. A. K. (2008). *Complementarities in Language*. Beijing: The Commercial Press.

Halliday, M. A. K. (2014). That "certarn cut": towards a characterology of Mandarin Chinese. *Functional Linghistics*, 1(2):4–23.

Halliday, M. A. K. and Matthiessen, C. M. I. M. (1999). *Construing Experience through Meaning: A Language-based Approach to Cognition*. Beijing: World Publishing Corporation.

Huddleston, R. and Pullum, G. K. (2002). *The Cambridge Grammar of the English Language*. Cambridge: Cambridge University Press.

Kierman, F. A. (1963). Ssu-ma Ch'ien's Historiographical Attitude as Reflected in Four Late Warring States Biographies. *Journal of the American Oriental Society*, 83(4):526.

Ku, H. M. (1898). *The Discourses and Sayings of Confucius: A New Special Translation, Illustrated with Quotations from Goethe and Other Writers*. Shanghai: Kelly and Walsh.

Lan, D. C. (1979). *The Analects, Lunyü*. New York: Penguin Books.

Legge, J. (1893/1971). Confucian Analects. In J. Legge. *Confucius: Confucian Analects, The Great Learning & The Doctrine of the Mean*. New York: Dover Publications, Inc.: 137-354.

Pound, E. (1950/1969). The Analects. In E. Pound. (1969). *Confucius: The Great Digest, the Unwobbling Pivot, the Analects*. New York: New Directions: 189-288.

Pulleyblank, E. G. (1995). *Outline of Classical Chinese Grammar*. Vancouver: UBC Press.

Robert, M. (1994). *Three Kingdoms*. Beijing: Foreign Language Press.

Tacitus, P. C. (2009[Ancieut Rome]). Annals and Histories. Translated by A.J. Church and W. J. Brodribb, with an introduction by R. L. Fox, notes revised by E. Cowan. Alfred A. Knopf, New York, London and Toronto: Everyman's Library.

Waley, A. (1938). *The Analects of Confucius*. London: G. Allen & Unwin Ltd.

Ware, J. R. (1955). *The Sayings of Confucius*. New York: New American Library.

Watson, B. (1963). *Records of the Grand Historian*. New York: Columbia University Press.

Watson, B. (1974). *Courtier and Commoner in Ancient China: Selections from the History of the Former Han* (by Pan Ku). New York and London: Columbia University Press.

Xu, Y. C. (2005). *Confucius Modernized: Thus Spoke the Master*. Beijing: Higher Education Press.

Yuan, Y. L. (auth.) and Wu, G. X. (trans.). (2017). *Cognition-based Studies on Chinese Grammar*. London/New York: Routledge.

Yang, X. Y. and Yang, G. (2007). *Selections from Records of the Historian*. Beijing: Foreign Languages Press.

班固.（1999）.《汉书》（简体字本）.北京：中华书局.

陈寿.（2005）.《三国志》（上、下）.长沙：岳麓书社.

方琰.（2001）.论汉语小句复合体的主位.《外语研究》,（2）：56-58.

黄燕婷.（2017）.语法复杂性在汉文史籍翻译中的应用.华侨大学学士论文.

蒋骁华.（1998）.互文性与文学翻译.《中国翻译》,（2）：19-24.

雷相奎.（2017）.三国演义译本对《三国志》外译的参考意义.华侨大学学士论文.

罗贯中.（2009）.《三国演义》.北京：中华书局.

欧阳修.（1974）.《新五代史》.北京：中华书局.

培根.（2008）.《新工具》.陈伟功编译.北京：北京出版社.

培根.（2008）.《培根文集》.江文编译.北京：中国戏剧出版社.

司马迁.（1982）.《史记》（简体字本）.北京：中华书局.

王洪涛.（2010）.互文性理论之于翻译学研究：认识论价值与方法论意义.《上海翻译》,（3）：6-11.

吴国向.（2012）.经典翻译与文化传承——"首届《论语》翻译研讨会"简述.《中国外语》,（1）：104-107.

吴国向.（2013）.《论语》翻译版本的语法复杂性研究.中山大学外国语学院博士论文.

吴国向.（2020）.译文词汇密度及其波动研究——以多重《论语》英译为例.《北京科技大学学报（社会科学版）》,36（5）：25-32，42.

杨衍松.（1994）.互文性与翻译.《中国翻译》,（4）：10-13.

袁毓林.（1994）.一价名词的认知研究.《中国语文》,（4）：241-253.

周一平.（2008）.中国二十四史：尽快英译，推向世界.《探索与争鸣》,（12）：27-30.

马建忠.（2007）.《马氏文通》.北京：商务印书馆.

附 录

部分"十国世家"的译文

Ten Hereditary Houses: A Selected Translation

Xiu Ouyang (A. D. 1007–1072)
Co-translated and revised by Guoxiang Wu

The Eighth Hereditary House of Min
  Translated by Guoxiang Wu
The Tenth Hereditary House of Eastern Han: Liu Min and Liu Chengjun
  Translated by Yanjie Zhang
The Seventh Hereditary House of Wu and Yue: Qian Liu
  Translated by Jiaqi Xue

The Eighth Hereditary House of Min①

Translated by Guoxiang Wu

Wang Shenzhi, with the courtesy name of Xintong, was a native of Gushi County of Guangzhou Commandery. His father was Wang Nen, who had been engaged in farming throughout his life, and his brother was Wang Chao, who had served as an assistant in the county government.

In the late Tang dynasty, as an increasing number of bandits were rising up, Wang Xu, a native of Shouzhou Commandery, led a group of soldiers to attack the county of Gushi. After they had conquered the county, Xu heard that Chao and his brothers were intrepid and talented, so he summoned them into the army and appointed Chao as lieutenant.

At that time, Qin Zongquan, who took control of Caizhou Commandery, was managing to recruit soldiers to expand his own troops. For this purpose, Zongquan appointed Xu as magistrate of Guangzhou and then tried to assemble Xu's soldiers to suppress the anti-imperial rebellion led by Huang Chao. Xu, however, hesitated to submit his soldiers under the command of Zongquan, so Zongquan dispatched his troops to trounce Xu. Knowing that he was not able to win the battle, Xu led his soldiers and fled southwards. They plundered everywhere they arrived until they entered the county of Linting via Nankang. Soon afterwards they captured the county of Zhangpu and now there were tens of thousands of men in the army. Xu was so suspicious and jealous in nature that those commanders who were capable and talented were mostly killed for one or another reason. Chao himself was quite frightened that he might also be killed one day.

When the troops arrived in the county of Nan'an, Chao persuaded his own forward commander to start up a revolt against Xu. "It is because of the threat under Xu," Chao said, "that we have abandoned our ancestral tombs and left our wives and children. We are now nothing but thefts and robbers! It isn't our own wish, is it? Now Xu is so skeptical that all capable commanders and talented officials are sure to be killed. None of us can guarantee our own safety even for a single day, let alone achieve any success!" The forward commander was

---

① Min is now an alias for the south-eastern Chinese province of Fujian. In ancient China, the nationality of Min was one of the most prominent southern minorities.

thoroughly disillusioned by what Chao had said. Recognising such a dangerous situation, they were supportive of each other, with tears trickling down from their eyes. Soon afterwards, Chao together with his forward commander selected dozens of vigorous soldiers to ambush Xu in the midst of the bamboo forest. These soldiers awaited Xu passing by and then jumped out from the forest to capture him. Xu was then imprisoned in the army and later he committed suicide.

Now that Xu had been deposed, the forward commander persuaded the generals and officials to uphold Chao as their new chief. "It is Chao," he said, "who has given us a second life." So Chao was promoted to be the lord. At that time, Liao Yanruo, magistrate of Quanzhou, led a corruptive and atrocious government, from which the people of Quanzhou suffered very much. When it was heard that Chao had invaded across territories to the border and that the army paraded in a disciplined order, the elder people, leading their youngsters, blocked the way with the hope that Chao and his troops would stay so as to replace the government by Yanruo. Chao then led his troops to outflank Yanruo and occupied Quanzhou the next year.

In the second year of the Guangqi period (A. D. 886), Chen Yan, surveillance commissioner of Fujian, nominated Chao as magistrate of Quanzhou. Yan passed away in the first year of the Jingfu period (A. D. 892). His son-in-law Fan Hui pronounced himself as the successor. Dissatisfied with Hui's claim of the title, Chao sent Shenzhi to attack Hui, but the war turned out to be a long stalemate and resulted in a large number of injuries and casualties. Shenzhi first requested to withdraw the troops, but it was disapproved of by Chao, so he further requested that Chao lead the troops in person and that more soldiers be summoned and sent. Chao replied with a simple report. "If both soldiers and generals have died out," he stated, "I shall surely go fighting myself." Shenzhi had no choice but to launch another campaign, leading commanders and soldiers in person. Hui's troops were eventually defeated and Hui himself was killed.

Later, the Tang dynasty appointed Chao as surveillance commissioner of Fujian and Chao in turn nominated Shenzhi as assistant. Shenzhi was a big, burly man, with his nose bridge highly upright and mouth widely square. He often rode a white horse, so he earned himself the name of "White Knight the Third" in the army. In the fourth year of the Qianning period (A. D. 897), Chao passed away and Shenzhi succeeded to his position.

The Tang dynasty established a provincial-level institution entitled "Weiwu Military Government" in Fuzhou and accordingly appointed Shenzhi as military commissioner. Since then, he had been promoted several times until he eventually became the joint manager of affairs with the secretariat chancellery and was granted with the title of "King of Langya". After the fall of the Tang dynasty, the Founding Emperor Taizu of the Liang dynasty nominated Shenzhi as general secretary of the imperial secretariat, granted him with "King of Min", and promoted Fuzhou as Metropolitan Government. At that time, Yang Xingmi occupied the Jianghuai area, blocking the land route in the region between the Yangtze River and the Huai River. Nevertheless, dispatching envoys to go by seaway via the seaport commanderies of Dengzhou and Laizhou, Shenzhi still contrived to pay loyal tribute to the Liang dynasty every year. Before his envoys reached the ports of destination, however, their boats had often capsized, and, among the envoys sailing into the sea, as many as three or four out of ten got drowned.

Shenzhi, though having risen up among the bandits, led a thrifty life, treated his subordinates with courtesy, and also received or recruited scholars or officials who had been dismissed from the central court after the downfall of the former Tang dynasty. Those who took official positions in Shenzhi's government included Wang Dan, whose father was Wang Pu, the former prime minister of the Tang dynasty, Yang Yi, whose elder brother was Yang She, the former prime minister of the Tang dynasty, and Xu Ying, who was a well-known scholar of the former Tang dynasty. In addition, a national academy was established to educate talented people in the region of Min, and policies were carried out to invite overseas and foreign merchants to boost the local economy. The merchant ships, however, could only berth across the sea at the Huangqi Island, between which and the mainland the mighty waves remained the last obstacle. One evening, after a fearful tempest had arisen with thunder and lightning, the sea was then split into two parts by a road leading to the island, which thus became a seaport overnight. The Min people believed that this was what the virtue of Shenzhi and his government had brought about, so they called it "Gantang Port", that is, the Sweet-Pear Port.

In the third year of the Tongguang period (A. D. 925) when he was 64 years old, Shenzhi passed away and was honoured with the posthumous title of

"Zhongyi", that is, the "Loyal Virtuous". His son Yanhan succeeded him in order of seniority.

Yanhan, with Ziyi as his courtesy name, was the eldest son of Shenzhi. In the fourth year of the Tongguang period (A. D. 926), the Tang dynastic court appointed Yanhan as military commissioner. In the same year, Emperor Zhuangzong was murdered and the nation suffered from many misfortunes. Yanhan took out *Historical Records* by the grand historian Sima Qian of the Han dynasty and showed the "Biography of Wuzhu the King of Min and Yue" to his generals and officials. "Min," he declared, "has been a kingdom since ancient times. If I do not claim the kingship now, what then should I be waiting for?"

So generals and officials in the military administration submitted written statements and advised him to proceed to restore the kingdom. In October (November or December, A. D. 926), Yanhan founded the kingdom and claimed the kingship, though still observing the calendar of the Tang dynasty.

Yanhan had a tall and large figure and he looked as beautiful and fair as a piece of jade, whereas his wife Mrs Cui was ugly in appearance and dissolute in nature, from which Yanhan himself was not able to restrain. Before the mourning period for Shenzhi came to an end, Yanhan removed the sacrificial offerings, and eagerly rushed into the act of selecting numerous girls of good breeding to be his concubines. Mrs Cui was so jealous-tempered that those well-bred girls who were beautiful tended to be imprisoned in a special room, fastened to a punishment device, whacked in the face with a bat which was made out of wood and carved into a hand-like shape, and then stabbed with an iron spike. Eighty-four of them were killed within one single year. Mrs Cui later got sick and dead of being reported to have seen their ghosts.

Yanbing, originally born in a Zhou family and later adopted as a son by Shenzhi, was appointed as magistrate of Jianzhou, but had been in a bad term with Yanhan ever since Shenzhi's time. Yanhan later succeeded to Shenzhi's position and appointed his younger brother Yanjun as magistrate of Quanzhou, for which Yanjun flew into a rage.

For these reasons, Yanbing and Yanjun worked out a conspiracy to revolt against their elder brother Yanhan. In December (January or February, A. D. 927), leading their soldiers respectively, Yanbing and Yanjun launched an invasion, in which Yanhan was captured, killed, and thus deposed. Yanjun succeeded to the throne soon afterwards with his given name changed into Lin.

Lin was the second son of Shenzhi. The Tang dynastic court soon afterwards appointed him as military commissioner, promoted him several times to the grand police inspector and the general secretary of the imperial secretariat, and eventually granted him with the title of "King of Min".

Earlier, when Yanbing conspired with Lin to murder Yanhan, Yanbing led his soldiers arrived first, and, not until the next day after they had captured and then killed Yanhan did Lin arrive with his soldiers. Nevertheless, regarding himself as the adopted son, Yanbing recommended Lin to succeed to the throne.

Yanbing was now returning to Jianzhou and Lin treated him with food and wine in the suburbs. As they bade farewell to each other, Yanbing instructed Lin in a superior tone, referring himself as the elder brother. "My younger brother!" he remarked. "Uphold the will of our forefather and never bother me to come over again!" Lin was offended with these words, and he had borne this in mind ever since. In the second year of the Changxing period (A.D. 931), Yanbing commanded his troops to assault Lin. He himself launched an attack at the west gate and sent his son Jixiong simultaneously to make another attack by seaway, attempting to make a breakthrough at the south gate. Lin dispatched Wang Renda to resist the attack launched by Jixiong. Renda designed a trap to avoid a direct encounter between the two forces, in which he first concealed soldiers in his boat and then held up a white flag, making a false plea for surrender. Jixiong was so gullible that he was tricked into the trap. He embarked onto the boat only to be ambushed and killed by Renda's soldiers. His head was transferred and hung over the west gate. On seeing this, the soldiers of Yanbing all fled away and Yanbing was then captured. When they got to see each other again, Lin mocked Yanbing in an inferior tone, referring himself as the younger brother. "My elder brother!" he remarked. "I cannot uphold the will of our forefather and ever bother you to come over again!" Yanbing could not make any reply, so he was killed soon afterwards. On hearing the failure, Jisheng, another son of Yanbing, who had stayed back to defend Jianzhou, escaped to the region of Qiantang in haste.

In the third year of the Changxing period (A.D. 932), Lin submitted a written application to the imperial court of the Tang dynasty. "Ma Yin was the King of Chu and Qian Liu was the King of Wu and Yue," he wrote. "Both of them served as general secretary of the imperial secretariat. Now that they have passed away, please grant me with the title of 'general secretary' ". Lin's application was not approved of, so Lin paid no further loyal tribute to the Tang dynastic court.

Taoist Chen Shouyuan was trusted because of his heterodox doctrines, so Lin built a holy palace to accommodate Shouyuan, in which a god called "Baohuang", that is, the Precious Emperor, was consecrated. Later Shouyuan made a prediction about Lin's fortune. "Baohuang orders," he said, "that Your Majesty refrain yourself from the throne for a short while and then Your Majesty will be made the son of heaven in the future sixty years." Lin was pleased with this, so he abdicated the throne and appointed his son Jipeng to take charge of the governmental affairs. Shortly afterwards Lin restored the dominion and sent Shouyuan to enquire Baohuang about his fortune again. "What destination," he said, "will I turn to after sixty years?" Shouyuan returned the words of Baohuang and said, "After sixty years, Your Majesty will become the saint of Dalou."

Soon afterwards, Lin claimed the emperorship with an imperial edict conferred by Baohuang, used the yellow dragon as a symbol to mark his mansion, and changed the designation of the reign into "Longqi", which meant that a dragon was rising up. Shenzhi was added to with the posthumous title of "Bright Martial Filial Emperor", or "Emperor Wu", and consecrated in the imperial temple as the "Founding Emperor". Five temples were established to consecrate the past five generations of forefathers, a hundred ranking officials were nominated, and Fuzhou was taken as the capital in the name of "Changle Fu", that is, Government of Long-lasting Happiness. The region of Min, however, was narrow in terms of its terrain and the revenue fell short of the expenditure. To cope with these problems, the military secretary Xue Wenjie was appointed as financial minister. Wenjie inspected numerous secret affairs among the folk and tended to convict those who were rich of various crimes and deprive them of their wealth in order to aid national expenditure. For this reason, much resentment arose among people in the state of Min. Wenjie also tried to recommend the talented wizard Xu Yan to Lin. "Your Majesty," he said, "there are too many crafty ministers by your side. If we don't reproach and rectify these ghosts and spirits, they will commit rebellion." Accordingly, Lin sent Yan to watch ghosts in the palace.

Wenjie and the inner military affairs commissioner Wu Ying had been dissatisfied with and resented each other to some extent. On one occasion, when Ying was off duty because he was not in good health, Wenjie informed Ying of a piece of false news, referring Ying as a duke. "His Majesty," he said, "entrusts you with an important position in the imperial court, but you have been off duty successively with the excuse of illness. His Majesty is going to dismiss you from the office." Ying asked, "How should I cope with this?" "If His Majesty sends someone to inquire about your health," Wenjie instructed Ying and said, "please do say that 'I have suffered from nothing but a headache'." Ying took it seriously. On the next day, Wenjie hinted Lin into sending a wizard to watch the health condition of Ying. The wizard said, "I had stepped into the Northern Temple only to see Ying being questioned by Chongshun King[①] with the sentence: 'How dare you have plotted a rebel?' The king then hit him in the head with a metal hammer." Lin consulted with Wenjie on these words and Wenjie said, "They are not yet believable for the moment. It would be suitable if we could inquire into Ying's health condition in person." Lin then sent someone to inquire Yin and Yin answered, "It is a headache." Ying was then imprisoned and Wenjie was sent by Lin to impeach him. Ying submitted, though acknowledging the false accusation, and was killed soon afterwards.

Ying had taken command of the troops and was generally supported by soldiers. When the news came that Ying died, they all burst into rage. Later in that year, the state of Wu sent troops to attack Jianzhou, so Lin dispatched his general Wang Yanzong to run a rescue campaign, but the soldiers simply stationed on the road, unwilling to march forward. "We will march on," they said, "until we have got Wenjie." Lin took pity on Wenjie and hesitated to give him up, but his son Jipeng made a plea to trade him for a possible relief of the emergent situation. As a result, Wenjie was escorted in a prison van on a trip to the army. Wenjie was good at numerology, so he made a prediction for himself and said, "There will be no worry for any ill luck in three days." This, however, was overheard by the soldiers who escorted him, so they speeded up and arrived at the destination in two days. The soldiers got excited and dismembered Wenjie in the downtown area. In addition, a large number of onlookers rushed to throw tiles

---

① Chongshun King, consecrated in the Northern Temple, is the posthumous title of Liu Xingquan, the forward general at the service of Wang Chao.

and stones at him and then carved up his flesh and bones. On the next day, messengers who had been sent by Lin to remit Wenjie from punishment arrived, but it was too late. Earlier, when Wenjie built the prison van at the service of Lin, he regarded the existing carriage as loose and wide, so he revised the traditional structure: The upper part and the lower part were combined into one single cell, within which sharp iron thorns were equipped, pointing to the center so that the prisoner would be pricked whenever the carriage moved. This done, Wenjie was the first victim of this new prison van.

In the third year of the Longqi period (A.D. 935), the designation of the reign was changed into Yonghe, that is, "Everlasting Harmony". Since Wang Renda took credit at the service of Lin for having killed Yanbing four years before, he had been in charge of the loyal bodyguards. Lin had scruple over this, so he turned to Renda on one occasion, making an inquiry about the second emperor of the Qin dynasty and Zhao Gao①, the prime minister of the dynasty. "Is it truly the case," Lin asked, "that Zhao Gao referred to a deer as a horse in order to fool the Second Emperor. "It is not that Gao could make a fool of the Second Emperor," Renda replied, "but that the second Emperor was a fool, so Gao referred to a deer as a horse. Now, Your Majesty is intelligent, and the number of court officials is no more than one hundred, of whose daily life and behaviours Your Majesty is kept well informed. If any one dares to abuse his power or stage any rebel, it is simple to extinguish his entire clan." Lin felt so ashamed that he granted money and silks to Renda as a comfort. After Lin retreated to his trusted followers, however, he warned them to guard against Renda. "Renda," he said, "though fairly usable in my generation, is too wise to be left over as a danger in the coming generation." Soon afterwards Renda was killed on a false accusation of crime.

Lin's wife died young, and his second wife Mrs Jin was taciturn though amiable. Shenzhi's maidservant Jinfeng, who came from a Chen family, was favoured by Lin and nominated as queen. Earlier, a government clerk named Gui Shouming, known by the name of "Brother Gui", was favoured by Lin because of his beauty. Lin later got a paralytic stroke and Mrs Chen fornicated with Brother

---

① Zhao Gao (? -207 B.C.) had formally served as advisor to Huhai, the 18th son of the Founding Emperor of the Qin dynasty. After Huhai succeeded to the throne and became the Second Emperor, Zhao Gao was the prime minister of the imperial court.

Gui. The directorate of general production Li Keyin also colluded with Mrs Chen by way of Brother Gui. This later became a rumour. When Lin ordered the brocade craftsmen to weave a curtain with the pattern of nine dragons, the rumour was then composed into a song and it was chanted among the nationals as follows, "For whom is the nine-dragon curtain woven? It accommodates more than one brother!"

Lin's maidservant Chunyan, born with adorable appearance, intrigued Lin's son Jipeng to a considerable degree. After Lin began to suffer from sickness, Jipeng made a proposal to Chunyan by way of Mrs Chen. Lin approved his son of the proposal though he was dissatified with the request. Lin's second son Jitao, however, was enraged by this, so he drafted a plan to kill Jipeng. Having overheard Jitao's plan, Jipeng was so frightened that he turned to Li Fang, directorate of the capital security division, seeking a solution. In October of the year (November or December, A. D. 935), when a banquet was held to entertain the army in Dapu Palace, Lin was sleepily seated and murmured that he saw Yanbing coming. Fang believed that Lin had been seriously sick, so he immediately ordered soldiers to break into Li Keyin's house and kill him. On the next morning, however, Lin turned out to be safe and sound at court and asked Fang about the crime for which Li Keyin had been killed. Fang was frightened and rushed out of the court, but, soon he came back together with Jipeng, leading the capital security guards, invaded the court. On hearing the sounds of drums, Lin retreated and hid in the midst of the nine-dragon curtain. The security guards stabbed him but he did not die. The servants could not bear the bitterness from which he suffered, so they helped in ending his life. Jitao, Empress Chen and Brother Gui were all killed by Fang. Lin got killed ten years after he had come to the throne. He was honoured with the posthumous title of "Hui Emperor", that is, Clement Emperor, and was consecrated in the imperial temple as "Taizong", that is, Grand Emperor.

Jipeng was the eldest son of Lin. After he had succeeded to the throne, his name was changed into "Chang" and the designation of reign was changed into "Tongwen", that is, Reasonably Cultured. Li Fang was then appointed to take charge of the six legions of armed forces and all security affairs. Fang, however, was well aware that he had committed regicide and he himself had been suspicious ever since he supported Chang to the throne, so a large number of loyal soldiers were raised to prepare for any unexpected incident. This, in turn, alerted and troubled Chang to such an extent that he ordered ambushing soldiers to capture and kill Fang in a grand banquet which was held to entertain the army. Fang was beheaded and his cut-off head was then hung over the city. His division became disobebient and thousands of his men revolted to burn down Qisheng Gate, take back the head of Fang and then seek refuge into the Qiantang area.

In the second year of the Tianfu period (A. D. 937), Chang sent envoys to pay loyal tribute to the imperial court of the Jin dynasty and the Founding Emperor in return sent the cavalier attendant-in-ordinary Lu Sun to confer Chang with the title of "King of Min" and also to granted his son Jigong with the title of "Prince of Linhai County". When Sun arrived in the state of Min, however, Chang did not receive him in person with the excuse of being in bad health. Instead, Jigong was instructed to host him and the council secretary Liu Yi was additionally sent to treat Sun in the guest-house. Yi looked brilliant with his hat and dress and even his servants who drove the carriage were gorgeous.

On another day, Sun incidentally met Yi on the way only to find that Yi simply wore cotton clothes and grass shoes, looking as ordinary as a civilian. Sun sent someone to mock him in the tone of an inferior. "Secretary of the Phoenix Cabinet①," the man said, "how can you embarrass us in such an extent?" Yi felt so ashamed that he went away quickly with his hands covering his face. These words were passed on to Chang and he felt offended at the thought that Sun had insulted him, so, when Sun was to make a return trip, Chang gave nothing in return. His son Jigong did send his adjuvant Zheng Yuanbi to keep company with Sun to the imperial capital, paying loyal tribute and presenting local products. In addition, Jigong also wrote to the ministers of the Jin dynasty, narrating that Chang was intending to seek for a mutual relation with the Jin dynasty so that the state of Min could be acknowledged independent. Bursting into rage at Chang's impertinence, the Founding Emperor issued an imperial decree to expose his crimes, returned all his presents and rejected any tribute he had paid. The vice minister of war Li Zhisun submitted a written statement to the emperor, requesting that his goods should be confiscated and his envoy should be arrested. Thus

---

① Secretary in the Grand Council was intentionally called Secretary of the Phoenix Cabinet in this conversation by the questioner. In the former Tang dynasty, the Grand Councile was referred to as the Phoenix Cabinet (凤阁 Fènggé), a ministry which was responsible for the imperial records.

Yuanbi was imprisoned, and when he was later bound up with shackles and introduced before the emperor, he lay prone and submitted. "Chang," he said, "is simply a barbarian king of the ethnic minorities. He does not know what are rite and righteousness. Your Majesty shows generous trustworthiness to invite people to the dynasty from far distance. I have obeyed the order humbly yet it has turned out to be offensive. I wish I had lain prone on the stake and been axed across the waist so that the crime of Chang might be atoned." On hearing this, the Founding Emperor remitted Yuanbi from punishment and repatriated him soon afterwards.

Chang was also intrigued by sorcerers. He granted Tan Zixiao, a Taoist, with the title of "Sir Right-One" and also granted Chen Shouyuan with the title of "Master of Heaven". In addition, another wizard Lin Xing was favoured for his witchcraft, and, no matter how big or small an event might be, Chang would act only according to the words expressed by him on behalf of Baohuang. Shouyuan instructed Chang to build a three-storey terrace called "Sanqing Tai". Several thousand *jin* of gold was used to cast the statues of the god Baohuang and the Founding Sovereign of Heaven, that is, the Lofty Laozi, and a large amount of borneol, frankincense and other incenses were burnt daily. Chang enjoyed himself at the foot of the terrace with instrumental music continued all day and all night. It was said that the elixir of life could be extracted in this way.

In the summer of the third year (A.D. 938), a rainbow was seen in the palace, so Lin Xing conveyed the words of the god. "This is an omen," he said, "which signals that a revolt be staged within the loyal clan." Xing then received an order to lead a group of soldiers to kill five of Shenzhi's sons or grandsons, including Yanwu, Yanwang and their sons, but Xing failed when taking actions, so he himself also got killed. Now that Chang became even more confused and reckless, he first nominated his father's maidservant Chunyan as his concubine and then promoted her as empress. Furthermore, he also sent the physician Chen Jiu to sell official titles with blank letters of appointment.

Chang's younger brother Jiyan had taken command of the six legions of armed forces and all security affairs. Chang was suspicious about the situation, so he removed Jiyan from the position and appointed his third younger brother Jiyong to take over it. In addition, Chang recruited soldiers and organised them into a division entitled "Chengwei Du" to ensure his own safety. What this division were granted and awarded was considerably favourable over other armed forces, including the other two divisions of security guards called "Konghe Du" and "Gongchen Du". Lian Chongyu, general-in-chief of "Konghe Du", and Zhu Wenjin, general-in-chief of "Gongchen Du", used this unfair treatment to irritate their own soldiers.

In the summer of this year, the prophets said that a disaster was to take place in Chang's palace, so Chang moved to the South Palace to keep away from the fire. His palace was on fire later. He suspected that Chongyu's soldiers had set the fire. The grand secretariant academician Chen Tan had been favoured and trusted by Chang because he was good at flattery. Chang consulted him about the fire, but Tan in turn told Chongyu about Chang's suspicion. Chongyu was so frightened that he led his soldiers to set fire on the South Palace one night. Taking his concubines and sons together, Chang led his security guards to fight a way out of the Yellow Gate and made camp in the wild. Chongyu received Yanyi and enthroned him. Yanyi commanded his son Jiye to make a final raid on Chang with a troop of soldiers. Facing Jiye's soldiers, Chang shot a number of them to death, and then, knowing that he could not escape, he threw his bow onto the ground. Jiye captured and killed Chang and none of his wives and his sons was spared. Yanyi came to the throne and honoured Chang with the posthumous title of "Kangzong", that is, the Peaceful Emperor.

Yanyi was the youngest son of Shenzhi. After he came to the throne, he changed his name into Xi, dispatched envoys to pay loyal tribute to the Jin dynasty and changed the designation of the reign into "Yonglong", that is, Ever-Prosperous. He also ordered to make big metal coins, each of which was set to be worth ten old coins. Although Xi had been obstinate and unyielding since Chang's time, when Chang's prime minister Wang Tan suppressed him, Xi also feared Tan and restrained himself from making further troubles. The state of Silla sent envoys to present a precious sword to the state of Min and Chang lifted the sword and showed it to Tan. "What is the use of this?" asked he. Tan answered, "It can be used to chop those who lack loyalty or filial piety." Xi was sitting aside and was shocked by what Tan had said. After Xi came to the throne, Silla presented another sword and this reminded Xi of Tan as well as what he had said before. Although Tan had died, Xi gave an order to excavate his tomb and expose his corpse. Tan's face looked as if he were still alive and his body was covered all over with blood.

Magistrate of Quanzhou Yu Tingying once robbed girls of good breeding from the civilian with a false command which was said to have been issued by Xi. For this reason, Xi flew into a rage and ordered censors to impeach and punish him, but Tingying tried to smooth this critical situation by handing in ten thousand grands of money for banquet expenditure to Xi. "What have you presented to the queen?" asked Xi. Accordingly, Tingying presented another ten million grands of money to the queen, and, as a result, he was not impeached. Xi once married his daughter to someone and those dynastic officials who failed to congratulate or present gifts were whipped. Vice censor-in-chief Liu Zan was to be punished for his unwillingness to impeach other ministers, and, as he was about to be whipped, grand master of remonstrance Zheng Yuanbi tried his best to dissuade the punishment, so Xi turned to Yuanbi and compared him to Duke Zheng of the Wei state in the Spring-Autumn period. "How can you compare yourself to Duke Zheng of Wei?" he asked, "and how dare you have dissuaded so far?" Yuanbi in return compared Xi to the founding emperor Taizong of the Tang dynasty, and answered, "If Your Majesty compare yourself to Taizong of Tang, I can humbly compare myself to Duke Zheng of Wei." Xi was so pleased that he released Zan and exempted him from the punishment of whipping.

Wang Yanzheng, who was one of Xi's elder brothers, had been appointed as military commissioner of Jianzhou and granted with the title of "King of Fusha" before the reign of Xi. Since Xi came to the throne, they had been in such a bad term with each other that they had even dispatched their troops to fight back and forth several times. Xi therefore vented his hatred on Yanzheng's clan and house and killed some of them for one or another reason. Grand master of remonstrance Huang Jun carried a coffin to the court and tried his best to remonstrate him from committing further misdeeds, but Xi was deeply enraged by his remonstrance, so he demoted Jun to an adjutant fiscal officer. The editor Chen Guangyi presented a written document in which more than fifty faults that Xi had or misdeeds that he committed were sorted out. Xi ordered his guards to put Guangyi to death: Guangyi was first whipped a hundred times but he was still alive, so he was hung in the neck by the guards with a rope under a tree only to be found dead after a long while. Minister of finance Chen Kuangfan presented a method to increase taxes on business and commerce. Xi was at first pleased with him and thought highly of him. "Kuangfan is rare and precious among men," said Xi. When it came to the end of the year, however, the annual revenue failed to reach to the expected amount, so Kuangfan had to make use of private borrowing to make it up. Kuangfan soon died of worries for this fault. Later, Xi discovered that Kuangfan had used private borrowing, so he ordered his men to split up Kuangfan's coffin, dismembered the body into pieces and discarded them into the water.

Xi was dissolute and tyrannical in nature, whereas his wife Mrs Li was ferocious and indulged in drinking. Xi employed people according to their appearance: Mrs Shang became the favourite princess simply because she looked fairly nice; Xi's nephew Li Renyu also had good appearance, so he was favoured and appointed by Xi as prime minister. Xi also indulged in drinking and always boozed; in addition, he requested his ministers to serve by his side and cater for the drinking, but most of them failed to sustain the excessive amount and often got heavily drunk. Those who refused to drink or discarded any wine in private were often punished or even got killed. On one occasion, his son Jirou discarded some drink, so he was killed together with a master of ceremonies. Meanwhile, since Lian Chongyu killed Chang, he had been frightened that he would be sanctioned by the nationals, so he made use of a marriage with Zhu Wenjin's family in order to strengthen his position and ensure his own safety. Xi later became suspicious with Chongyu and his colleagues and often blamed them for the guilt that they had committed to the loyal clan, but what they could do was simply to defend themselves with their running noses. This was well noticed of by Mrs Li, who had been envious of Princess Shang since the latter was favoured by Xi. Mrs Li worked out a conspiracy against Xi and intended to enthrone her son Yacheng, so she sent someone to take words to Chongyu and his colleagues. The man came to Chongyu and Wenjin and referred them as dukes. "His Majesty treats you both in an unfair manner," he said, "and how can this situation be coped with?" Chongyu and his colleagues were all panicked, so they planned to take an action to solve this problem. In March in the sixth year of the Yonglong period (April or May, A. D. 944), after Xi took an excursion, he drank as usual and returned to the palace, but he was dragged down from the horse on mid-way and then killed by soldiers who had been dispatched by Chongyu and his colleagues. Xi was honoured with the posthumous title of "Jingzong", that is, the

Grand Emperor.

Earlier, Yanzheng, who was also son of Shenzhi, had submitted several written statements of remonstrance to Xi because Xi was dissolute in nature and tyrannical in government since Xi had succeeded to the throne. These remonstrations, however, irritated Xi to such an extent that he in return sent Du Jiancong as commissioner to supervise Yanzheng's army. Yanzheng rejected Xi's military supervision by expelling and sending Jiancong back to Fuzhou, and, as a result, a war was brought about between these two brothers. Xi first dispatched his troops to attack Yanzheng, but his troops were defeated. Soon afterwards, Yanzheng founded a new kingdom with "Yin" as the name on the basis of Jianzhou Commandery and changed the designation of the reign into "Tiande", that is, "Heavenly Virtue".

It had been one year also since Lian Chongyu killed Chang and, one day, Chongyu summoned all of the ministers in the Min government and declared that they were to break away from the ruling of the Wang's clan. "In the past," he said, "the Founding Emperor Wu went through battlefields in spite of arrows and stones, and since then the state of Min has been established. His sons and grandsons, however, are dissolute and tyrannical and they have gone too far away from the right path so that the heaven has begun to hate the Wang's clan. Now that the common people begin to recommend men of talent to replace them, we should accept those who are virtuous so as to make this land peaceful." None of the ministers dared to have any further discussion as to whether it was justifiable or not, and, seeing that there was no explicit protest, Chongyu in person supported Zhu Wenjin to ascend into the palace, seated him on the throne, and led all the officials to face north and submit to Wenjin. Wenjin in turn appointed Chongyu to take charge of the six legions of armed forces and all security affairs. Those brothers and sons from the Wang's clan who resided in Fuzhou were mostly killed, regardless of their ages. Huang Shaopo was sent to defend Quanzhou, Chen Yun was to defend Zhangzhou, and Xu Wenzhen was to defend Tingzhou. The new government adopted the designation of the Jin dynasty; it was the first year of the Kaiyun period (A.D. 944).

The general commander of Quanzhou Liu Congxiao deceived the men of Quanzhou in the belief that Yanzheng, King of Fusha, was dispatching armed forces to capture Fuzhou. "King of Fusha," he said, "is now leading troops to occupy Fuzhou and all traitors in Fuzhou are sure to be sanctioned. We have served as ministers for the Wang's house for all our life, and how can we submit to those traitors and even serve them as accomplices?" The men of Quanzhou were fully convinced of this unreal situation, so they rose up together against Shaopo, put him to death and then received and nominated Wang Jixun as magistrate. After the news from Quanzhou arrived, the men of Zhangzhou also killed Yun and then received Wang Jicheng as magistrate. Both Jixun and Jicheng were princes of the Wang's clan. When the news came to Tingzhou, Wenzhen was so frightened that he surrendered Tingzhou to Yanzheng directly. Seeing that Yanzheng had taken control of the three commanderies of Quanzhou, Zhangzhou and Tingzhou, Chongyu had to kill Wenjin and transferred his head to Jianzhou, showing his willingness to surrender Fuzhou to Yanzheng, but he was in turn killed by Lin Renhan, assistant general of Fuzhou; Renhan planned to receive Yanzheng to move the capital from Jianzhou to Fuzhou.

At this point, Li Jing, King of Southern Tang, heard that the state of Min was in disorder, so he dispatched his troops to invade it with the aim to taking over its land. While Yanzheng himself stayed in Jianzhou, he sent his nephew Jichang to defend Fuzhou. As the troops of Southern Tang were launching a fierce attack on Yanzheng in Jianzhou, Li Renda, general commander of Fuzhou, took this opportunity and persuaded his followers to start a revolt against Jichang so as to separate Fuzhou from Jianzhou. "The troops of Southern Tang were now conquering Jianzhou," Renda said, "but King of Fusha cannot even protect himself, so how can he possess this land?" Soon afterwards, Renda and his men captured and killed Jichang. Now Renda intended to claim the kingship, but he was afraid that no one would support him, so he invited a monk named Zhuo Yanming out of the Snow Peak Temple, showed him to the public, and tried to pursuade them to accept the monk as king. "This is not an ordinary man!" announced Renda before the public. He then wore Yanming with the dragon crown and guided generals and officials to face north and submit themselves to Yanming as ministers, but Yanming was killed by Renda soon afterwards. Renda took over the throne after Yanming died, and he sent his sincerity to Li Jing; Li Jing in turn appointed Li Renda, who was later renamed into "Hongyi", as commissioner of the Weiwu Military Government. After Jianzhou was conquered and occupied by Li Jing's troops, Li Jing migrated Yanzheng's family and clan to the capital city of Jinling and granted Yanzheng with the title of "King of Boyang". It was the fourth year of the Baoda period during the reign of Li Jing (A. D. 946).

On hearing that Yanzheng had surrendered to the state of Southern Tang, Liu Congxiao arrested Wang Jixun and sent him to Jinling, showing his sincerity and submission to Li Jing. Li Jing in turn set up a military institution entitled "Qingyuan Military Government" in Quanzhou and Congxiao was accordingly appointed as commissioner. After Li Jing conquered Jianzhou and settled Yanzheng's clan down in Jinling, he sent someone to Fuzhou and summoned Li Renda to the central court in Jinling. Instead of obeying Li Jing's instruction, however, Li Renda directly surrendered to the state of Wu and Yue. Meanwhile, Liu Congxiao also expelled the garrison soldiers of Li Jing and took control of the two commanderies of Quanzhou and Zhangzhou, and Li Jing still granted Congxiao with the title of "King of Jinjiang" though. During the reign of Emperor Shizong of the Zhou dynasty (A. D. 954–959), Congxiao dispatched his company commander Cai Zhongxing in the guise of a merchant to the dynastic court, so Zhongxing went through some bypaths to the capital city and managed to establish a representative office, seeking solutions to a possible submission to the Zhou dynasty as a dependent state. Except for this, since Emperor Shizong and Li Jing took Yangtze River as their border, no direct connection could be easily established, so loyal tribute was no longer paid to the Zhou dynasty, and Congxiao was still subject to the state of Southern Tang. What came later was documented in the state history of Southern Tang.

The third year of the Kaiyun period (A. D. 946) of the Jin Danasty, a year of M. Fire Horse, was the fourth year of the Baoda period of the state of Northern Tang. In this year, Li jing's troops attacked and conquered Jianzhou. The reign of the Wang's house came to an end. According to *Records of Jiangnan*, Li Jing captured the Wang's clan and then moved them to the capital city of Jinling in the third year of the Baoda period (A. D. 945). This is erroneous. With regard to the initial year, it was in the first year of the Jingfu period (A. D. 892) of the Tang dynasty that Wang Chao entered Fuzhou and was appointed as surveillance commissioner. Recorders of the later generations, however, made use of the superstitious prophecy as evidence that the Wang's clan come with one (year of) horse and go with another (year of) horse, so the second year of the Guangqi period (A. D. 886), also a year of M. Fire Horse, was mistaken by them as the initial year when Wang Chao was appointed as magistrate of Quanzhou. Therefore, it is sixty-one years from this mistaken initial year of M. Fire Horse to the second successive year of M. Fire Horse, that is, the fourth year of the Baoda period (A. D. 946), when the state of Min came to an end. The time, however, when the house of Wang had a sudden control over the state of Min, should begin with the first year of the Jinfu period (A. D. 892). It was actually fifty-five years. Now it is correctly recorded by a number of historians that the state came to an end in a year of M. Fire Horse, but it is erroneous to quote the initial year from books of prophets. Though the initial year in *Records of Jiangnan* is correct, the final year is unfortunately incorrect.

The Tenth Hereditary House of Eastern Han: Liu Min and Liu Chengjun

Translated by Yanjie Zhang

Liu Min, originally named Liu Chong, was biologically a younger brother of the Founding Emperor "Gaozu" of the Han dynasty. Liu Min had dense beard and double pupils in his eyes. When he was young, Liu Min was quite a rascal, addicted to alcohol and indulging in gambling. As a punishment, he was once branded in his face and served as a private in the army. When Emperor "Gaozu" of Han served for the Jin dynasty as military commissioner of the Hedong District, including an area to the east of the middle reach of the Yellow River, Liu Min was appointed as commander-in-chief. After Emperor "Gaozu" of Han came to the throne, Liu Min was nominated as governor of Taiyuan, regent of the imperial capital and joint manager of affairs with the secretariat-chancellery. During the reign of Emperor "Yindi" (A. D. 948-950), he was promoted to president of the council.

Emperor "Yindi" was young, and the regime fell in the hand of ministers. The Founding Emperor "Taizu" of the Zhou dynasty, who took charge of military affairs, had newly won considerable merits by suppressing three rebellions. However, he had an enmity with Liu Min long before, and Liu Min had worried about this ever since. Liu Min consulted his assistant Zheng Gong for a solution, referring to "Taizu" as Duke Guo (Wei). "His Majesty is at this moment young and weak," he said, "and the regime falls in the hand of powerful ministers, among whom Duke Guo is the most powerful now. I have been at odds with him from the beginning, so what would happen when it is the time?" Zheng Gong answered, "The reign of the Han dynasty will become chaotic. The metropolis of Jinyang is surrounded by steep mountains, so no troops under heaven are able to take it away easily. In addition, the revenue collected from its ten prefectures is well enough to meet the expenditure. Your lordship is a member of the royal clan, but, if you have no plan at this moment, it will certainly be controlled by someone else in the near future." "What you have said," Liu Min said, "is just what I have been thinking of and worried about." Therefore, Liu Min stopped paying taxes to the imperial court and recruited heroes under heaven and adult citizens to expand the scale of the army. In the third year of the Qianyou period (A. D. 950), the Founding Emperor "Taizu" of the Zhou dynasty revolted in the region of Wei (now Hebei Province). Emperor "Yindi" was then killed and Liu Min planned to dispatch his troops.

When Emperor "Taizu" of Zhou entered the capital city of Bianzhou from the region of Wei, his ambition of rebellion was made explicit. The ministers of the Han dynasty, however, did not granted him with a prompt recognition at that time, so he did not dare to come to the throne immediately. After Emperor "Yindi" died, the ministers decided to enthrone Liu Chengxun. Liu Chengxun was the youngest son of Emperor "Gaozu" of Han. However, Liu Chengxun was seriously ill in bed then, so Emperor "Taizu" of Zhou reported to the empress of the Han dynasty (the mother of Emperor "Yindi") that Liu Yun, the son of Liu Min, should be the successor of the throne. Prime Minister Feng Dao was then dispatched to receive Liu Yun from the commandery of Xuzhou (now in Jiangsu Province). Liu Yun was the military commissioner. At that moment, people all knew that Emperor "Taizu" of Zhou was actually hiding his ambition that he wanted to claim the emperorship. Only Liu Min was pleased and satisfied with what Emperor "Taizu" of Zhou had said and done. "If my son becomes the emperor," Liu Min said, "what trouble should I ever need to consider?" So he withdrew his troops, and sent someone to the capital to show his gratitude and loyalty to the court. Emperor "Taizu" of Zhou had lived as a grass root when he was young, and he tattooed his neck with a flying sparrow, so he was called "Little Sparrow Guo". When Emperor "Taizu" of Zhou met the envoys sent by Liu Min, he told them in detail about his intention of supporting Liu Yun as the emperor. To convince the envoys, he pointed to his neck and showed them the tattoo of a sparrow, referring to Liu Min as Duke. "Since ancient times," he said, "there has been no Son of Heaven who has a tattoo, hasn't there? Fortunately, Duke Liu has his trust in me." Liu Min was so pleased that he fully believed what Emperor "Taizu" of Zhou said and did. Li Xiang, vice governor of Taiyuan, remonstrated with Liu Min. "Duke Guo," he said, "had raised his army to offend Emperor 'Yindi'. This implies that he would neither be a courtier of the Han court, nor help the loyal clan to succeed the throne." Li Xiang further suggested that Liu Min should lead his army to cross the mountain of Taihang and control the city of Mengjin (now in Henan Province) to wait for any change that would take place. He insisted that it would be unwise to withdraw the troops until Liu Yun was enthroned by then. Liu Min was fully convinced that his son would come to the throne unconditionally, so he regarded Li Xiang's remonstrance as a danger to the relationship between him and his son. He burst into a rage and scolded Li Xiang before the public. "Li Xiang is so stupid," he said, "that he plot to sow the seed of hatred between my son and me!" Liu Min commanded the henchmen to capture and kill Li Xiang. Li Xiang made a sigh before he was killed. "I followed an unwise man," he said, "and I knew that it is destined for me to be dead. I do not regret, but my wife is ill, and she cannot survive without me, so I hope that she can die with me." When Liu Min heard of Li Xiang's last words from others, he ordered to kill Li Xiang's wife as well in the marketplace. Liu Min reported the death of Li Xiang and his wife to the Han court to show his loyalty. As it had been expected, however, Emperor "Taizu" of Zhou claimed the emperorship later and the Han dynasty was replaced by the Zhou dynasty. Liu Yun was soon afterwards demoted and entitled with "Duke of Xiangyin" (now in Hunan Province). Liu Min sent his company commander Li Chan to deliver a letter to Emperor "Taizu" of Zhou, requesting that Liu Yun be sent back to Taiyuan. However, Liu Yun had already been killed. On hearing of the death of Liu Yun, Liu Min cried sorrowfully and recalled what Li Xiang's had remonstrated. He felt so sorry that he built a memorial temple for Li Xiang and held memorial ceremony for Li Xiang at every festival and at New Year.

On M. Earth Tiger, January in the first year of Guangshun period of the Zhou dynasty (February 24, A.D. 951), Liu Min claimed the emperorship in Taiyuan and appointed his second son Liu Chengjun as Taiyuan governor. He granted former administrative assistant Zheng Gong and Zhao Hua as prime ministers, former chief lackey Chen Guangyi as commissioner of palace attendants. He also dispatched secretary of the imperial council Li Chan as envoy to Khitan in order to set up a diplomatic tie with Khitan. The King of Khitan, Wuyu, also known as King of Yongkang (that means "forever healthy"), proposed to Liu Min that Khitan and Han were states of father and son. At that time, Liu Min was 57 years old and Wuyu was 35. In return, Liu Min asked his prime minister Zheng Gong to write to Wuyu and referred himself as "nephew emperor", stating that he would simply served Wuyu as his uncle. Wuyu sent Shuzha, King of Yan, and Gao Xun, commander of the administration chamber, to grant Liu Min as Emperor "Shenwu" of Han (that is, the "Wise Mighty"), and Liu Min's wife as empress. Wuyu was quite forthright and stubborn in nature. Whenever Liu Min's envoys came, he bothered them with meat and strong liquor. Zheng Gong had used to be weak and ill, but Wuyu ignored the fact and forced him to drink a lot once. Zheng Gong was so drunk that he died after a banquet. Though Wuyu knew that Liu Min sought for independence, he felt fortunate that great changes took place in the nation, so he sent his great ministers Shuzha and Gao Xun to reply to Liu Min with his favorite horse Huangliu and a jade belt on which nine dragons and twelve ears of rice were engraved.

Wuyu was later murdered by Shuzha and his place was taken by Shulue. Liu Min sent chancellor of the privy council Wang Dezhong to visit Khitan, and asked Shulue for troops to launch an attack on the Zhou dynasty. Shulue dispatched Xiao Yujue leading 50 thousand soldiers to help Liu Min. Liu Min led his troops to attack the commandery of Jinzhou (now in Shanxi Province), but his attack was defeated by Wang Jun of the Zhou dynasty. Since it was freezing cold in that winter, Liu Min's soldiers suffered from coldness and hunger. As a result, more than half his soldiers were dead or lost. Next year, Liu Min attacked the commandery of Fuzhou, but he was defeated by Zhe Deyi, military commissioner of Yong'an army. Zhe Deyi seized the opportunity to take over the army stationed in the county of Kelan (now in Shanxi Province).

After Emperor "Taizu" of Zhou collapsed, Liu Min was glad to hear the news so that he sent envoys again to Khitan to request for army assisting him to attack the Zhou dynasty. To help Liu Min, Khitan sent their excellent general Yang Gun to come with a calvary of 10 thousand and troops of 50 or 60 thousand soldiers coming from different divisions of the state of Xi (a region between the north of the Yan Mountain and the southeast of Mongolia). This army was claimed to be of 100 thousand. Liu Min nominated Zhang Yuanhui as pioneer general, and he himself led a calvary of 30 thousand to attack the commandery of Luzhou (now in Shanxi Province). Magistrate of Luzhou Li Jun sent Mu Lingjun with a cavalry of 3 thousand to fight against Zhang Yuanhui at the Taiping Station (now the county of Xiangyuan). Zhang Yuanhui defeated Mu Lingjun and then laid siege to Luzhou.

At that time, Emperor "Shizong" of the Zhou dynasty newly came to the throne. According to the judgement of Emperor "Shizong", since Liu Min took pleasure in the national funeral and the son of heaven was newly enthroned, he would not expect that the Zhou dynasty was able to raise the army. Therefore, Emperor "Shizong" insisted that he should lead the army himself to attack Liu Min. Though most ministers including his prime minister Feng Dao regarded this as dangerous, he firmly stuck to his idea. In March of the first year of the Xiande period (April, A. D. 954), Emperor "Shizong" led the army himself to meet Liu Min's army. On M. Wood Horse (April 25, A. D. 954), a battle took place in the county of Gaoping (now in Shanxi Province). Li Chongjin and Bai Chongzan led the left wing, Fan Ai'neng and He Hui led the right wing, Xiang Xun and Shi Yanchao led the central division, and Zhang Yongde led the imperial guards to protect Emperor "Shizong". Liu Min's army was also lined into three parts: Zhang Yuanhui stationed his troops in the east, Yang Gun stationed in the west and Liu Min stationed in the center. Looking at their enemy troops, Yang Gun advised Liu Min and said, "We are facing with a strong opponent, so we cannot underestimate the enemy or act rashly." Liu Min, however, blew his beard and said, "Don't talk nonsense! We must seize this opportunity and make sure not to lose it." Yang Gun got angry and left without a word. Liu Min ordered that the east division initiate the attack. Wang Dezhong controlled his horse and advised, saying, "The south wind is violent, and it is not in favour of the north division. It is better to wait for a while till the wind become favourable." Liu Min felt angry and said, "You old, poor and boorish man! Do not ever try to upset my army!" He turned to Zhang Yuanhui without hesitation and commanded him to launch an attack on the Zhou's army. Zhang Yuanhui attacked the right wing of the Zhou's army. At the beginning of the battle, Fan Ai'neng and He Hui retreated, and their cavalry ran into disorder. Thousands of the infantries abandoned their armors, and surrendered themselves to Zhang Yuanhui. The army roared, "Long live! Long live!" hovering above rivers and mountains. Emperor "Shizong" was so frightened that he supervised the army in person. All the soldiers became brave and dashed ahead. Meanwhile, the wind went even wilder. To avoid the downsides made by the violent wind, Liu Min waved the red flag in order to take control of his army, but they still ran into an unmanageable manner. Liu Min was therefore defeated. At sunset, Liu Min gathered the remaining ten thousand soldiers, and stationed by a mountain stream.

Since Emperor "Shizong" of Zhou had forged ahead with determination, Zhou's backup troops led by Liu Ci failed to follow up until the battle was won. After Liu Ci's troops arrived, they chased and attacked Liu Min. Liu Min suffered from a second defeat. Military supplies including weapons and annunition, helmets and armours, vehicles and utensils were all collected by Liu Ci. Liu Min alone rode his Khitan horse "Huangliu" and ran away by a footpath of the Diaoke hill, but he lost his way in the valleys at night. With the assistance and guidance of a local villager, he went astray towards the county of Pingyang (now in Shanxi Province), but he found another way to get back to Taiyuan. Zhang Yuanhui fought to his death on the battlefield. Yang Gun had got angry with Liu Min, so he halted the west troops and did not involve in the battle. As a result, this troops came back without casualty. When Liu Min returned to Taiyuan, he was so grateful for his horse Huangliu that he built a special stable for him. The horse was decorated with gold and silver, treated the same as third-rank officials, and granted with the title of "General Freedom".

Emperor "Shizong" rested the army in the commandery of Luzhou, and feasted his generals and soldiers as an award for their braveness in the battle, put to death over 70 defeated generals including Fan Ai'neng and He Hui, and gained tremendous military prestige. Emperor "Shizong" then launched an attack on Taiyuan. Meanwhile, he dispatched Fu Yanqing and Shi Yanchao to control the pass of Xinkou in the north of Taiyuan in order to block reinforcements from Khitan to Liu Min. The city of Taiyuan, with an area of some forty square *li*, was besieged tightly by the army of Zhou. Troops were disposed only three hundred steps away from the city wells. Continuous attacks had been made from April to June but they failed to conquer the city. Meanwhile, Fu Yanqing and his troops were defeated by Khitan, and Shi Yanchao fought to death in the war. Considering all of these, Emperor "Shizong" decided to withdraw troops.

Earlier, before Taiyuan was besieged, Liu Min dispatched Wang Dezhong to accompany Yang Gun on this return trip, and asked further aid from Khitan. Before Khitan dispatched some thirty or forty thousand cavalrymen to help Liu Min, they sent Wang Dezhong back in advance. When Wang Dezhong arrived at the commandery of Daizhou (in the north of Taiyuan), general commander Sang Gui murdered defense commissioner Zheng Chuqian, and surrendered the city to the Zhou dynasty. Wang Dezhong was captured and sent to Zhou as well. Emperor "Shizong" summoned and asked Wang Dezhong how many soldiers he had obtained from Khitan. Wang Dezhong answered that he asked for nothing but to accompany Yang Gun back to Khitan. Emperor "Shizong" believed him, but, on hearing that Khitan defeated Fu Yanqing at Xinkou, Wang Dezhong was put to death.

After Liu Min failed in the Gaoping campaign and was besieged within Taiyuan by troops led by Emperor "Shizong", he fell ill from stress and depress. He died at the age of sixty in November of the second year (A. D. 955). His son Liu Chengjun succeeded to the throne.

Liu Chengjun was the second son of Liu Min. When he was young, he was studious and became excellent at calligraphy. After Liu Min collapsed, Liu Chengjun sent someone to present a report to Khitan, in which he referred to himself as "baron". The king of Khitan Shulue replied him with an imperial edict, in which Chengjun was referred to as "my son" and his succession to the throne was approved of. Originally, Liu Min used to tell Zhang Yuanhui and other ministers why he did not claim the emperorship. "On account of the great cause of Emperor 'Gaozu' and the tragedy of my son Liu Yun," he said, "I refuse to succumb to Duke Guo for the sake of morality and justice. All that I want is to revenge for my country and my family with the help of you. As for proclaiming to be emperor of this land, is it really with my willingness? Simply examine ourselves: What son of heaven am I? What military commissioners are you?" Though he arrogated the title of emperor, he did not change the reign of designation. The title of "Qianyou", adopted by Emperor "Gaozu" of Han, was maintained. No imperial temple was built and, in sacrificial ceremonies in the four seasons, rites and etiquettes for the family were followed instead of those for the nation. It was not until Liu Chengjun succeeded to the throne that he firstly announced amnesty in his land, changed the title of "the tenth year of the Qianyou period (A.D. 957)" into "the first year of the Tianhui period", and built seven temples in the Xiansheng Palace.

Khitan dispatched Gao Xun to help Liu Chengjun. Liu Chengjun sent Li Cungui and Gao Xun to attack the county of Shangdang, but they returned with no achievement. In the next year (A.D. 958), Emperor "Shizong" of Zhou went north to suppress Khitan, and controlled three passes. The envoys of Khitan came to Taiyuan to ask for emergency help. When Liu Chengjun was about to send his army to support Khitan, Emperor "Shizong" withdrew his troops, so no military action was taken further.

After the Zhou dynasty was replaced by the Song dynasty, military commissioner Li Yun rebelled in the commandery of Zhaoyi. He dispatched his general Liu Jichong and administrative assistant Sun Fu to submit to Liu Chengjun a document, in which he expressed his intention to become a courtier of Han. He also arrested his military supervisors Zhou Guangxun and Li Tingyu and sent them to Taiyuan. In addition, Li Yun asked Liu Chengjun for relief troops. Liu Chengjun planned to discuss with Khitan but Liu Jichong told him the intention of Li Yun that no Khitan troops be used. Liu Chengjun agreed and then led all his army himself out of the Tuanbai valley (now in the county of Qi in Shanxi Province). His ministers saw him off at Fenhe River. His major-domo Zhao Hua advised him. "Your majesty," Zhao Hua said, "Li Yun has been always indiscreet. For such a man, you deploy all soldiers and resources of the state without taking success or failure into consideration. I am really worried about this." Anyhow, Liu Chengjun came to the Taiping station and granted him with the title of Duke of Longxi. However, Li Yun saw that Liu Chengjun neither had honourable escorts or guards, nor looked like an emperor, so he regretted submitting to be a minister of Liu Chengjun. He then explained that he owed the royal house of Zhou a debt of gratitude, so he could not bear to betray them. Since Liu Chengjun had a family feud with the house of Zhou, he became displeased with Li Yun's explanation. Liu Chengjun dispatched commissioner of palace attendants Lu Zan to supervise Li Yun's army. Li Yun became ever discontent and he held different opinions with Lu Zan in many things. To ease the contradictions between them, Liu Chengjun therefore sent his prime minister Wei

Rong to reconcile them.

Li Yun was soon defeated and he committed suicide. Accordingly, Wei Rong was captured to the capital of the Song dynasty. When Emperor "Taizu" of Song asked Wei Rong why Liu Chengjun helped Li Yun in staging the revolt, Wei Rong spoke rudely to him. Emperor "Taizu" commanded his man to hit Wei Rong with an iron rod in the head. His head began to bleed and was covered with blood at once, but Wei Rong did not compromise. "I die in a right path!" shouted he. Emperor "Taizu" looked around at his ministers and said, "This is a loyal minister." He released Wei Rong and gave an order that Wei Rong's wound be treated with effective medicine. Emperor "Taizu" asked Wei Rong to write Liu Chengjun a letter, in which Emperor "Taizu" asked for Zhou Guangxun and other generals. He also promised that Wei Rong could be sent back to Taiyuan. Liu Chengjun did not reply to the agreement, however, so Wei Rong was detained in the capital city of Kaifeng. Later, Liu Chengjun expressed his regret to Zhao Hua. "I failed to listen to you," he said, "and I was nearly defeated. For the loss of Wei Rong and Lu Zan, I feel ever pitiful and regretful."

From then on, Liu Chengjun took Confucianist scholars into special consideration and appointed Guo Wuwei as general councillor. Guo Wuwei came from the commandery of Dizhou and lived as a hermit in the Baofu mountain. He had a square face and a sticky mouth which made him look like a bird. He was studious and knowledgeable, skilled in debating. He once was a Taoist priest with cambric clothes and lived in the Wudang mountain. When Emperor "Taizu" of Zhou (he was a general of the Han dynasty) suppressed Li Shouzhen in Hezhong District, Guo Wuwei went to the gate of a military camp and visited him. Emperor "Taizu" consulted him about the contemporary affairs and he was surprised at Guo Wuwei's response. Emperor "Taizu" planned to recruit Guo Wuwei as his consultant. However, someone advised him and said, "My lord, you are now a minister of the Han dynasty. You have a large number of troops and stay far away from the capital. It is not wise in the long run to recruit any political strategist." As a result, Emperor "Taizu" did not receive Wuwei as his consultant. Guo Wuwei then left the Wudang mountain and had lived as a hermit in the Baofu mountain since then. Liu Chengjun's inner military affairs commissioner Duan Chang knew Guo Wuwei and recommended him to Liu Chengjun. Liu Chengjun summoned Guo Wuwei as grand master of remonstrance and then appointed him as prime minister. In the fifth year of the Tianhui period (A. D. 961), Wang Yin, Liu Shao, Zhao Luan and other leaders of palace guards and palace eunuchs plotted a revolt, but the plot was uncovered, so they were all killed. Their confession implicated Duan Chang, so Liu Chenjun demoted Duan Chang from inner military affairs commissioner to magistrate of the Fenzhou commandery and then hanged him to death.

From Liu Min's reign, it was obligatory to report to Khitan whatever decision had been made. After Liu Chengjun succeeded, however, most reports were omitted, including when he changed the designation of the reign, echoed Li Yun to break away from the Song dynasty, and put Duan Chang to death. As a result, Khitan dispatched envoys to blame Liu Chengjun for his failure to inform them of these decisions. Liu Chengjun panicked and apologized for his offence to Khitan. In addtion, envoys sent by Liu Chenjun were often detained in Khitan. The more Liu Chengjun served Khitan sincerely, the more Khitan treated Liu Chengjun harshly. Since Li Yun's death, Liu Chengjun had lost support from Khitan and Khitan had no further desire to invade southwards. With a small territory and lack of products, Liu Chenjun still had to paid loyal tribute to Khitan annually, so national expenditure was gradually reduced. To solve this problem, Liu Chengjun nominated the monk Jiyong as chief minister of dependencies. Jiyong was a son of Liu Shouguang, the late "King of Yan". When Liu Shouguang was defeated and killed, Liu Jiyong survived because he was born by a concubine. He shaved his head and became a monk. Later, he moved to the Wutai mountain. Since Jiyong was reasonably wise and skilled at managing money, he was trusted by the royal clan since Liu Min's time. Besides, Jiyong was able to teach the Buddhist classics *Avatamsaka Sutra*, so sacrifices and donations were offered from four quarters. Jiyong collected most of these offerings to aid the national expenditure. Since the Wutai mountain was located on the territory of Khitan, Jiyong also presented his horses to Liu Chengjun. These horses was called "Tiandu Horses", that is, horses that are used to aid the army. Hundreds of horses were sent to Liu Chenjun annually. Moreover, he built a metallurgical factory at the Bai valley, and employed workers to dig mountains and collect silver mine. Silver was produced and delivered to the house of Liu. With this, Liu Chengjun was able to establish the Baoxing army. Jiyong was promoted several times until he was nominated as grand preceptor and then as secretariat director. He died of disease in his old age and was conferred with a posthumous title of "King of Ding".

By means of a spy at the boundary, Emperor "Taizu" of Song once sent words to Liu Chengjun, referring to him as king. "I understand," he said, "that you have family feud with the house of Zhou, so it is right for you not to yield. There is, however, no misunderstanding or hatred between you and me now, but why should you confine yourself in that quarter of land? If you have set your mind on the whole nation, it is wise for you to cross the Taihang mountain to fight a showdown battle." Liu Chengjun dispatched the spy to answer Emperor "Taizu" of Song. "The land and the military force in the area of Hedong," he said, "accounts for less than one tenth of the whole nation. My house is not a rebelling one. The simple purpose for me to protect this piece of land is to prevent my ancestors from having no sacrifice." Emperor "Taizu" of Song felt sorry for Liu Chengjun's sad words, and told the spy with smile. "Please tell Chengjun for me," he said, "that I would like to give him a chance." Until Liu Chengjun's reign ended, Emperor "Taizu" imposed no further troops.

The Seventh Hereditary House of Wu and Yue: Qian Liu

Translated by Jiaqi Xue

Qian Liu, whose courtesy name was Jumie, was a native of Lin'an, a county in the Hangzhou commandery. In Lin'an, there was a huge tree, under which Qian Liu used to played games with other children in his childhood. Sitting on a stone, Qian Liu commanded other children to do this or to do that as if he were the leader. His instructions were well-conducted and other children also feared him to some extent. When he grew up, he neither had a career to make a living nor did he wish to land a job to make money. Later, he made some profits by selling salt.

Zhong Qi, an official of Lin'an, had several sons who always gambled and drank with Qian Liu. At first, Zhong Qi strictly prevented his sons from playing with Qian Liu. To his mind, it was pointless for his sons to make friends with such a vagrant. However, they still followed Qian Liu. At that time, there was a famous prophet in the county of Yuzhang, who claimed that there appeared the sign of a king between the constellations of Niu and Dou. These two constellations corresponded to Qiantang River in Hangzhou. Thereupon, the prophet visited the region of Qiantang and predicted that the king was in Lin'an, so he arrived in

Lin'an, concealing himself in the marketplace as a physiognomizer in order to seek for the true man. Coincidentally, Zhong Qi shared a close relationship with the prophet and he was told about the sign of king on one occassion. "There is a distinguished man in your town," the prophet said, "but I fail to find him in the marketplace. Distinguished as you are, I am afraid that you are not comparable with that man." Then, Zhong Qi hosted a banquet for the prophet, in which all gentlemen and heroes were invited. The prophet hid himself among them and sized up guests, but he could discern no enough sign of a king. On another day, when the prophet paid a visit to Zhong Qi's house, Qian Liu was about to come from outside. Noticing Zhong Qi, Qian Liu left. The prophet watched him with surprise and said, "Here is truly the distinguished man!" Hearing his words, Zhong Qi smiled and said, "That is simply a yong man of the Qian family in my neighborhood." Later, the prophet summoned Qian Liu, and, after observing the young man carefully, he confirmed his prediction with Zhong Qi, "You are distinguished", he said, "because of this man." He then turned to Qian Liu and comforted him. "You are not an ordinary man and will achieve great success in the future," he said, "so please treasure yourself." When the prophet was about to leave the county, he had a conversation with Zhong Qi. "It is not my desire," he said, "to seek this very man. The only thing I want to do is to verify whether my physiognomy still works or not." He left on the next day. Since then, Zhong Qi started to let his sons and other young men follow Qian Liu. From time to time, he would give Qian Liu some money to help him get out of poverty.

Qian Liu was good at archery and maths and knew a little about astronomy. In the second year of the Qianfu period (A.D. 875) of the Tang dynasty, Wang Chen, deputy general of the province of West Zhejiang, staged a revolt. Dong Chang, who had been dispatched as general commander to station in the county of Shijian, started to recruit soldiers in his neighborhood to fight against Wang Chen. Qian Liu was appointed as assistant general and defeated Wang Chen. At that time, Huang Chao, leading several thousand rebels, attacked and occupied large areas in the province of East Zhejiang. As they approaching the county of Lin'an, Qian Liu said, "Since rebels are far more numerous than soldiers in the county, it is difficult to defend them directly. What we should do is to dispatch raiders to fight." Thereupon, Qian Liu and twenty gallant soldiers ambushed in the valley. As Huang Chao sent single soldiers as pioneers to explore the risk,

Qian Liu's archer shot their general to death. As a result, Huang Chao's troops ran into disorder. Qian Liu led his soldiers to attack Huang Chao's troops, killing several hundred soldiers. Though he won the battle, Qian Liu said, "This kind of strategy we took just now can be utilized only once. How could we defend when their principal force come?" So he led his troops to a place called "Babaili", which literally meant "a far distance of eight hundred li". On the midway, Qian Liu told an old woman about the troops. "If someone comes and asks, please tell them that soldiers are stationed at 'Babaili' in Lin'an." When Huang Chao's troops came, they heard what the old woman said, but they failed to realise that "Babaili" was simply the name of a place. "We were newly defeated by some twenty soldiers," they said. "How can we fight against an army of eight hundred li?" At the thought of that, Huang Chao's troops passed by Lin'an quickly. Lieutenant general Gao Pian heard that Huang Chao did not dare to attack Lin'an. To strengthen the defence, he summoned Dong Chang and Qian Liu together to the city of Guanglin. A long time later, since Gao Pian had no will to fight the rebellious generals, so Dong Chang and others were not employed further. Consequently, they asked to return. Gao Pian appointed Dong Chang as magistrate of Hangzhou. At that time, the nation was in disorder. Dong Chang then organised troops of different counties into eight divisions and appointed Qian Liu as commander in chief, and Cheng Ji as general commander of the Jingjiang Du division.

In the second year of the Zhonghe period (A. D. 882), Liu Hanhong, surveillance commissioner of the Yuezhou commandery, had grudge against Dong Chang. At that time, Liu Hanhong dispatched his brother Liu Hanyu and the inspector-in-chef Xin Yue to station troops at the county of Xiling. When informed of this situation, Qian Liu led the Eight-Division Troops to travel across the river, getting the secret military code of the rival and attacking their barracks. The soldiers were so disturbed and frightened that their barracks were burnt down. Liu Hanhong and other generals all retreated. Liu Hanhong later dispatched Huang Gui and He Xiao to station troops in the counties of Zheji and Xiaoshen, but both of them were defeated by Qian Liu. Main forces of both sides encountered and a battle followed. Liu Hanhong's troops were defeated. Both He Xiao and Xin Yue got killed. Liu Hanhong changed his clothe and escaped with a chopper in hand, looking like a butcher. When he was caught up by Qian Liu's soldiers, Liu

Hanhong showed them his chopper and said, "I am just a butcher." Therefore, he escaped safe and sound.

In the fourth year of the Zhonghe period (A. D. 884), Emperor "Xizong" appointed his private envoy Jiao Jupan as peace envoy to mediate between Hangzhou and Yuezhou. An imperial edict was issued that Dong Chang and Liu Hanhong should cease arms immediately, but neither of them followed the emperor's order. After a short period, Liu Hanhong dispatched his general, Zhu Bao, Hang Gongwen, Shi Jianshi and other commanders to lead the sailors to station in Wanghai, a small town near to Yuezhou. While Qian Liu moved his soldiers to Pingshui, Cheng Ji led a troop of raiders, destroyed Zhu Bao's forces at night under cover of darkness, and stood by in Fengshan. Shortly afterwards, Shi Jianshi and other generals had no choice but to surrender and Cheng Ji occupied Yuezhou soon afterwards. Liu Hanhong fled to the commandery of Taizhou for a recess but the magistrate of Taizhou arrested him and sent him to Qian Liu. Finally, Liu Hanhong was beheaded in Kuaiji and all his family were killed. Qian Liu wrote the emperor a report, hoping that Dong Chang could replace Liu Hanhong to govern Yuezhou, while he himself stayed in Hangzhou.

In the third year of the Guangqi period (A. D. 887), Qian Liu was appointed as the left army general and magistrate of Hangzhou and Dong Chang was appointed as the surveillance commissioner of Yuezhou. In that year, Gao Pian was jailed by Bi Shiduo. Bi Shiduo once was a general of Huang Chao and surrender to Gao Pian in the fifth year of the Qianfu period (A. D. 878). As a result, the province of Huinan ran into overwhelming disorder. Xu Yue, a general of the Liuhe town, occupied Suzhou. Liu Hao, an assistant general in Ruizhou, drove his commander Zhou Bao away. Zhou Bao fled to the commandery of Changzhou. Liu Hao recommended Xue Lang, an officer of the revenue section, as general commander. For this reason, Qian Liu dispatched his generals Cheng Ji and Du Leng to attack Changzhou. They returned with Zhou Bao. Qian Liu held a military ceremony in suburb to welcome them and arranged Zhou Bao to live in a house called Zhangting. Zhou Bao died of illness later. Du Leng and other generals attacked Runzhou, drove Liu Hao away and captured Xue Lang. Xue Lang was killed and his heart was taken out and offered as a sacrifice to the spirit of Zhou Bao. Shortly afterwards, Qian Liu sent his brother Qian Qiu to attack Xu Yue. Xu Yue was defeated, abandoned the city and fled away. He was caught and got killed later.

Emperor "Zhaozong" appointed Qian Liu as defense commissioner of Hangzhou. At that time, Yang Xingmi and Sun Ru were fighting against each other to occupy the province of Huainan. Qian Liu also engaged in battles in the area between Suzhou and Changzhou. After a while, Yang Xingmi killed Sun Ru, occupied Huainan, and captured Runzhou. Meanwhile, Qian Liu also conquered Suzhou and Changzhou. The Tang dynastic court promoted the army in Yuezhou as a provincial-level institution entitled "Weisheng Military Government", appointed Dong Chang as military commissioner, and entitled him "King of Longxi". Hangzhou was promoted as Wusheng Military Government, Qian Liu was appointed as chief military training commissioner, and Cheng Ji as vice commissioner. Cheng Ji, whose courtesy name was Hongji, worked with Qian Liu to fight against others for many years and came up with numerous tactics. Qian Liu married his daughter to Cheng Ji's son, Cheng Renxiu. In addition, Qian Liu appointed Du Leng, Ruan Jie, Gu Quan and others as generals, and nominated Shen Song, Pi Guangye, Lin Ding and Luo Ying as distinguished guests. All of them shared matchless and paramount talents and have made contributions before.

In the second year of the Jingfu period (A. D. 893), Qian Liu was promoted as military commissioner of "Zhenhai Military Government" and magistrate of Runzhou. In the first year of the Qianning period (A. D. 894), Qian Liu was further appointed as secretariat-chancellery. In the second year of the Qianning period (A. D. 895), Dong Chang rose in rebellion in Yuezhou. Dong Chang was always silly and slow in making decisions. When hearing people's cases, he always resorted to the dices. Those who won the game were judged to be righteous. Ying Zhi, Wang Wen, Han Yun and other sorcerers or witches confused Dong Chang with heresies. They also presented him birds and beasts as auspicious omens. Ni Deru, an assistant general, further suggested that Dong Chang claim the emperorship. "In ancient times," he said, "there was a rumour that the bird of 'Luoping' decided people's fate in the region of Yue. Therefore, common people often drew pictures of the bird and enshrined them. I find that your signature is quite similar to those pictures." With these words, Ni Deru showed Dong Chang a picture. Dong Chang was so pleased with this that he proclaimed himself as emperor, named the empire as Luoping, and changed the designation of the reign into "Shuntian", which meant "in conformity to the heaven". His soldiers were divided into two divisions. The inner division wore yellow uniforms and the outer division wore white. All uniforms were inscribed with the word "Guiyi", that is, "returning to rightness". The vice general Huang Jie regarded it as unacceptable and tried his best to dissuade Dong Chang from doing so, but Dong Chang was so angry that he ordered to decollate Huang Jie. When Huang Jie's head was presented before him, Dong Chang further abused him. "The evil-doer fails to live up to my expectation." He said, "He refused to be a duke, but chose himself to be killed." With these words, he threw Huang Jie's head to the washroom. Thereby, Dong Chang wrote a letter to Qian Liu. Qian Liu soon informed the imperial court of Dong Chang's rebellion.

Emperor "Zhaozong" promulgated an imperial edict to deprive Dong Chang of his official ranks. Qian Liu was entitled with "Prince of Pengcheng" and appointed as bandit-suppression commisioner of the West Zhejiang Province. "Mr. Dong owns me a favour," Qian Liu said, "so no action should be taken to suppress him directly." While he stationed thirty thousand soldiers at the Ying'en Gate (that is, "Gate of Thanksgiving"), his adviser Shen Pang was sent to order Dong Chang to amend his mistakes. Dong Chang presented Qian Liu two million grands of money as military expenditure, captured and sent Ying Zhi and other sorcerers to the army, and also pleaded punishment for his guilt. Qian Liu then withdrew his troops. However, Dong Chang went back on his words and sent Chen Yu, Cui Wen and other generals to station troops in the counties of Xiangyan and Shihou. In addition, he asked Yang Xingmi for relief troops. Yang Xingmi sent An Renyi to rescue Dong Chang. In that case, Qian Liu dispatched Gu Quanwu to attack Dong Chang, killing Cui Wen. Most of Dong Chang's generals, including Xu Xun, Tang Jiu and Yuan Bin, were mediocre, having no talent on commanding soldiers. When encountering Gu Quanwu's troops, they were defeated immediately. Dong Zhen, whose father was a brother of Dong Chang, was brave and skillful in fighting. Gu Quanwu and other commanders launched joint attacks on him for more than a year, but they were not able to defeat him. Dong Zhen, however, had grudge against his assistant general Ci Yu. Ci Yu made a false charge against Dong Zhen, so Dong Zhen was put to death by Dong Chang. After the death of Dong Zhen, Dong Chang's troops were defeated by Gu Quanwu. Gu Quanwu arrested and took Dong Chang to Hangzhou. When they arrived at the river of Xixiaojiang, Dong Chang looked around his men, referring Qian Liu as duke. "Both Duke Qian and I came from a humble place," he said. "I was once a general commander, but now, who am I and who is he? What face do I have to meet him again?" All his men looked at each other and burst into tears. All of a sudden, Dong Chang goggled and cried, jumping into the water to get drowned.

Emperor "Zhaozong" intended to sent his prime minister Wang Pu to defend Yuezhou, but Wang Pu proposed that it was better to appoint Qian Liu. Accordingly, the "Weisheng Military Government" was changed into "Zhendong Military Government" and Qian Liu was appointed as military commissioner of both "Zhenhai" and "Zhendong" Military Governments as well as police inspector. In addition, he was granted with a metal and was exempt from nine death penalties. While Qian Liu went to Yuezhou with the imperial order, he also governed the area of Qiantang. Yuezhou was called "Dongfu", that is, the "East Government". In the first year of the Guanghua period (A. D. 898), "Zhenhai Military Government" was moved to Hangzhou and Qian Liu was promoted as grand preceptor of inspection. The title of Qian Liu's home village was changed into "Xungui Neighbourhood, Guangyi Vallige", that is, "a neighbourhood of noble merit in the vallige of generous righteousness". The barrack in which Qian Liu had settled was called "Yijin Barrack", that is, the "barrack of nobility". At that time, magistrate of Wuzhou Wang Tan rebelled and surrendered to Yang Xingmi. Yang Xingmi dispatched his general Kang Ru to echoed Wang Tan, so he attacked the nearby commandery of Muzhou. Qian Liu dispatched his brother Qian Jinqiu to meet the attack and Qian Jinqiu defeated Kang Ru in the county of Xuanzhu. Wang Tan fled to the commandery of Xuanzhou. Therefore, Emperor "Zhaozong" decided to draw a portrait for Qian Liu in the Linyan Cabinet, promoted "Yijin Barrack" to "Yijin City". In addition, the Shijian mountain is changed into "Yijin Mountain" and the Daguan Mountain is renamed as "Gongcheng Mountain", that is, the "mountain of meritorious minister". Later, Qian Liu paid a visit to "Yijin City" and held a banquet to entertain his home fellows. The hills and the forest were covered with brocade and the huge tree where he used to play games with other children in his early childhood was called "Yijin General".

In the second year of the Tianfu period (A. D. 898), Qian Liu was entitled with "King of Yue". While Qian Liu was away on a tour to the Yijin City, Xu

Guan, commander-in-chief of the right division of Wuyong Du, and Xu Zaisi, commander-in-chief of the left division, rebelled. After they set fires everywhere and plundered the outer city, they attacked the inner city. Qian Chuanying, a son of Qian Liu, and his generals, inlcuding Ma Zhuo and Chen Wei, closed the gate and defended the city. When Qian Liu returned, the north gate of the outer city was closed, he was not able to enter the city. On behalf of Qian Liu, Cheng Ji fought against Xu Guan and killed more than a hundred soldiers. Xu Guan stationed his troops in the Xinglong temple. Meanwhile, Qian Liu wore plain clothes and entered the city stealthily. He dispatched Ma Zhuo, Wang Rong, Du Jianwei and other generals to defend different gates, respectively. In addition, he planned to send Gu Quanwu to defend the East Government. Gu Quanwu said, "We do not have to worry about the East Government. What we should take into consideration is the Huainan Province. Since Xu Guan was defeated by our troops, he is sure to ask relief troops from Huainan. If this is the case, the trouble will not be a small one. Nevertheless, Yang Xingmi is known to be a man of character. If he is informed of our plight, he is sure to do us a favor." Qian Liu thought what Gu Quanwu said made sense. "However," Gu Quanwu continued, "if I visit Yang Xingmi alone, I do not think that he will trust me and help us. Please choose one of the princesses who you think is suitable to go with me." Qian Liu said, "Previously, I had planned to marry Qian Yuanzhi to the Yang house." Hence, Qian Yuanzhi was sent to accompany Gu Quanwu on the visit to Guangling, the capital city of Huainan. As was expected, Xu Guan planned to meet Tian Jun in the commandery of Xuanzhou. After Gu Quanwu and other envoys arrived in Guangling, Yang Xingmi married his daughter to Qian Yuanzhi and ordered Tian Jun to return at once. Tian Jun returned after he took a hundred grands of money from Qian Liu and Qian Yuanguan as hostage, another son of Qian Liu.

In the first year of the Tianyou period (A. D. 904), Qian Liu was entitled with "King of Wu". He built the Hall of Meritorious Ministers and set up a monument to record their achievements. In total, five hundred officials and generals were praised and their names were inscribed on the back of the monument. In the fourth year (A. D. 907), the Yijin City was promoted to "An'guo Yijin Military Government", that is, a military government of peace and nobility.

When the Founding Emperor of "Taizu" of the Liang dynasty came to the throne, he granted Qian Liu with the title of "King of Wu and Yue" and appointed him as military commissioner of Huainan. One of his advisers persuaded Qian Liu to reject the appointment. Qian Liu answered with a smile, comparing himself with Sun Zhongmou, King of Wu in the three-kingdom period. "Am I not comparable to Sun Zhongmou?" said he. Anyway, he accepted the appointment. Emperor "Taizu" once asked a reporting official of the Wu and Yue state about Qian Liu's hobbies. "Is Qian Liu fond of anything in his casual life?" said he. The official answered, "He is fond of jade belts and fine horses." Emperor "Taizu" smiled and said, "He is truly a hero!" Emperor "Taizu" awarded Qian Liu with a bunch of jade belts and ten of the horses which he himself rode when he played ball games. After Wei Quanfeng and other generals of the Jiangxi Province were defeated by Yang Wo, Wei Zaichang in the commandery of Xinzhou sought refuge with Qian Liu. Qian Liu did not like his surname "Wei", which meant "danger", so it was changed into "Yuan". In the second year of the Kaiping period (A.D.908), Qian Liu was further nominated as the president of the council. He renamed the county of Lin'an into "An'guo", that is, "Peaceful State", and renamed Guangyi Vallige into "Yijin Village", that is, "Noble Village". In the third year (A.D.909), he was appointed as grand guardian.

Yang Wo dispatched his generals Zhou Ben and Chen Zhang to attack and besiege Suzhou. Qian Liu dispatched his brothers Qian Ju and Qian Biao to run a rescue campaign. The attacking troops fended off the city with barriers above the water to stop boats and sank nets, to which copper bells were fastened, into the water to stop divers. Sima Fu, a marine in the defending troops, was wise and good at diving. He first used a huge bamboo pole to touch the net, so the bells rang. While soldiers in the attacking troops were alerted by the sound to pull the net, Sima Fu passed under water and entered the city. He went out of the city in the same way. Therefore, the order of a general offensive was sent to the defending troops in the city and the relief troops outside the city. These two troops launched a simultaneous attack on Zhou Ben and Chen Zhang's troops. Since they echoed each other as if they were commanded by the god, Zhou Ben and Chen Zhang's troops were totally shocked and completely defeated. Zhou Ben and other generals retreated, but Lue Qiuzhi, He Ming and other generals were captured.

In the fourth year (A.D.910), when Qian Liu toured the Yijin Military Government, he composed a poem titled "Song of Going Home" as follows:

Returning home at festivals in gorgeous garments,
I am welcomed and followed by folks coming from afar.
Just as the constellations Niu and Dou are no comets and men are no deceivers,
So the King of Wu and Yue with four horses is home.

In the first year of the Qianhua period (A.D.911), Qian Liu was nominated as general secretary of the imperial secretariat and lieutenant general of four field headquarters in Huainan, Xuanruan and other provinces. Qian Liu set up a life-time temple for himself in the Yijin Military Government. In that year, Qian Liu's brother Qian Biao, who defended the commandery of Huzhou, killed his garrison general Pan Chang without permission from Qian Liu. Qian Biao felt guilty and fled to the province of Huainan for fear of punishment. In the second year (A.D.912), after Zhu Yougui, King of Ying, became the emperor of the Liang dynasty, he revered and conferred Qian Liu as Shangfu, that is, senior minister. In the third year of the Zhengming period (A.D.917) during the reign of the final Emperor "Modi" of Liang, Qian Liu was granted as grand marshal of soldiers and horses under heaven. In the fourth year (A.D.918), Yang Longyan conquered the commanderary of Qianzhou, and Qian Liu started to pay loyal tributes to the Liang dynasty by sea. In the first year of the Longde period (A.D.921), Qian Liu's title rather than his name was written in the imperial edic.

After Emperor "Zhuangzong" of the Tang dynasty moved the capital to Luoyang, Qian Liu dispatched envoys to pay tributes and requested for a jade book. Emperor "Zhuangzong" had relevant departments to discuss Qian Liu's request. It was commonly held among the ministers that he who was no son of heaven was not allowed to use the jade book. Among them, Guo Chongtao expressed strong objection to the request. Emperor "Zhuangzong", however, approved later and granted Qian Liu with a jade book and a gold seal. Since Qian Liu appointed his son Qian Yuanjing as military commissioner of "Zhenhai Military Government" and other military governments, he claimed the title of "King of Wu and Yue". The place where he lived was referred to as palace and his government was called imperial court. His officials and subordinates began to refer to themselves as ministers. Qian Liu established three buildings in the "Yijin Military Government" to store the jade book, gold certificates and edicts. In addition, he dispatched envoys to acknowledge the kingdoms of Xinluo and Bohai. Overseas kingdoms in return acknowledged Qian Liu as their senior.

After Emperor "Mingzong" came to throne, An Zhonghui took charge of state affairs. Qian Liu wrote a letter to An Zhonghui, in which arrogant words were used. An Zhonghui was enraged by the letter. At that time, palace servitors Wu Zhaoyu and Han Mei were sent as envoys to the state of Wu and Yue. When they returned, Han Mei made a false accusation that Wu Zhaoyu submitted to Qian Liu as minister and danced for him. An Zhonghui reported to the emperor to deprive Qian Liu of all his titles and ranks, including "King of Wu and Yue", grand marshal and senior minister, and ordered him to resign as grand preceptor. In that case, Qian Yuanjing and others dispatched envoys through some bypaths to hand in letters and reports in which affairs were explained in detail. After An Zhonghui died, Emperor "Mingzong" restored Qian Liu's titles and ranks. In the third year of the Changxing period (A. D. 932) when he was 81 years old, Qian Liu passed away and was honoured with the posthumous title of "Wusu", that is, the Mighty Solemn.